THE YOUNG RUGBY PLAYER

The Young Rugby Player: Science and Application provides a comprehensive and accessible overview of the recent research behind the preparation, development and performance of the young rugby player. Each chapter concludes with key take-home messages and practical applications demonstrating how practitioners can provide evidence-informed delivery with the young rugby athlete. The book highlights how research and science can inform practice including coaching, sport science, player development and performance with the young rugby player. Each author is a world leader within their respective discipline including academics and practitioners who research and practice across youth rugby.

The book includes chapters on:

- Introducing the young rugby player, including topics related to growth and maturation, talent identification and development and understanding the demands of youth rugby.
- Understanding and developing the young rugby player, including topics related to physical, psycho-social, technical and tactical development, alongside training practices and fatigue and recovery.
- Other hot topics including nutrition, injury, concussion and injury prevention and the female young rugby player.

This text is vital reading for all coaches, sport scientists, strength and conditioning coaches and all academics with an interest in the science and practical application of working with the young rugby player.

Kevin Till, PhD, is a Professor of Athletic Development in the Carnegie School of Sport at Leeds Beckett University, UK.

Jonathon Weakley, PhD, is a Lecturer of Strength and Conditioning and Human Physiology at Australian Catholic University, Australia. He is also an Associate Research Fellow at Leeds Beckett University, UK.

Sarah Whitehead, PhD, is a Senior Lecturer in Strength and Conditioning within the Carnegie School of Sport at Leeds Beckett University, UK.

Ben Jones, PhD, is a Professor of Sport and Exercise Physiology within the Carnegie School of Sport at Leeds Beckett University, UK. He is also a Visiting Professor at the University of Cape Town, South Africa, and the University of New England, Australia.

THE YOUNG RUGBY PLAYER

Science and Application

Edited by
Kevin Till, Jonathon Weakley,
Sarah Whitehead and Ben Jones

NEW YORK AND LONDON

Cover image: digicamchic/Getty Images

First published 2023
by Routledge
605 Third Avenue, New York, NY 10158

and by Routledge
4 Park Square, Milton Park, Abingdon, Oxon, OX14 4RN

Routledge is an imprint of the Taylor & Francis Group, an informa business

© 2023 selection and editorial matter, Kevin Till, Jonathon Weakley, Sarah Whitehead, and Ben Jones; individual chapters, the contributors

The right of Kevin Till, Jonathon Weakley, Sarah Whitehead, and Ben Jones to be identified as the authors of the editorial material, and of the authors for their individual chapters, has been asserted in accordance with sections 77 and 78 of the Copyright, Designs and Patents Act 1988.

All rights reserved. No part of this book may be reprinted or reproduced or utilised in any form or by any electronic, mechanical, or other means, now known or hereafter invented, including photocopying and recording, or in any information storage or retrieval system, without permission in writing from the publishers.

Trademark notice: Product or corporate names may be trademarks or registered trademarks, and are used only for identification and explanation without intent to infringe.

ISBN: 978-0-367-61238-2 (hbk)
ISBN: 978-0-367-61232-0 (pbk)
ISBN: 978-1-003-10479-7 (ebk)

DOI: 10.4324/9781003104797

Typeset in Bembo
by codeMantra

CONTENTS

List of Figures	*vii*
List of Tables	*xi*
About the Editors	*xiii*
About the Contributors	*xv*
Foreword	*xxiii*
Acknowledgements	*xxv*

1 Youth Rugby: Setting the Scene 1
   Kevin Till, Martin MacTaggart and Ben Jones

2 Long-Term Athletic Development of the Young Rugby Player 16
   Kevin Till, Rhodri S. Lloyd and Joey C. Eisenmann

3 Developmentally Appropriate Coaching Practice for
   Children Playing Rugby 34
   David Morley and Donna O'Connor

4 Davids and Goliaths: Kinanthropometry and Grouping
   Strategies in Youth Rugby 51
   John Sampson, Job Fransen, Ric Lovell and Kevin Till

5 Talent Identification in Male Youth Rugby 67
   *Adam L. Kelly, Alexander B. T. McAuley, Francesco Dimundo
   and Kevin Till*

6	The Demands of Youth Rugby Match-Play *Sarah Whitehead, Dan Weaving, Rich Johnston, Dale B. Read,* *Ryan White and Ben Jones*	91
7	Profiling Physical Qualities in Youth Rugby: The ProPQ Tool *Jonathon Weakley, Cameron Owen, Ben Jones and Kevin Till*	107
8	Strength and Conditioning Training for Physical Development *Jonathon Weakley, Josh Darrall-Jones and Nicholas Gill*	127
9	The Psychosocial Development of Youth Rugby Players *Ross A. Shand, Lea-Cathrin Dohme and Stephen D. Mellalieu*	150
10	Technical and Tactical Development in Youth Rugby *Michael Ashford and Jamie Taylor*	166
11	Improving Young Rugby Player's Tackle Ability *Sharief Hendricks, Gregory Tierney and Steven den Hollander*	194
12	Training Practices in Youth Rugby Players *Padraic Phibbs, Timothy Hartwig and Sarah Whitehead*	222
13	Monitoring Fatigue and Recovery in Youth Rugby *Carlos Ramírez-López, Cédric Leduc, Mathieu Lacome* *and Ben Jones*	236
14	Nutrition for the Young Rugby Player *Marcus Hannon, Sarah Chantler and Nessan Costello*	250
15	Injury Risk and Reduction Strategies in Young Rugby Players *Michael Hislop and Keith Stokes*	270
16	The Young Female Rugby Player *Sean Scantlebury and Omar Heyward*	315
17	Planning Your Coaching for Young Rugby Players *Michael Ashford and Jamie Taylor*	331
Index		*347*

FIGURES

1.1	Overview of England Rugby Football Union's Age Grade Rugby	5
1.2	England Rugby Football Union's Player Pathway	9
2.1	Factors to Consider for the Long-term Athletic Development of Young Rugby Players	18
2.2	Athletic Motor Skill Competencies (adapted from Lloyd et al., 2015)	27
3.1	Coach's Decision-Making Processes in Providing a Developmentally Appropriate Environment for Children (Becoming CAYPABLE; adapted from Morley & Muir, 2012)	35
4.1	The Variability in Body Mass in Youth Rugby Players Aged 12–15 years	52
4.2	Summary of Kinanthropometry, Maturation and Outcomes within Youth Rugby	56
5.1	Ecological Dynamic Factors to Consider when Identifying Male Youth Rugby Players (adapted from Kelly et al., 2022)	69
5.2	Examples of two different frozen Screen Clips used to Differentiate Selection, Position and Player Potential during the Perceptual Cognitive Expertise Video Simulation Test. The Clips Were Used as Examples that Represented Different Real-Life Game Situations (e.g., A, Defending; B, Attacking) in Which Time, Scores and Position on the Pitch Was Provided to Contextualise Each Option.	73
5.3	The Birth Quartile (BQ) Distribution Percentages of the English Professional Pathway, Senior Professional and Senior International Players (adapted from Kelly et al., 2021d)	76
5.4	Players (left) and Coaches' (right) Perceptions of the Talent Identification and Development Processes in English Rugby Union	83

5.5	The Locking Wheel Nut Model – Hypothetical Patterns from Three Different Players (adapted from Kelly et al., 2018)	84
6.1	The Modification of Drill Design to Influence the Physical and Technical Demands	98
6.2	The Process of Using the Global Navigation Satellite System (GNSS) Raw Velocity Trace to Analyse and Evaluate Training, an Example Report	101
7.1	Process for Profiling Physical Qualities in Team Sports	108
7.2	Principal Component Analysis for Evaluating Physical Performance	119
7.3	Principal Component Analysis for Comparison between Two Players using Interactive Settings	119
7.4	Longitudinal Analysis according to Chronological Age for Strength, Power, Speed and Aerobic Capacity	120
8.1	Resistance Training Progressions to Guide Exercise Prescription	139
9.1	The Planning for Psychosocial Skills and Characteristics Development across Short, Medium, and Long-term in a Rugby Talent Development Environment	159
10.1	An Example Mental Model of Rugby Union	184
11.1	Technical Skill Training Framework (adapted from Hendricks et al., 2019)	209
12.1	The Athlete Monitoring Cycle	229
12.2	Longitudinal Analysis of Weekly High-Speed Running Exposures Using Z-Scores	230
12.3	Squad Load and Recovery Summary Table including Weekly High-Speed Running, sRPE Load, and Subsequent Daily Perceived Recovery Scale Scores	230
12.4	Visualisation of Squad Load and Recovery Interactions from Rolling Weekly sRPE Load and Daily Perceived Recovery Scale Z-scores	231
13.1	Practical Considerations for the Development of a Fatigue Monitoring System	244
15.1	Venn Diagram Outlining Considerations for Developing the Activate Injury Prevention Exercise Programme to Account for both Logistical and Environmental Barriers to using the Programme and the Existing Scientific Evidence Base for Preventive Exercise Programme Structure and Content (adapted from Hislop, 2017)	295
15.2	Changes to Activate Programme Structure Following End User Feedback (adapted from Hislop, 2017)	298
15.3	Sample Running and Change of Direction Exercises from Level 1 of U15 Version of Programme (sourced from World Rugby, 2022)	299
15.4	Sample Lower Limb Balance and Landing Exercises from Level 1 of U15 Version of Programme (sourced from World Rugby, 2022)	300

15.5	Sample Resistance Training Exercises from Level 1 of U15 Version of Activate Programme (sourced from World Rugby, 2022)	301
15.6	Sample Landing and Plyometric Exercises from Level 1 of U15 Version of Activate Programme (sourced from World Rugby, 2022)	302
15.7	Sample Pitch Layout for Completing the Activate Programme (sourced from World Rugby, 2022)	302
16.1	The number of Studies per Sports Science and Medicine Theme in Female Rugby (information from Heyward et al., 2022)	319
16.2	Key Injury Surveillance Figures from the 2021 Women's Rugby League Super League	320
16.3	The Combined Mean Ratings of Importance and Feasibility for each of the Injury Risk Factors (Scantlebury et al., 2022)	322
17.1	A Sample Nested Plan for a U15 Rugby Union Team (adapted from Abraham & Collins, 2011a; Abraham et al., 2014, 2022)	338

TABLES

2.1	Ten Pillars for Successful Long-Term Athletic Development (Lloyd et al., 2016)	24
2.2	RAMPAGE Coaching Session Framework	26
3.1	Bio-Psycho-Social Development of Children and Young People in Sport (Adapted from Morley & Sanctuary, 2016)	37
3.2	A 'Throwing' Example of RFL Skills according to the Lifespan Motor Development Model Matrix Analysis	43
3.3	Player's Needs at the Beginner, Intermediate and Advanced Stages of Development	45
3.4	Session Structure for a Movement-Based Approach to Coaching Children in Rugby	46
5.1	Participation History for Forwards and Backs and Top-10 Potentials and Bottom-10 Potentials in a Rugby Union Academy (adapted from Dimundo et al. 2022)	71
7.1	Examples of Testing Methods used in Youth Rugby and Measures of Reliability Reported in the Literature	110
8.1	Training Programmes of Studies that have Investigated Resistance Training in Youth Rugby Players	130
8.2	Example of a Beginner's Resistance Training Programme	140
8.3	Example of an Advanced Resistance Training Programme	141
9.1	Psychosocial Characteristics Facilitative of Young Players' Development (adapted from Dohme et al., 2019)	152
9.2	Psychosocial Skills Facilitative of Young Players' Development (adapted from Dohme et al., 2019)	153
10.1	Summary of the Research Studies Measuring Technical and Tactical Qualities	168

10.2	Definitions for Measures of Technical and Tactical Qualities offered within the Research Literature as Key Game Skills (Definitions Derived Directly from; Bennett et al., 2016; Den Hollander et al., 2016, 2019; Gabbett et al., 2010; Ungureanu et al., 2019)	175
10.3	Summary of the Research Studies Developing Technical and Tactical Qualities in Youth Rugby	178
10.4	Summary of the Research Studies using Competition to Address Technical and Tactical Development	183
10.5	The Seven Key Principles when Applying Deliberate Practice in your Coaching (adapted from Eccles et al., 2022, p. 3)	186
10.6	List of the Wellington Rules introduced in 2017 (Ashford et al., 2020, p. 2672)	188
11.1	Summary of Studies Evaluating the Tackle in Youth Rugby Union	196
11.2	Summary of Studies Evaluating the Tackle in Youth Rugby League	198
11.3	Tackle Techniques Associated with Injury Prevention and Performance in Rugby Union (Hollander et al., 2021)	200
11.4	Ball-carry Techniques Associated with Injury Prevention and Performance in Rugby Union (Hollander et al., 2021)	201
11.5	Criteria to Assess Tackler and Ball-Carrier Technical Skills (Adapted from Hendricks et al., 2018)	204
11.6	Tackle Contact Skill Training Variables (adapted from Hendricks et al., 2018)	207
11.7	An Example Tackle Contact Training Program	211
13.1	Commonly Used Methods and Tools for Measuring Fatigue	238
14.1	Dietary Carbohydrate Recommendations for Young Rugby Players across Training and Match Days. Values Represent a Guide, which should be Individually Tailored to the Requirements of Each Player	253
14.2	Example Dietary Energy, Macronutrient, and Fluid Intake on a Training Day for a Young Rugby Player. Dietary Energy and Macronutrient Distribution Targets and Coaching Points are Examples for Practitioners Working with Young Rugby Players	261
15.1	Summary of Overall Match and Training Injury Incidence Rates in Youth Rugby Union (separated by recording definition)	273
15.2	Summary of Overall Match and Training Injury Incidence Rates in Youth Rugby League (separated by recording definition)	281
15.3	Summary of Existing Preventive Exercise Programmes Reviewed as part of the First Stage in the Development Process	294
16.1	The Number of Research Studies in Female Rugby by Decade	319
17.1	Alignment of Book Chapters to the Five Rings of Athlete Development	336
17.2	Options for Using the Big 5 as a Planning Audit (Adapted from Collins & Collins, 2021)	337

ABOUT THE EDITORS

Kevin Till, PhD, ASCC, is a Professor of Athletic Development within the Carnegie School of Sport at Leeds Beckett University. Kevin is the Co-director of the Carnegie Applied Rugby Research (CARR) Centre. Kevin has published over 180 international scientific peer-reviewed publications over the last decade related to youth athletes, talent identification and development, sport science and coaching (mainly within the sport of rugby). His research and applied work has led to policy and practice changes within rugby. He is also a Strength and Conditioning Coach at Leeds Rhinos RLFC within their academy programs.

Jonathon Weakley, PhD, is a Lecturer in Strength and Conditioning and Human Physiology at Australian Catholic University. Additionally, he holds a Visiting Research Fellow position at Leeds Beckett University. Jonathon has worked with professional sporting teams across Europe and Australasia, with a particular focus on the development of strength, power and muscle hypertrophy through resistance training and nutritional interventions. He currently consults for several sporting organisations and technology companies and has over 75 peer-reviewed manuscripts on the topics of strength and conditioning, exercise physiology, applied biomechanics and nutrition.

Sarah Whitehead, PhD, is a Senior Lecturer in Strength and Conditioning at Leeds Beckett University. Sarah completed her PhD with the CARR Centre at Leeds Beckett investigating the match characteristics of rugby league, alongside working as a practitioner with the Leeds Rhinos Academy. Within her current academic role Sarah is an active researcher within sport science and performance. Additionally, Sarah is the Head of Athletic Performance and Development for Leeds Rhinos Netball and works with the Rugby Football League (RFL) Injury Surveillance Project.

Ben Jones, PhD, ASCC, is a Professor of Sports Physiology and Performance within the Carnegie School of Sport at Leeds Beckett University. He is Co-director of the Carnegie Applied Rugby Research (CARR) Centre and a Visiting Professor at the University of Cape Town, South Africa, and the University of New England, Australia. Ben has published over 200 international scientific peer-reviewed publications. Ben is also Strategic Lead for Performance and Research for England Rugby League at the Rugby Football League, and Pathway Performance Director at Leeds Rhinos Rugby League Club. Ben has worked on policy and practice changes within rugby for a number of years.

ABOUT THE CONTRIBUTORS

Michael Ashford, PhD, is a Coach Developer for Grey Matters Performance, UK, a Lecturer in Sport Coaching at the University of Edinburgh and the Head of Coach Development for Wasps Rugby Academy. Michael's research has explored areas of talent development, player decision making, coach decision making, coach development and coaching planning and practice. As a Coach Developer, he currently supports a range of coaches with their practice, across individual, team and Olympic sport contexts. Michael is also an experienced Rugby Union Coach, having been Head Coach of Harrogate RFC and the University of Leeds men's teams.

Sarah Chantler, RD, MSc, is a Registered Dietitian and Senior Lecturer at Leeds Beckett University. Originally from South Africa, she qualified as a Dietitian at the University of Cape Town and consulted for the practice associated with the Sports Science Institute of South Africa before moving to the United Kingdom to complete her PhD. Her research focuses around gastrointestinal health and nutrition literacy in athletes, in conjunction with applied work across a wide variety of sports.

Nessan Costello, PhD, is SENr Accredited Sports Nutritionist and Senior Lecturer at Leeds Beckett University. His research interests lie in evaluating the energy and macronutrient requirements of team sport athletes, having completed an applied PhD with Leeds Rhinos RFLC academy. Alongside his research, Nessan is currently consulting with two professional soccer teams across the English Premier League and English Football League Championship.

Josh Darrall-Jones, PhD, ASCC, is a Research Fellow at Leeds Beckett University, with previous applied experience as Head of Academy Strength and

Conditioning and Sport Science at Wasps Rugby, and First team Rehabilitation Strength and Conditioning Coach at Bath Rugby. Josh completed his PhD with the Carnegie Applied Rugby Research (CARR) Centre at Leeds Beckett University investigating the physical characteristics of Academy Rugby Union players in collaboration with Yorkshire Carnegie RUFC.

Steven den Hollander, PhD, is the Head of Data and Sport Science at UXI Sport, an organisation that runs five rugby institutes across South Africa. Steve completed his PhD at the University of Cape Town, evaluating the assessment and development of contact technique in rugby. His research expertise includes performance analysis, skill acquisition and development, player monitoring and biokinetics.

Francesco Dimundo, MSc, FHEQ, is a PhD Candidate at Birmingham City University, investigating the *talent identification and development in professional rugby union*. His research is sponsored by Worcester Warriors RFC, the club in which he worked as Strength and Conditioning Coach for the last three seasons. His working experiences include organisations and teams as ALTIS athletics, Scottish Institute of Sport, Scottish football Premiership, Italian football Serie B, Italian volleyball Premiership, Nike F.C. Academy, English college and rugby academy and Pro-combat clubs. Francesco provides lectures in different universities in the UK and works to improve the talent system in Italy.

Lea-Cathrin Dohme, PhD, is a Lecturer in Sport and Exercise Psychology at Cardiff Metropolitan University. Her research focuses on the positive development of youth athletes by teaching coaches and parents how to promote athletes' psychological development through sport. This includes examining the knowledge and strategies employed by coaches and parents individually and collaboratively that foster or inhibit this development. To improve athletes' positive development, Dr. Dohme also engages in the development, delivery and evaluation of national and international coach education initiatives.

Joey C. Eisenmann, PhD, is a Diverse Scholar-Practitioner with 25 years of experience in paediatric exercise science and youth athletic development. He has published 200 peer-reviewed scientific papers, lectured widely, served on several national-level committees and projects involving pediatric sports medicine, youth fitness, youth sports and strength and conditioning, and has coached and developed thousands of youth and high school athletes and coaches. Most recently, he was the Director of Spartan Performance at Michigan State University and Director of High Performance and Education at USA Football. Currently, he is a Visiting Professor at Leeds Beckett University and the Head of Strength and Conditioning at IMG Academy.

Job Fransen, PhD, is an Assistant Professor at the University Medical Centre Groningen and an Adjunct Fellow at the University of Technology Sydney. He studies motor skill acquisition, talent, expertise and performance analysis in team sports.

Nicholas Gill, PhD, is the Strength and Conditioning Coach for the New Zealand All Blacks Rugby and Associate Professor in Human Performance within the Faculty of Health, Sport and Human Performance at the University of Waikato. Nick has combined the role of 'scientist' and 'coach' for the last 18 years and alongside his professional role has published over 100 scientific papers.

Marcus Hannon, PhD, is a Sport and Exercise Nutrition registered (SENr) Performance Nutritionist and is currently Lead Performance Nutritionist at Aspire Academy in Doha, Qatar. He has worked with a range of youth and adult athletes across a variety of sports including football (previously Aston Villa and Everton), rugby (previously Northampton Saints and Ulster Rugby) and professional boxing. Marcus completed his PhD at Liverpool John Moores University (LJMU), investigating the energy requirements of Premier League academy footballers. He is still actively involved in applied sports science and nutrition research and is also a Visiting Research Fellow at LJMU.

Timothy Hartwig, PhD, is a Senior Lecturer at Australian Catholic University, Sydney. Tim completed his PhD in partnership with Rugby Australia and has spent over 15 years exploring the training practices of youth rugby players. His main research focus is a better understanding of training and competition loads and youth player load management to improve performance and participation and reduce overtraining and injuries.

Sharief Hendricks, PhD, is a Senior Lecturer at the University of Cape Town (UCT) and a Visiting Fellow at Leeds Beckett University (UK). He has been awarded the prestigious UCT Fellows Young Researcher Award (2019), a two-time finalist for the TW Kambule-NSTF Researcher Award (2020 and 2021) (an award for South Africa's top scientists) and the European College of Sport Science Fellowship (FECSS) (2020). He is also currently the President-Elect of the South African Sports Medicine Association, and Chair of Research and Science for the South African Sports Confederation and Olympic Committee (SASCOC).

Omar Heyward, MSc, ASCA PCAS-P, is a PhD Candidate with the Carnegie Applied Rugby Research (CARR) Centre at Leeds Beckett University. His PhD research investigates the applied sport science of the female rugby athlete. In addition to his research, he is currently the Lead Strength and Conditioning Coach for England Rugby's Women's Pathway and the Sports Scientist for the Leeds Rhinos Rugby League Academy Team.

Michael Hislop, PhD, is an Injury Prevention and Surveillance Researcher at World Rugby (Ireland), where he is responsible for conducting and coordinating a number of research projects that aim to advance player welfare across rugby union. Prior to joining World Rugby, Mike obtained his PhD from the University of Bath (UK), where, in partnership with England Rugby, he was involved in researching injury risk factors and risk reduction strategies in schoolboy rugby union.

Rich Johnston, PhD, is a Senior Lecturer at Australian Catholic University, Brisbane. Rich has worked as a Practitioner across a number of sports, including both rugby league and union. With his role at the university, he is an Active Researcher across a number of areas of sport science, with over 50 peer-reviewed publications. He also works as a Consultant for a number of teams, providing data analytical services to optimise training and streamline reporting of information.

Adam L. Kelly, PhD, CSci, is a Senior Lecturer and Course Leader for Sports Coaching and Physical Education at Birmingham City University, UK. Alongside attaining his PhD from the University of Exeter, Adam is a BASES Sport and Exercise Scientist and UEFA A Licenced Coach. Broadly, his research interests explore organisational structures in youth sport to better understand the athlete development process and help create more appropriate settings. He is currently collaborating with various regional organisations and national governing bodies across a range of sports including basketball, cricket, football, rugby union, squash and swimming.

Mathieu Lacome, PhD, was recently at Paris Saint-Germain FC as Head of Research and Innovation and is now the Chief Performance and Analytics Officer for Parma. Mathieu built his career in sports science and has been working in athlete performance for well over a decade in elite football. He has done his PhD in Applied Physiology and Performance while working for the French Rugby Union as Sports Scientist and Strength and Conditioning Coach for the U20 and U19. He also co-founded the Sports Performance and Science Report journal aiming at democratising research. Over the last ten years, he focused a lot on advancing knowledge of load monitoring and injuries and its relationship to interventions for training and match.

Cédric Leduc, PhD, holds a master's degree in Exercise Physiology and Strength and Conditioning. Additionally, he has recently been awarded a PhD exploring the importance of sleep in the recovery process for team sport athletes. Alongside his academic background, Cédric has been a sport scientist for a variety of elite team sport environments and is currently the Sport Scientist at Crystal Palace Football Club

Rhodri S. Lloyd, PhD, FNSCA, is a Professor of Paediatric Strength and Conditioning and Chair of the Youth Physical Development Centre at Cardiff Metropolitan University. His research interests surround the impact of growth and maturation on long-term athletic development and the mechanisms underpinning neuromuscular training adaptations and injury risk in youth. He is an accredited Strength and Conditioning Coach with the UK Strength and Conditioning Association and the National Strength and Conditioning Association. He has authored in excess of 140 research publications, 30 book chapters and three textbooks in the area of paediatric strength and conditioning.

Ric Lovell, PhD, is an Associate Professor in Sport and Exercise Science at Western Sydney University. Ric researches and provides consultancy in sports physiology and performance science, primarily in football codes. His predominant research focus investigates optimal preparation and athletic development strategies for players, including injury risk and fatigue mitigation, talent identification and monitoring training and match loads. During his career, Ric has worked with a range of national and international football teams and several governing bodies on policy development, research and innovation and education.

Martin MacTaggart is currently an MSc Student at Leeds Beckett University alongside his role at England Rugby Union as Player Pathway Manager, working with the Regional Academies and Constituent Bodies (Counties) to establish and support the implementation of pathway programmes and the development of coaches. He is an Experienced Coach developer and Mentor within the union supporting coaches across the advanced and performance coaching awards.

Alexander B. T. McAuley is a PhD Researcher in Sport Genomics and Assistant Lecturer in the Sport and Exercise and Life Science departments within the Faculty of Health, Education and Life Sciences (HELS) at Birmingham City University. He is the Primary Investigator of the Football Gene Project, a multidisciplinary investigation that aims to identify genotype-phenotype associations in football to enhance understanding of the biological mechanisms underpinning performance and ultimately facilitate greater individualised athlete development.

Stephen D. Mellalieu, PhD, is a Professor in Applied Sport Psychology at Cardiff Metropolitan University, UK. He is the Co-founder and Network Editor of the World Rugby Science Network. His research interests lie in the area of athlete welfare, including stress, coping, wellbeing and performance, psychological skills training and behaviour change, and the organisational environment of elite sport. Stephen is a Chartered Psychologist of the British Psychological Society, a Registered Practitioner Psychologist and Partner with the Health and Care Professions Council and a British Association of Sport and Exercise Sciences Accredited Sport Scientist. He has 25 years of consultancy experience in Olympic and Professional sport, working predominantly within professional rugby union for the past 15 years.

David Morley, PhD, is Carnegie Professor of Physical Education at Leeds Beckett University, UK and Adjunct Professor of Sport Coaching at La Trobe University,

Australia. Dave has led national and global projects concerned with improving children's health, wellbeing, physical activity, movement and physical literacy on behalf of national and international sport organisations. He has been responsible for designing and evaluating programs reaching thousands of coaches and teachers. He has also led on the evaluation of multiple national interventions, including 'Let's talk Rugby League', as well as supporting the developments of child and adolescent interventions for the Rugby Football League and Rugby Football Union in England. He is currently Lead Advisor for Nike and the Youth Sport Trust developing and evaluating a games-based, movement assessment intervention involving 25 million children across over 20 countries and has a passion for developing children's enjoyment in sport and those who support such environments.

Donna O'Connor, PhD, is a Professor of Sports Coaching and coordinates the postgraduate Sports Coaching Program at the University of Sydney. She is a Former Strength and Conditioning Coach with an NRL club and the Australian Women's basketball team. Donna is an Active Researcher and Consultant on coaching practice, athlete and coach development, and sports performance. She is also an ICCE-trained Coach Developer, and a Member of the World Congress Science and Football Steering Committee and International Council of Coaching Excellence research committee.

Cameron Owen, MSc, is a PhD Student at Leeds Beckett University. His PhD focuses on identifying the between player differences and within players development of physical qualities in academy rugby union players. Alongside this Cameron has worked as a Strength and Conditioning Coach in an RFU Regional Academy and Super League Netball Franchise Pathway, and currently provides support for England Wheelchair Rugby League and the British Diving World Class Programme.

Padraic Phibbs, PhD, is currently an Athletic Development Coach with Leinster Rugby and the Irish Rugby Football Union, as well as a Visiting Research Fellow at Leeds Beckett University. Padraic completed his PhD with the Carnegie Applied Rugby Research (CARR) Centre at Leeds Beckett University investigating the training demands of adolescent rugby union players, and subsequently held a Postdoctoral Research Fellow position on the Talented Developing Player project in conjunction with the Rugby Football Union.

Carlos Ramírez-López is a Research Fellow at Leeds Beckett University and the National Team Sports Scientist at Scottish Rugby Union. Carlos completed his PhD with the Carnegie Applied Rugby Research (CARR) Centre at Leeds Beckett University investigating fatigue, recovery and performance in youth elite rugby players in collaboration with five different unions during the U18 Six Nations Tournament, alongside working as a Practitioner with Yorkshire Carnegie

Academy. In addition to his Practitioner role with Scottish Rugby Union, Carlos is currently conducting research in scientific innovation, injury surveillance and physical and physiological profiling of international-level rugby players.

Dale B. Read, PhD, is a Lecturer in Sports Performance at Manchester Metropolitan University. He is an Accredited Strength and Conditioning Coach with the UKSCA and an Accredited Sport and Exercise Scientist with BASES. He has worked with youth rugby union players in schools and academies across England and Australia. Dale studied his PhD within the Carnegie Applied Rugby Research (CARR) Centre at Leeds Beckett University and remains a Visiting Research Fellow. His research explores the physiology and performance of rugby union players, and to date, he has published over 30 peer-reviewed academic articles in this area.

John Sampson, PhD, is an Associate Professor in the School of Medicine at the University of Wollongong, NSW, Australia. John worked with Premier League Football, and Super League Rugby clubs in the UK, before moving to Australia to complete his PhD. John is currently an Active Member of Rugby Australia's National Safety Committee. His primary focus is injury surveillance, and injury risk reduction where he has worked with Rugby League, Rugby Union, Football (soccer), American Football Clubs and the Australian Army. He has over 45 research publications (book chapters and peer-reviewed manuscripts) to date.

Sean Scantlebury, PhD, CSCS, is a Research Fellow at Leeds Beckett University. Sean completed his PhD with the Carnegie Applied Rugby Research (CARR) Centre at Leeds Beckett University investigating factors associated with training load in adolescent athletes. His current research focusses on injury surveillance, match demands and the anthropometric and physical qualities of the women's rugby league Super League. Additionally, he is the Lead Performance Coach for the England women's rugby league team.

Ross A. Shand, CPsychol, is a Chartered Sport and Exercise Psychologist at Leeds Beckett University. His applied work includes providing psychological support to teams and organisations at senior and developmental levels. In addition to this, Ross is undertaking a PhD investigating the psychosocial development of young players within a rugby union academy.

Keith Stokes, PhD, is a Professor of Applied Physiology within the Department for Health at the University of Bath and Medical Research Lead for the Rugby Football Union.

Jamie Taylor, PhD, is a Senior Coach Developer at Grey Matters, an Assistant Professor at Dublin City University and a Lecturer in Sport Coaching at the University of Edinburgh. His background is as an Experienced Coach and continues to work as an Academy Coach at Wasps RFC. Previous roles include coaching at Leicester Tigers and Pathway Coaching Lead at the English Institute of Sport. As a Coach Developer, he consults across a variety of organisations and has worked with over 150 coaches in a developmental capacity. This has included working with coaches at the elite and academy levels in football, rugby union, rugby league, tennis and a variety of Olympic sports. He has ongoing research interests in coaching, performance, talent development and coach development.

Gregory Tierney, Meng, PhD, is a Lecturer in Biomechanics at Ulster University. Gregory has conducted consultancy work and research with national and international sport governing bodies, and his research has formed the basis for policy and law changes in sport to reduce head injuries and their potential long-term consequences. Gregory is an Active Member of the Scientific Review Committee for the International Research Council on Biomechanics of Injury, Science and Medicine Research Committee at the Rugby Football League and was recently awarded the 'Hans Gros Emerging Researcher Award' by the International Society of Biomechanics in Sport.

Dan Weaving, PhD, is a Senior Lecturer in Sports Performance at Leeds Beckett University. His research interests lie in the use of technology and data analytics to inform the training process in team sports and has published over 50 articles in the area. Alongside his research, Dan has concurrently worked in professional rugby league for the past decade, providing applied sport science support across the multidisciplinary team and is currently Sport Scientist at Leeds Rhinos RLFC. He also provides consultancy to sporting organisations and governing bodies relating to these areas.

Ryan White, MSc, is a PhD Candidate with the Carnegie Applied Rugby Research (CARR) Centre at Leeds Beckett University. His PhD research investigates data mining techniques to further the understanding of the movement patterns and characteristics of professional team sport athletes. In addition to his research, Ryan is the first team sport scientist with the Leeds Rhinos rugby league men's team.

FOREWORD

Rugby has been an instrumental part of my life. I was lucky to play professionally for almost twenty years and loved every minute of it. In recent years, I have coached within Rugby League and Rugby Union at Leeds Rhinos and Leicester Tigers, respectively. But rugby has also provided many other great things – friendships, experiences, life skills, life lessons – it has so much to offer.

My love of rugby started as a young child, growing up in Oldham, North England and training and playing with my local amateur club Waterhead ARLFC. This is where my early experiences began, and I started to learn my trade but benefit from what the sports have to offer. It is vitally important we continue to grow the sports of rugby so that young people can have the opportunity to potentially experience and learn the things that I have in my career. And that starts with the young rugby player – and it is our responsibility as stakeholders in the sports to do that in an appropriate and healthy way.

On that note, it is great to see a book focussed on the science and application for the young rugby player. This text summarises the current research within young rugby players but more importantly provides practical examples, recommendations and key take home messages for how national governing bodies, organisations and stakeholders (coaches, practitioners, parents, players) can use this information to maximise the development of their players. It covers a wide range of topics including growth and maturation, talent identification, player development (including technical, tactical, physical and psychosocial), nutrition, injury risk and planning your practice. It is both educational and informative to help support our practices with young players.

It is more important than ever before that we use this information to inform our practices to maximise participation of young people in the game and support those that have the chance of being successful. I highly recommend this book for all involved in youth rugby and look forward to seeing how this information can continue to grow the sports of rugby in the future.

Kevin Sinfield, OBE

ACKNOWLEDGEMENTS

Many thanks to my co-editors for their ideas, discussions and hard work in producing this book. A further thank you to every contributor who has offered their expertise in summarising the research literature and sharing their practical applications or recommendations for practice. Thank you to Leeds Beckett University, the Carnegie School of Sport and the Carnegie Applied Rugby Research (CARR) Centre for their continued support in all our research and knowledge exchange activity. A big thank you to all the organisations, stakeholders and players we get the chance to work with. Finally, thank you to my family for everything you do!

Kevin Till

First, thank you to the co-editors and my close friends, Kevin, Ben, and Sarah. Without your hard work, guidance, and support, this book would not be possible. Second, thank you to the authors and contributors. Your wisdom and knowledge help make this an excellent applied text which will support young rugby players into the future. Finally, thank you to my whānau. Particularly, Murray and Brigid. I hope this goes a small way for all the hours driving me to matches, standing on sidelines, and believing in me.

Jonathon Weakley

Thank you to all contributors for your knowledge and expertise throughout the book. A big thank you to my co-editors for your hard work and dedication in pulling the book together. Finally, thank you to Leeds Beckett University and the Carnegie School of Sport for their continued support.

Sarah Whitehead

Thank you to my co-editors, especially Kevin, for keeping us all on track. Thank you to all the contributors who were willing to share their expertise and knowledge. This book is underpinned by all the coaches, sport scientists, strength and conditioning coaches, teachers, administrators, policy makers, physiotherapists, doctors and players who continue to ask questions that we don't know the answer to – leading to more research! Thank you to Leeds Beckett University, the Carnegie School of Sport and all the sports teams and organisations we work with for the continued trust, challenge and support.

Ben Jones

1
YOUTH RUGBY
Setting the Scene

Kevin Till, Martin MacTaggart and Ben Jones

Introduction

Rugby is a collective name for the family of team sports, Rugby Union and Rugby League. Rugby was believed to have originated as a sport in the 1830s at Rugby School when during a game of football, William Webb Ellis (whom the Rugby Union World Cup is now named after) picked up the ball and started to run with it. The rugby codes then split in 1895 when rugby league turned professional, starting to pay players. It was not until 100 years later that rugby union became professional, after the 1995 World Cup in South Africa. Over the last 125–130 years, the sports have evolved their own rules, competitions and world governing bodies (i.e., World Rugby, International Rugby League) to become established independent, international and professional team field sports.

Whilst these differences have emerged over time, similarities remain within the codes of rugby. Rugby league and rugby union are contact-skill-based sports characterised by intermittent, high-intensity and invasive activities (Till et al., 2020). The aim of rugby is to outscore the opposition, primarily by progressing the ball over the opposition's try line to score a try. This can be achieved by running with the ball, kicking the ball and/or passing (only backwards) the ball by hand to another team member. One key component of rugby is that players are frequently required to engage in physical contact and collision events with opposing players through either tackling the opposition in defence or carrying the ball in attack. As such, the sports of rugby place multiple technical, tactical, physical and psychosocial demands on its athletes requiring players to develop multiple characteristics to participate, perform and compete across multiple playing levels (i.e., from amateur to elite) and age grades (from U6s to Masters).

As this book presents and discusses the science and application of the young rugby player this chapter has several purposes. First, the chapter aims to introduce the codes of rugby union and rugby league, identifying the clear differences between the sports. Second, the chapter presents the structure of youth rugby for participation, performance and development purposes. To support the readers understanding of the structure of youth rugby, the chapter presents England Rugby Football Union (RFU)'s Age Grade Rugby playing pathway as a practical application of the organisation of youth rugby within a national governing body. The chapter then concludes by explaining why scientific research and practical application within youth rugby is important for maximising health, development and performance within young rugby players and therefore presenting the topics discussed within each chapter of this text.

Rugby Union

Since turning professional in 1995, the expansion of rugby union has increased rapidly with millions of participants across over 100 nations worldwide. For example, it is estimated that there are over 2.1 million participants within England alone (Freitag et al., 2015), with many of these participants being young rugby players. Adult rugby union consists of two teams of 15 players (and up to eight interchange players) competing against each other for two halves of 40-minutes separated by a 10–15 minute half-time recovery. However, at younger age grades, the number of players, game length (in minutes) and the rules are adapted to suit the needs of young players.

Players are primarily split across two positional groups (i.e., forwards and backs) and ten specific playing positions. Forwards are classified as either front row forwards (inclusive of two props and one hooker) or back row forwards (two second row, two flankers and one lock) and are typically involved in more contact and collision events than backs. Backs are classified as inside backs (one scrum-half, one fly-half) and outside backs (two centres, two wingers and one fullback) and are typically involved in more free running and skill-based opportunities than forwards.

Rugby union is a territorial game with the laws of the sport enforced by World Rugby, the international governing body. The primary aim is to progress the ball over the opposition's try line (i.e., score a 'try'). The team in possession of the ball has an unlimited tackle count and may lose possession through an error (e.g., dropping the ball, losing possession in a ruck), penalty infringement (e.g., failing to release the ball when tackled) or through kicking the ball. When in possession, a breakdown occurs when the attacker is stopped by the defence by bringing them to ground (a tackle, which is frequently followed by a ruck), or by contesting for possession with the ball-carrier on their feet (a maul). Rugby union matches can be restarted via set pieces including scrums (following an error), lineouts (after the ball goes out of play), kicks (following a penalty or a point is scored) or a tap (following a penalty). Points are awarded through scoring tries (five points), penalty kicks (three points), drop goals (three points) or conversions following a try (two points).

Rugby League

Rugby league is predominantly played within Australia, England, Fiji, France, New Zealand, Papua New Guinea, Samoa and Tonga. The International Rugby League governs the international game (e.g., Rugby League World Cup) with two professional club competitions in Europe (i.e., Super League) and Australasia (i.e., National Rugby League). Participation in rugby league in most countries is lower than rugby union; however, it continues to be a popular sport for youth players in the primary playing nations.

Adult rugby league consists of two teams of 13 players (and four interchange players) who compete for two halves of 40-minutes, separated by a 10–15 minute half-time recovery. As with rugby union, different versions of the game are applied within younger age grades. The 13 players are generally split across two positional groups (i.e., forwards and backs) and nine different playing positions. Forwards are made up of two props, one hooker, two second row and one loose forward. Backs are made up of one scrum-half, one stand-off/five-eight, two centres, two wingers and one fullback. Further positional classification can include hit up 'middle' forwards (inclusive of front row forwards, loose forward), wide-running forwards (second row), adjustables (hooker, scrum half, stand-off/five-eight) and outside backs (centres, wingers, fullback).

Rugby league teams have six tackles to progress the ball over the opposition's try line and score a '*try*'. A tackle is complete when an attacker is either held stationary or put to the ground by the opposing defensive team. The attacker then plays the ball between their feet (i.e., by rolling the ball backwards with their foot) to progress to the next phase of play; the same team is then allowed to pass (only backwards), run or kick the ball until the next tackle. Up to two players from the opposing team are permitted to stand in front of the tackled player, known as markers, while the rest of the team must retreat the defensive line 10 m. Possession of the ball is relinquished either after the sixth tackle is completed, the opposing team kicks the ball, makes a mistake or a penalty is awarded. This results in the successive interchange of ball possession, requiring players to continuously attack and defend throughout the game (Gabbett, 2005). Points are awarded through scoring a try (four points), kicking a penalty or conversion (two points) or a drop goal (one point).

Youth Development

The period of youth represents both childhood (i.e., generally up to 11 years in girls and 13 years in boys) and adolescence (i.e., ranging from 12 to 18 years in girls and 14–18 years in boys; Lloyd et al., 2015). Hence, within this book a young rugby player is referred to as anyone up to the age of 18 years. The International Olympic Committee consensus statement on youth athletic development commenced by stating, the goal is clear: Develop healthy, capable and resilient young athletes, while attaining widespread, inclusive, sustainable and enjoyable participation and success for all levels of individual athletic achievement (Bergeron et al., 2015, p. 843). This statement emphasises the importance that sports participation (e.g., for health benefits) and sports performance (e.g., talent development) are key pathways to consider for all youths. However, achieving this is a challenge for all stakeholders working within youth sports (i.e., youths, parents, coaches and administrators) due to the careful balancing act between health and performance alongside meeting the needs of the many rather than the few. With so many options (e.g., sport, recreation, education, entertainment) now available for youths, providing developmentally appropriate practice that means young players continue to participate and develop is key. As such, sporting organisations and national governing bodies must structure and support their youth player pathways to maximise youth athletic development and provide training, competition and development opportunities for all individuals involved in the sport from participation to performance. In addition, sporting organisations and national governing bodies have a responsibility to ensure all stakeholders are appropriately ready to deliver these training, competition and development opportunities for these young players.

Youth Rugby

Within rugby, like most youth sports, national governing bodies most used option for organising training and competition is to group players using annual-age grades (e.g., U8s, U13s, U18s). Participation within rugby can start as young as five years of age, whereby participants train and compete using modified versions of the sport by adapting the number of players (e.g., 4 *vs.* 4), the pitch size (e.g., 40 × 20 m), the equipment used (e.g., ball size) and the rules implemented (e.g., touch or tag). Rugby can be played within schools or local community clubs with such strategies aiming to ensure all players enjoy rugby in a safe environment whilst developing a wide array of skills, focused upon healthy development. Rugby is traditionally a late specialisation sport (Côté & Vierimaa, 2014) especially compared to other team sports (e.g., soccer; Noon et al, 2015). Specialising within rugby is recommended towards late adolescence (i.e., 15–16 years). Traditionally, this is where the talent identification, selection and development of players demonstrating the potential for future success within rugby is implemented (Till et al., 2021). In these talent identification and development systems, players are typically identified from community or school rugby and invited to train with a professional rugby academy (from 14 to15 years of age), prior to potentially signing a professional contract at 16–18 years of age (the age may depend upon the code and country).

While these talent identification and development programmes are commonly implemented, challenges of being a youth rugby player can emerge at this timepoint. First, biological, psychological and social development (e.g., maturation; the process of becoming an adult) results in significant changes to the youth rugby player that may impact upon both their performance and health. Second, prior to 16 or 18 years of age (depending upon the code and country) the organisational system in which players may train and compete can be complex. This can result in young players training and competing within multiple rugby programmes (i.e., club, school, representative and academy) alongside undertaking other sporting activities (i.e., playing other sports) and school-based commitments (e.g., Physical Education; Hendricks et al., 2019). Therefore, players can compete and train in a complex multi-sport, multi-environment and multi-coach development programme. Within youth rugby union, such a programme has been previously termed as '*organised chaos*', whereby '*organised*' is defined as making arrangements or preparations for an event, and '*chaos*' is defined as the property of a complex system whose behaviour is so unpredictable it appears random (Phibbs et al., 2018). Therefore, due to both human development principles (e.g., biological, psychological and social development) and organisational structures (e.g., organisation of youth rugby), understanding youth rugby and the youth rugby player is vital to ensure appropriate and sustainable participation and player development for as many youth players as possible. This should therefore be at the forefront of all rugby governing bodies, clubs and schools, and stakeholders involved within youth rugby, strategies to ensure healthy and appropriate youth athletic development and achieve the goals of the International Olympic Committee (Bergeron et al., 2015).

The following section aims to explain the England RFUs' Age Grade Rugby programme to support and guide appropriate development opportunities for all young rugby players.

England Rugby Football Unions' Age Grade Rugby

Fun and friendship are often expressed as the most important reasons to play sport. However, both expert opinion and the England Rugby's own research have shown that the emphasis has historically been placed on winning, with evidence of over playing the more able players and under playing those less able players to achieve results during matches. Following the conclusion of pilot programmes, the national governing body in England, the RFU, developed a system to support young rugby players to maximise participation and performance within the sport. This system is known as Age Grade Rugby (AGR; Figure 1.1)

FIGURE 1.1 Overview of England Rugby Football Union's Age Grade Rugby.

with the intention to introduce the sport of rugby and develop appropriate technical, tactical, physical and psychosocial skills in incremental stages without the full complexity of the laws and regulations used within the adult game. This is essentially a long-term curriculum towards full adult rugby union.

England RFU established five core values that support being involved in the game; Teamwork, Respect, Enjoyment, Discipline and Sportsmanship. These values are central to the game as a whole and are essential to the philosophy in supporting young rugby players. Taking these values, AGR utilises three core principles; Player Centred, Development Driven, and Competition Supported in the development of the AGR system;

- Player Centred means meeting the needs of that individual player with a focus on potential rather than current ability, and the importance is on enjoyment and encouraging a life-long love of rugby.
- Development Driven means recognising the various stages in a player's journey and providing the opportunities to develop physical competence, rugby skills and self-confidence to enjoy rugby.
- Competition Supported means providing appropriate meaningful playing opportunities that enable further development and exploration of resilience, leadership and rugby's core values, Teamwork, Respect, Enjoyment, Discipline and Sportsmanship.

The AGR aims to ensure that every individual, regardless of age, experience and ability, can enjoy the game in a safe environment and develop their personal and social skills, alongside their rugby skills, which will lead to lifelong involvement in the sport. By having this emphasis, it is hoped that young people will enjoy the game for longer and into their adult years.

Age Grade Rugby Structure

Most of the AGR structure occurs within community clubs. Whilst many community clubs will provide activity for young rugby players from five years old, the AGR game formally begins at six years old and has specific regulations through to U18s that operate alongside the laws of the game. However, once a player reaches their 17th birthday, players may apply through a formal process to play adult rugby. To support players development from six years to 18 years, AGR has rules and recommendations to provide age and stage-appropriate training and competition opportunities for all players. The stages are described below considering the number of players, pitch size and rules of the game;

- Starting the journey at U7, players play a non-contact version of the game, usually tag, in a four *vs.* four game with pitch dimensions of 20 m × 20 m. Teams have an unlimited number of 'tags' to score and the emphasis is on teamwork, running, evasion and passing. It's suggested to 'game coaches'

that the rules of the game are not strictly enforced in the early stages (e.g., forward pass/knock on or even running out of the pitch area) with engagement and encouragement the primary considerations.
- U8 players play the same non-contact game with increased numbers, six *vs.* six, larger pitch; 45 m × 22 m, and tags are now limited to six to try and score before the ball is given to the opposition.
- At U9, the game moves to a contact version through the introduction of the tackle, numbers are increased to seven a side and the pitch to 60 m × 30 m. There is still no contest for possession as the primary consideration is players learning the skill of tackling.
- The scrum, given for a forward pass or a knock on, is introduced for the first time at U10. It is uncontested with the nearest three players from each team taking part. Player numbers are increased to eight *vs.* eight, and one player from each team may now contest for the ball after a tackle developing both ruck and maul skills.
- Kicking out of hand is introduced in the U11 game, and the number of players involved in the contest of possession increases to maximum two per team, and the numbers on each team increase to nine *vs.* nine, whilst the pitch size is again increased. This is also the first stage where the game defines two positional sets of players; forwards who are involved in the scrum, and backs
- At U12, the scrum is enlarged to five per team and although the strike to win possession is contested, there is no pushing allowed. Team size now increases to 12 *vs.* 12 and unlimited numbers may now contest possession.
- For the U13 game the scrum increases to six players per team and pushing up to a maximum of 1.5 m is now allowed. The maximum number of players per team also increases to 13 *vs.* 13 and again the pitch adjusts to accommodate the increased number of players.
- U14 is the first age at which the full 15 a side game is played, with an eight-player scrum, kicks for goal are introduced for penalties and try conversions. The uncontested lineout is also introduced for the first time, with jumping only. At U15 lifting is introduced within the lineout, but still uncontested.
- The U16, U17 and U18 ages play the full adult laws except the scrum where players may still only push for 1.5 m.

Strategies to Support Youth Development

The design of AGR places inclusivity and each player's skill development first, with an increasing intensity of competition later. To support this philosophy, the RFU have implemented several strategies to deliver the AGR structure. For U7–U11 this includes festivals and triangular competitions, U12–U13 play in Waterfall style competitions, at U14 more formal competition is introduced through knockout cups, with leagues introduced at U15 for the first time (see Box 1.1 for definitions).

> **Box 1.1**
>
> - A Festival is a competitive round-robin playing opportunity where equal team and player participation is the emphasis. Winning doesn't affect your ongoing participation as every team plays the same appropriate number of matches.
> - A Triangular competition is a playing opportunity for three teams where equal player participation is the emphasis. Focus is on maximising all your player's involvement, development and enjoyment rather than the score.
> - A Waterfall competition is a competitive playing programme where equal participation and progression are the emphasis. The outcome of a pool games is recorded to enable every team to advance to later rounds for an equal number of matches against similar-level teams.
> - A Knockout Cup is a competitive playing programme where the outcome of the game is recorded and dictates your progression to later knock-out rounds or decides your final standing. Usually includes a winner's trophy.
> - A League is a competitive playing programme where the outcome of the game is recorded, and points are applied to dictate your position and final standing in the league table. Usually includes a winner's trophy. This may lead to a play-off system to establish final champions.

In September 2019, the RFU also introduced the Half Game rule (i.e., all players must play a minimum of a half of a game) into its regulations to ensure that all players (across all age grades) within a match-day squad will receive an equal amount of playing time and maintain the core values of England Rugby into late adolescence. Furthermore, the demands on players in the U14–U18 age grades is ever increasing, with many players participating at club, school and development programmes, possibly alongside other school sport.

In order to implement an approach that supports the player and minimises the impact on 'core' playing and training programmes, AGR is supported by the Age Grade Calendar. The AGR calendar aims to align playing and training opportunities across different school, club and representative programmes. The playing calendar provides a model which supports inclusivity of all players, guards against overplaying and underplaying and limits conflict between club and school/college rugby maintaining choice for players to play with their peer groups. This calendar ensures that national competition and representative rugby are delivered across the country at a consistent time. It enables key county and regional age grade stakeholders to arrange, balance and publish their local activities in advance of the season. The Age Grade Playing Calendar is part of the age grade rugby regulations of the game.

Talent Identification and Development Programme

To support talented players, the England Rugby Player Pathway (see Figure 1.2) is an integral part of the structure that supports England teams and is in place to provide a coherent, challenging and nurturing journey for individuals regardless of their eventual playing context. This pathway is delivered alongside the club, school, college and university game via 14 Regional academies that are spread geographically across England. It aims to keep a broad base and delay final selection until late adolescence when players have developed the necessary physical, cognitive, social and emotional skills. There are three stages identified as essential to delivering success, each aspect derives from and draws from the elements in the previous stage; Explore-Adapt-Win. At U14–U18, players are exposed to the 'Explore' stage where players are encouraged to 'explore' their boundaries. When progressing into the U20 programme players focus on the tactical understanding required to overcome game problems and adapt to situations. At the senior end of the pathway there is a clear ambition – to Win.

Working with experts, both within rugby and from other environments, the following ethos has been established to help shape how the programme operates;

- Decisions are based on long-term and appropriate development goals rather than early success.
- A shared understanding of, and access to a common framework and language is important, which can vary across each regional academy.
- Clear, open communication on what is required, that ensures the athlete is an engaged and an active participant.
- Highly individualised, evidence-based support where we develop a player's psychosocial competencies alongside their rugby competencies to support reaching their potential.

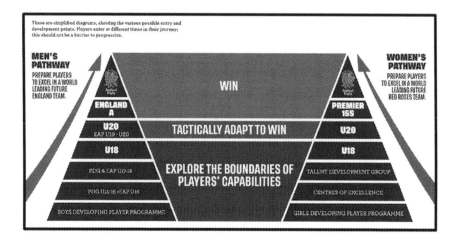

FIGURE 1.2 England Rugby Football Union's Player Pathway.

Starting with the England Rugby Developing Player Programme (ERDPP), players are introduced to the Player Pathway for the first time at U14 for boys and U15 for girls. Players are mainly nominated by coaches from clubs and schools and attend assessment events to determine their suitability for the programme. The Purpose of the ERDPP is to provide an early experience of a talent nomination, identification and development, with a focus on skill development and acquisition, game understanding and the physical components that help a player unlock their potential. When players have been identified for the ERDPP it is expected that they remain in the programme for its duration, finishing in April of the U16 year.

Through this longitudinal assessment approach, coaches are better able to determine who might be suitable for the next stage. As each step progresses, the expectations in terms of time commitment, training intensity and off-field commitment increase. It is important to note that players move between, and in and out of the pathway, and early selection is not a predictor of success. Following the conclusion of the ERDPP, selected male players will progress into the Player Development Group (PDG) and female players into the Centres of Excellence (CoE). The purpose of this stage is to build upon the platform created in the ERDPP by further developing and confirming core skills and tactical application (with positional specificity) in competitive environments and different game situations.

Due to the smaller numbers involved a more individualised approach is also taken with players expected to develop their individual development plan. A higher emphasis is also placed on the more holistic nature of development with nutrition, wellbeing, strength and conditioning advice given. England teams are introduced for the first time at U18 for both male and female players, where players are primarily drawn from the PDG and CoE programmes. Once a male player concludes their U18 season, they may be offered a contract into a junior academy and then later potentially senior academy before a full playing contract. Most female players move into the adult game on conclusion of their U18 season, whereby some players may be offered contacts with Premier 15's clubs.

In summary, the England RFU have an AGR system to support the participation, performance and development of all young rugby players. This system is based upon clear values of Player Centred, Development Driven and Competition Supported that strongly considers the needs of young players based upon their age and stage of development. This is delivered by a number of strategies including the AGR playing structure from U6 to U18, competition rules (e.g., Half Game rule) alongside a talent identification and development system that commences at U14 aligned with rugby union being a late specialisation sport.

Book Overview

This chapter has introduced the sports of rugby, the importance of youth athletic development and the young rugby player, whilst providing an example of a national governing bodies structure to support the participation, performance and development of young rugby players. Routledge's The *Young Rugby Player: Science and Application* book aims to support practitioners in increasing their knowledge base and then delivering evidence-informed practice to help support all young rugby players. Each chapter showcases the latest cutting-edge research and provides either practical examples or recommendations of this research applied in practice. It is hoped that this content will support national governing bodies, organisations and stakeholders (i.e., coaches, support staff, parents, players) wanting to develop world class, evidence-informed programmes for their young rugby players. To achieve this, 16 chapters have been written to cover the key areas of youth athletic development related to the development of the young rugby player. The chapters in this science and application book include:

Chapter 2 – Long-Term Athletic Development

This chapter introduces key concepts of long-term athletic development related to the youth rugby player. This includes growth and maturation, physical development, injury risk, training load management and psycho-social development, each of which will be further explored throughout the book. The chapter then presents the ten pillars of long-term athletic development and a coaching session framework to help practitioners deliver effective long-term athletic development programmes for young rugby players.

Chapter 3 – Developmentally Appropriate Coaching for Children

This chapter focuses on coaching children and introduces the main developmental features of children that influence their sporting experiences. The chapter then presents a range of coaching practices that respond to their developmental needs of children with a case study provided for how these developmentally appropriate practices have been implemented into player development environments using a movement-based approach.

Chapter 4 – Kinanthropometry and Grouping Strategies

This chapter presents the kinanthropometry of youth rugby players and discusses how maturity can affect rugby performance, physical development, talent identification and injury risk. The chapter also considers the evidence and efficacy of grouping strategies used within youth rugby. Practical recommendations for understanding and assessing growth and maturity, considerations for training and competition, talent identification and development strategies and stakeholder communication are provided.

Chapter 5 – Talent Identification

This chapter overviews the youth rugby talent identification research using the ecological dynamic framework. This framework considers the task (e.g., participation history), the performer characteristics (e.g., psychological characteristics) and the environmental factors (e.g., sociocultural influences) related to the youth rugby player. A range of practical recommendations are then provided in relation to talent and how practitioners can effectively ad ethically identify talent within young rugby players.

Chapter 6 – The Match-Play Demands

This chapter summarises and presents the research quantifying the technical-tactical and physical demands of youth rugby league and rugby union match-play, and compares between playing positions, standards and age grades. A practical overview of how practitioners can utilise such data to assist in appropriate training prescription is then presented.

Chapter 7 – Profiling Physical Qualities

This chapter summarises how anthropometry, body composition, strength, power, speed, agility and change-of-direction, aerobic and anaerobic capacity and athletic movement skills are measured within young rugby players. The chapter then presents the practical application of a national standardised fitness testing assessment within the United Kingdom rugby league whereby a profiling tool was created for enhancing the physical development of young rugby players.

Chapter 8 – Strength and Conditioning Training

This chapter describes and discusses the strength and conditioning training interventions that have been investigated within the scientific literature with youth rugby players. Furthermore, this chapter will provide researchers with an overview of the various training interventions used and the physical performance outcomes that can be expected by manipulating the acute training variables in youth rugby players. Based on this information, the chapter then presents recommendations for designing strength and conditioning programmes for young rugby players.

Chapter 9 – Psychosocial Development

This chapter synthesises and reviews the research on youth rugby players' psychosocial development including psychosocial skills and characteristics. The chapter then provides six recommendations to support coaches and practitioners in establishing and maintaining rugby environments that intentionally, and systematically, facilitate the psychosocial development of their players.

Chapter 10 – Technical and Tactical Development

This chapter summarises the relevant research for the technical and tactical development within young rugby players including the measurement of technical and tactical qualities, technical and tactical development and the role of competition. The chapter then offers practical implications across: (1) how coaches and practitioners can measure technical and tactical development over time, (2) coaching methods that support technical and tactical development and (3) modes of competition.

Chapter 11 – The Tackle

This chapter examines the youth rugby tackle research and considers the implications for player health, development and performance. It discusses how to improve players knowledge, attitudes and behaviours around tackle technique, the optimal location to tackle the ball-carrier, and how to assess and monitor tackle technique in training and matches. The chapter concludes with a practical application on how to design effective tackle training programmes.

Chapter 12 – Training Practices

This chapter presents the research that has focussed upon the training practices and training loads of youth rugby players, from individual sessions to the annual macro-cycle (i.e., season). The second part of the chapter provides a practical overview on methods of training load measurement, data analysis, visualisation and communication, as well as considerations on training to competition ratios in youth rugby.

Chapter 13 – Fatigue and Recovery

This chapter summarises the research on fatigue and recovery in youth rugby including measuring fatigue, fatigue following training, match-play and congested fixtures alongside considering recovery strategies. A range of practical recommendations are presented to monitor and influence the fatigue and recovery of young rugby players.

Chapter 14 – Nutrition

This chapter considers nutrition for both health and performance based on the unique demands of the rugby codes. This includes nutritional assessment methods, typical dietary behaviours of young rugby players and strategies for maximising appropriate and healthy nutrition. The chapter achieves this by answering a range of common nutrition questions for the young rugby player.

Chapter 15 – Injury Risk and Prevention

This chapter summarises the existing evidence evaluating the risk of injury and concussion with rugby. It also considers the most common injury sites and types and consider the major risk factors associated with injury. Injury prevention strategies are then reviewed. The chapter then details the practical application of designing and developing a pre-activity movement control exercise programme to reduce injury risk in schoolboy rugby players aged 14–18 years, known now as the Activate Injury Prevention Exercise Programme.

Chapter 16 – The Female Player

The popularity of female rugby is increasing rapidly around the world. However, the underpinning female-specific sports science evidence base has not increased concurrently with the game's growth. This chapter summarises the available literature, including female-specific considerations and provides practical recommendations for enhancing player development within female players.

Chapter 17 – Planning Your Coaching

This chapter aims to draw upon all the chapters and content of the book to explore the concept of planning training for young rugby players. This concludes with a contextualisation of nested planning in youth rugby, offering worked examples and considerations faced in day-to-day practice.

References

Bergeron, M. F., Mountjoy, M., Armstrong, N., Chia, M., Cote, J., Emery, C. A., Faigenbaum, A., Hall, G., Jr., Kriemler, S., Leglise, M., Malina, R. M., Pensgaard, A. M., Sanchez, A., Soligard, T., Sundgot-Borgen, J., Van Mechelen, W., Weissensteiner, J. R., & Engebretsen, L. (2015). International Olympic Committee consensus statement on youth athletic development. *British Journal of Sports Medicine*, *49*, 843–851. https://doi.org/10.1136/bjsports-2015-094962

Côté, J., & Vierimaa, M. (2014). The developmental model of sport participation: 15 Years after its first conceptualization. *Science and Sports*, *29*, S63–S69. https://doi.org/10.1016/j.scispo.2014.08.133

Freitag, A., Kirkwood, G., & Pollock, A. M. (2015). Rugby injury surveillance and prevention programmes: Are they effective? *British Medical Journal*, *350*, h1587. https://doi.org/10.1136/bmj.h1587

Gabbett, T. (2005). Science of rugby league football: A review. *Journal of Sports Sciences*, *23*, 961–967. https://doi.org/10.1080/02640410400023381

Hendricks, S., Till, K., Weaving, D., Powell, A., Kemp, S., Stokes, K., & Jones, B. (2019). Training, match and non-rugby activities in elite male youth rugby union players in England. *International Journal of Sports Science and Coaching*, *14*, 336–343. http://doi.org/10.1177/1747954119829289

Lloyd, R. S., Oliver, J. L., Faigenbaum, A. D., Howard, R., Croix, M. B. D. S., Williams, C. A., Best, T. M., Alavar, B. A., Micheli, L. J., Thomas, D. P., Hatfield D. L., Cronin J. B., & Myer, G. D. (2015). Long-term athletic development - part 1: A pathway for all youth. *The Journal of Strength and Conditioning Research*, *29*, 1439–1450. https://doi.org/10.1519/JSC.0000000000000756

Noon, M. R., James, R. S., Clarke, N. D., Akubat, I., & Thake, C. D. (2015). Perceptions of well-being and physical performance in English elite youth footballers across a season. *Journal of Sports Sciences*, *33*, 2106–2115. https://doi.org/10.1080/02640414.2015.1081393

Phibbs, P. J., Jones, B., Roe, G., Read, D., Darrall-Jones, J., Weakley, J., Rock, A., & Till, K. (2018). The organised chaos of English adolescent rugby union: Influence of weekly match frequency on the variability of match and training loads. *European Journal of Sport Science*, *18*, 341–348. http://doi.org/10.1080/17461391.2017.1418026

Till, K., Barrell, D., Lawn, J., Rock, A., Lazenby, B., & Cobley, S. (2021). 'Wide and emergent - narrow and focussed': A dual-pathway approach to talent identification and development in England Rugby Union. In J. Baker, J. Schorer, & S. Cobley (Eds.), *Talent identification and development in sport: International perspectives* (pp. 170–183). (2nd ed.). Routledge.

Till, K., Weakley, J., Read, D. B., Phibbs, P., Darrall-Jones, J., Roe, G., Chantler, S. D., Mellalieu, S., Hislop, M., Stokes, K., Rock, A., & Jones, B. (2020). Applied sport science for male age-grade rugby union in England. *Sports Medicine-Open*, *6*, 1–20. https://doi.org/10.1186/s40798-020-0236-6

2
LONG-TERM ATHLETIC DEVELOPMENT OF THE YOUNG RUGBY PLAYER

Kevin Till, Rhodri S. Lloyd and Joey C. Eisenmann

Introduction

Children play sports for fun, to develop skills and for the psychosocial benefits associated with sports participation (Visek et al., 2013). Furthermore, an often stated mantra in paediatric exercise science is that children are not simply 'miniature adults' and they should be treated and exposed to sport-related activities appropriate with their age and stage of development. Due to the unique physiology, psychology and sociology of childhood (generally up to the age of 11 years in girls and 13 years in boys) and adolescence (typically including girls aged 12–18 years and boys aged 14–18 years; Lloyd et al., 2015), it is important to understand the fundamental principles of paediatric exercise science in order to design and deliver successful long-term athletic development programmes. The poetic verses below (edited on the original poem 'He's just a little boy' by Chaplain Bob Fox) are a timely reminder of these principles.

> *"He is just a little boy" (Chaplain Bob Fox)*
>
> He waits in position with his heart pounding fast,
> The ball is won, the pass made and the die is cast.
> Mum and Dad can't help him, he stands alone,
> A catch, a dive for glory and his team has won.
> He tries but the ball slips from his grasp,
> A groan from the "supporters" and hands-in head gasp.
> "He should never have been picked" shouts a thoughtless fan,
> Tears fill his eyes…the game is no longer fun.
> Open your heart and give him a break,
> In moments like this a man you can make.
> Keep this in your mind and do not forget,
> He is just a little boy, and not a man yet.

DOI: 10.4324/9781003104797-2

Based on the scientific research literature, the notion of long-term athletic development has grown in popularity over the last two decades. This has included the adoption of models by sport national governing bodies and resulted in the publication of consensus (Bergeron et al., 2015) and position (Lloyd et al., 2016) statements on the topic with key definitions shown in Box 2.1.

Box 2.1

Long-term athletic development is the habitual development of *athleticism* over time to improve health, fitness and physical performance, reduce injury risk and develop confidence and competence in all youth.

Athleticism is the ability to consistently perform a range of movements with precision and confidence in a breadth of environments, requiring competent levels of motor skills, strength, power, speed, agility, balance, coordination and endurance.

(Lloyd et al., 2016)

There are several factors to consider for the journey of a young rugby player from childhood to adolescence that will influence an individual's development and their experience of the journey. Whilst not an exhaustive list, these factors are displayed in Figure 2.1 and are represented in cogs because it is the culmination of many interacting factors that will govern the overall development, performance and experience of any young rugby player. In turn, long-term athletic development requires the integration of multiple disciplines (e.g., sports coaching, strength and conditioning, sports medicine, child development) to ensure that young athletes develop in a holistic manner.

The purpose of this chapter is to introduce and summarise key research on the key concepts of long-term athletic development including growth and maturation, developing athleticism, injury risk, training load management and psychosocial development. These topics will be discussed in more detail throughout the book. The chapter will then present the ten pillars of long-term athletic development proposed by the National Strength and Conditioning Association (NSCA; Lloyd et al., 2016) and show how these can be delivered through a coaching session framework (Till et al., 2021).

Research Overview

Growth and Maturation

Perhaps one of the most influential and fundamental factors to long-term athletic development is growth and maturation. All youth experience growth and maturation as part of natural development during the first two decades of life. In

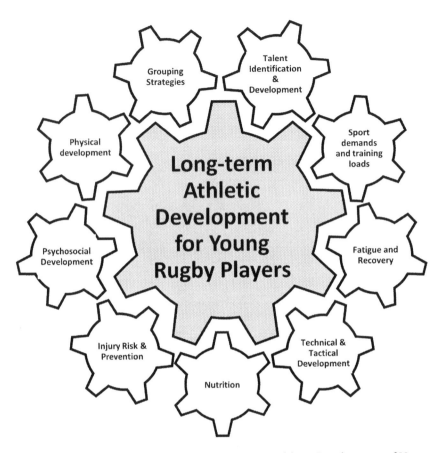

FIGURE 2.1 Factors to Consider for the Long-term Athletic Development of Young Rugby Players.

turn, normal physical growth and biological maturation (and psycho-social development) have a profound impact on both sport participation and performance. Indeed, as an area of study, growth and maturation has, and continues to, receive great attention in the scientific literature due to its influence on other factors including fitness development (Lloyd & Oliver, 2012), injury risk (Johnson et al., 2020; Wik et al., 2020) and talent identification and development (Till et al., 2017). In essence, we must first understand the process of normal growth and maturation before we consider their impact on training and sports performance.

Growth is defined as an increase in the size of the body or its parts (Baxter-Jones et al., 2005). Most often this is considered as the changes in height and body mass but could also include segmental lengths (e.g., leg length), circumferences (e.g., arm, calf) or the organs (e.g., heart). Maturation is defined as the timing and tempo of progress towards a fully biologically mature state, and this process varies markedly between individuals (Faigenbaum et al., 2019; Malina, 2004). Maturation occurs during childhood and adolescence but is most pronounced during puberty when youth can be classified as *early-maturing*, *on-time* or *late-maturing* depending on the timing of certain pubertal events (e.g., age at peak height velocity). Another way to think about maturation is considering that chronological age increases linearly, while biological maturation progresses in a non-linear fashion with high variability (Box 2.2). Changes to the body with growth and maturation include natural developments in structure and function (e.g., increased size of heart, muscle architecture) and associated improvements in fitness (e.g., cardiorespiratory fitness, muscle strength). Therefore, one of the challenges when working with young rugby players is to distinguish between relative improvements due to normal growth and maturation versus sports and structured training (Baxter-Jones et al., 2005). Being able to assess and account for growth and/or maturity status allows for greater interpretation of data and a better understanding of performance in young rugby players. An overview of the methods available to assess maturity is provided in Chapter 4.

Box 2.2

The large individual variability in the timing, tempo and magnitude of biological maturation emphasises the importance of growth and maturation within long-term athletic development pathways (Lloyd et al., 2014).

Research within youth male rugby players has shown that *early-maturing* players are typically bigger, faster and stronger, often outperforming their less mature peers in physical fitness tests including upper-body explosive strength (Till et al., 2014) and sprinting (Till & Jones, 2015). Furthermore, height and maturity status account for a significant percentage of power-related performance in adolescent players (Howard et al., 2016; Till et al., 2011). These maturity-related differences in body size and physical performance often result in a bias towards *early maturing* youth rugby players being identified and selected for representative teams (Howard et al., 2016), which naturally de-selects *later-maturing* players irrespective of their potentially higher skill levels. This should be given consideration since research has shown that *later-maturing* players catch up in size and physical fitness between the ages of 13–15 years (Till et al., 2014).

In addition to maturity status, further selection bias in young rugby players (and many youth sports) often emanates from the relative age effect (RAE). The RAE reflects the uneven distribution of birth dates relative to the selection date for the sport amongst an age-grouped cohort, favouring the relatively older individuals (e.g., those born September–November in the United Kingdom). Because of the nature of chronological age grouping, a child that is born late in the year could be playing against someone born earlier in the year despite having ~12 months age difference. Indeed, relatively older players have been shown to have greater participation rates (Cobley & Till, 2017) and selection opportunities within talent identification programmes (Kelly et al., 2021; Till et al.,

2010) in youth rugby. However, RAE should not be confused with or equated to biological maturity. These are two entirely separate constructs. These factors demonstrate the importance of understanding growth and maturation and the associated biases in the selection and long-term development of youth players.

Athleticism

Developing athleticism (see Box 2.1) from childhood to adulthood is important for health and fitness and reducing injuries alongside meeting the physical demands of rugby. This is especially important for rugby given the short-burst, high-intensity, intermittent and collision-based nature of the sports (see Chapter 6). Existing international youth athletic development guidelines advocate the use of strength and conditioning activities to develop appropriate levels of athleticism in both children and adolescents (Bergeron et al., 2015; Lloyd et al., 2016). Previous models of athletic development have proposed principles that integrate growth and maturation alongside the trainability of youths (e.g., Developmental Model of Sports Participation [Côté et al., 2007]; Long-term Athlete Development Model [Balyi & Hamilton, 2004]; Youth Physical Development Model [Lloyd & Oliver, 2012]; FTEM [Foundations, Talent, Elite, Mastery] framework [Gulbin et al., 2013]). It is outside the scope of this chapter to critically review these models in detail (see Pichardo et al., 2018), however, adopting an organised, long-term approach to youth athletic development is important. Recent systematic reviews have also provided evidence that motor skills (Collins et al., 2019), aerobic fitness (Harrison et al., 2015), agility (Asadi et al., 2017), sprint speed (Moran et al., 2017) and muscular strength and power (Behm et al., 2017) are trainable in youth populations (Box 2.3).

> **Box 2.3**
>
> Strength and conditioning activities are appropriate and important for individuals of any age. They should be introduced to rugby players at the earliest possible steps of the pathway in a developmentally appropriate way (Radnor et al., 2020).

Injury Risk

While it is impossible to eliminate injuries altogether, it is important to build resilient young players that are better prepared for both the demands of the sport alongside the influence of growth and maturation on injury risk. For example, injury incidence increases with higher levels of play in school-aged rugby (Barden & Stokes, 2018; Palmer-Green et al., 2015; see Chapter 15). Furthermore, research (albeit in soccer) demonstrates injury risk increases during periods of significant growth in height (Kemper et al., 2015). The large increases in height and significant increases in body mass during the adolescent growth period can disrupt movement control and loadings on soft tissue structures, thus increasing injury risk (Johnson et al., 2022). To protect against this, strength and conditioning that includes resistance training can reduce the risk of injury (Zwolski et al., 2017). For example, in youth rugby union, a preventive movement control exercise programme was shown to reduce injury risk in schoolboy players, with multiple weekly exposures to the programme (three times per week) proving most effective (Hislop et al., 2017; see chapter 15).

Balancing the Training Schedule

Although the previous section emphasised the importance of strength and conditioning, it is important to consider effective programming involves successfully balancing training with adequate opportunity for recovery (see Chapter 12). The training load of athletes can be sub-divided into *internal load* (i.e., how an individual experiences training; subjective) and *external load* (i.e., how much was work performed; objective; Bourdon et al., 2017). Depending on the phase of season, training loads should be carefully manipulated to promote adaptation, manage fatigue and facilitate performance (Halson, 2014). Research has shown that a risk factor for sport-related injury includes high volumes of single sport participation (Jayanthi et al., 2015; Pasulka et al., 2017) and congested playing schedules (LaPrade et al., 2016; Luke et al., 2011). Specifically for young athletes, training loads need to be considered in regards to maturation as the growth processes experienced by young athletes will result in structural and functional adaptations, which will consume some of their daily energy expenditure (Faigenbaum et al., 2019).

To improve performance and stimulate adaptation, some form of acute fatigue is required (Meeusen et al., 2013). However, when youth athletes are exposed to excessive training loads in the absence of adequate recovery, they are at risk of experiencing *non-functional overreaching* (i.e., unintentional decrements in performance resulting from an imbalance between the training dose and opportunities for recovery), or in extreme cases, *overtraining* (i.e., a syndrome that induces prolonged impairments in performance and maladaptation of biological, neurochemical and hormonal systems; (Meeusen et al., 2013)). Previous research has shown that approximately 30–40% of youth athletes have self-reported non-functional overreaching and/or overtraining (Matos et al., 2011). Cumulatively, balancing the training load and recovery for youth athletes is crucial to promote physical adaptation and adequately prepare youth players for the demands of sport, but also manage negative health outcomes (e.g., injury, non-functional overreaching). Chapters 12 and 13 present more detail on monitoring training load, fatigue and recovery in the young rugby player.

Psychosocial Development

Whilst the physical side of training receives much attention, psychosocial wellbeing is an often overlooked yet crucial component of long-term athletic development programmes (Lloyd et al., 2016). Enjoying positive experiences, being challenged and having fun are major reasons why children play sport (Allender et al., 2006). Research shows a lack of fun and enjoyment are common causes of dropout from youth sport (Crane & Temple, 2015). To this end, the International Olympic Committee advocate that sports participation should promote wellbeing, but that the process should be fulfilling to sustain participation and success at all levels (Bergeron et al., 2015; Mountjoy et al., 2008). While some players will successfully transition through development pathways to the professional level, the majority will not. Irrespective of the level of the game that a player reaches, it is imperative that positive psychosocial skills and characteristics are nurtured in young players and that they are provided with sporting environments that foster positive development.

Many psychosocial skills and characteristics that should be targeted through long-term athletic development programmes (Lloyd et al., 2016) are reflected in youth rugby research (see Chapter 9). Specifically, psychosocial skills and characteristics that young rugby players perceive as important for their development include: enjoyment, responsibility for self, adaptability, squad spirit, being a self-aware learner, determination, confidence, optimal performance state, game sense, appropriate attentional focus and mental toughness (Holland et al., 2010). The players also revealed that personal performance strategies, reflection on action, use of supportive climates and team-based strategies were some of the techniques that they used to facilitate this development (see more in Chapter 9).

Furthermore, the role significant others (e.g., coaches, parents) play in the development process of youth athletes is crucial. Coaches and parents can serve as strong influencers on youth players and are able to facilitate positive wellbeing and aid performance through their behaviours and actions (Harwood & Knight, 2015). Ultimately, along with sports coaches, it is imperative that parents are armed with the knowledge, understanding and, where necessary, the practical tools that allow them to be responsive, discussive and empathetic with youth players, to promote positive psychosocial attributes and better enable them to navigate the complexities of sport (Box 2.4).

Box 2.4

Parents should consider where and when is the appropriate time to discuss their child's sporting performance, with constructive and supportive discussion in private settings more favourable (Tamminen et al., 2017).

Practical Applications

The above section has summarised a range of research related to the long-term athletic development of the young rugby player. Whilst it is not possible to review all research here, further depth will be explored within each chapter of the book. The following practical applications section aims to summarise some key implications from the research into practice and offer a solution for how some of these considerations for long-term athletic development can be applied by coaches and practitioners.

Across the rugby codes around the world, leading nations have adopted, designed and implemented their own long-term athletic development models (or equivalents). Examples include the 'Small Blacks' programme in New Zealand (New Zealand Rugby Union, 2021), the '6 to 6 Nations' development programme from the Irish Rugby Football Union (Irish Council for Sports, 2006), and the long-term player development model promoted through World Rugby (World Rugby, 2014). The specific detail and content of each 'model' differ (and some may be outdated), but most pathways will endeavour to ensure holistic development. This includes the development of rugby skills and tactical understanding, enhance athleticism, promote positive and negate negative (e.g., injury) outcomes especially considering growth and maturation, promote positive psychological attributes and social interaction, while maintaining enjoyment and enthusiasm for the game.

Ten Pillars of Long-Term Athletic Development

To ensure all youths, regardless of age, stage or ability, are provided opportunities for long-term athletic development, the NSCA published a position statement on long-term athletic development (Lloyd et al., 2016). The NSCA position statement aimed to (a) help foster a more unified and holistic approach to long-term athletic development, (b) promote the benefits of a lifetime of healthy physical activity and (c) prevent and/or minimise sport and physical activity-related injuries for all boys and girls. This was deemed important because long-term athletic development reflects an interdisciplinary concept important for health, physical activity and sports performance, while considering the physical, motor skill and psychosocial factors (e.g., confidence) associated with youth development. To support practitioners, the NSCA position statement proposed ten pillars for successful long-term athletic development based upon previous models (Côté & Vierimaa, 2014) and up-to-date research evidence (e.g., Baker et al., 2018; Bergeron et al., 2015; Côté et al., 2009; Faigenbaum & Myer, 2010; Granacher et al., 2016), which should be the hallmarks of any development pathway for youth (Table 2.1). However, please note that any long-term athletic development programme should be context specific, and the ten pillars provide the 'big picture' components to consider. Each of the factors presented within Figure 2.1 is linked to the ten pillars of long-term athletic development and is covered in more detail throughout the remaining chapters of this book. Although these ten pillars are not sport (or rugby) specific, they highlight the importance of promoting and implementing a range of strategies to maximise the health and performance of young individuals during training and competition.

TABLE 2.1 Ten Pillars for Successful Long-Term Athletic Development (Lloyd et al., 2016)

Pillar	Description	Book Chapter
1	Long-term athletic development pathways should accommodate for the highly individualised and non-linear nature of the growth and development of youth.	3, 4, 5, 14
2	Youth of all ages, abilities and aspirations should engage in long-term athletic development programmes that promote both physical fitness and psychosocial wellbeing.	7, 8, 9
3	All youth should be encouraged to enhance physical fitness from early childhood, with a primary focus on motor skill and muscular strength development.	8, 15
4	Long-term athletic development pathways should encourage an early sampling approach for youth that promotes and enhances a broad range of motor skills.	5, 10, 11
5	Health and wellbeing of the child should always be the central tenet of long-term athletic development programmes.	All
6	Youth should participate in physical conditioning that helps reduce the risk of injury to ensure their on-going participation in long-term athletic development programmes.	3, 8, 15
7	Long-term athletic development programmes should provide all youth with a range of training modes to enhance both health- and skill-related components of fitness.	3, 6, 8, 9, 10, 11, 12, 15
8	Practitioners should use relevant monitoring and assessment tools as part of a long-term athletic development strategy.	5, 6, 7, 9, 10, 11, 12, 13, 14, 15
9	Practitioners working with youth should systematically progress and individualise training programmes for successful long-term athletic development.	All
10	Qualified professionals and sound pedagogical approaches are fundamental to the success of long-term athletic development programmes.	All

RAMPAGE: A Coaching Session Framework

Whilst the ten pillars were provided as a guiding framework, it is important to consider how practitioners can achieve these ten pillars in their own contextual situation. However, developing interventions for multiple practitioners (e.g., sports coaches, teachers, strength and conditioning coaches) is challenging, considering the wide range of knowledge and understanding required from a physical, psychosocial, technical and tactical and health perspective. Integrating the principles of long-term athletic development into rugby development programmes requires detailed planning. Therefore, it is important to consider how long-term athletic development can be operationalised within regular youth rugby programmes rather than being viewed as an independent entity.

To achieve this, Till et al. (2021) developed a coaching session framework, named RAMPAGE, based upon evidence-based principles that could be practically applied across multiple coaching contexts. RAMPAGE is an acronym standing for Raise, Activate, Mobilise, Prepare, Activity, Games, and Evaluate. The coaching session framework was designed to (a) be applied across multiple youth levels (i.e., participation to performance) and sports (e.g., team to individual), (b) be applied across all stages of development (i.e., childhood to adulthood), (c) integrate all areas for holistic long-term athletic development (i.e., physical, technical, tactical and psychosocial) and (d) consider 'how' coaches may implement this. The framework provides a generalised structure (see Table 2.2) for all practitioners to implement coaching sessions focused on long-term athletic development principles in a way that is flexible with their context, their participants and the goals of their programme/players. Based on this justification, the RAMPAGE coaching session framework allows for flexibility, variety and coach autonomy, while providing guidance for coaches on what activities should be delivered and when during a session they can be delivered. Table 2.2 presents and details the stages of a RAMPAGE coaching session framework.

Table 2.2 shows six areas of a coaching session that can achieve multiple holistic goals. For example, the *Raise* section can increase body temperature and develop locomotor and object control skills through purposeful and engaging activity (e.g., obstacle courses or tag games in children, or linear running mechanics with older and more advanced athletes). The *Activate* and *Mobilise* sections focus upon key dynamic movements to support athletic development and to reduce injury risk, and include lower-body, upper-body and anti-rotation and core bracing movements through traditional body weight strength circuits, animal walks/movements, partner-based games or inclusion of stability, strength and mobility challenges. The *Prepare* section is focused on executing high-intensity movements such as sprinting, jumping or throwing with maximal effort. Activities within the prepare section typically include speed, agility and power-based activities, with a specific focus upon acceleration, deceleration and reacceleration, jumping and rebounding or contact/wrestling activities in rugby. Practitioners can vary *how* these exercises are structured and delivered, ranging from

TABLE 2.2 RAMPAGE Coaching Session Framework

Section		Aim	Example Activities	Tech-Tact
R	Raise	Raise the body temperature and introduce locomotor and object control skills	Obstacle courses, running mechanics, tag games, ball handling drills	***
A	Activate	Activate the muscles and mobilise the joints to develop strength, stability and mobility and help reduce injury occurrence	Strength exercises, animal movements, partner challenges, circuits	*
M	Mobilise			
P	Prepare	Increase the intensity of the activity through speed, agility and power-related activities	Races, relays, agility courses, jumping, throwing, wrestling	**
A	Activity	To develop the key technical skills and tactical understanding of rugby through a variety of scenarios	Catching, passing, kicking, tackling, ruck, decision making	*****
G	Games	Implement the technical or tactical activity within a game situation with a focus on endurance or metabolic conditioning	Small, medium and large sided games	****
E	Evaluate	Evaluate the session during a cool down whilst providing opportunity for individual work ons	Flexibility, landing mechanics, core skills, use of questioning and reflection to evaluate	**

Psycho-Social: Coaches observation and behaviours linked to session objectives should be used and emphasised throughout the session to develop psycho-social attributes (e.g., communication, control, confidence, concentration, presence, resilience, self-awareness, commitment)

Tech-Tact: The star system identifies the emphasis and integration of rugby skills within each section of the session. *Limited focus to *****Always a focus

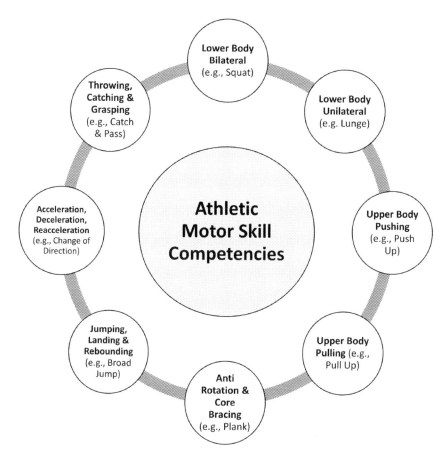

FIGURE 2.2 Athletic Motor Skill Competencies (adapted from Lloyd et al., 2015).

individual isolated efforts (e.g., maximal vertical jumps) to relays and races, or even dynamic games depending on the developmental stage of their participants. Athletic motor skill competencies to include in these sections are shown in Figure 2.2.

The *Activity* and *Games* sections of the RAMPAGE coaching session framework are most likely viewed as the main focus of the session by the rugby technical coach. Again, the developmental stage of the participants would determine the activities planned and delivered. For example, fundamental movement skill development may remain the central focus for young, inexperienced children (e.g., 11 and younger) to help enhance a range of catching, passing, kicking and contact skills. Ideally, they should be gradually progressed considering a long-term development approach (e.g., increasing the difficulty and challenge of catching skills) whilst maintaining fun and inclusivity. For more experienced adolescents (e.g., 11 and older), rugby-specific skills developing towards tactical understanding should be implemented with advancing age and playing level.

Games provide a great opportunity to have fun and challenge players whilst also developing technical, tactical, physical and psycho-social aspects of development. Games can also provide an opportunity to indirectly develop endurance or metabolic capacities as well as speed and agility. It is recommended to conclude a session with time devoted to *Evaluate* the session. This can be incorporated within the traditional cool down, where a focus could be placed upon individual 'add-ons' including flexibility, landing mechanics (when fatigued), core skills or an opportunity for a focus on psychosocial skills and characteristics. In addition, this part of the session can be used for mental skills and/or nutrition and recovery education. Practitioners are encouraged to use questioning and reflective skills to evaluate the session.

Whilst the RAMPAGE framework provides a structure to deliver technical, tactical and physical skills, the whole session should be underpinned by psychosocial development. Till and colleagues (2021) proposed RAMPAGE focuses upon communication, control, confidence, concentration, resilience, presence, self-awareness and commitment as key cornerstones of a psychosocial curriculum for long-term athletic and personal development. Chapter 9 will provide more details on developing and implementing a psychosocial curriculum. However, practitioners purposefully planning and delivering activities and coaching behaviours to develop psychosocial skills is important. For example, coaches may plan how to develop the psychosocial characteristic of communication by creating session activities that could involve players working in small groups to solve a problem, to develop speaking, listening and verbal reasoning skills, supported by facilitative coaching behaviours (e.g., asking questions).

The RAMPAGE framework provides an opportunity to achieve many of the NSCA ten pillars of long-term athletic development (Lloyd et al., 2016). However, it is also recommended to consider longer-term/multi-year planning to truly achieve long-term athletic development. This should also include the monitoring of growth and maturity (pillar 1), encouragement of sampling of other sports (pillar 4), monitoring and assessment (pillar 8) and progression and individualisation of training (pillar 9). Such strategies can be achieved through single and long-term planning and delivery. Finally, qualified practitioners and appropriate pedagogical approaches are key and should be at the planning forefront of all governing bodies, organisations and practitioners to optimise long-term athletic development.

Key Take Home Messages

- Youths play sports for fun, to develop skills, and for the psychosocial benefits associated with sports participation. We should never lose sight of the fact that children pick up a rugby ball to play the game. The role of all practitioners is to support a lifetime of engagement in the sport.
- To support this, it is important to understand the principles of long-term athletic development including growth and maturity, developing athleticism

(and reducing injury occurrence), and psychosocial skills and characteristics, all while balancing training loads and the overall demands of childhood and adolescence (e.g., schooling, family, friends, etc.).
- The NSCA ten pillars of long-term athletic development can help governing bodies, organisations and practitioners to reflect upon, and consider, their practices for developing each and every young rugby player.
- The RAMPAGE coaching session framework provides a planning tool to help practitioners implement holistic development by considering the technical, tactical, physical and psychosocial development of young people.
- Regular exposure to athletic development opportunities and sport-specific skill development, underpinned by appropriate coaching behaviours delivered by qualified coaches and appropriate pedagogical strategies, will likely keep young players involved in the sport for life.

References

Allender, S., Cowburn, G., & Foster, C. (2006). Understanding participation in sport and physical activity among children and adults: A review of qualitative studies. *Health Education Research, 21,* 826–835. https://doi.org/10.1093/her/cyl063

Asadi, A., Arazi, H., Ramirez-Campillo, R., Moran, J., & Izquierdo, M. (2017). Influence of maturation stage on agility performance gains after plyometric training: A systematic review and meta-analysis. *Journal of Strength and Conditioning Research, 31,* 2609–2617. https://doi.org/10.1519/JSC.0000000000001994

Baker, J., Schorer, J., & Wattie, N. (2018). Compromising talent: Issues in identifying and selecting talent in sport. *Quest, 70,* 48–63. https://doi.org/10.1080/00336297.2017.1333438

Balyi, I., & Hamilton, A. (2004). *Long-term athlete development: Trainability in childhood and adolescence. Windows of opportunity. Optimal trainability.* National Coaching Institute & Advanced Training and Performance.

Barden, C., & Stokes, K. (2018). Epidemiology of injury in elite English Schoolboy Rugby Union: A 3-year study comparing different competitions. *Journal of Athletic Training, 53,* 514–520. https://doi.org/10.4085/1062-6050-311-16

Baxter-Jones, A. D. G., Eisenmann, J. C., & Sherar, L. B. (2005). Controlling for maturation in pediatric exercise science. *Pediatric Exercise Science, 17,* 18–30. https://doi.org/10.1123/pes.17.1.18

Behm, D., Young, J., Whitten, J., Reid, J., Quigley, P., Low, J., Li, Y., Lima, C., Hodgson, D., Chaouachi, A., Prieske, O., & Granacher, U. (2017). Effectiveness of traditional strength versus power training on muscle strength, power and speed with youth: A systematic review and meta-analysis. *Frontiers in Physiology, 30,* 8. https://doi.org/10.3389/fphys.2017.00423

Bergeron, M. F., Mountjoy, M., Armstrong, N., Chia, M., Cote, J., Emery, C. A., Faigenbaum, A., Hall, G., Jr., Kriemler, S., Leglise, M., Malina, R. M., Pensgaard, A. M., Sanchez, A., Soligard, T., Sundgot-Borgen, J., van Mechelen, W., Weissensteiner, J. R., & Engebretsen, L. (2015). International Olympic Committee consensus statement on youth athletic development. *British Journal of Sports Medicine, 49,* 843–851. https://doi.org/10.1136/bjsports-2015-094962

Bourdon, P. C., Cardinale, M., Murray, A., Gastin, P., Kellmann, M., Varley, M. C., Gabbett, T. J., Coutts, A. J., Burgess, D. J., Gregson, W., & Cable, N. T. (2017).

Monitoring athlete training loads: Consensus statement. *International Journal of Sports Physiology and Performance*, *12*, S2161–S2170. https://doi.org/10.1123/IJSPP.2017-0208

Cobley, S. P., & Till, K. (2017). Participation trends according to relative age across youth UK Rugby League. *International Journal of Sports Science & Coaching*, *12*, 339–343. https://doi.org/10.1177/1747954117710506

Collins, H., Booth, J. N., Duncan, A., & Fawkner, S. (2019). The effect of resistance training interventions on fundamental movement skills in youth: A meta-analysis. *Sports Medicine Open*, *5*, 17. https://doi.org/10.1186/s40798-019-0188-x

Côté, J., Baker, J., & Abernethy, B. (2007). Practice to play in the development of sport expertise. In R. Eklund & G. Tenenbaum (Eds.), *Handbook of sport psychology* (pp. 184–202). Wiley.

Côté, J., Lidor, R., & Hackfort, D. (2009). ISSP position stand: To sample or to specialize? Seven postulates about youth sport activities that lead to continued participation and elite performance. *International Journal of Sport and Exercise Psychology*, *7*, 7–17. https://doi.org/10.1080/1612197X.2009.9671889

Côté, J., & Vierimaa, M. (2014). The developmental model of sport participation: 15 Years after its first conceptualization. *Science & Sports*, *29*, S63–S69. https://doi.org/10.1016/j.scispo.2014.08.133

Crane, J., & Temple, V. (2015). A systematic review of dropout from organized sport among children and youth. *European Physical Education Review*, *21*, 114–131. https://doi.org/10.1177/1356336X14555294

Faigenbaum, A. D., Lloyd, R. S., & Oliver, J. L. (2019). *ACSM essentials of youth fitness*. Human Kinetics.

Faigenbaum, A. D., & Myer, G. D. (2010). Resistance training among young athletes: Safety, efficacy and injury prevention effects. *British Journal of Sports Medicine*, *44*, 56–63. https://doi.org/10.1136/bjsm.2009.068098

Granacher, U., Lesinski, M., Büsch, D., Muehlbauer, T., Prieske, O., Puta, C., Gollhofer, A., & Behm, D. G. (2016). Effects of resistance training in youth athletes on muscular fitness and athletic performance: A conceptual model for long-term athlete development. *Frontiers in Physiology*, *7*, 164. https://doi.org/10.3389/fphys.2016.00164

Gulbin, J. P., Croser, M. J., Morley, E. J., & Weissensteiner, J. R. (2013). An integrated framework for the optimisation of sport and athlete development: A practitioner approach. *Journal of Sports Sciences*, *31*, 1319–1331. https://doi.org/10.1080/02640414.2013.781661

Halson, S. L. (2014). Monitoring training load to understand fatigue in athletes. *Sports Medicine*, *44*, S139–S147. https://doi.org/10.1007/s40279-014-0253-z

Harrison, C. B., Gill, N. D., Kinugasa, T., & Kilding, A. E. (2015). Development of aerobic fitness in young team sport athletes. *Sports Medicine*, *45*, 969–983. https://doi.org/10.1007/s40279-015-0330-y

Harwood, C. G., & Knight, C. J. (2015). Parenting in youth sport: A position paper on parenting expertise. *Psychology of Sport and Exercise*, *16*, 24–35. https://doi.org/10.1016/j.psychsport.2014.03.001

Hislop, M. D., Stokes, K. A., Williams, S., McKay, C. D., England, M. E., Kemp, S. P. T., & Trewartha, G. (2017). Reducing musculoskeletal injury and concussion risk in schoolboy rugby players with a pre-activity movement control exercise programme: A cluster randomised controlled trial. *British Journal of Sports Medicine*, *51*, 1140–1146. https://doi.org/10.1136/bjsports-2016-097434

Holland, M. J. G., Woodcock, C., Cumming, J., & Duda, J. L. (2010). Mental qualities and employed mental techniques of young elite team sport athletes. *Journal of Clinical Sport Psychology*, *4*, 19–38. https://doi.org/10.1123/jcsp.4.1.19

Howard, S. M., Cumming, S. P., Atkinson, M., & Malina, R. M. (2016). Biological maturity-associated variance in peak power output and momentum in academy rugby union players. *European Journal of Sport Science, 16*, 972–980. https://doi.org/10.1080/17461391.2016.1205144

Jayanthi, N. A., LaBella, C. R., Fischer, D., Pasulka, J., & Dugas, L. R. (2015). Sports-specialized intensive training and the risk of injury in young athletes: A clinical case-control study. *American Journal of Sports Medicine, 43*, 794–801. https://doi.org/10.1177/0363546514567298

Johnson, D. M., Cumming, S. P., Bradley, B. & Williams, S. (2022). The influence of exposure, growth and maturation on injury risk in male academy football players. *Journal of Sports Sciences, 40*, 1127–1136, https://doi.org/10.1080/02640414.2022.2051380

Johnson, D. M., Williams, S., Bradley, B., Sayer, S., Murray Fisher, J., & Cumming, S. (2020). Growing pains: Maturity associated variation in injury risk in academy football. *European Journal of Sport Science, 20*, 544–552. https://doi.org/10.1080/17461391.2019.1633416

Kelly, A. L., Till, K., Jackson, D., Barrell, D., Burke, K., & Turnnidge, J. (2021). Talent identification and relative age effects in english male rugby union pathways: From entry to expertise. *Frontiers in Sports and Active Living, 3*, 12. https://doi.org/10.3389/fspor.2021.640607

Kemper, G., Van Der Sluis, A., Brink, M., Visscher, C., Frencken, W., & Elferink-Gemser, M. (2015). Anthropometric injury risk factors in elite-standard youth soccer. *International Journal of Sports Medicine, 36*, 1112–1117. https://doi.org/10.1055/s-0035-1555778

LaPrade, R. F., Agel, J., Baker, J., Brenner, J. S., Cordasco, F. A., Cote, J., Engebretsen, L., Feeley, B. T., Gould, D., Hainline, B., Hewett, T., Jayanthi, N., Kocher, M. S., Myer, G. D., Nissen, C. W., Philippon, M. J., & Provencher, M. T. (2016). AOSSM Early sport specialization consensus statement. *Orthopaedic Journal of Sports Medicine, 4*, 2325967116644241. https://doi.org/10.1177/2325967116644241

Lloyd, R. S., Cronin, J. B., Faigenbaum, A. D., Haff, G. G., Howard, R., Kraemer, W. J., Micheli, L. J., Myer, G. D., & Oliver, J. L. (2016). National Strength and Conditioning Association position statement on long-term athletic development. *Journal of Strength and Conditioning Research, 30*, 1491–1509. https://doi.org/10.1519/JSC.0000000000001387

Lloyd, R. S., & Oliver, J. L. (2012). The youth physical development model: A new approach to long-term athletic development. *Strength and Conditioning Journal, 34*, 61–72. https://doi.org/10.1519/SSC.0b013e31825760ea

Lloyd, R. S., Oliver, J. L., Faigenbaum, A. D., Howard, R., Croix, M. B. D. S., Williams, C. A., Best, T. M., Alvar, B. A., Micheli, L. J., & Thomas, D. P. (2015). Long-term athletic development-part 1: A pathway for all youth. *The Journal of Strength & Conditioning Research, 29*, 1439–1450. https://doi.org/10.1519/JSC.0000000000000756

Lloyd, R. S., Oliver, J. L., Faigenbaum, A. D., Myer, G. D., & De Ste Croix, M. B. (2014). Chronological age vs. biological maturation: Implications for exercise programming in youth. *Journal of Strength and Conditioning Research, 28*, 1454–1464. https://doi.org/10.1519/JSC.0000000000000391

Luke, A., Lazaro, R. M., Bergeron, M. F., Keyser, L., Benjamin, H., Brenner, J., d'Hemecourt, P., Grady, M., Philpott, J., & Smith, A. (2011). Sports-related injuries in youth athletes: Is overscheduling a risk factor? *Clinical Journal of Sports Medicine, 21*, 307–314. https://doi.org/10.1097/JSM.0b013e3182218f71

Malina, R. M. B., C.; & Bar-Or, O. (2004). *Growth, maturation and physical activity.* Human Kinetics.

Matos, N., Winsley, R., & Williams, C. (2011). Prevalence of nonfunctional overreaching/overtraining in young English athletes. *Medicine and Science in Sports and Exercise, 43*, 1287–1294. https://doi.org/10.1249/MSS.0b013e318207f87b

Meeusen, R., Duclos, M., Foster, C., Fry, A., Gleeson, M., Nieman, D., Raglin, J., Rietjens, G., Steinacker, J., Urhausen, A., European College of Sport Science, & American College of Sports Medicine (2013). Prevention, diagnosis, and treatment of the overtraining syndrome: Joint consensus statement of the European College of Sport Science and the American College of Sports Medicine. *Medicine and Science in Sports & Exercise, 45*, 186–205. https://doi.org/10.1249/MSS.0b013e318279a10a

Moran, J., Sandercock, G., Rumpf, M. C., & Parry, D. A. (2017). Variation in responses to sprint training in male youth athletes: A meta-analysis. *International Journal of Sports Medicine, 38*, 1–11. https://doi.org/10.1055/s-0042-111439

Mountjoy, M., Armstrong, N., Bizzini, L., Blimkie, C., Evans, J., Gerrard, D., Hangen, J., Knoll, K., Micheli, L., Sangenis, P., & Van Mechelen, W. (2008). IOC consensus statement: "Training the elite child athlete". *British Journal of Sports Medicine, 42*, 163–164. https://doi.org/10.1136/bjsm.2007.044016

New Zealand Rugby Union. (2021). *Small blacks*. https://www.smallblacks.com

Palmer-Green, D. S., Stokes, K. A., Fuller, C. W., England, M., Kemp, S. P., & Trewartha, G. (2015). Training activities and injuries in English youth academy and schools rugby union. *The American Journal of Sports Medicine, 43*, 475–481. https://doi.org/10.1177/0363546514560337

Pasulka, J., Jayanthi, N., McCann, A., Dugas, L. R., & LaBella, C. (2017). Specialization patterns across various youth sports and relationship to injury risk. *Phys Sportsmed*, 1–9. https://doi.org/10.1080/00913847.2017.1313077

Pichardo, A. W., Oliver, J. L., Harrison, C. B., Maulder, P. S., & Lloyd, R. S. (2018). Integrating models of long-term athletic development to maximize the physical development of youth. *International Journal of Sports Science and Coaching, 13*, 1189–1199. https://doi.org/10.1177/1747954118785503

Radnor, J. M., Moeskops, S., Morris, S. J., Mathews, T. A., Kumar, N. T. A., Pullen, B. J., Meyers, R. W., Pedley, J. S., Gould, Z. I., Oliver, J. L., & Lloyd, R. S. (2020). Developing athletic motor skill competencies in youth. *Strength and Conditioning Journal, 42*, 54–70. https://doi.org/10.1519/SSC.0000000000000602

Tamminen, K. A., Poucher, Z. A., & Povilaitis, V. (2017). The car ride home: An interpretive examination of parent–athlete sport conversations. *Sport, Exercise, and Performance Psychology, 6*, 325. https://doi.org/10.1037/spy0000093

Till, K., Cobley, S., O'Hara, J., Brightmore, A., Cooke, C., & Chapman, C. (2011). Using anthropometric and performance characteristics to predict selection in junior UK Rugby League players. *Journal of Science and Medicine in Sport, 14*, 264–269. https://doi.org/10.1016/j.jsams.2011.01.006

Till, K., Cobley, S., O'Hara. J., Cooke, C., & Chapman, C. (2014). Considering maturation status and relative age in the longitudinal evaluation of junior rugby league players. *Scandinavian Journal of Medicine in Science and Sports, 24*, 569–576. https://doi.org/10.1111/sms.12033

Till, K., Cobley, S., Wattie, N., O'Hara, J., Cooke, C., & Chapman, C. (2010). The prevalence, influential factors and mechanisms of relative age effects in UK Rugby League. *Scandinavian Journal of Medicine & Science in Sports, 20*, 320–329. https://doi.org/10.1111/J.1600-0838.2009.00884.x

Till, K., Eisenmann, J., Emmonds, S., Jones, B., Mitchell, T., Cowburn, I., Tee, J., Holmes, N., & Lloyd, R. S. (2021). A coaching session framework to facilitate long-term athletic development. *Strength & Conditioning Journal*, *43*, 43–55. https://doi.org/10.1519/SSC.0000000000000558

Till, K., & Jones, B. (2015). Monitoring anthropometry and fitness using maturity groups within youth rugby league. *Journal of Strength and Conditioning Research*, *29*, 730–736. https://doi.org/10.1519/JSC.0000000000000672

Till, K., Morley, D., O'Hara, J., Jones, B. L., Chapman, C., Beggs, C. B., Cooke, C., & Cobley, S. (2017). A retrospective longitudinal analysis of anthropometric and physical qualities that associate with adult career attainment in junior rugby league players. *Journal of Science in Medicine and Sport*, *20*, 1029–1033. https://doi.org/10.1016/j.jsams.2017.03.018

Visek, A. J., Harris, B. S., & Blom, L. C. (2013). Mental training with youth sport teams: Developmental considerations and best-practice recommendations. *Journal of Sport Psychology in Action*, *4*, 45–55. https://doi.org/10.1080/21520704.2012.733910

Wik, E. H., Martinez-Silvan, D., Farooq, A., Cardinale, M., Johnson, A., & Bahr, R. (2020). Skeletal maturation and growth rates are related to bone and growth plate injuries in adolescent athletics. *Scandinavian Journal of Medicine in Science and Sports*, *30*, 894–903. https://doi.org/10.1111/sms.13635

World Rugby. (2014). *Rugby ready*. https://passport.world.rugby/injury-prevention-and-risk-management/rugby-ready/long-term-player-development/

Zwolski, C., Quatman-Yates, C., & Paterno, M. (2017). Resistance training in youth: Laying the foundation for injury prevention and physical literacy. *Sports Health*, *9*, 436–443. https://doi.org/10.1177/1941738117704153

3
DEVELOPMENTALLY APPROPRIATE COACHING PRACTICE FOR CHILDREN PLAYING RUGBY

David Morley and Donna O'Connor

Introduction

Whilst other chapters in this book provide an in-depth exploration of specific developmental areas (e.g., physical qualities, Chapter 8; psycho-social skills and characteristics, Chapter 9; technical and tactical development, Chapter 10) for the young rugby player, mainly focussed at adolescent ages (e.g., 14 years plus), this chapter is concerned with the holistic developmental needs of children. The United Nations Convention on the rights of children defines a child as any person under the age of 18 (UNICEF, 2022). For the purpose of this chapter, mainly as a result of other chapters exploring different phases of a child's development in rugby, we will define a child between the ages of 6 and 13 years of age.

To support coaches and stakeholders in achieving these holistic developmental needs, this chapter summarises the main developmental features (i.e., biopsycho-social) of children that influence their sporting experiences and provides a range of coaching practices that respond to their developmental needs. Further on in the chapter, a perspective of coaching effectiveness is presented specifically for those coaches working with children in rugby. A case study of applied research will be used to articulate how these developmentally appropriate practices are implemented into player development environments using a movement-based approach. The chapter concludes with a range of recommendations and implications for practice that a coach would find useful when coaching young rugby players.

Research Overview

Using 'Becoming CAYPABLE' as a Developmentally Appropriate Framework for Coaching Children

When coaching children, a coach needs to be aware of a myriad of intertwined perspectives that affect their coaching practice. These perspectives include (1) an understanding of the unique needs and wants of this particular cohort of players, (2) the activities at their disposal to address these needs and wants and (3) the learning environment the coach is striving to establish in terms of how these activities are structured and, most importantly, the behaviours the coach uses. The decision-making processes a coach employs within the cycle of planning, delivering and reviewing a developmentally appropriate environment for children have been effectively articulated within professional development programmes for rugby coaches, building on the work of others (Abraham & Collins 2011; Muir et al., 2011), as displayed in Figure 3.1.

The 'Becoming CAYPABLE' framework (Morley & Muir, 2012) was primarily developed for coaches attending a coach qualification course and was designed to illustrate the different mechanisms involved in coaching children. A number of dynamic influencing factors will affect children's experiences within rugby, which are contained within 'dynamic systems theory' (DST; Davids et al., 2003; Grehaigne & Godbout, 2014). Therefore, the CAYPABLE framework is based on the notion that a child's development is facilitated or constrained by an interplay between:

- The capabilities, needs and wants of the *Individual* child,
- The *Task* that is used to meet the needs of the Individual(s) and

FIGURE 3.1 Coach's Decision-Making Processes in Providing a Developmentally Appropriate Environment for Children (Becoming CAYPABLE; adapted from Morley & Muir, 2012).

- The *Environment* established by the Coach, predominantly determined by the behaviours that the coach uses.

These three factors must be viewed simultaneously to recognise practices that are constraining or supporting a young player's development. It is evident that these dynamic factors are interdependent in as much as if a task is established that fails to take account of the individual developmental needs of the young players completing the task, it is doomed to fail. Similarly, if the coach uses behaviours specifically designed to relate to the developmental stage of young players it is likely to result in increased engagement, enjoyment, skills competence and subsequent retention. By using DST, it is clear that the 'individual' relates to *Children And Young People*, the task relates to *Activity Base* and the environment relates to *Learning Environment* to form the 'CAYPABLE' acronym.

Who Are We Coaching?

Within the Becoming CAYPABLE model, an understanding of 'who' we are coaching can be further explained through an understanding of the biological, psychological and sociological developmental needs of the child. Combining these biopsychosocial factors of human development in a way that affords us the opportunity to understand the multifaceted and nonlinear nature of children's development acknowledges the inherent failure in focussing too narrowly on single factors affecting development (e.g., only physiological), therefore rendering that approach inadequate (Abbot et al., 2005). This 'biopsychosocial' modelling of human development has been used to review participant development in sport (Bailey et al., 2010) and as a way of appreciating human development more broadly (Kiesler, 1999).

A biopsychosocial perspective of children's needs requires the coach to think differently about the purpose of coaching children, moving away from commonly evidenced notions of employing adult-framed, sport-specific practices (Bailey et al., 2013). Such practices are commonly laced with high-volume, repetitive, high-pressure situations, and often use a child's sport performance as an early predictor of future success (Martindale et al., 2005). The residual effect of these approaches exposes a child to a significant risk of drop out caused by physical fatigue, stress and anxiety (Weiss & Williams, 2004). Evidence suggests that children are dropping out of sport in large numbers (Visek et al., 2015) because they lose interest, feel disempowered by the coach, and there is an overemphasis on winning and not enough fun (Wall & Côté, 2007; Witt & Dangi, 2018).

Table 3.1 outlines the key biopsychosocial needs of young children in sport and physical activity as a guide for coaches to be able to establish their coaching practices accordingly. These biopsychosocial developmental processes should be understood when working with young players to understand how development in childhood and adolescence affects sport participation and performance.

TABLE 3.1 Bio-Psycho-Social Development of Children and Young People in Sport (Adapted from Morley & Sanctuary, 2016)

Stage	Aspect of Development	Child's Development	Coaching Considerations
Early 4–7 years	Biological	Gross motor skills	Development of gross motor skills is paramount (e.g., skipping, running, riding bike, catching, etc.).
	Psychological	Slow processing speeds; Limited use of control processes; Over-inclusion.	Keep cues short, few and simple. Use general instruction/feedback. Continuous reminders of cues. Need to focus attention on task-relevant stimuli.
	Social	Development of early peer relationships; Child unable to see a situation from another child's point of view.	Peer relations primarily revolve around shared activities and interests. Struggles to understand different roles within the team, other than their own.
Intermediate 8–12 years	Biological	Fine motor skills developing more rapidly; Body scaling (shape variation becoming more pronounced).	Fine motor skills are developing on the gross motor skill foundation already laid. Refine and develop a 'feel' for the ball, (e.g., when carrying, catching and passing).
	Psychological	Increase in processing speed; Uses strategies to interpret instructions and tactical demands; Rehearses responses to tasks and situations as they emerge.	Start using more precise instruction/feedback, shorter encoding processes mean skill development is now accelerated. Less need for cue reminders, but still needed occasionally. Still need to focus attention on task-relevant stimuli.
	Social	Peer group acceptance.	Offer regular opportunities for players to demonstrate/develop their skills in making friends and getting along with teammates.

(*Continued*)

TABLE 3.1 (Continued)

Stage	Aspect of Development	Child's Development	Coaching Considerations
Later 13+ years	Biological	Puberty	Understand individual variation in maturation during this stage. Physical changes in the body require athletes to relearn some skills to accommodate for physical changes. Kinesthetic awareness and body in space are critical elements. Understand influence of fat storage and muscular development at varying levels for different players.
	Psychological	Continued increase in processing speed; Increased use and quality of control processes; May only pay attention to the areas that the player feels are important for their own development.	Avoid inappropriate excessive questioning, which can create anxiety and defensiveness within players, who feel as though they are being tested. Provide opportunities for deliberate practice to further refine the use of skills in sport-specific ways to increase confidence in participation. Support the establishment, and achievement of, clearly defined goals related to individual areas for improvement.
	Social	Close, face-to-face communication between pairs or sub-units of players	Emphasise the importance of the individual within the collective. De-emphasise the importance of competitive outcomes and stress the importance of fun and learning with friends

A note of caution: the age ranges used are typically representative of young players' development but should always be viewed in relation to individual needs, rather than chronological age development.

In specific reference to the game of rugby, coaches need an awareness of how children differ in relation to the practices used within game construction. It is recognised that children have differing development needs to those of adults and participate for very different reasons (Bailey et al., 2013). There is a natural crossover between 'who' we are coaching with 'what' we are coaching, in the way that both practice and competitive games can be structured (the 'what') with the needs of children (the 'who'). Game structure for children is often based on the adult version of the game with limited understanding of the developmental appropriateness of this adult version for the children playing it (Capranica & Millard-Stafford, 2011). There is also evidence to suggest that children enjoy high levels of interaction within the game and learning skills are seen as a primary reason for children's participation (Weiss et al., 2012). Furthermore, children's enjoyment of the sport is elevated when they feel more competent in being able to perform the core skills of a game (Beni et al., 2017; Rottensteiner et al., 2013). It is clear that a child's involvement in a game is largely premised on their ability to practice the skills that they require to participate in the game on a regular basis including in training and in competition.

How Are We Coaching?

Understanding 'how' we coach is another area of consideration when making decisions in providing a developmentally appropriate environment for children. Table 3.1 presents some stage-specific considerations for the coach, based on the biopsychosocial needs of children. The ability of the coach to place the child at the centre of their coaching process and practices through understanding the player's developmental needs, motivations, behaviours, capabilities and competences is clearly warranted. Recent modelling that explores the notion of centralising the athlete in a sport environment has been framed as 'athlete-centred coaching' (ACC; see Pill, 2018). The use of ACC entails a fundamental shift in the relationship between athletes and coaches that re-frames the role of the coach, moving away from an authoritarian, autocratic leader (i.e., a coach-centred coach) to a humanistic, democratic leader that empowers athletes in the development process (i.e., athlete-centred coach; Nelson et al., 2014; Potrac & Cassidy, 2006). Headley-Cooper (2020, 2011) suggested that where athlete empowerment is central to a coach's intended outcomes, the perception from coaches is that the resultant improvement in the coach–athlete relationship helps foster not only individual development, but team development and cohesion. She goes on to suggest that to fully empower athletes, the coach's role is to define what success looks like and facilitate opportunities for athletes to take ownership of the process of their development (Headley-Cooper, 2020). Whilst most of the theory and research related to ACC is related to coaching adults, it's clear that the principles of empowerment and athlete ownership are still applicable to ensure children playing rugby are fully engaged in their own development. Of course, the amount of ownership the child can take for their development will be affected by the child's emotional maturity and access to broader support structures that help them in this regard.

ACC provides a framework for locating the athlete's developmental needs at the centre of the coaching process, by using a range of key pedagogical principles, one of which is how we use game modifications, to facilitate athlete learning (Griffin et al., 2017). Modifications to the game within practice can be made through three distinct strategies; representation, exaggeration and adaptation (Griffin et al., 2017). Representation involves the maintenance of some contextual aspects of the game but slowing play down (e.g., walking players through moving forwards and passing backwards along a line). Exaggeration involves overemphasising some aspects of play to encourage a tactical or technical experience (e.g., using four attackers against three defenders to emphasise space behind defenders). Adaptation can be used to vary the challenge to the athlete according to their developmental stage, using a range of game constraints (e.g., space, score, rules, number of players; Hopper, 2011).

There is evidence to suggest modified, game-like activities can be used in practice situations to support a player's skill (Klusemann et al., 2012), decision-making (Miller et al., 2017; O'Connor et al., 2017) and physiological (Jones & Drust, 2007) development. The ways in which coaches creatively manipulate constraints (e.g., even/uneven teams, size of playing area, rules) in an attempt to replicate the competitive environment will influence player interactions and the opportunities for players to interpret cues, make decisions, execute skills and adapt to the opposition (Davids et al., 2013; O'Connor et al., 2017). For example, following a review of rugby league for players aged 5–11 years, prompted by growing concerns around engagement and retention of young ruby players, research was conducted to explore the impact of a newly introduced 'modified' game in comparison to the 'traditional' primary rugby league game being played at the time (Morley et al., 2016). The research found that a modified game that decreased the space and number of players and adjusted some of the rules resulted in an increase in the total number of technical skills performed, particularly for the younger players. More specifically, the modified game featured more passes, catches, plays and effective tackles, with players crossing the advantage and defensive lines and scoring more frequently than in the traditional game. These increases in offensive action are of particular significance when considering previous evidence suggesting that children enjoy this element of the game and that enjoyment is one of the main reasons cited for their participation in sport (Coakley, 1980; Weiss et al., 2012). In other sports, players had greater ball contacts in a 4v4 game compared to an eight *vs.* eight football/soccer game (Jones & Drust, 2007) while the size of the team (three *vs.* three; five *vs.* five) may influence the tactical behaviours of players (e.g. more shots at goal in three *vs.* three and more support play in five *vs.* five; Castelão et al., 2014).

Renshaw and Chow (2019) highlight some key principles for coaches to consider when designing modified activities to enhance player learning: (1) coaches are problem setters and players explore the 'how, why, where and when'; (2) coaches check the representativeness of the activity by asking 'does this look and feel like the real thing to you?'; and (3) coaches ensure the amount of variability in an activity is matched to the learner (e.g., low variability for beginners). Finally, another example where 'modifications' have been implemented is the change in actual competition matches. Whilst in flag football, one of the few studies (Burton et al., 2011) that have examined the use of modified games with children during competition, variations to the size of the ball and rules restricting the movements of players during attack in flag football increased the points scored (745–1,158 points) and nearly doubled the number of players scoring (47%) between the season without and with the modifications, respectively. Affecting changes in offensive outcomes through modified games is critical in a child's development and participation as children suggest that this form of play results in the most fun for them and, as a result, improves their intrinsic motivation (Coakley et al., 1980). A more recent study in Rugby Union in the UK explored the impact of a game modification that stipulated all players selected in the squad on match day must play at least half a game (Jones et al., 2021). Players who played more regularly reported more enjoyment and an increased intention to continue to play rugby than players who played less regularly.

The 4C's framework is another way of understanding 'how are we coaching?' and emphasises the outcomes related with positive youth development; competence, confidence, connection and character (Côté et al., 2016). Player competence (physical and cognitive skill) can be developed through a combination of deliberate practice and deliberate play where coaches individualise information that is positive, but that is also realistic in relation to what players can observe through peer comparison. A coach can support a child's 'confidence' by creating a mastery climate enabling a child's competence to be evaluated by themselves according to self-referenced improvement and effort rather than comparing themselves to others. 'Connection' is often why children play sport and can be encouraged by the coach in the way they promote positive participant-peer, parent and coach interaction. Finally, character can be developed by the coach being a positive role model; reinforcing the behaviours of players who demonstrate sportsperson ship by engaging in pro-social behaviours while not condoning antisocial behaviours. The 4Cs framework is applicable to both participation and high-performance youth sport frameworks. For example, elite youth soccer players ($N = 455$) reported relatively high levels of self-confidence and competence, strong coach-athlete relationships and higher prosocial compared to antisocial behaviour (O'Connor et al., 2020).

What Are We Coaching?

The third component of the CAYPABLE model considers 'what we are coaching' and refers to skill development – both rugby specific and movement specific. This is examined in detail in the practical application section.

Practical Application: A Movement-Based Approach to Developing Children Playing Rugby

Why Is It Needed?

Research suggests that young rugby league players are not being exposed to a full range of movement competencies that are required to produce versatile, co-ordinated athletes able to function effectively within the game (Morley, 2011; Morley et al., 2011; Morley & Webb, 2009). It has also been suggested that the deficiency of movement skills being coached within rugby is a bi-product of coaching development programs that fail to effectively support the delivery of sessions relevant to the developmental needs of young players, commonly reverting to adult-based methods and approaches (Morley & Webb, 2009). As previously mentioned, treating children in the same way as adults fails to recognise their unique developmental needs. It is clear that effective movement development of children is crucial within their technical development as they acquire skills relevant to their playing rugby. The ability of a coach to differentiate the task to meet the developmental needs of the Individual is consistent with Davids et al.'s (2003) appreciation of the dynamic systems that exist within coach decision-making and is crucial when working with children. Table 3.2 provides an example of the fundamental differences in how a child progresses in the development of a skill (e.g., throwing) within rugby.

More broadly, children need to develop movement skills such as balance, co-ordination, reaction and timing, which are the building blocks of sport and most forms of recreational physical activity (Gallahue & Ozmun, 2006). The focus on the establishment of fundamental movement skills, irrespective of their significance in terms of rugby, is vital to a child's subsequent inclusion in any form of sport or physical activity (Morley et al., 2016). Using the appropriate movement-based approach at the correct stage of a child's development can contribute to the overall pathway of the athlete as they progress through certain developmental stages in relation to their capabilities.

Coach Support for Movement Development in Rugby League

A movement-focussed coach development course has been developed previously by the Rugby Football League (RFL) in England, based on the 'Becoming CAYPABLE' framework (Figure 3.1) and now used as the Level 1 coaching qualification by the RFL (Morley, 2012). The outcomes of the course were to support coaches in (1) describing how the CAYPABLE framework helped them to plan, deliver and evaluate their coaching practice; (2) delivering safe and fun coaching sessions, based on pre-prepared cards; and (3) reflecting on coaching practice and what can be done to improve coaching.

TABLE 3.2 A 'Throwing' Example of RFL Skills according to the Lifespan Motor Development Model (Gallahue & Ozmun, 2006) Matrix Analysis

Areas of Skill	Current Skill Demands	Early (four to seven years)	Middle (8–12 years)	Later (13 years +)	Elite (existing skill sets)

Throwing Ability to impart force to an object in the general direction of intent	• Static
	  • Weighting
	  • Timing
	  • Accuracy
	• Moving
	  • Weighting
	  • Timing
	  • Accuracy
		Thumbs point inwards
		Difficulty in judging
		Action from elbows
		Resembles a push
		Follow-through forwards and downwards
		Little rotary action
		Limited weight transfer
		Feet remain stationary
			Thumbs point upwards
			Ball is recoiled before release
			Ball does not pass centre or side of body line in preparation
			Trunk and shoulders rotate towards throwing side
			Sideward and forwards shift of body weight
			Opposite leg strikes ground to throwing side
				Ball passes centre or side line of body offering full recoil in preparation
				Trunk, shoulders and hips fully rotate
				Able to demonstrate proficiency on both sides
				Opposite leg to throwing side acts as block to produce force
				Arms extend fully in direction of throw
					6 o'clock
					Over the front foot
					Ball pointed down
					Shoulders rotated
					Wrist hands
					Dummy half-pass
					Approach
					Move into sit position (step to ball)
					Scans sit

Understanding Children's Movement within Rugby League

The course was constructed around the movement needs of children at various developmental phases, according to the Lifespan Motor Development model (Gallahue & Ozmun, 2006). These movements were categorised into Stability, Object Control and Locomotion (SOL) and the sequential development of each movement was mapped into the various stages (i.e., beginner, intermediate and advanced) of a young player's development. Each player could then be assessed and supported in relation to their development through these stages by assessing them at the Beginner, Intermediate or Advanced stage of movement competence. So if a young rugby player was still coming to terms with fundamental movement skills such as running, throwing and catching in isolation they would be considered at the beginner stage. If they could combine two or more of these movements into more complex sequences and start to demonstrate more fluency and consistency in their movement, they would be considered Intermediate. For example, they could evade a player and pass using stability (side-step), object control (carrying, grip, throwing on the run) and locomotion (running a zig-zag). Finally, if they were able to demonstrate complex movement skills consistently and with fluently on repeated occasions, they would be their movement competence would be regarded as advanced. We could see this in tackling, whereby the child uses stability to be able to crouch, twist, turn and bend before and during in the tackle, wrap the player as an aspect of object control by gripping and controlling their movements and run in a variety of directions prior to the tackle to position themselves effectively. Further, detailed, examples of how these developmental stages can be seen within rugby-specific movement skills were provided as an overview (Table 3.3).

Structuring a Session for Children in Rugby League

Also covered within the design of the course was how to structure a session and what to cover within each aspect of the session. The general framework proposed four aspects of a session for coaching children: (1) warm ups, (2) game introduction, (3) movement development (SOL) and (4) game application and is described in more detail in Table 3.4.

Key Take Home Messages

Becoming CAYPABLE outlines how coaches can create learning environments that are developmentally appropriate and athlete centred. The following implications and recommendations for practice centre on (1) an understanding of the child, (2) an understanding of skill development within rugby and (3) an understanding of teaching and learning principles (Muir et al. 2011).

TABLE 3.3 Player's Needs at the Beginner, Intermediate and Advanced Stages of Development

Levels and Stages of Learning a New Movement Skill	Children and Young People
	Players Thinking… Individual
Beginner/Novice level	Player tries to form a conscious mental plan of the movement task
Awareness stage	Wants to know how the body *should* move
Exploratory stage	Knows what to do, but unable to do it with consistency
Discovery stage	Forms a conscious mental plan for performing the task
Intermediate/Practice level	Player has good general understanding of the movement task
Combination stage	Puts skills together with less conscious attention to their elements
Application stage	Makes effort to refine skill
Advanced/Fine tuning level	Player has a complete understanding of the movement task
Performance stage	Gives little or no conscious attention to the elements of the task
Individualised stage	Fine tunes performance based on personal attributes and limitations

Understanding the Child

Consider the differing biological, psychological and sociological (biopsychosocial) needs of children playing rugby as they develop:

- Children's skeletal, muscular and nervous systems develop rapidly and a coach must be aware of the risk of burn out and injury caused by excessive exercise, load and stress.
- Biological developmental differences will affect each child's capacity to demonstrate the movement skills fundamental to sports participation (e.g., balancing, travelling, controlling objects). Therefore, be aware of the differences within your groups.
- Children have a variety of reasons for participating in sport, comprising a mixture of fun, motor competence, challenge and social interaction (Beni et al., 2017).
- Over time, children's motivations for participation will change. Younger children seek excitement and pleasure, while older children strive for achievement and satisfaction (Bailey et al., 2010).

46 David Morley and Donna O'Connor

TABLE 3.4 Session Structure for a Movement-Based Approach to Coaching Children in Rugby

Aspect of Session Structure	Purpose	
	Enables Players to	Enables Coaches to
Warm Ups	<ul><li>Start slowly and build speed</li><li>Practice skills</li><li>Be creative</li><li>Think</li><li>Develop self-confidence</li><li>Work effectively with others</li></ul>	Prepare the players for the specific focus of the session
Game introduction	<ul><li>Get a feel for the environment</li><li>Think about what they are doing and how to improve</li><li>Understand which skills they need to improve upon before re-applying back into the game later</li></ul>	Assess the level of competence within the group and ask questions about:<ul><li>Key points related to the skill</li><li>Modifications that can be made to help layers develop</li></ul>
Sol development	<ul><li>Develop movement skills that underpin the core skills</li><li>Explore effective ways of moving</li><li>Develop awareness of their own movement abilities</li><li>Understand why some movement patterns are more effective than others</li><li>Understand the relevance of movements to performance within the game</li></ul>	<ul><li>Provide demonstrations and encourage players to demonstrate</li><li>Provide specific individual feedback</li><li>Question the development of SOL skills – 'what did you need to improve upon in the game intro?'</li><li>Progress the challenge within the activity</li></ul>
Game application	<ul><li>Apply the skills they have just been practicing into a game</li><li>Progress skills</li><li>Develop tactical awareness</li><li>Think about how the skills they are developing apply to rugby league</li></ul>	<ul><li>Re-start the game in the same format as the game intro used at the start of the session</li><li>Introduce progressions to the game being played</li><li>Make links between intro, application and SOL</li><li>Ask players to suggest ways in which SOL movements and skills can be applied into a game situation, e.g., penetrating a defence, kicking for territorial advantage</li></ul>

Understanding Skill Development

Equally, a greater understanding of developmentally appropriate movement and rugby skills would come from developing a sound knowledge of the following principles:

- Incorporate a wide variety of cognitive (i.e., knowledge and understanding of what they are doing), perceptual (i.e., what they do in relation to what they see – the ball, the pitch, other players) and motor skills (SOL) into development programmes.
- From roughly ages four to seven years, offer a broad range of fundamental movement skills based on the SOL categories of movement in a playful context, as these contribute to participation in sport more broadly and assist in developing more advanced skills in later years.
- From around ages 8–12 years, appropriate opportunities should be provided for participants to learn a wide range of transferable sport skills (e.g., creating space for self and others) and specific skills used in rugby.
- Provide opportunities for children to engage in free play which promotes enjoyment, engagement and autonomy – this can be before, during or after scheduled practice sessions.

Understanding Coaching and Learning

Finally, a greater understanding of coaching and learning would come from developing a sound knowledge of the following principles:

- Judge and acknowledge performance in relation to the children's bio-psycho-social needs to establish a positive learning climate.
- When planning, establish targets that meet the bio-psycho-social and sport-specific needs of players, through consideration of the overall management of sessions (i.e., what and how they manipulate the task – use of space, time and equipment), selection of learning cues and identification of learning assessment methods.
- When designing practice activities and games, coaches can manipulate constraints to scaffold player learning. Modified practice games enhance involvement through manipulating space and rules to increase the frequency of technical skills and enjoyable outcomes for children.
- Use demonstrations when players are learning new skills and sparingly to reinforce correct skill development (Horn & Williams, 2004).
- Regularly provide immediate feedback for younger children trying to master new tasks and less, delayed, instructional feedback for older children (Wulf & Shea, 2004).
- Plan to maximise learning opportunities by considering how often you stop the activity to intervene and provide solutions. With older children give

them time to trial new strategies, make mistakes and correct their own errors (O'Connor et al., 2018).
- Adopt a facilitative approach and ask questions that provoke children's curiosity, improve understanding of skills, focus attention, increase confidence and develop decision-making/problem-solving skills. Avoid excessive questioning which can create anxiety and defensiveness within children.
- During the early stages (i.e., 6–12 years) of a child's participation in sport, with an emphasis on playful activities (i.e., deliberate play). The coach's role should be to modify the environment or supply directive feedback and instructions in order to quickly correct errors.
- The coach should also encourage children to sample a range of sports as early diversification allows for experiences across a range of contexts supporting positive youth development and long-term sport involvement (Côté & Vierimaa, 2014).

References

Abbott, A., Button, C., Pepping, G. J., & Collins, D. (2005). Unnatural selection: Talent identification and development in sport. *Nonlinear Dynamics, Psychology, and Life Sciences, 9*, 61–88.

Abraham, A., & Collins, D. (2011). Taking the next step: Ways forward for coaching science. *Quest, 63*, 366–384. https://doi.org/10.1080/00336297.2011.10483687

Bailey, R., Collins, D., Ford, P., MacNamara, Á., Toms, M., & Pearce, G. (2010). Participant development in sport: An academic review. *Sports Coach UK, 4*, 1–134.

Bailey, R., Cope, E., & Pearce, G. (2013). Why do children take part in, and remain involved in sport? A literature review and discussion of implications for sports coaches. *International Journal of Coaching Science, 7*, 55–71.

Beni, B., Fletcher, T., & Chroinin, D. (2017). Meaningful experiences in physical education and youth sport: A review of the literature. *Quest, 69*, 291–312. https://doi.org/10.1080/00336297.2016.1224192

Burton, D., O'Connell, K., Gillham, A. D., & Hammermeister, J. (2011). More cheers and fewer tears: Examining the impact of competitive engineering on scoring and attrition in youth flag football. *International Journal of Sports Science & Coaching, 6*, 219–228. https://doi.org/10.1260/1747-9541.6.2.219

Capranica, L., & Millard-Stafford, M. L. (2011). Youth sport specialization: How to manage competition and training? *International Journal of Sports Physiology and Performance, 6*, 572–579. https://doi.org/10.1123/ijspp.6.4.572

Castelão D., Garganta J., Santos R., & Teoldo, I. (2014). Comparison of tactical behaviour and performance of youth soccer players in 3v3 and 5v5 small-sided games. *International Journal of Performance Analysis in Sport, 14*, 801–813. https://doi.org/10.1080/24748668.2014.11868759

Coakley, J. J. (1980). Play, games, and sport: Developmental implications for young people. *Journal of Sport Behavior, 3*, 99.

Côté, J., Turnnidge, J., & Vierimaa, M. (2016). A personal assets approach to youth sport. In *Routledge handbook of youth sport* (pp. 243–255). Routledge.

Côté, J., & Vierimaa, M. (2014). The developmental model of sport participation: 15 years after its first conceptualization. *Science and Sports, 29*, S63–S69. https://doi.org/10.1016/j.scispo.2014.08.133

Davids, K., Araújo, D., Correia, V., & Vilar, L. (2013). How small-sided and conditioned games enhance acquisition of movement and decision-making skills. *Exercise and Sport Sciences Reviews, 41*, 154–161. https://doi.org/10.1097/JES.0b013e318292f3ec

Davids, K., Glazier, P., Araujo, D., & Bartlett, R. (2003). Movement systems as dynamical systems. *Sports Medicine, 33*, 245–260. https://doi.org/10.2165/00007256-200333040-00001

Gallahue, D., & Ozmun, J. (2006). *Understanding motor development: Infants, children, adolescents, adults* (6th ed.). McGraw-Hill.

Grehaigne, J., & Godbout, P. (2014). Dynamic systems theory and team sport coaching. *Quest, 66*, 96–116. https://doi.org/10.1080/00336297.2013.814577

Griffin, L. L., Butler, J. I., & Sheppard, J. (2017). Athlete-centred coaching: Extending the possibilities of a holistic and process-oriented model to athlete development. In S. Pill (Ed.), *Perspectives on athlete-centred coaching* (pp. 9–23), Routledge.

Headley-Cooper, K. (2011). Athlete-centred coaching: What does it mean to you. *Coaches Plan/Plan du Coach, 17*, 18–20.

Headley-Cooper, K. (2020). Challenges that coaches face in empowering athletes to "think for themselves. In D. Cooper, & B. Gordon (Eds.), *Tactical decision-making in sport: How coaches can help athletes to make better in-game decisions* (pp. 39–49), Routledge.

Hopper, T. (2011). Game-as-teacher: Modification by adaptation in learning through game-play. *Asia-Pacific Journal of Health, Sport and Physical Education, 2*, 3–21. https://doi.org/10.1080/18377122.2011.9730348

Horn, R. R., & Williams, A. M. (2004). Observational learning: Is it time we took another look? In A. M. Williams, & N. J. Hodges (Eds.), *Skill acquisition in sport: Research, theory and practice* (pp. 175–206), Routledge.

Jones, B., Hope, E., Hammond, A., Moran, J., Leeder, T., Mills, J., & Sandercock, G. (2021). Play more, enjoy more, keep playing; Rugby is a simple game. *International Journal of Sports Science & Coaching, 16*, 636–45. https://doi.org/10.1177/1747954121991444

Jones, S., & Drust, B. (2007). Physiological and technical demands of 4 v 4 and 8 v 8 games in elite youth soccer players. *Kinesiology, 39*, 150–156.

Kiesler, D. J. (1999). *Beyond the disease model of mental disorders.* Praeger.

Klusemann, M. J., Pyne, D. B., Foster, C., & Drinkwater, E. J. (2012). Optimising technical skills and physical loading in small-sided basketball games, *Journal of Sports Sciences, 30*, 1463–1471. https://doi.org/10.1080/02640414.2012.712714

Martindale, R., Collins, D., & Daubney, J. (2005). Talent development: A guide for practice and research within sport, *Quest, 57*, 353–375. https://doi.org/10.1080/00336297.2005.10491862

Miller, A., Harvey, S., Morley, D., Nemes, R., Janes, M., & Eather, N. (2017). Exposing athletes to playing form activity: outcomes of a randomised control trial among community netball teams using a game-centred approach. *Journal of Sports Sciences, 35*, 1846–1857. https://doi.org/10.1080/02640414.2016.1240371

Morley, D. (2012). A 'fit for purpose strategy' for the Rugby Football League. In A. Navin (Ed.), *Sports coaching: A reference guide for students, coaches and competitors* (pp 237–175), Crowood Press.

Morley, D., & Muir, B (2012) *Becoming CAYPABLE: Level 1 coach qualification support resource.* Leeds: Coachwise.

Morley, D., Ogilvie, P., Till, K., Rothwell, M., Cotton, W., O'Connor, D., & McKenna, J. (2016). Does modifying competition affect the frequency of technical skills in junior rugby league? *International Journal of Sport Science and Coaching, 10*, 623–636. https://doi.org/10.1177/1747954116676107.

Morley, D., & Sanctuary, C. (2016). The young rugby player. In K. Till & B. Jones (Eds.), *The science of sport: Rugby* (pp. 93–110), Crowood Press.

Morley, D. & Webb, V. (2009). A 'fit purpose' approach to skills development in Rugby Football League. *UK Coaching Summit*, Glasgow, 27–29 Apr.

Muir, B., Morgan, G., Abraham, A., & Morley, D. (2011). Developmentally appropriate approaches to coaching children. In I. Stafford (Ed.), *Coaching children in sport* (pp. 39–59). Routledge.

Nelson, L., Cushion, C. J., Potrac, P., & Groom, R. (2014). Carl Rogers, learning and educational practice: Critical considerations and applications in sports coaching. *Sport, Education and Society*, 19, 513–531. https://doi.org/10.1080/13573322.2012.689256

O'Connor, D., Gardner, L., Larkin, P., Pope, A., & Williams, A. M. (2020). Positive youth development and gender differences in high performance sport. *Journal of Sports Sciences*, 38, 1399–1407. https://doi.org/10.1080/02640414.2019.1698001.

O'Connor, D., Larkin, P., & Williams, A. M., (2017). What learning environments help improve decision-making? *Physical Education and Sport Pedagogy*, 22, 647–660. https://doi.org/10.1080/17408989.2017.1294678

O'Connor, D., Larkin, P., & Williams, A. M. (2018). Observations of youth football training: How do coaches structure training sessions for player development. *Journal of Sports Sciences*, 36, 39–47. https://doi.org/10.1080/02640414.2016.1277034

Pill, S. (Ed.). (2017). *Perspectives on athlete-centred coaching*. Routledge.

Potrac, P., & Cassidy, T. (2006). The coach as a 'more capable other. In R. Jones (Ed.), *The sports coach as educator* (pp. 57–68). Routledge.

Renshaw, I., & Chow, J.-Y. (2019). A constraints-led approach to sport and physical education pedagogy. *Physical Education and Sport Pedagogy*, 24, 103–116, https://doi.org/10.1080/17408989.2018.1552676

Rottensteiner, C., Laakso, L., Pihlaja, T., & Konttinen, N. (2013). Personal reasons for withdrawal from team sports and the influence of significant others among youth athletes. *International Journal of Sports Science & Coaching*, 8, 19–32. https://doi.org/10.1260%2F1747-9541.8.1.19

United Nations Children's Fund (UNICEF). (2022). Convention on the rights of the child. Available at: https://www.unicef.org/cuba/en/reports/convention-rights-child-child friendly-text [Accessed 27 May 2022].

Visek, A. J., Achrati, S. M., Mannix, H. M., McDonnell, K., Harris, B. S., & DiPietro, L. (2015). The fun integration theory: Toward sustaining children and adolescents sport participation. *Journal of Physical Activity and Health*, 12, 424–433. https://doi.org/10.1123/jpah.2013-0180.

Wall, M., & Côté, J. (2007). Developmental activities that lead to dropout and investment in sport. *Physical Education and Sport Pedagogy*, 12, 77–87. https://doi.org10.1080/17408980601060358.

Weiss, M. R., Amorose, A. J., & Kipp, L. E. (2012). Youth motivation and participation in sport and physical activity. In R. M. Ryan (Ed.), *The Oxford handbook of human motivation* (pp. 520–553). Oxford University Press.

Weiss, M. R., & Williams, L. (2004). The why of youth sport involvement: A developmental perspective on motivational processes'. In M. R. Weiss (Ed.), *Developmental sport and exercise psychology: A lifespan perspective* (pp. 223–268). Fitness Information Technology.

Witt, P., & Dangi, T. (2018). Why children/youth drop out of sports. *Journal of Park and Recreation Administration*, 36, 191–199. https://doi.org/10.18666/JPRA-2018-V36-I3-8618

Wulf, G., & Shea, C. H. (2004). Understanding the role of augmented feedback: The good, the bad and the ugly. In A. M. Williams & N. Hodges (Eds.), *Skill acquisition in sport* (pp. 145–168). Routledge.

4
DAVIDS AND GOLIATHS: KINANTHROPOMETRY AND GROUPING STRATEGIES IN YOUTH RUGBY

John Sampson, Job Fransen, Ric Lovell and Kevin Till

Introduction

Youth rugby players are often organised into (bi)annual-age groups using specific cut-off dates (e.g., 1st September in England, 1st January in Australia) in attempts to create equal competition and development opportunities for all players. However, chronological age-grouping can result in large differences in body size between players of the same age. Furthermore, an age grouping structure in rugby alongside the natural processes of growth, maturation and development within children and adolescents can have implications for player participation and development within the codes. To date, a range of research has examined kinanthropometry (i.e., the study of size, shape, proportion, composition and maturation) in youth rugby players and the relationships with rugby performance, talent identification and injury. This has opened debate around appropriate grouping strategies within youth rugby to ensure equal competition and development opportunities for all.

This chapter aims to highlight and provide an overview of the research on the kinanthropometry of youth rugby players and its relevance for player development, talent identification and injury risk. A range of practical implications for coaches, sport scientists and practitioners working within youth rugby to consider in relation to kinanthropometry and grouping strategies within youth rugby development programmes are then presented.

Research Overview

Kinanthropometry in Youth Rugby

The most reported measurements in young rugby players are stature and body mass. Herein, a review of the literature (Patton et al., 2016) highlights that male

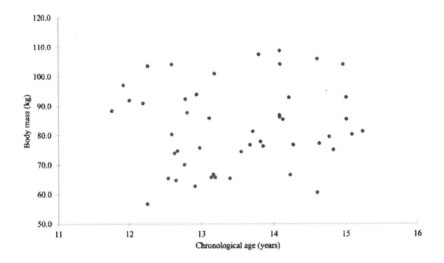

FIGURE 4.1 The Variability in Body Mass in Youth Rugby Players Aged 12–15 Years

rugby league and union players aged 12–18 years typically lie above the 50th percentile for stature, with body mass approaching the 95th percentile when compared to normative population data (http://www.cdc.gov/growthcharts). However, substantial variability in both stature and body mass is observed within young rugby players (Patton et al., 2016). For example, Krause et al. (2015) showed differences in stature of over 40 cm and body mass of almost 100 kg between players competing within both Under 12 (U12)–13 and U14–U15 rugby union age grades. Whilst these differences may seem substantial, the combination of age groups (i.e., biannual) in this study may exemplify the variability. Nonetheless, such data demonstrates the large variation in body size between players of a similar chronological age. Figure 4.1 shows exemplar data for the body mass distribution of a group of competitive rugby players aged 12–15 years playing in the same rugby competition.

Alongside stature and body mass, other kinanthropometric measures presented in male youth rugby research literature include body composition, somatotype, skeletal lengths, skeletal breadths and circumferences. Research has shown increases in absolute fat mass and fat-free mass (i.e., lean mass) with age (Gavarry et al., 2018). Yet, relative measures (e.g., sum of skinfolds, body fat percentage) remain relatively stable across adolescent rugby players (Darrall-Jones et al., 2015) and skeletal lengths, breadths, and circumferences of youth rugby players have been shown to increase with age aligned to growth and maturation (Cheng et al., 2014; Waldron et al., 2014). Body shape changes are observed, and somatotype develops from predominantly ectomorphic (i.e., tall and thin) to become more endomorphic (i.e., heavier and rounder) and mesomorphic (i.e., muscular development) during late adolescence (Cheng et al., 2014). However, like stature and body mass, large variability occurs within these kinanthropometric measures. For example, in consideration of ethnicity, Australian Polynesian players possess greater humeral and femoral breadths, bicep and calf circumferences and endomorphic and mesomorphic somatotypes than non-Polynesian players (Cheng et al., 2014). The observed variability can influence positional allocation with differences across a range of kinanthropometric measures between forwards and backs in youth rugby (e.g., Delahunt et al., 2013).

Biological Maturation

The large range of kinanthropometric measures between players of a similar age can occur due to maturation (the transition from childhood to adolescence). Maturation is defined as the timing and tempo of the progress towards the mature adult state (Malina et al., 2004). There are different types of maturation, including, but not limited to skeletal (i.e., development of the skeletal system usually presented as skeletal age), sexual (i.e., secondary sexual characteristics development or age at menarche in girls, or testicular volume in boys) or somatic (i.e., changes in height and mass, age at peak height velocity [APHV]) (see Lloyd et al., 2014; Sampson et al., 2022). While skeletal and sexual maturation can be estimated using a variety of techniques such as self-reported secondary sex characteristics or skeletal x-rays, somatic methods are most common in sport practice due to their relatively unobtrusive nature (i.e., using kinanthropometric measurements).

Somatic maturation can be evaluated by measuring stature longitudinally to obtain characteristics of the adolescent growth spurt. For example, for boys the growth spurt generally commences between 10.3 and 12.1 years (standard deviation [SD] = 0.9–1.0 years), lasts for between 2 and 5 years with peak height velocities (PHV) of ~8.2–10.3 cm/year (SD = 0.9–1.6 cm/year) observed around 13.4–14.3 years (SD = 0.8– 1.1 years). For girls, the adolescent growth spurt commences between 8.5 and 10.3 years (SD = 0.6–1.6 years) with PHVs of ~7.5–9.1 cm/year (SD = 0.7–1.7) observed around 11.4–12.1 years (SD = 0.7–1.2 years) (Beunen & Malina, 1988). To the authors' knowledge, no studies have used longitudinal growth data spanning the adolescent growth spurt to obtain the timing of PHV or maturity status of youth rugby players. Instead, most researchers have used mathematical equations to estimate maturity offset (Box 4.1; Mirwald et al., 2002) or percentage of predicted adult height (PAH; Box 4.2; Khamis & Roche, 1994).

Box 4.1

The Mirwald maturity offset method (Mirwald et al., 2002) uses chronological age, stature, seated stature and body mass in sex-specific regression equations to calculate a maturity offset (i.e., years from PHV). Negative and positive maturity offset values generally classify individuals as pre-PHV and post-PHV, respectively. A maturity offset can then be used to estimate an individual's APHV by subtracting the maturity offset from chronological age. Estimated maturity offsets and APHVs have been used to classify players according to their *maturity status* by comparing an individual's estimated APHV with that of the sample mean from which the individual originates. For example, an individual with an estimated APHV <1 year compared to the mean APHV of the sample to which they belong can be considered relatively early maturing. On the other hand, an individual with an estimated APHV >1 year compared to the sample mean is considered relatively late maturing. Estimated APHVs within one year plus/minus the sample estimated APHV can be considered to be relatively on time (Malina & Kozieł, 2014). Other maturity status classification methods such as using the sample standard deviation as a cut-off value are also reported (Malina et al., 2004). It should be noted that significant estimating errors of ±1 year have been reported and that this method should only be used in youths who are near their APHV (see Fransen et al., 2021).

Box 4.2

The Khamis-Roche (1994) PAH method uses stature and parental stature (corrected for overestimation) in sex-specific regression equations to predict a child's adult height and calculate %PAH. Young players can then be grouped into respective maturity bands: <85% PAH, prepubertal; ≥85% to <90%, early pubertal; ≥90% to ≤95%, mid-pubertal, or ≥95%, late pubertal (Cumming et al., 2017). Of note, PHV will typically occur during 88–96% of PAH, often peaking, on average, at ~92% (Baxter-Jones, 2013). It should be noted that this method was developed using predominantly white youths and may be inappropriate in multi-ethnic populations such as youth rugby. The median error for the Khamis-Roche PAH method is ~2.0 cm within the 50th percentile but this error can increase to ~0.3 cm at the 90th percentile, and when considering age groups of interest in relation to maturation tempo (11–15 years), the median error is reported as 2.4–2.8 cm to 5.5–7.3 cm for the 50th and 90th percentiles, respectively (Towlson et al., 2021).

Maturity Status in Youth Rugby

Studies in rugby league (Till et al., 2010; Waldron et al., 2014) and union (Howard et al., 2016) have assessed somatic maturity status using prediction equations. Howard et al. (2016) assessed the maturity status using the percentage of PAH (%PAH) method of 51, 14–17-year-old academy rugby union players with

44 players classified as on-time, seven as early maturing and no players as late maturers. Similarly in rugby league players, Till et al. (2010) estimated APHV (using the Mirwald maturity offset method) as 13.6±0.6 in U13–U15. These studies subsequently demonstrate that early to on-time maturing players are favoured within player identification and selection in youth rugby.

Relationships with Injury Risk, Physical Performance and Talent Identification

The variability and observed differences in body size and maturity status of young rugby players have raised public debate. Media reports (Gould, 2011; Lewis, 2014) and parental concerns (Boufous et al., 2004) have raised fears that size and maturity mismatches within age-grade rugby competitions may effect development and influence injury risk. However, the only research study to date has shown no association between injury risk and body size in youth rugby (Krause et al., 2015). Yet, injury risk (in general) may be heightened during maturation as large increases in the length of bones, increased tendon stiffness and muscle growth can place additional strain on the growing body resulting in overuse injuries (e.g., Osgood Schlatter's) and increased risk of other injuries (e.g., anterior cruciate ligament injuries in girls) (Gerrard, 1993; Radnor et al., 2018).

When considering rugby performance in adult rugby, a larger body size has been positively associated with scrummage performance (Quarrie & Wilson, 2000), competition success (Gabbett, 2009) and running momentum (body mass x running velocity) (Hendricks et al., 2014). Whilst limited research exists exploring maturity and youth rugby performance, positive associations between 10 m momentum and successful ball carries have been observed in elite U15–U17 rugby league players (Waldron et al., 2014), but in U12–U15 recreational rugby union players body size had no effect on rugby performance (Krause et al., 2015). Increased body mass may favour the expression of maximal strength, power and initial sprint momentum in youth rugby (Baker & Newton, 2008) and one would expect advanced body size to facilitate physical components of the game at the youth level considering the positive relationships between maturation and physical performance (e.g., strength, power, speed; Till & Jones, 2015). This is evidenced in youth players who are identified and selected to talent development programmes being usually advanced in body size and maturation (Cheng et al., 2014; Howard et al., 2016; Till et al., 2010). However, research has actually shown that later maturing players between 13 and 15 years gained more height and improved their 60 m sprint performance and upper body power more than earlier maturing players (Till et al., 2014) and that body size and maturity status at 13–15 years were not associated with future career outcomes in rugby league (Till et al., 2016).

These research findings infer that the physical advantages afforded to bigger and earlier maturing youth players may lead to increased opportunities within youth rugby (Figure 4.2). However, such advantages may be transient in nature, potentially masking weaknesses in technical, decision-making and/or

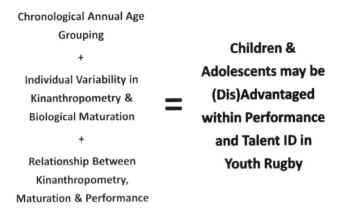

FIGURE 4.2 Summary of Kinanthropometry, Maturation and Outcomes within Youth Rugby

psycho-social attributes. A challenge for player development stakeholders in rugby is thus to create opportunities for, and avoid the early deselection of relatively younger, smaller and/or later maturing players.

Grouping Strategies

Based on the above research and knowledge, classifying youth rugby players by age has become a matter of debate. Whilst age grouping is the most common grouping strategy, several federations have adopted the intuitive method of grouping youth players according to body mass (see Lentin et al., 2021; Patton et al., 2016). Players with advanced anthropometric characteristics may be 'accelerated' (i.e., play up) to participate against older players. Conversely, the term 'dispensation' is used for smaller players who are eligible to compete in younger age categories (i.e., play down) and is considered a strategy that may increase participation (Cassidy, 2018). Lentin et al. (2021) showed a weight grading model helped to reduce the variability in body size of young players whilst maintaining the identity of age category in French rugby. However, such a grouping strategy resulted in mainly obese players being 'accelerated' which subsequently resulted in large variability and body composition mismatches. Furthermore, anthropometric-based grading does not consider important performance features such as body composition (Fontana et al., 2017), mental maturity (Patton et al., 2016) and skill competency (Pienaar et al., 1998). Whilst bio-banding (i.e., the grouping of individuals according to maturation instead of chronological age) has been used in other sports (e.g., soccer; Cumming et al., 2017), to date no research on this topic is available in rugby. Thus, whilst alternative 'grouping' strategies may offer advantages for player development and participation, there is a lack of research in youth rugby to substantiate this claim and as such future research is needed.

Practical Applications

Based on the research overview, this practical applications section aims to provide practitioners (e.g., coaches, sport scientists) and administrators/organisations (e.g., clubs, national governing bodies) with a series of recommendations of how and where they can apply this knowledge into practice.

Understand Growth and Maturation

Practitioners and administrators must acknowledge, be aware of, and consider the substantial variability in body size within young rugby players when applying appropriate development opportunities for all players. The key concept is that players may be of a similar chronological age but may demonstrate large differences in size, especially during adolescence (i.e., 11–13 years in girls and 12–16 years in boys) when differences in maturity status are apparent. The knowledge described above can help practitioners and administrators across the micro- (e.g., coaching sessions), meso- (e.g., clubs, management) and macro- (e.g., national governing bodies, policy) levels of the youth sport system (Eisenmann et al., 2020). For example, at the micro-level coaches working with young rugby players may adapt their training focus to provide a greater challenge for earlier maturing players and more support for later maturing players to aid their development. At the meso- and macro-levels, organisations may implement multiple grouping strategies (e.g., age, size, maturity, skill) within training and competition and implement policies around competition and talent identification (Eisenmann et al., 2020). Specifically, rugby unions have delayed the age when talent identification into academy programmes occurs to post-maturation, in an attempt to reduce maturity selection biases (Till et al., 2020). However, to understand and apply this within practice requires gaining an accurate understanding of an individual's maturation status. In a non-clinical context, the recommended method is to estimate the occurrence of PHV either by %PAH or an estimation of the attainment of PHV. These estimations are sufficiently sensitive to assign players into categories (i.e., pre, circum or post puberty), which can, alongside players' chronological age, offer valuable insights into youth players' growth and development (Fransen et al., 2021). Researchers and practitioners should yet carefully contemplate the large variability in timing and tempo of maturational events and shortcomings of non-invasive estimations of somatic maturity (Fransen et al., 2021).

Measurement Guidelines and Protocols

The implementation of consistent kinanthropometric measurement and assessment protocols is recommended in youth rugby players. Detailed instructions for kinanthropometric assessments are detailed elsewhere (e.g., Malina et al., 2004), however, too often practitioners and researchers use these methods without considering if they present the right fit for the sport, the athletes and the logistical means of the organisation. Therefore, some guidelines and recommendations for rugby scientists and practitioners tasked with assessing rugby players' anthropometry, growth and maturation are presented. A number of pragmatic methods are available to measure kinanthropometry (specifically stature and body mass) and estimate an individual's maturity status in youth rugby (e.g., longitudinal monitoring of stature or mass; maturity offset [Mirwald et al., 2002]; %PAH [Khamis & Roche, 1994]). Whilst these methods have strengths and limitations, important considerations are described below.

a   Appropriate measurement tools and standardised procedures

Random and systematic error both require consideration in the context of measuring kinanthropometry and estimating maturity in the context of rugby. Random error can be the result of variations in the subjects being measured, or the assessors performing the measurements (Malina et al., 2004). It is considered random because it is randomly greater or smaller than the actual phenomenon and may therefore not cause an issue (i.e., sometimes there is an over-measurement, and sometimes under-measurement, and both cancel each other out). Systematic measurement error is usually skewed in one direction and can include a data entry mistake in a spreadsheet aimed at estimating a player's APHV. To overcome measurement error issues, scientists or practitioners can take two important steps. First, as a single assessor is unlikely to be consistently available to record all measures for the same player(s), the development of standardised protocols to dictate how anthropometric measurements should be developed. Second, the measurement instruments (e.g., skinfold calipers, stadiometer) should be consistently and properly calibrated to optimise their validity and reliability. For example, plastic stadiometers for measuring stature can bend easily during assessment threatening measurement consistency.

b   Measuring *vs.* estimating maturity

Using non-invasive anthropometric measurements to estimate maturity in youth athletes is practical, but it must be recognised that they are estimations with inherent systematic error (Fransen et al., 2021). For example, Mirwald et al. (2002) recognised the systemic error stating that: 'maturity offset can be estimated within an error of ± one year, 95% of the time'. Furthermore, it should be considered that estimations of APHV derived from a participant's chronological age and maturity offset (Mirwald et al., 2002; Moore et al., 2015) or maturity ratio (Fransen et al., 2018) are most accurate when measured at a chronological age close to APHV, but become increasingly biased as chronological age is further removed from their APHV. The inaccuracies of non-invasive estimations of maturity are also magnified in exactly those athletes where the estimations are of most value (e.g., those who are late or early maturing [Cumming et al., 2017]), with anthropometric measurements tending to overestimate APHV in early maturing, and underestimate in late maturing individuals (Malina et al., 2015). Maturity status classified by the percent of predicted adult stature is a relatively simple and feasible to administer somatic measure. Errors (linked to the reliance on self-reporting of parental stature) should yet be recognised with estimates ranging from poor-moderate (Malina et al., 2007, 2012, 2015); that said, equations are available to adjust for their systematic over-estimation (Epstein et al., 1995). The technique is yet redundant in circumstances where accurate reporting of both biological parents stature is unavailable. Maturity estimations should as such, only be used as they were intended (i.e., to qualitatively classify players according to their maturity status rather than as a quantification of the timing of the adolescent growth spurt).

c   The 4C's of Implementation

Regular implementation of growth and maturity monitoring is challenging based on the contact time available and the number of athletes to assess. It has been recommended that a robust measurement and assessment programme requires the following four key principles to be applied to data collection and result in actionable implementation into the coaching practice (Eisenmann et al., 2020);

1   Commitment of an individual(s) to direct the process, select appropriate measures and educate stakeholders.
2   Consistent collection of the relevant data on a quarterly basis.
3   Communication of data along with training recommendations for athletes. Spreadsheets from Towlson et al. (2021) are useful for predicting maturity status.
4   Collaboration between multiple practitioners (if available) to develop appropriate training strategies.

Player Assessment and Talent Identification

Applying growth and maturation information to player assessment and talent identification processes (see more in Chapter 5) is an important consideration for practitioners. Such practices would allow practitioners to demonstrate greater awareness and understanding of the effect of growth and maturity on player performance and potential (Till & Baker, 2020). This is demonstrated by two examples below (Boxes 4.3 and 4.4).

Box 4.3

Player A is a relatively small, later maturing U14 fullback with less developed physical attributes compared to his/her age grouped peers. This often results in Player A not carrying the ball into contact at high speeds and failing to make tackles when opponents break the line. However, Player A demonstrates high technical skills (e.g., passing), tactical awareness (e.g., decision making) and psycho-social skills and characteristics (e.g., resilience, communication) that may suggest future potential capabilities for rugby within this position.

> **Box 4.4**
>
> Player B is an earlier maturing U14 player who also plays fullback. He is referred to as the most 'talented' player on his school team. Player B is very fast and athletic, often making numerous line breaks and scoring tries every game based on his athleticism. Whilst Player B has these transient physical advantages (owing to advanced maturity), he often fails to make the right decision in a two v one situation (preferring to use his pace) and fails to communicate with his teammates defensively.

Whilst these examples only provide a short snapshot of two players, they help coaches and practitioners consider how advanced size and maturity for players within the same position may influence performance and whether these performance attributes are related to long-term potential and hence talent identification.

Training Programme Design

Linked to practical application 1, coaches and practitioners can design and adapt training sessions and programmes that consider the body size and maturity status of the players related to (1) temporary plateaus or decrements in motor performance (referred to as adolescent awkwardness), (2) increased overuse injury risk (e.g., Osgood Schlatter's disease) and (3) large variability in size and maturity. First, related to adolescent awkwardness, practitioners should realise this is a temporary stage of decline and focus upon long-term not short-term selection decisions. Second, to improve co-ordination, implementing physical development, especially gross motor coordination and strength-based work within training sessions and programmes in relation to maturity status would be beneficial. Third, practitioners can implement constraints or challenges within games or training according to player maturity status. This could be to harvest the gains (i.e., increased physical attributes) that occur during maturation or to adjust the level of challenge for early/later maturing individuals. For example, to encourage an early maturing, physically dominant rugby player (like Player B example, Box 4.4) to use and develop evasive running and passing skills instead of using their physical prowess to run through their smaller and later maturing opponents, a constraint could be applied to them that states if they run straight into contact it is an automatic turnover. Including these in the participants' goal setting and development plan (whether informal or formal) also adds greater focus and perceived value from the participant. Chapter 15 provides further information on the implementation of an injury prevention programme. Lastly, the growth spurt can be a period of high training volumes for adolescent rugby players (Hendricks et al., 2019). Therefore, practitioners should consider the volume and intensity of training sessions, especially when players undertake multiple modes of training (see Chapter 12) alongside other periods of stress (e.g., school exams).

Grouping Strategies and Practices within Training and Competition

Annual-age grouping remains the most prevalent grouping strategy within youth rugby. However, to create different developmental experiences that support or challenge individual and groups of players, practitioners may consider implementing alternative grouping strategies within their training and competition programmes. These alternative grouping strategies may include:

a   The organisation of small-sided games within training that groups individuals by age, maturity, body size and positions. Herein, the appropriateness of including both age-, size-, maturity- and skill-matched and mis-matched training opportunities should also be considered to encourage the development and preparedness of the varied demands of game-play.
b   Provide participants with opportunities to progress and be challenged through a change of training environment. For example, joining sessions with relatively older participants (move up to train with the next age group). This could be within a planned transition period, for a specific session, on a regular basis, or more informally. Such practices could also be replicated in competition allowing player dispensation rules to allow players to play up or down.
c   Include rules to allow equal playing time. The Rugby Football Union in England now has a Half Game rule that means all players must play for a minimum of half a game.
d   Create competitions and adapt rules of the games to increase or decrease the challenge and technical and psychological aspects of rugby (and general athletic) performance and development (Côté & Vierimaa, 2014). For example, games could be implemented that reward technical skill, effort and psychosocial skills and characteristics (e.g., communication) rather than traditional scoring systems. Such competitions may encourage wider participation within the sport and the development of skills required for all players and reduce the physical emphasis associated with size and maturity variability.

Create 'Wider' Pathways

Based on research demonstrating the increased opportunities for large and earlier maturing players, rugby organisations should consider how they create development opportunities for all players. For example, the Leeds Rhinos RLFC designed and implemented a parallel later maturing developing programme as part of their talent pathway (see Till & Bell, 2019). As there is a restriction on the number of opportunities within the talent pathway within the United Kingdom rugby league from U15 (i.e., 20 player opportunities), the club implemented a parallel pathway for those players classified as later maturing individuals who were not recruited by any other professional rugby league club to increase the talent pool consistent with recommendations in other sports (e.g., soccer; Bennett et al., 2019). This created an additional talent development opportunity for players, who do not normally receive such support and included rugby player development and high-quality coaching, strength and conditioning coaching and home programme, player and parent education sessions (e.g., nutrition, psychology), fitness testing, individual player feedback and regular monitoring and feedback with parents and community club. Such a strategy could be considered by other sports and professional clubs within their talent identification and development processes, hopefully providing more developmental opportunities to more players in the future.

Communication and Collaboration

Whilst the above practical implications are recommended for consideration by practitioners and organisations, one vital aspect to successful implementation is the communication of the above information in relation to growth and maturation with a range of stakeholders (e.g., players, parents/guardians, other coaches). Being able to explain the changes and why you are organising training or policies in such a way may increase player buy-in and motivation to take part. This will help in the messaging and collaboration between others (e.g., parents and coaches) in providing explanations for these decisions. Furthermore, helping parents/guardians to understand the stages of development and nonlinear nature of growth and maturation is crucial. Being aware of how this impacts upon rugby performance enables parents/guardians to embrace the journey their child is on, rather than unhealthy expectations and unrealistic pressure to 'perform'.

Key Take Home Messages

- Youth rugby players are taller and heavier than normal populations but large variations in body size exists that mean players of all shapes and sizes compete within the codes of rugby.
- Maturation is defined as the timing and tempo of the progress towards the mature adult state. Large variability can exist in the timing and tempo of maturation. Studies in rugby show early to on-time maturing players are usually favoured within player identification and selection in youth rugby.
- The physical advantages afforded to bigger and earlier maturing youth players alongside the chronological annual age grouping system used may result

in advantages for earlier maturing and disadvantages for later maturing players. As such, practitioners need to understand maturation and where possible, measure maturation to inform their decision-making.
- When assessing maturation, the use of appropriate measurement tools and standardised procedures are needed to ensure as accurate information as possible.
- Practitioners can use growth and maturity information to inform their talent identification decisions, training and competition practices.
- It is recommended to create different developmental experiences and grouping strategies to support and challenge individual and groups of players. This could include organisation of small-sided games within training by age, maturity or body size; implementation of rules to allow equal competition time; provide opportunities for playing up or down; and adapt competition rules to focus on technical skill rather than traditional scoring systems.
- National governing bodies and professional organisations could consider developing wider talent pathways for the inclusion of later maturing individuals.
- Communication with stakeholders (e.g., parents, coaches, players) is key to successful implementation.

References

Baker, D. G., & Newton, R. U. (2008). Comparison of lower body strength, power, acceleration, speed, agility, and sprint momentum to describe and compare playing rank among professional rugby league players. *The Journal of Strength & Conditioning Research*, 22, 153–158. https://doi.org/10.1519/JSC.0b013e31815f9519

Baxter-Jones, A. D. (2013). Growth, maturation, and training. In D. J. Caine, K. W. Russell, & L. Lim (Eds.), *Handbook of sports medicine and science: Gymnastics* (pp. 17–27). John Wiley & Sons, Ltd.

Bennett, K. J., Vaeyens, R., & Fransen, J. (2019). Creating a framework for talent identification and development in emerging football nations. *Science and Medicine in Football*, 3, 36–42. https://doi.org/https://doi.org/10.1080/24733938.2018.1489141

Beunen, G., & Malina, R. M. (1988). Growth and physical performance relative to the timing of the adolescent spurt. *Exercise and Sport Sciences Reviews*, 16, 503–540. https://doi.org/https://doi.org/10.1249/00003677-198800160-00018

Boufous, S., Finch, C., & Bauman, A. (2004). Parental safety concerns–A barrier to sport and physical activity in children? *Australian and New Zealand Journal of Public Health*, 28, 482–486. https://doi.org/ https://doi.org/10.1111/j.1467-842X.2004.tb00032.x

Cassidy, T. (2018). 'I didn't have to tackle humungus people': An ecological investigation into a dispensation policy in New Zealand junior rugby. *International Journal of Sports Science & Coaching*, 13, 947–957. https://doi.org/10.1177/1747954118769181

Cheng, H. L., O'Connor, H., Kay, S., Cook, R., Parker, H., & Orr, R. (2014). Anthropometric characteristics of Australian junior representative rugby league players. *Journal of Science and Medicine in Sport*, 17, 546–551. https://doi.org/10.1016/j.jsams.2013.07.020

Côté, J., & Vierimaa, M. (2014). The developmental model of sport participation: 15 Years after its first conceptualization. *Science & Sports*, 29, S63–S69. https://doi.org/https://doi.org/10.1016/j.scispo.2014.08.133

Cumming, S. P., Lloyd, R. S., Oliver, J. L., Eisenmann, J. C., & Malina, R. M. (2017). Bio-banding in sport: Applications to competition, talent identification, and strength and conditioning of youth athletes. *Strength & Conditioning Journal*, *39*, 34–47. https://doi.org/10.1519/SSC.0000000000000281

Darrall-Jones, J. D., Jones, B., & Till, K. (2015). Anthropometric and physical profiles of English academy rugby union players. *The Journal of Strength & Conditioning Research*, *29*, 2086–2096. https://doi.org/10.1519/JSC.0000000000000872

Delahunt, E., Byrne, R. B., Doolin, R. K., McInerney, R. G., Ruddock, C. T., & Green, B. S. (2013). Anthropometric profile and body composition of Irish adolescent rugby union players aged 16–18. *The Journal of Strength & Conditioning Research*, *27*, 3252–3258. https://doi.org/10.1519/JSC.0b013e3182915ea6

Eisenmann, J. C., Till, K., & Baker, J. (2020). Growth, maturation and youth sports: Issues and practical solutions. *Annals of Human Biology*, *47*, 324–327. https://doi.org/10.1080/03014460.2020.1764099

Epstein, L. H., Valoski, A. M., Kalarchian, M. A., & McCurley, J. (1995). Do children lose and maintain weight easier than adults: A comparison of child and parent weight changes from six months to ten years. *Obesity Research*, *3*, 411–417. https://doi.org/10.1002/j.1550-8528.1995.tb00170.x

Fontana, F. Y., Colosio, A. L., Da Lozzo, G., & Pogliaghi, S. (2017). Player's success prediction in rugby union: From youth performance to senior level placing. *Journal of Science and Medicine in Sport*, *20*, 409–414. https://doi.org/10.1016/j.jsams.2016.08.017

Fransen, J., Bush, S., Woodcock, S., Novak, A., Deprez, D., Baxter-Jones, A. D., Vaeyens, R., & Lenoir, M. (2018). Improving the prediction of maturity from anthropometric variables using a maturity ratio. *Pediatric Exercise Science*, *30*, 296–307. https://doi.org/https://doi.org/10.1123/pes.2017-0009

Fransen, J., Skorski, S., & Baxter-Jones, A. D. (2021) Estimating is not measuring: the use of non-invasive estimations of somatic maturity in youth football. *Science and Medicine in Football*, *5*, 261–262. https://doi.org/10.1080/24733938.2021.1975808

Gabbett, T. J. (2009). Physiological and anthropometric correlates of tackling ability in rugby league players. *The Journal of Strength & Conditioning Research*, *23*, 540–548. https://doi.org/10.1519/JSC.0b013e31818efe8b

Gavarry, O., Lentin, G., Pezery, P., Delextrat, A., Chaumet, G., Boussuges, A., & Piscione, J. (2018). A cross-sectional study assessing the contributions of body fat mass and fat-free mass to body mass index scores in male youth rugby players. *Sports Medicine-Open*, *4*, 1–9. https://doi.org/10.1186/s40798-018-0130-7

Gerrard, D. (1993). Overuse injury and growing bones: The young athlete at risk. *British Journal of Sports Medicine*, *27*, 14–18. https://dx.doi.org/10.1136/bjsm.27.1.14

Gould, P. (2011). *Crunch time for juniors weighty issue*. Sydney morning Herald. Retrieved 27th July from https://www.smh.com.au/sport/nrl/crunch-time-for-juniors-weighty-issue-20110319-1c1ba.html

Hendricks, S., Karpul, D., & Lambert, M. (2014). Momentum and kinetic energy before the tackle in rugby union. *Journal of Sports Science & Medicine*, *13*, 557.

Hendricks, S., Till, K., Weaving, D., Powell, A., Kemp, S., Stokes, K., & Jones, B. (2019). Training, match and non-rugby activities in elite male youth rugby union players in England. *International Journal of Sports Science & Coaching*, *14*, 336–343. https://doi.org/10.1177/1747954119829289

Howard, S. M., Cumming, S. P., Atkinson, M., & Malina, R. M. (2016). Biological maturity-associated variance in peak power output and momentum in academy rugby union players. *European Journal of Sport Science, 16*, 972–980. https://doi.org/10.1080/17461391.2016.1205144

Khamis, H. J., & Roche, A. F. (1994, Oct). Predicting adult stature without using skeletal age: The Khamis-Roche method. *Pediatrics, 94*, 504–507. https://doi.org/10.1542/peds.94.4.504

Krause, L. M., Naughton, G. A., Denny, G., Patton, D., Hartwig, T., & Gabbett, T. J. (2015). Understanding mismatches in body size, speed and power among adolescent rugby union players. *Journal of Science and Medicine in Sport, 18*, 358–363. https://doi.org/10.1016/j.jsams.2014.05.012

Lentin, G., Cumming, S., Piscione, J., Pezery, P., Bouchouicha, M., Gadea, J., Raymond, J.-J., Duché, P., & Gavarry, O. (2021). A comparison of an alternative weight-grading model against chronological age group model for the grouping of schoolboy male rugby players. *Frontiers in Physiology, 12*, 670720. https://doi.org/10.3389/fphys.2021.670720

Lewis, T. (2014). *Is rugby now too dangerous for children*. The Observer. Retrieved 27th July from https://www.theguardian.com/sport/2014/sep/28/is-rugby-now-too-dangerous-for-children-to-play

Lloyd, R. S., Oliver, J. L., Faigenbaum, A. D., Myer, G. D., & Croix, M. B. D. S. (2014). Chronological age vs. biological maturation: Implications for exercise programming in youth. *The Journal of Strength & Conditioning Research, 28*, 1454–1464. https://doi.org/10.1519/JSC.0000000000000391

Malina, R. M., Bouchard, C., & Bar-Or, O. (2004). *Growth, maturation, and physical activity*. Human Kinetics. https://doi.org/10.5040/9781492596837

Malina, R. M., Coelho E Silva, M. J., Figueiredo, A. J., Carling, C., & Beunen, G. P. (2012). Interrelationships among invasive and non-invasive indicators of biological maturation in adolescent male soccer players. *Journal of Sports Sciences, 30*, 1705–1717. https://doi.org/10.1080/02640414.2011.639382

Malina, R. M., Dompier, T. P., Powell, J. W., Barron, M. J., & Moore, M. T. (2007). Validation of a noninvasive maturity estimate relative to skeletal age in youth football players. *Clinical Journal of Sport Medicine, 17*, 362–368. https://doi.org/10.1097/jsm.0b013e31815400f4

Malina, R. M., & Kozieł, S. M. (2014). Validation of maturity offset in a longitudinal sample of Polish boys. *Journal of Sports Sciences, 32*, 424–437. https://doi.org/10.1080/02640414.2013.828850

Malina, R. M., Rogol, A. D., Cumming, S. P., e Silva, M. J. C., & Figueiredo, A. J. (2015). Biological maturation of youth athletes: Assessment and implications. *British Journal of Sports Medicine, 49*, 852–859. https://doi.org/10.1136/bjsports-2015-094623

Mirwald, R. L., Baxter-Jones, A. D., Bailey, D. A., & Beunen, G. P. (2002). An assessment of maturity from anthropometric measurements. *Medicine & Science in Sports & Exercise, 34*, 689–694. https://doi.org/10.1097/00005768-200204000-00020

Moore, S. A., McKay, H. A., Macdonald, H., Nettlefold, L., Baxter-Jones, A. D., Cameron, N., & Brasher, P. M. (2015). Enhancing a somatic maturity prediction model. *Medicine & Science in Sports & Exercise, 47*, 1755–1764. https://doi.org/10.1249/mss.0000000000000588

Patton, D. A., McIntosh, A. S., & Denny, G. (2016). A review of the anthropometric characteristics, grading and dispensation of junior and youth rugby union players in Australia. *Sports Medicine, 46*, 1067–1081. https://doi.org/10.1007/s40279-016-0481-5

Pienaar, A. E., Spamer, M. J., & Steyn Jr, H. S. (1998). Identifying and developing rugby talent among 10-year-old boys: A practical model. *Journal of Sports Sciences, 16*, 691–699. https://doi.org/10.1080/026404198366326

Quarrie, K. L., & Wilson, B. (2000). Force production in the rugby union scrum. *Journal of Sports Sciences, 18*, 237–246. https://doi.org/10.1080/026404100364974

Radnor, J. M., Oliver, J. L., Waugh, C. M., Myer, G. D., Moore, I. S., & Lloyd, R. S. (2018). The influence of growth and maturation on stretch-shortening cycle function in youth. *Sports Medicine, 48*(1), 57–71. https://doi.org/10.1007/s40279-017-0785-0

Sampson, J. A., Fransen, J., Lovell, R., & Till, K. (2022). Body size and age grouping in youth rugby. In K. Till, J. Weakley, S. Whitehead, & B. Jones (Eds.), *Youth rugby*. Routledge.

Till, K., & Baker, J. (2020). Challenges and [possible] solutions to optimizing talent identification and development in sport. *Frontiers in Psychology, 11*, 664. https://doi.org/10.3389/fpsyg.2020.00664

Till, K., Barrell, D., Lawn, J., Lazenby, B., Rock, A., & Cobley, S. (2020). 'Wide and emergent - narrow and focussed': A dual-pathway approach to talent identification and development in England rugby union. In J. Baker, S. Cobley, & J. Schorer (Eds.), *Talent identification and development in sport: International perspectives* (pp. 170–183). Routledge.

Till, K., & Bell, S. (2019). A talent development programme for later maturing players in UK rugby league: Research to practice. *UK Coaching Applied Coaching Research Journal. 4*, 16–23.

Till, K., Cobley, S., Morley, D., O'hara, J., Chapman, C., & Cooke, C. (2016). The influence of age, playing position, anthropometry and fitness on career attainment outcomes in rugby league. *Journal of Sports Sciences, 34*, 1240–1245. https://doi.org/10.1080/02640414.2015.1105380

Till, K., Cobley, S., O'Hara, J., Chapman, C., & Cooke, C. (2010). Anthropometric, physiological and selection characteristics in high performance UK junior rugby league players. *Talent Development and Excellence, 2*, 193–207.

Till, K., Cobley, S., O'Hara, J., Cooke, C., & Chapman, C. (2014). Considering maturation status and relative age in the longitudinal evaluation of junior rugby league players. *Scandinavian Journal of Medicine & Science in Sports, 24*, 569–576. https://doi.org/10.1111/sms.12033

Till, K., & Jones, B. (2015). Monitoring anthropometry and fitness using maturity groups within youth rugby league. *Journal of Strength and Conditioning Research, 29*, 730–736.

Towlson, C., Salter, J., Ade, J. D., Enright, K., Harper, L. D., Page, R. M., & Malone, J. J. (2021). Maturity-associated considerations for training load, injury risk, and physical performance in youth soccer: One size does not fit all. *Journal of Sport and Health Science, 10*, 403–412. https://doi.org/10.1016/j.jshs.2020.09.003

Waldron, M., Worsfold, P., Twist, C., & Lamb, K. (2014). Changes in anthropometry and performance, and their interrelationships, across three seasons in elite youth rugby league players. *The Journal of Strength & Conditioning Research, 28*, 3128–3136. https://doi.org/10.1519/JSC.0000000000000445

5
TALENT IDENTIFICATION IN MALE YOUTH RUGBY

Adam L. Kelly, Alexander B. T. McAuley, Francesco Dimundo and Kevin Till

Introduction

The modern-day landscape of professional sport is arguably more competitive than ever. Within the rugby codes, the professionalisation of the sports has increased over the last two–three decades. This has resulted in national governing bodies and professional rugby clubs investing significant sums towards resources in order to identify and support the development of future players. Meanwhile, many young players aspire to follow in the footsteps of iconic players and achieve success in the sports. To support the goals of organisations and individual players, talent identification and development systems (generally referred to as academies) are now commonly applied. The process of identifying and selecting the appropriate players into these programmes is therefore a prominent challenge for all involved in the development of future rugby players (Dimundo et al., 2021a).

The purpose of this chapter is to provide a summary of the current research literature that examines talent identification in male youth rugby. To achieve this, and due to the dynamic nature of talent, the chapter will use the Ecological Dynamics Framework (EDF; Davids et al., 2013) considering the task, performer and environment (see the section below for further details) to summarise the literature. Based on the literature presented, the chapter will then provide a range of practical recommendations for key stakeholders (e.g., coaches, practitioners, policy makers) working within talent identification and player development in youth rugby to consider for their future practices.

What Is Talent?

Talent is a commonly used word in society often applied across multiple domains (e.g., education, arts, sport). However, the use of *talent* is often unclear and inconsistent. To support the key goal of talent identification and development, within youth sport, *talent* has been termed as 'the presence or absence of particular skills or qualities identified at earlier time points that correlate to or predict expert future performance' (Cobley et al., 2012, p. 3). Although often used interchangeably, talent identification and talent development are different concepts and both are part of the broader developmental process. *Talent identification* can be considered as the process of recognising current participants with the potential to excel in a particular sport, whereas *talent development* is the process of providing the most appropriate learning environment to realise this potential (Williams & Reilly, 2000). These definitions support the notion of understanding the relationships between current performance and future potential within sport, which is a definite challenge for all involved in rugby.

One factor to consider when identifying youth players with the potential to excel at adulthood is the multidimensional nature of *talent* (McAuley et al., 2022). Hence, it is important to adopt a suitable framework to consider this complex topic. One particularly useful framework to suit the rugby codes and the aims of this chapter is the EDF (Davids et al., 2013). The EDF states that talent should be considered as a dynamically varying relationship constrained by the task, performer and environment, which underscores how talent cannot be the result of a single independent factor (Sarmento et al., 2018; Seifert et al., 2017). The EDF was previously used by Dimundo et al. (2021a) during their systematic review on talent identification and development in rugby union, thus allows the collation of factors that influence the talent identification process in rugby, including: (a) *task* (e.g., participation history), (b) *performer* (e.g., psychological skills and characteristics, technical and tactical skills, physical characteristics) and (c) *environmental* (e.g., relative age effects (RAEs), sociocultural influences). See a summary in Figure 5.1 (Kelly et al., 2022).

Research Overview

Task Constraints

Task constraints encapsulate the specific activities athletes engage in during development, as well as the overarching structure with which their participation is governed. Two converging sport participation developmental trajectories have been proposed by the Development Model of Sport Participation (DMSP) towards achieving sporting expertise: (a) *early diversification* (typically between the ages of 6–11 years) and later specialisation, and (b) *early specialisation* (see Côté et al., 2007 for an overview). Despite the significant pitfalls (e.g., dropout, injury) widely reported with earlier age specialisation (see Bergeron et al., 2015), numerous team sports have established developmental systems that encourage this approach. Moreover, there are concerns over the prognostic accuracy of early identification with performance at adulthood (see Till & Baker, 2020 for an overview). Interestingly, however, it appears many of the talent development

Talent Identification in Male Youth Rugby 69

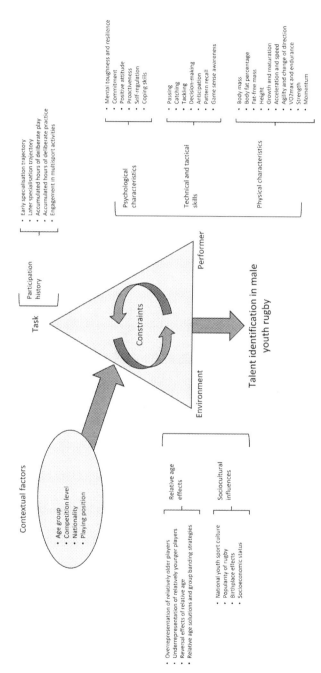

FIGURE 5.1 Ecological Dynamic Factors to Consider when Identifying Male Youth Rugby Players (adapted from Kelly et al., 2022).

pathways that exist in rugby actually encourage an early diversified approach, whereby formal selection does not often take place until approximately aged 15 years.

Participation History

Research in rugby has revealed potential shortcomings in specialising and selecting players at young ages. For instance, Pienaar and Spamer (1998) reported that during a talent identification phase in U10 rugby, physical abilities (e.g., linear speed, agility) were a discriminating factor in selection. However, the subsequent selection at U12 compared those who were (de)selected and showed that superior technical skills (e.g., passing distance, passing accuracy) differentiated selection decisions in the U10 age group. This demonstrates potential inconsistencies in early (e.g., childhood) talent identification, as the selection was initially based on physical abilities, but then oriented towards technical skills.

With regard to older age groups, Durandt et al. (2011) studied the effectiveness of talent identification procedures in U13 players and their progression towards U16 and U18 squads. They reported that 31.5% and 24.1% of the U13 players were reselected to play in the U16 and U18 squads, respectively. The low proportion of players who were reselected could suggest that early selection processes may be flawed and subject to selection biases. This may be due to the considerable maturational differences in U13 players (Kelly & Williams, 2020), alongside the introduction of more structured rules (i.e., 15-a-side) and competition (i.e., league formats) that could significantly impact talent identification between players of the same chronological age (Till et al., 2020).

More recently, a longitudinal study by Booth et al. (2020) showed that developmental U16 and U18 players with a higher participation history in rugby league had greater improvements in physical qualities (i.e., change of direction, maximal aerobic capacity and strength endurance) over two seasons. However, during a retrospective analysis of professional rugby league players, results did not show any evidence of an athlete adhering to an *early specialisation* trajectory (Cupples et al., 2018). Instead, trajectories shared behavioural patterns adhering to the DMSP's sampling pathway as players transitioned through similar stages, but at different developmental time-points. Importantly though, findings diverged from the DMSP as to when behavioural transitions were made (e.g., cessation of other sporting activity and reductions in play occurred at later ages than proposed by the DMSP model), suggesting the potential for DMSP refinement in rugby (Cupples et al., 2018). In addition, as summarised in Table 5.1, Dimundo et al. (2022) reported that academy rugby union players who were ranked as having more potential to achieve senior professional status by their coaches, engaged in more hours of game exposure at a younger age (i.e., aged 8–11 years) and accumulated more time in peer-led play during late childhood and early adolescence (i.e., aged 12–15 years), when compared to those players ranked with

TABLE 5.1 Participation History for Forwards and Backs and Top-10 Potentials and Bottom-10 Potentials in a Rugby Union Academy (adapted from Dimundo et al. 2022).

Task constraints	All forwards	All backs	Top-10 potentials	Bottom-10 potentials
Participation history	Mean±SD	Mean±SD	Mean±SD	Mean±SD
Number of sports	2.9 ±1.8	3.7±1.9	3.5±2.1	3.5±2.2
Game exposure U8-U11 (hours)	74.1±47.5	99.0±50.1	120.7±52.3	59.8±24.3
Coach-led U8-U11 (hours)	300.8±182.3	216.5±131.3	296.4±112.1	216.0±193.8
Peer-led U8-U11 (hours)	126.8±159.0	81.0±72.3	139.0±209.1	82.7±62.9
Game exposure U12-U15 (hours)	226.1±114.4	222.4±93.0	234.8±122.2	215.5±71.7
Coach-led U12-U15 (hours)	411.9±274.1	343.6±150.7	391.0±175.5	368.4±225.3
Peer-led U12-U15 (hours)	255.2±233.1	287.5±316.2	311.5±274.8	124.1±48.3

lower potential. In the same study, it was reported that all players practiced two sports or more during both childhood and early adolescence. This perhaps indicates that, in general, young rugby players are exposed to a diverse environment (perhaps due to the later-age specialised), which could positively impact holistic and rugby specific.

Moving forward, researchers are encouraged to explore the developmental trajectories (e.g., practice history profiles) and experiences (e.g., interviews) of professional and international rugby players to better understand their pathways towards achieving expertise. In turn, this may help key stakeholders employed in youth rugby settings devise an evidence-based approach as part of their talent identification strategies.

Performer Constraints

Performer constraints are structural or functional and refer to the characteristics and capabilities of individuals. These can include physical characteristics, psychological skills and characteristics and technical and tactical skills, which are summarised in detail in Chapters 8–10, respectively. A summary in relation to research studies exploring these performer constraints from a talent identification perspective is offered below.

Psychological Skills and Characteristics

Psychological skills and characteristics have been reported as important factors for achieving success in rugby and consequently talent identification. For example, Cupples and O'Connor (2011) interviews of national youth coaches suggested that cognitive indicators (i.e., communication, mental toughness, attitude, discipline, character, personality, learning ability) were deemed as crucial to reach high-performance levels. In addition, Hill et al. (2015) identified six psychological characteristics that discriminate successful and unsuccessful players (i.e., commitment, self-regulation, resilience, realistic performance evaluation, growth mind-set, being proactive). More recently, Chiwaridzo et al. (2019c) interviewed 22 coaches in Zimbabwe to explore their perceptions of the attributes that characterise good adolescent rugby players showing psychological qualities (i.e., mental strength, emotionally stable, positive attitude, courageous, determined, disciplined, teachable, passionate, communication) were important. In addition, Taylor and Collins (2019) interviewed ten academy rugby coaches in the UK to explore the reasons why high potential/apparently gifted rugby players failed to realise their potential. Lacking psychological skills (i.e., commitment, coping skills, self-regulatory capacity, motivation, excessive need for recognition and praise, narcissistic tendencies) was one key factor that emerged.

Other findings in this area show that psychological characterises can differentiate higher and lower performers (i.e., self-confidence, personal coping resources, coping with adversity, levels of hardiness; Andrew et al., 2007; Sheard & Golby, 2010) and playing positions (i.e., active coping strategies; Dimundo et al., 2022). As such, this research suggests that psychological characteristics are a key indicator of performance in rugby. However, their usefulness as part of the talent identification process requires further exploration. Moreover, further study is required to better understand the complex ecological relationship between psychological traits and other tasks, performers and environmental constraints during talent identification procedures.

Technical and Tactical Skills

Technical testing often appears as part of a battery of multidimensional assessments in rugby literature. For example, Plotz and Spamer (2006) and Spamer et al. (2009) adopted a cross-cultural comparison when examining youth rugby players. Plotz and Spamer (2006) found South African U18 players outperformed their English and New Zealand counterparts on several technique-specific tests. In contrast, Spamer et al. (2009) revealed New Zealand U16 players possessed superior ground and kicking skills compared to English and South African equivalents. Together, these findings suggest nationality is an important consideration whilst exploring technical characteristics as part of the talent identification process.

Other findings in this area also highlight how higher-performing youth players possess superior technical skills (i.e., tackling, catching, passing, ball carrying, ruck clearing and diverse evasive manoeuvres; Chiwaridzo et al., 2019a, 2019b, 2020; den Hollander et al., 2019; Pearce et al., 2019, 2020). Crucial technical skills (i.e., passing, catching, tackling, ball handling) have also been identified by coaches as important (Chiwaridzo et al., 2018). However, the discriminative ability of technical skills is often dependent on age category and playing position (Chiwaridzo et al., 2019a, 2020; Cupples & O'Connor, 2011).

Tactical understanding is also an essential skill for rugby players that have been shown in senior players (e.g., Runswick et al., 2020; Sherwood et al., 2018). Research in youth players revealed higher performing players had better attentional focus scores (Di Corrado et al., 2014). In addition, crucial tactical skills (i.e., reading the game, decision making, game-sense awareness, anticipation, visual and auditory skills) were also reported in coach perception research (Chiwaridzo et al., 2019a; Cupples & O'Connor, 2011). Cognitive skills have been shown to be important aspects in sport for both anticipation and tactical awareness (Mann et al., 2007). Although, in the context of rugby, recent findings showed that perceptual-cognitive expertise (i.e., measured via video simulation tests; see Figure 5.2 for examples) was inconsistent for discriminating U15 players selection (Dimundo et al., 2021b), academy ranking (Dimundo et al., 2022) and rugby-specific positions in U15 players (Dimundo

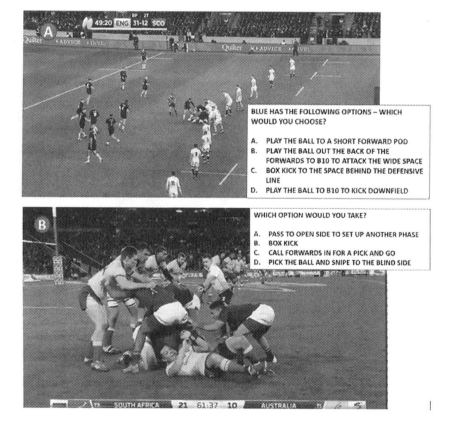

FIGURE 5.2 Examples of two different frozen Screen Clips used to Differentiate Selection, Position and Player Potential during the Perceptual Cognitive Expertise Video Simulation Test. The Clips Were Used as Examples that Represented Different Real-Life Game Situations (e.g., A, Defending; B, Attacking) in Which Time, Scores and Position on the Pitch Was Provided to Contextualise Each Option.

et al., 2021b, 2022). However, research on tactical skills in youth rugby remains limited despite most probably being a key aspect of a coach's practice within talent identification.

Physical Characteristics

Physical characteristics are very much central to the talent identification research in youth rugby, and in comparison to the other performer constraints, they have been more extensively studied. Indeed, there is a plethora of empirical studies which have reported on the influence of these factors in both rugby union and rugby league using multiple research designs (cross-sectional, longitudinal, retrospective), which has ultimately led to numerous review papers (e.g., Owen et al., 2020; Till et al., 2017).

Empirical studies of particular interest are those which have examined the predictive value of physical qualities possessed at younger ages on selection into talent development programmes and future career attainment (Till et al., 2011, 2016; Tredrea et al., 2017). Regarding selection, Dimundo et al. (2021b) found that selected U15 players possessed superior body mass, handgrip strength, and speed compared to their non-selected counterparts, with only the 20 m sprint being a key discriminating factor for selection. Regarding career attainment, Till et al. (2016) identified overall significant effects for anthropometric and fitness characteristics in U14 and U15 players, but not in U13s. Specifically, professional players at U14 and U15 significantly outperformed amateur players on sum of four skinfolds, speed, change of direction speed, and estimated $\dot{V}O_2$max. This research demonstrates that the development of physical qualities in youth rugby players contributes to selection and career attainment at adulthood.

Growth and maturation can also play an important role in the talent identification process in youth rugby (see Chapters 2 and 4). Advanced maturation can have a significant effect on the physical qualities and subsequent opportunities to be identified. Since rugby is deemed a physical, invasive sport, those who mature earlier are at an advantage when athletes are grouped by age since their anthropometric and physical qualities will be at an advanced stage. Recent findings from an English Premiership academy cohort demonstrated physical characteristics differentiated age-grade and rugby-specific positions (Dimundo et al., 2021c). In the same study, it was suggested that the successful progression of players through a professional academy should be based on the development of greater parameters of body mass, power, sprint momentum and aerobic capacity. However, further research is required to better understand the role of maturity status on selection into talent pathways in rugby. It is also important to consider the evolution of rugby and the subsequent physical requirements. For example, French youth rugby players have become progressively taller and heavier (e.g., selected players have increased by 6 cm in height and 12.3 kg in body mass from 1988 to 2008; Sedeaud et al., 2013). Thus, growth, maturation and the evolution of rugby over time are important elements to consider during the talent identification process in rugby.

Environmental Constraints

Environmental constraints are external to individuals and represent influences they often have little control over, such as when and where they are born, as well as accessibility and economic barriers. These include factors such as relative age and sociocultural influences, which can have important implications on talent identification. A research overview focussed on the context of rugby is offered below.

Relative Age Effects

Players in youth sport competitions are regularly grouped into (bi)annual-age groups. RAEs refer to the overrepresentation of those born earlier in the selection year (e.g., September-November; birth quarter one [BQ1] in England) and the underrepresentation of those born later (e.g., June-August; BQ4 in England). Pronounced RAEs have been reported by several studies throughout the literature in both rugby codes (e.g., Cobley & Till, 2017; Kelly et al., 2021c; Till et al., 2010). Indeed, a recent overview of RAEs reported that players born in BQ1 (ranging from 29 to 60%) are 1.4 to 6.2 times more likely to be selected into competitive youth rugby union teams compared to those born in BQ4 (ranging from 8 to 24%) (Kelly et al., 2021a). As an example, in an English Premiership academy (Dimundo et al. 2021c), early born U16 and U18 players were overrepresented (U16: BQ1 = 50% vs. BQ4 = 7.1%; U18: BQ1 = 40.4% vs. BQ4 = 7.1%) compared to their later-born peers, with 71.1% of backs born in the first half of the year (BQ1 and BQ2). This led to the understanding that the collision and invasive nature of rugby may exacerbate the physical advantages of relatively older youth players (Baker et al., 2009). Furthermore, enhanced psychosocial development and an older training age may explain why younger players are outperformed by their chronologically older counterparts in sports such as rugby (e.g., Doncaster et al., 2020).

The broader development outcomes due to RAEs in rugby have been extensively explored throughout the literature. For instance, McCarthy and Collins (2014) and McCarthy et al. (2016) identified *reversal effects* of relative age (i.e., how a greater number of relatively younger rugby players [e.g., BQ1 = 20% vs. BQ4 = 50%] successfully transitioned to the professional level). These differences may suggest that competitive play against relatively older players benefits relatively young players during their long-term development (Collins & MacNamara, 2012; Kelly et al., 2020b). Indeed, it is suggested that relatively younger players may experience greater 'growth', as they are at an initial disadvantage during their development due to these additional challenges (McCarthy et al., 2016). Similarly, Kelly et al. (2021d) explored RAEs during entry into professional and international rugby union pathways in England, as well as comparing them to their respective senior cohort (i.e., U15 Regional Academy Player vs. Senior Professional Player; U16–U23 England Academy Player vs. Senior International Player). Their findings revealed a significant overrepresentation of relatively older players compared with their relatively younger peers within both youth cohorts (BQ1 = 43% vs. BQ4 = 10%: BQ1 = 37% vs. BQ4 = 15%: see Figure 5.3). In comparison, there was no significant difference in the BQ distributions within both senior cohorts. Further, BQ4s were 3.9 times more likely to achieve senior professional and international levels than BQ1s and BQ2s once selected into the talent pathways, respectively. As such, relatively younger players may have a greater likelihood of achieving expertise following entry into a rugby talent pathway due to benefitting from more competitive play against relatively older counterparts during their development (e.g., the *underdog hypothesis*; Gibbs et al., 2012). However, further research is required to substantiate these claims.

Despite RAEs being extensively studied in rugby, potential solutions have not yet been widely explored within this context (see Webdale et al., 2020 for a review). Although, possible relative age solutions in rugby have been recently discussed by Kelly et al. (2021d), in which they take inspiration from research in comparable sports such as *age and anthropometric* bandings (e.g., Jones et al., 2019), a *flexible chronological approach* (e.g., Kelly et al., 2021e) and *birthday-banding* (Kelly et al., 2020a). Despite these suggestions, further research is required to design, implement and evaluate a range of potential relative age solutions in youth rugby.

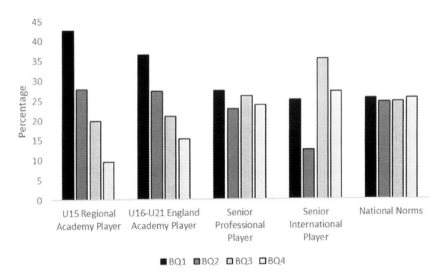

FIGURE 5.3 The Birth Quartile (BQ) Distribution Percentages of the English Professional Pathway, Senior Professional and Senior International Players (adapted from Kelly et al., 2021d).

Sociocultural Influences

Inter- and intra-sociocultural factors can influence talent identification opportunities in rugby. For instance, individuals from countries with high participation rates in rugby (e.g., New Zealand) are more likely to engage in rugby activities. Whereas individuals from low participating (e.g., Germany) or emerging (e.g., Canada) rugby nations are not going to experience the same prospects due to inter-cultural differences (Asselstine & Edwards, 2019). As such, this will affect the long-term development of youth players, alongside having an impact on proceeding senior performance levels.

With regard to intra-sociocultural factors, birthplace effects have been shown to play an important role. For instance, in the Australian rugby league, there was a significant under-representation of players that initiated their participation in cities (i.e., >1,000,000 residents), along with a contrasting over-representation of players that initiated their participation in small communities (i.e., <20,000 residents; Cobley et al., 2014). Interestingly, there was also an interaction between birthplace and relative age, as the odds of being a relatively older professional player were reduced when their first club was in a small community. This may suggest that over time clubs in smaller communities facilitate more advantageous micro-system processes to alleviate or attenuate relative age inequalities.

It has also been reported that a greater access to talent development pathways and professional sport are experienced by white and privately educated athletes (Lawrence, 2017). From a socioeconomic viewpoint (using a player's home postcode as a proxy to measure their potential levels of deprivation), it has been shown that players from more deprived groups participate in fewer sports and accumulate less hours of structured rugby practice when compared to those from less deprived groups (Winn et al., 2016). Moreover, Dimundo et al. (2022) revealed that: (a) back players were generally more deprived than forwards, (b) top-10 potentials were more deprived compared to bottom-10 potentials, (c) none were considered 'critically deprived' and (d) players with a lower socioeconomic status were physically smaller and lighter than those players from a higher status. This potentially indicates that levels of deprivation could help in forming rugby-specific attributes (e.g., anthropometric, physical, psychological, social identity, perceptual-cognitive expertise) based on playing positions (Dimundo et al., 2022). Overall, sociocultural influences can have significant implications on individual talent identification opportunities and should be considered during recruitment processes. This may be explained by several factors, such as limited access to coaching, resources and facilities, as well as disparities in parental support and financial expenditure (Côté et al., 2014).

Practical Applications

Based on the research overview presented above, it is evident that the talent identification process in rugby is impacted by a variety of task, performer and environmental constraints. As such, it is important that stakeholders (e.g., administrators, coaches, sport scientists) and organisations (e.g., clubs, national governing bodies) employed in rugby settings consider the following practical recommendations of how and where they can apply this knowledge into practice.

Task Constraints

Participation History

It appears many talent pathways in rugby are already facilitating a later age-specialisation approach, whereby formal selection does not usually take place until approximately aged 15 years (Till et al., 2020). Indeed, this approach seems logical since it appears to be a challenge to predict future performance capabilities at younger ages (e.g., pre-adolescence), eliminates possible drawbacks (e.g., dropout, injury) and negates potential selection biases (e.g., maturity status, RAEs) that coincide with earlier identification (Till & Baker, 2020). However, it is also important for practitioners to consider the possible benefits of earlier engagement in rugby in order to develop the physical and technical skillset required to achieve expertise. Thus, a fine balance remains between offering rugby participation for all, providing additional rugby-specific developmental opportunities for those who may require it and recognising the appropriate age to initiate formal selection processes in rugby talent pathways.

Based on the *participation history* research presented throughout this chapter, practitioners should consider the following suggestions in their applied settings:

- Support long-term developmental outcomes for *all* players based on an age-specific perspective.
- The long-term outcomes associated with early specialisation in rugby (e.g., attainment of expertise, continued participation, personal development) are poorly understood. Thus, during the selection process, inter-individual variation should be considered and formal recruitment at early ages should be discouraged.
- Later age talent identification and evaluation procedures may facilitate greater efficacy and validity within developmental systems. Thus, try and delay talent identification and hence specialisation until after maturity.

Performer Constraints

Psychological Skills and Characteristics

The specific psychological trait that has been most evidenced as an important factor for achieving expertise in rugby is *mental toughness* (i.e., hardiness, mental strength, resilience). As such, it may prove beneficial for practitioners to profile young rugby players to identify such characteristics when recruiting them into talent development systems. Additional understanding on position-specific attributes is also necessary to fully optimise individualised psychological skills and characteristics as part of the talent identification process in rugby.

Based on the *psychological skills and characteristics* research presented throughout this chapter, practitioners should consider the following suggestions in their applied settings:

- The majority of sport psychology literature in rugby has gathered the perspectives and experiences of coaches and players. Stakeholders should draw from these understandings when identifying and selecting players, through gauging psychological skills and characteristics such as mental toughness, attitude, discipline and confidence.
- Incorporating psychological profiling or assessments into talent identification strategies could help gain a better understanding of an individual's psychological skills and characteristics. This may also help facilitate markers of long-term potential over performance-related outcomes.
- Sport psychologists appear to be underrepresented amongst support staff in rugby, particularly in comparison to strength and conditioning coaches. Stakeholders are encouraged to better understand the role of a sport psychologist and how they could facilitate talent identification procedures in their youth rugby settings.

Technical and Tactical Skills

Technical attributes, based on age, competition level, nationality and playing position, are important considerations when identifying talent and selecting young players into talent pathways. However, due to the limited cross-sectional designs, it is unclear whether higher-performing players have superior tactical skills with less experience at younger ages or develop this progressively with accumulated domain and task-specific practice. Nevertheless, the development of these cognitive skills will inevitably be dependent of the opportunities to participate and develop in rugby settings (i.e., task constraints). Moving forward, practitioners in youth rugby are encouraged to explore a combination of technical skills (e.g., passing, catching, tackling, ball handling, kicking) based on tactical situations (e.g., structured vs. unstructured), position-specific considerations (i.e., forwards vs. backs), participation experiences (i.e., early vs. later specialisation) and playing levels (e.g., selected vs. deselected) to offer a more accurate and ecological profile that is applicable to practical talent identification environments. Moreover, researchers are encouraged to synthesise the existing literature to enable practitioners working in youth rugby to apply key indicators/benchmarks of potential talent that are fundamental to their respective cohort and environment.

Based on the *technical and tactical skills* research presented throughout this chapter, practitioners should consider the following suggestions in their applied settings:

- The majority of technical and tactical observations are based on the coach's subjective opinion. Thus, stakeholders are encouraged to consider how they could better incorporate such measures into their talent identification processes to help inform their decision-making.

- Objective measures that may facilitate talent identification procedures include match analysis data, skills testing, video-based simulations and game-based situation tests. This will help complement subjective opinions and negate the individual weaknesses of each approach used in isolation.
- Consider adopting a range of conditioned or small-sided games as part of talent identification procedures in order to capture more technical and tactical actions.

Physical Characteristics

It is clear that physical characteristics significantly contribute to player performance and career prospects within rugby. However, age, maturity and playing position are important variables to consider when assessing player ability. Future research is needed to expand on age group and position-specific characteristics of those selected into talent pathways to help practitioners better understand how these mechanisms can inform the selection processes. Moreover, the position-specific predictive value of physical traits possessed at younger ages on future career attainment may be of interest to practitioners. Although, it is critical that the evolution of sport is always considered, as predictive characteristics in the past may not be as important in the present, or indeed the future. Therefore, practitioners should consider maturational variability within their talent identification decisions and consider alternative grouping strategies (e.g., *bio-banding*, which groups young players based on anthropometric and maturational status; Malina et al., 2019). However, it is important to consider how this may look in the context of youth rugby. Indeed, current studies have primarily focussed their attention on across other sports, thus it is difficult to fully interpret how it will be conveyed within a rugby setting that is comprised of a diverse talent development system. Moving forward, an introduction to grouping players by height, weight and/or some maturational variables may prove beneficial in moderating maturity-related biases in youth rugby.

Based on the *physical characteristics* research presented throughout this chapter, practitioners should consider the following suggestions in their applied settings:

- Gather growth and maturity data as part of a holistic talent identification process. This will help ensure selectors are aware of each individual's maturity status and how they compare amongst their age-matched peers. Do not mistake an advanced maturity status for talent or long-term potential.
- It's important to consider physical characteristics based on the maturity status (i.e., biological age) of an individual rather than their chronological age. Since rugby is a physical sport, those who mature earlier will likely have advanced physical characteristics and thus outperform their less-mature peers during competition.
- Consider alternative grouping strategies during trials (e.g., bio-banding), training or competition rather than chronological age grouping to offer a different perspective of players.

Environmental Constraints

Relative Age Effects

First, it is important for practitioners to recognise that RAEs currently exist as a result of the (bi) annual age groups structures that are adopted to organised youth rugby. Indeed, RAEs are creating an inequitable youth rugby system that may not truly represent the long-term potential of players, and as a consequence, could result in inaccurate decisions during talent identification procedures. Practitioners are encouraged to work collaboratively with researchers to move beyond typical research examining RAEs in rugby, and instead focus their attention on designing, implementing and evaluating strategies with the purpose of moderating RAEs. In-turn, this may widen the pool of potential talent for practitioners when recruiting young players that may be missed due to such selection biases. For instance, the explicit cuing of RAEs during selection processes (e.g., trials) may prove useful for practitioners to better understand the relative age of individuals (Mann & van Ginneken, 2017), which could help create a more accurate perception of a player based on their own birth date rather than comparing them within their respective age group.

Based on the *relative age effects* research presented throughout this chapter, practitioners should consider the following suggestions in their applied settings:

- Ensure stakeholders are aware of each individuals birthdate and how that could influence their performances and their subsequent perceptions. For instance, age-ordered shirt numbering systems or supplying selectors with clear information and education may help achieve this.
- Consider grouping athletes differently during trials to ensure you gain a more holistic understanding of each player (see Chapter 4).
- Use markers of long-term potential (e.g., psychological skills and characteristics, biological age) over performance-related outcomes (e.g., winning, points scored). Remember, those who are relatively older will likely outperform their relatively younger but age-matched peers, although this may not necessarily translate into positive long-term developmental outcomes.

Sociocultural Influences

Practitioners employed in youth rugby settings should reflect upon national youth sport culture, birthplace effects, ethnicity and socioeconomic factors when designing, implementing and evaluating talent identification procedures. In addition, researchers are encouraged to further explore these sociocultural implications in youth rugby to better understand the possible outcomes related to talent identification procedures. In doing so, it is hoped this will facilitate more equal opportunities to a wider pool of potential young talent for practitioners in the short-term, as well as subsequently enhancing the standard of senior rugby competition in the long-term.

Based on the *sociocultural influences* research presented throughout this chapter, practitioners should consider the following suggestions in their applied settings:

- Since nations are not going to experience the same prospective talent due to inter-cultural differences, it is important to consider the popularity of rugby and national culture when designing talent identification programmes.
- Provide talent identification opportunities for more players in more diverse environments. In particular, clubs based in larger cities and/or communities should reflect how they can create more advantageous micro-systems within their organisational structures.
- Consider how levels of deprivation can impact upon task (e.g., access to organised sport and rugby) and performer (e.g., development of psychological skills and characteristics) constraints. Thus, socioeconomic status should be used during talent identification processes, through proxies such the index of multiple deprivation (i.e., via home postcode) and school type attended (i.e., private or state), to help better understand individual circumstances.

A Multidisciplinary Approach

A less used but highly effective approach when investigating and identifying talented rugby players is adopting a mixed methods (i.e., both quantitative and qualitative) approach (McCormack et al., 2021). Such an approach enables both objective (e.g., results from physical tests) and subjective (e.g., perceptions of coaches) data to help inform more accurate talent decisions (Sieghartsleitner et al., 2019). This mixed-methods approach reflects the multifaceted nature of talent and represents a key aspect in a professional rugby academy since it can merge data from areas belonging to task, performer and environmental constraints. In fact, a recent qualitative study from an English Premiership rugby union academy interviewed coaches and players to gain a better understanding of their perceptions of the talent identification and development processes (Dimundo et al., under review). It was reported that the identification and progression of players were based on a combination of factors appertaining to a broader EDF (see Figure 5.4). Despite several authors attempted to provide practical guidelines for talent identification using a qualitative approach (e.g., Chiwaridzo, et al. 2019c; Roberts & Fairclough, 2012), limitations concerning the method adopted (i.e., focus groups) have restricted the field of exploration to the area concerning the performer and contextual constraints. Therefore, more appropriate qualitative strategies of investigation (e.g., journals, interviews, timelines) along with quantitative data originated from tests and questionnaires can present a useful approach towards achieving a multidisciplinary approach to talent identification in youth rugby.

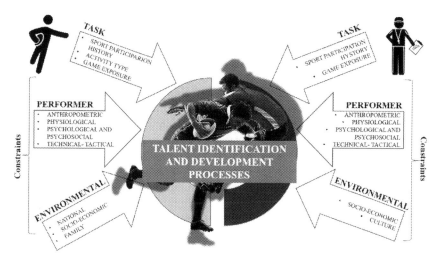

FIGURE 5.4 Players (Left) and Coaches' (Right) Perceptions of the Talent Identification and Development Processes in English Rugby Union.

Various tools have been designed by researchers in an attempt to support practitioners with their decision-making during talent identification. Player profiling is a popular method that has been advocated as it offers a user-friendly framework relevant to the applied environment (Baker et al., 2018), which moves beyond prescriptive models that can be challenging to implement into practical settings (MacNamara & Collins, 2014). Butler and Hardy's (1992) early theory and application of performance profiling in sport highlight its flexible approach together with the support for practitioners to understand rugby players across several aspects. As an example, Kelly et al. (2018) created the *Locking Wheel Nut Model* using discipline-specific characteristics that have been identified as influential factors during the talent identification process (see Figure 5.5). This model has been designed using the methodology and visual design of the locking wheel nut, through recognising the concept of an individualised approach while observing various performer constraints based on the task and environmental constraints. Similarly to the locking wheel nut, it is important to understand how the player fits within the model, through identifying and categorising individual markers of potential through player profiling. Conversely, without all the relevant information, the coach may not have the precise 'key' to support optimum talent identification from a fully integrated, multidisciplinary perspective. Indeed, this also helps understand that talent is not a 'one-size-fits-all' approach and that the locking wheel nut can vary from player to player based on their personal attributes and markers of potential.

Whilst observing the Locking Wheel Nut Model, the environmental and task constraints surround the psychological, sociological, physiological, technical and tactical disciplines (i.e., performer constraints), because of the interchangeable outcomes that are created from particular settings and activities. Practitioners can

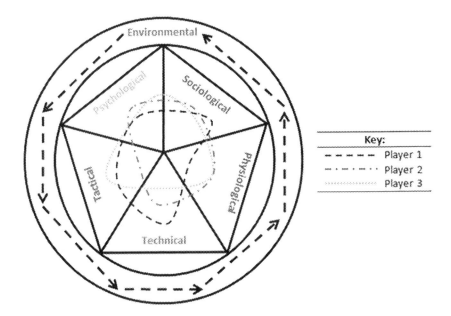

FIGURE 5.5 The Locking Wheel Nut Model – Hypothetical Patterns from Three Different Players (adapted from Kelly et al., 2018).

observe an individual's potential within each discipline on a Likert scale (e.g., one = poor; ten = excellent) that can be supported using both subjective and objective measures. Once these characteristics have been identified, they can get drawn together to identify the player's 'locking wheel nut' profile. Such profiling can be determined based on the performance model of the environment.

Key Take Home Messages

- Talent is a combination of current performance and future potential, and practitioners must establish the factors for these in making their talent identification decisions.
- The EDF provides a useful framework to consider talent identification in youth rugby. It highlights how male youth rugby cannot be based upon any individual performance characteristic in isolation, and that the interaction amongst all constraints should be considered when identifying youth talent.
- Specifically, these constraints include: (a) *task* (e.g., participation history), (b) *performer* (e.g., psychological skills characteristics, technical and tactical skills and physical factors) and (c) *environmental* (e.g., RAEs and sociocultural influences).
- From a task perspective, practitioners should consider participation history and activity types in rugby, as well as employ talent identification processes at a later age.

- From a performer perspective, practitioners should consider adopting a multidimensional approach considering psychological skills characteristics, technical and tactical skills and physical factors whilst accounting for age and maturity.
- From an environmental perspective, practitioners should consider the sociocultural environment and provide opportunities to maximise participation within rugby to increase the talent pool.
- It is recommended that because talent is a complex and misunderstood phenomenon, we should stop thinking about talent per se (especially at younger ages). It may be more effective, and ethical, to apply appropriate and research-informed practices to everyone (or as many as possible) for as long as possible, which may result in greater utilisation of resources and a more efficacious system.

References

Andrew, M., Grobbelaar, H. W., & Potgieter, J. C. (2007). Sport psychological skill levels and related psycho-social factors that distinguish between rugby union players of different participation levels. *South African Journal for Research in Sport, Physical Education and Recreation, 29*, 1–14. https://doi.org/10.10520/EJC108850

Asselstine, S., & Edwards, J. R. (2019). Managing the resource capabilities of provincial rugby unions in Canada: An understanding of competitive advantage within a sport development system. *Managing Sport and Leisure, 24*, 78–96. https://doi.org/10.1080/23750472.2019.1583078

Baker, J., Schorer, J., Cobley, S., Bräutigam, H., & Büsch, D. (2009). Gender, depth of competition and relative age effects in team sports. *Asian Journal of Exercise & Sports Science, 6*, 7–13.

Baker, J., Schorer, J., & Wattie, N. (2018). Compromising talent: Issues in identifying and selecting talent in sport. *Quest, 70*, 48–63. https://doi.org/10.1080/00336297.2017.1333438

Bergeron, M. F., Mountjoy, M., Armstrong, N., Chia, M., Côté, J., Emery, C. A., Faigenbaum, A., Hall, J. G., Kriemler, S., Léglise, M, Malina, R. M., Pensgaard, A. M., Sanchez, A., Soligard, T., Sundgot-Borgen, J., van Mechelen, W., Weissensteiner, J. R., & Engebretsen, L. (2015). International Olympic Committee consensus statement on youth athletic development. *British Journal of Sports Medicine, 49*, 843–851. http://doi.org/10.1136/bjsports-2015-094962

Booth, M., Cobley, S., Halaki, M., & Orr, R. (2020). Is training age predictive of physiological performance changes in developmental rugby league players? A prospective longitudinal study. *International Journal of Sports Science & Coaching, 15*, 306–315. https://doi.org/10.1177/1747954120919909

Butler, R., J., & Hardy, L. (1992). The performance profile: Theory and application. *The Sport Psychologist, 6*, 253–264. https://doi.org/10.1123/tsp.6.3.253

Chiwaridzo, M., Chandahwa, D., Oorschot, S., Tadyanemhandu, C., Dambi, J. M., Ferguson, G., & Smits-Engelsman, B. C. (2018). Logical validation and evaluation of practical feasibility for the SCRuM (School Clinical Rugby Measure) test battery developed for young adolescent rugby players in a resource-constrained environment. *Plos One, 13*, e0207307. https://doi.org/10.1371/journal.pone.0207307

Chiwaridzo, M., Ferguson, G. D., & Smits-Engelsman, B. C. M. (2019a). Anthropometric, physiological characteristics and rugby-specific game skills discriminating

Zimbabwean under-16 male adolescent rugby players by level of competition. *BMJ Open Sport & Exercise Medicine*, *5*, e000576. https://doi.org/10.1136/bmjsem-2019-000576

Chiwaridzo, M., Ferguson, G. D., & Smits-Engelsman, B. C. M. (2019b). Qualities or skills discriminating under 19 rugby players by playing standards: A comparative analysis of elite, sub-elite and non-rugby players using the SCRuM test battery. *BMC Research Notes*, *12*, 536. https://doi.org/10.1186/s13104-019-4563-y

Chiwaridzo, M., Ferguson, G. D., & Smits-Engelsman, B. C. M. (2020). Anthropometric, physiological characteristics and rugby-specific game skills of schoolboy players of different age categories and playing standards. *BMC Sports Science, Medicine and Rehabilitation*, *12*, 3. https://doi.org/10.1186/s13102-019-0155-3

Chiwaridzo, M., Munambah, N., Oorschot, S., Magume, D., Dambi, J. M., Ferguson, G., & Smits-Engelsman, B. C. M. (2019c). Coaches' perceptions on qualities defining good adolescent rugby players and are important for player recruitment in talent identification programs: The SCRuM project. *BMC Research Notes*, *12*, 132. https://doi.org/10.1186/s13104-019-4170-y

Cobley, S., Hanratty, M., O'Connor, D., & Cotton, W. (2014). First club location and relative age as influences on being a professional Australian rugby league player. *International Journal of Sports Science & Coaching*, *9*, 335–346. https://doi.org/10.1260/1747-9541.9.2.335

Cobley S., Schorer J., & Baker J. (eds.) (2012). Identification and development of sport talent: A brief introduction to a growing field of research and practice. In *Talent identification and development in sport: International perspectives* (pp. 1–10). London: Routledge.

Cobley, S. P., & Till, K. (2017). Participation trends according to relative age across youth UK rugby league. *International Journal of Sports Science & Coaching*, *12*, 339–343. https://doi.org/10.1177/1747954117710506

Collins, D., & MacNamara, Á. (2012). The rocky road to the top. *Sports Medicine*, *42*, 907–914. https://doi.org/10.2165/11635140-000000000-00000

Côté, J., Baker, J. & Abernethy, B. (2007). Practice and play in the development of sport expertise. In R. Eklund & G. Tenenbaum (Eds.), *Handbook of Sport Psychology* (pp.184–202). (3rd Ed.): Hoboken, NJ: Wiley. https://doi.org/10.1002/9781118270011.ch8

Côté, J., Turnnidge, J., & Evans, M. B. (2014). The dynamic process of development through sport. *Kinesiologica Slovenica*, *20*, 14–26.

Cupples, B., & O'Connor, D. (2011). The development of position-specific performance indicators in elite youth rugby league: A coach's perspective. *International Journal of Sports Science & Coaching*, *6*, 125–141. https://doi.org/10.1260/1747-9541.6.1.125

Cupples, B., O'Connor, D., & Cobley, S. (2018). Distinct trajectories of athlete development: A retrospective analysis of professional rugby league players. *Journal of Sports Sciences*, *36*, 2558–2566. https://doi.org/10.1080/02640414.2018.1469227

Davids, K., Araújo, D., Vilar, L., Renshaw, I., & Pinder, R. (2013). An ecological dynamics approach to skill acquisition: Implications for development of talent in sport. *Talent Development and Excellence*, *5*, 21–34.

den Hollander, S., Lambert, M., Jones, B., & Hendricks, S. (2019). Tackle and ruck technique proficiency within academy and senior club rugby union. *Journal of Sports Sciences*, *37*, 2578–2587. https://doi.org/10.1080/02640414.2019.1648121

Di Corrado, D., Murgia, M., & Freda, A. (2014). Attentional focus and mental skills in senior and junior professional rugby union players. *Sport Sciences for Health*, *10*, 79–83. https://doi.org/10.1007/s11332-014-0177-x

Dimundo, F., Cole, M., Blagrove, R., McAuley, A. B. T., Till, K., & Kelly, A. L. (2021b). Talent identification in an English Premiership rugby union academy:

Multidisciplinary characteristics of selected and non-selected male under-15 players. *Frontiers in Sports and Active Living*, 3, 1–10. https://doi.org/10.3389/fspor.2021.688143

Dimundo, F., Cole, M., Blagrove, R., McAuley, A. B. T., Till, K., & Kelly, A. L. (2021b). Talent identification in an English Premiership rugby union academy: Multidisciplinary characteristics of selected and non-selected male under-15 players. *Frontiers in Sports and Active Living*, 3, 1–10. https://doi.org/10.3389/fspor.2021.688143

Dimundo, F., Cole, M., Blagrove, R. C., McAuley, A. B., Till, K., Hall, M., Pacini, D., & Kelly, A. L. (2021c). The anthropometric, physical, and relative age characteristics of an English Premiership rugby union academy. *International Journal of Strength and Conditioning*, 1. https://doi.org/10.47206/ijsc.v1i1.67

Dimundo, F., Cole, M., Blagrove, R. C., Till, K., & Kelly, A. L. (2022). A multidisciplinary investigation into the talent development processes in an English Premiership rugby union academy: A preliminary study through an ecological lens. *Sports*, 10, 13. https://doi.org/10.3390/sports10020013

Dimundo, F., Cole, M., Blagrove, R. C., Till, K., McAuley, A. B. T., Hall, M., Gale, C. J., & Kelly, A. L. (2021a). Talent identification and development in male rugby union: A systematic review. *Journal of Expertise*, 4, 33–55.

Doncaster, G., Medina, D., Drobnic, F., Gómez-Díaz, A. J., & Unnithan, V. (2020). Appreciating factors beyond the physical in talent identification and development: Insights from the FC Barcelona sporting model. *Frontiers in Sports and Active Living*, 2, 91. https://doi.org/10.3389/fspor.2020.00091

Durandt, J., Parker, Z., Masimla, H., & Lambert, M. (2011). Rugby-playing history at the national U13 level and subsequent participation at the national U16 and U18 rugby tournaments. *South African Journal of Sports Medicine*, 23, 103–105. https://doi.org/10.17159/2078-516x/2011/v23i4a321

Gibbs, B. G., Jarvis, J. A., & Dufur, M. J. (2012). The rise of the underdog? The relative age effect reversal among Canadian-born NHL hockey players: A reply to Nolan and Howell. *International Review for the Sociology of Sport*, 47, 644–649. https://doi.org/10.1177/1012690211414343

Hill, A., MacNamara, Á., & Collins, D. (2015). Psychobehaviorally based features of effective talent development in rugby union: A coach's perspective. *The Sport Psychologist*, 29, 201–212. https://doi.org/10.1123/tsp.2014-0103

Jones, C., Visek, A. J., Barron, M. J., Hyman, M., & Chandran, A. (2019). Association between relative age effect and organisational practices of American youth football. *Journal of Sports Sciences*, 37, 1146–1153. https://doi.org/10.1080/02640414.2018.1546545

Kelly, A. L., Barrell, D., Burke, K., & Till, K. (2021a). Relative age effects in rugby union: A narrative review. In A. L. Kelly, J. Côté, M. Jeffreys, & J. Turnnidge (Eds.), *Birth advantages and relative age effects in sport: Exploring organizational structures and creating appropriate settings*. London: Routledge.

Kelly, A. L., Jackson, D., Barrell, D., Burke, K., & Baker, J. (2021b). The relative age effect in international rugby union: Consequences of changing the cut-off date and exploring youth to senior transitions. *High Ability Studies* [ePub ahead of print]. http://doi.org/10.1080/13598139.2021.1997722

Kelly, A. L., Jackson, D. T., Barrell, D., Burke, K., & Till, K. (2021c). The relative age effect in male and female English age-grade rugby union: Exploring the gender-specific mechanisms that underpin participation. *Science and Medicine in Football* [ePub ahead of print]. https://doi.org/10.1080/24733938.2021.1955145

Kelly, A. L., Jackson, D. T., Taylor, J. J., Jeffreys, M. A., & Turnnidge, J. (2020a). "Birthday-banding" as a strategy to moderate the relative age effect: A case study into the England squash talent pathway. *Frontiers in Sports and Active Living, 2*, 1–9. https://doi.org/10.3389/fspor.2020.573890

Kelly, A. L., McAuley, A. B. T., Dimundo, F., & Till, K. (2022) Talent identification in male youth rugby: An ecological perspective. In: K. Till, J. Weakley, S. Whitehead, & B. Jones. Youth Rugby, Routledge.

Kelly, A. L., Till, K., Jackson, D., Barrell, D., Burke, K., Turnnidge, J. (2021d). Talent identification and relative age effects in English male rugby union pathways: From entry to expertise. *Frontiers in Sports and Active Living, 3*, 1–9. https://doi.org/10.3389/fspor.2021.640607

Kelly, A. L., & Williams, C. A. (2020). Physical characteristics and the talent identification and development processes in male youth soccer: A narrative review. *Strength & Conditioning Journal, 42*, 15–34. https://doi.org/10.1519/SSC.0000000000000576

Kelly, A. L., Wilson, M. R., Gough, L. A., Knapman, H., Morgan, P., Cole, M., Jackson, T. D., & Williams, C. A. (2020b). A longitudinal investigation into the relative age effect in an English professional football club: Exploring the 'underdog hypothesis'. *Science and Medicine in Football, 4*, 111–118. https://doi.org/10.1080/24733938.2019.1694169

Kelly, A. L., Wilson, M. R., Jackson, D. T., Goldman, D. E., Turnnidge, J., Côté, J., & Williams, C. A. (2021e). A multidisciplinary investigation into "playing-up" a chronological age group in an English football academy. *Journal of Sports Science, 39*, 854–864. https://doi.org/10.1080/02640414.2020.1848117

Kelly, A. L., Wilson, M. R., & Williams, C. A. (2018). Developing a football-specific talent identification and development profiling concept – The locking wheel nut model. *Applied Coaching Research Journal, 2*, 32–41.

Lawrence, D. W. (2017). Sociodemographic profile of an Olympic team. *Public Health, 148*, 149–158. https://doi.org/10.1016/j.puhe.2017.03.011

MacNamara, A., & Collins, D. (2014). More of the same? Comment on "An integrated framework for the optimisation of sport and athlete development: A practitioner approach". *Journal of Sports Sciences, 32*, 793–795. http://dx.doi.org/10.1080/02640414.2013.855805

Malina, R. M., Cumming, S., Rogol, A., Coelho-e-Silva, M., Figueiredo, A., Konarski, J. & Kozieł, S. (2019). Bio-banding in youth sports: Background, concept, and application. *Sports Medicine, 49*, 1671–1685. https://doi.org/10.1007/s40279-019-01166-x

Mann, D. L., & van Ginneken, P. J. M. A. (2017). Age-ordered shirt numbering reduces the selection bias associated with the relative age effect. *Journal of Sports Sciences, 35*, 784–790. https://doi.org/10.1080/02640414.2016.1189588

Mann, D. T., Williams, A. M., Ward, P., & Janelle, C. M. (2007). Perceptual-cognitive expertise in sport: A meta-analysis. *Journal of Sport and Exercise Psychology, 29*, 457–478. https://doi.org/10.1123/jsep.29.4.457

McAuley, A. B., Baker, J., & Kelly, A. L. (2022). Defining "elite" status in sport: From chaos to clarity. *German Journal of Exercise and Sport Research, 52*, 193–197. https://doi.org/10.1007/s12662-021-00737-3

McCarthy, N., & Collins, D. (2014). Initial identification & selection bias versus the eventual confirmation of talent: Evidence for the benefits of a rocky road? *Journal of Sports Sciences, 32*, 1604–1610. https://doi.org/10.1080/02640414.2014.908322

McCarthy, N., Collins, D., & Court, D. (2016). Start hard, finish better: Further evidence for the reversal of the RAE advantage. *Journal of Sports Sciences, 34*, 1461–1465. https://doi.org/10.1080/02640414.2015.1119297

McCormack, S., Jones, B., Elliott, D., Rotheram, D., & Till, K. (2021). Coaches' assessment of players physical performance: Subjective and objective measures are needed when profiling players. *European Journal of Sport Science*, 1–11. https://doi.org/10.1080/17461391.2021.1956600

Owen, C., Till, K., Weakley, J., & Jones, B. (2020). Testing methods and physical qualities of male age grade rugby union players: A systematic review. *Plos One*, *15*, e0233796. https://doi.org/10.1371/journal.pone.0233796

Pearce, L. A., Leicht, A. S., Gómez-Ruano, M. Á., Sinclair, W. H., & Woods, C. T. (2020). The type and variation of evasive manoeuvres during an attacking task differ across a rugby league development pathway. *International Journal of Performance Analysis in Sport*, *20*, 1134–1142. https://doi.org/10.1080/24748668.2020.1834490

Pearce, L. A., Sinclair, W. H., Leicht, A. S., & Woods, C. T. (2019). Passing and tackling qualities discriminate developmental level in a rugby league talent pathway. *International Journal of Performance Analysis in Sport*, *19*, 985–998. https://doi.org/10.1080/24748668.2019.1689750

Pienaar, A. E., & Spamer, M. J. (1998). A longitudinal study of talented young rugby players as regards their rugby skills, physical and motor abilities and anthropometric data. *Journal of Human Movement Studies*, *34*, 13–32.

Plotz, A., & Spamer, M. (2006). A comparison of talented South African and English youth rugby players with reference to game-specific-, anthropometric-, physical and motor variables. *South African Journal for Research in Sport, Physical Education and Recreation*, *28*, 101–107. https://doi.org/10.4314/sajrs.v28i1.25934

Roberts, S. J., & Fairclough, S. J. (2012). The influence of relative age effects in representative youth rugby union in the North West of England. *Asian Journal of Exercise & Sports Science*, *9*, 86–98.

Runswick, O. R., Green, R., & North, J. S. (2020). The effects of skill-level and playing-position on the anticipation of ball-bounce in rugby union. *Human Movement Science*, *69*, 102544. https://doi.org/10.1016/j.humov.2019.102544

Sarmento, H., Anguera, M., Pereira, A., & Araújo, D. (2018). Talent identification and development in male football: A systematic review. *Sports Medicine*, *48*, 907–931. https://doi.org/10.1007/s40279-017-0851-7

Sedeaud, A., Vidalin, H., Tafflet, M., Marc, A., & Toussaint, J. F. (2013). Rugby morphologies: "Bigger and taller", reflects an early directional selection. *The Journal of Sports Medicine and Physical Fitness*, *53*, 185–191.

Seifert, L., Orth, D., Button, C., Brymer, E., & Davids, K. (2017). An ecological dynamics framework for the acquisition of perceptual-motor skills in climbing. In F. Feletti (Ed.), *Extreme sports medicine* (pp. 365–382). New York: Springer.

Sheard, M., & Golby, J. (2010). Personality hardiness differentiates elite-level sport performers. *International Journal of Sport and Exercise Psychology*, *8*, 160–169. https://doi.org/10.1080/1612197X.2010.9671940

Sherwood, S., Smith, T., & Masters, R. (2018). Pattern recall, decision making and talent identification in rugby union. *European Journal of Sport Science*, *19*, 834–841. https://doi.org/10.1080/17461391.2018.1545051

Sieghartsleitner, R., Zuber, C., Zibung, M., & Conzelmann, A. (2019). Science or coaches' eye? – Both! Beneficial collaboration of multidimensional measurements and coach assessments for efficient talent selection in elite youth football. *Journal of Sports Science and Medicine*, *18*, 32–43.

Spamer, E. J., Du Plessis, D. J., & Kruger, E. H. (2009). Comparative characteristics of elite New Zealand and South African u/16 rugby players with reference to game specific skills, physical abilities and anthropometric data. *South African Journal of Sports Medicine*, *21*, 53–57.

Taylor, J., & Collins, D. (2019). Shoulda, coulda, didnae—Why don't high-potential players make it? *The Sport Psychologist*, *33*(2), 8596. https://doi.org/10.1123/tsp.2017-0153

Till, K., & Baker, J. (2020). Challenges and [possible] solutions to optimizing talent identification and development in sport. *Frontiers in Psychology, 11*, 664. https://doi.org/10.3389/fpsyg.2020.00664

Till, K., Cobley, S., Morley, D., O'Hara, J., Chapman, C., & Cooke, C. (2016). The influence of age, playing position, anthropometry and fitness on career attainment outcomes in rugby league. *Journal of Sports Science, 34*, 1240–1245. https://doi.org/10.1080/02640414.2015.1105380

Till, K., Cobley, S., O'Hara, J., Brightmore, A., Cooke, C., & Chapman, C. (2011). Using anthropometric and performance characteristics to predict selection in junior UK rugby league players. *Journal of Science and Medicine in Sport, 14*, 264–269. https://doi.org/10.1016/j.jsams.2011.01.006

Till, K., Cobley, S., Wattie, N., O'hara, J., Cooke, C., & Chapman, C. (2010). The prevalence, influential factors and mechanisms of relative age effects in UK rugby league. *Scandinavian Journal of Medicine & Science in Sports, 20*, 320–329. https://doi.org/10.1111/j.1600-0838.2009.00884.x

Till, K., Scantlebury, S., & Jones, B. (2017). Anthropometric and physical qualities of elite male youth rugby league players. *Sports Medicine, 47*, 2171–2186. https://doi.org/10.1007/s40279-017-0745-8

Till, K., Weakley, J., Read, D. B., Phibbs, P., Darrall-Jones, J., Roe, G., Chantler, S., Mellalieu, S., Hislop, M., Stokes, K., Rock, A., & Jones, B. (2020). Applied sport science for male age-grade rugby union in England. *Sports Medicine Open, 6*, 14. https://doi.org/10.1186/s40798-020-0236-6

Tredrea, M., Dascombe, B., Sanctuary, C. E., & Scanlan, A. T. (2017). The role of anthropometric, performance and psychological attributes in predicting selection into an elite development programme in older adolescent rugby league players. *Journal of Sports Sciences, 35*, 1897–1903. https://doi.org/10.1080/02640414.2016.1241418

Webdale, K., Baker, J., Schorer, J., & Wattie, N. (2020). Solving sport's 'relative age' problem: A systematic review of proposed solutions. *International Review of Sport and Exercise Psychology, 13*, 187–204. https://doi.org/10.1080/1750984X.2019.1675083

Williams, A., & Reilly, T. (2000). Talent identification and development in soccer. *Journal of Sports Sciences, 18*, 657–667. https://doi.org/10.1080/02640410050120041.

Winn, C., Ford, P., McNarry, M., Lewis, J., & Stratton, G. (2016). The effect of deprivation on the developmental activities of adolescent rugby union players in Wales. *Journal of Sports Sciences, 35*, 2390–2396. https://doi.org/10.1080/02640414.2016.1271136

6
THE DEMANDS OF YOUTH RUGBY MATCH-PLAY

Sarah Whitehead, Dan Weaving, Rich Johnston, Dale B. Read, Ryan White and Ben Jones

Introduction

Within the rugby codes, time-motion and performance analysis quantify the technical, tactical and physical demands of match-play. While both performance and time-motion analysis were traditionally conducted using video-based notational analysis, developments in technology have improved their efficiency. Wearable microtechnology devices including global navigation satellite systems (GNSS) and micro-electrical-mechanical systems (MEMS; including tri-axial accelerometers, gyroscopes and magnetometers) have facilitated more widespread quantification of the time motion characteristics of youth rugby match-play, with video-based methods still the predominant method for quantifying technical-tactical performance. The data derived from the analysis of match-play on the technical-tactical and physical demands across different age grades and playing standards can be used inform training practices in young rugby players.

The area of performance analysis commonly refers to the quantification of the technical-tactical components of team sport match-play. Given the nature of the rugby codes and the significance of these aspects towards playing success (Kempton et al., 2017), capturing performance indicators is important. This may include defensive (e.g., number of tackles, rucks) and offensive (e.g., passes, kicks) statistics at a team or individual level, as well as more in-depth analysis on tactical performance and playing styles (Woods et al., 2017b). Time motion analysis (i.e., change in location over time) allows multiple variables to be calculated including average and maximum speed, changes in speed (e.g., acceleration) and distances covered above certain speeds (e.g., low-speed or high-speed distance). More recently, developments in algorithms using MEMs allow valid and automated measurement of collision counts (Hulin et al., 2017). The intermittent and dynamic nature of rugby match-play means several variables need to be considered.

Quantifying the match demands through time motion and performance analysis has practical applications in youth rugby. It provides an understanding of the positional (e.g., forwards and backs) differences in locomotor, collision and technical-tactical characteristics between playing standards (e.g., club *vs.* international) and age grades (e.g., U16 *vs.* U18 *vs.* U20). Such information can support youth rugby coaches in the prescription of training practices to assist in optimal player development and progression through playing pathways.

Current research on the demands of match-play has highlighted several considerations within the prescription of training and drill design, including the appropriate metrics (e.g., average speed, accelerations, collisions) to use and their specificity and appropriateness for positions, phase-of-play specificity and age grade. Additionally, the quantification of match volume should be considered in training prescription by considering the previous match, and the subsequent weekly training volume. The systematic monitoring of match-play demands over a season can identify the match-to-match variability in demands to assist in the planning and manipulation of weekly volume and training practices based on the difficulty of the previous match (Dalton-Barron et al., 2020; McLaren et al., 2016). Training volume and intensity should be manipulated by the coach to elicit performance-enhancing adaptations (Weaving et al., 2020) to assist in optimal match-preparation and progression through playing pathways. In this chapter, volume refers to the amount of actions/movement, and intensity refers to the amount of actions/movement per unit of time, both of which are important in the use of match-demands data in the design and monitoring of training practices in youth rugby.

The purpose of this chapter is to first summarise the research that details the technical-tactical and physical demands of youth rugby league and union match-play, and second consider the practical application of the match-demands data and research in terms of training prescription and monitoring. These practical applications can assist coaches in understanding the specific demands of match-play, which can be used to help player preparation.

Research Overview

Rugby League

Technical-Tactical Demands

The technical-tactical demands of youth rugby league match-play have been quantified in several studies (e.g., Bennett et al., 2016; Dempsey et al., 2017; Woods et al., 2017a). The total ball-in-play time for elite U20 match-play (80-minute game) has been reported as 49:40±4:29 minutes, with an average activity cycle of 72±15 seconds, and the longest activity cycle of 289±58 seconds (Gabbett, 2012). Collision frequency is the most evaluated performance indicator. Specifically, during international U18 match-play, Dempsey et al. (2017)

reported defensive collisions of 10±7 for backs and 19±10 for forwards, compared to offensive carries into contact of 7±4 and 5±4 for backs and forwards respectively. Others have investigated the frequency of missed or unsuccessful tackles (Waldron et al., 2014; Woods et al., 2017a), with a squad total of 36±11 missed tackles during elite U20 match-play reported (Woods et al., 2017a). Additionally, hit-up forwards have greater skill involvements than adjustables (total: 0.5 ± 0.2 $n \cdot min^{-1}$) and outside backs (total: 0.3 ± 0.2 $n \cdot min^{-1}$; Bennett et al., 2016). It is evident that there needs to be a position-specific consideration towards technical-tactical training, specifically around contact training.

Studies have compared technical-tactical performance indicators (PI) between playing standards and age grades (Johnston et al., 2015; Kempton et al., 2013; Waldron et al., 2014). Teams competing in a higher division at a school tournament carried out a greater number of total (15 ± 7 $n \cdot min^{-1}$) and relative (0.4 ± 0.2 $n \cdot min^{-1}$) collisions compared to the lower divisions (total = 9 ± 3; relative 0.3 ± 0.1 $n \cdot min^{-1}$; Gabbett, 2014; Johnston et al., 2015). Additionally, there are dissimilarities in the team PI profiles of the U20 and senior professional match-play (Woods et al., 2017a) and defensive play-the-ball losses alone can classify between U19 and senior professional match-play for forwards, with number of quick play-the-balls, carries and collisions deemed as important for the classification between the two levels for backs (Whitehead et al., 2021b). These studies demonstrate differences in these match-play behaviours between playing standards, providing specific focuses for coaches when preparing players for the next level of competition.

Physical Demands

In youth rugby league, whole match total distances of ~2516–6773 m, with ~116–404 m high-speed running, ~ 9–26 collisions (Dempsey et al., 2017; Gabbett, 2013; Johnston et al., 2015), and peak 10-minute average running speeds of ~94–106 $m \cdot min^{-1}$ (Whitehead et al., 2018, 2020) have been reported. The large range in values reported is in part due to the different match lengths (40–80 min), however, positional differences and differences between playing standards and age grades have also been identified.

The total distance covered during match-play reported for youth backs (~5707–6767 m) is greater than that reported for forwards (~4063–4911 m), but with minimal differences apparent for whole match average running speeds (backs: ~83–96 $m \cdot min^{-1}$ *vs.* forwards: ~89–97 $m \cdot min^{-1}$; Dempsey et al., 2017; Gabbett, 2013; McLellan & Lovell, 2013; Whitehead et al., 2018), highlighting the need to take into consideration differences in playing time when comparing positions. Positional differences in the peak locomotive characteristics have been identified in elite U16 (Thornton et al., 2019) and U19 (Whitehead et al., 2020) match-play. Under 19 fullbacks have the greatest peak average running speeds across all durations (e.g., 10 minutes: 106 ± 9 $m \cdot min^{-1}$ *vs.* ~94–101 $m \cdot min^{-1}$), but other positional differences are duration dependent (Whitehead et al. 2020).

At the U16 age group, hookers have a *very likely* higher acceleration demands compared to fullbacks (Thornton et al., 2019). Such research highlights the differences in locomotor profiles between positions which should be considered when prescribing training.

Differences in the physical match demands have also been identified between playing standards and age grades (Johnston et al., 2015; Thornton et al., 2019; Whitehead et al., 2018). Higher standards of competition in a school tournament have the greatest average match-speed and high-speed running distance compared to the lower standards (Gabbett, 2014; Johnston et al., 2015), which could be reflective of the team's ability to cope with an intensified period of competition through enhanced physical qualities (Johnston et al., 2015). Position-specific differences between U16 club and international standard have been reported for the whole and peak match demands; backs have greater whole match, and peak 60-second average running speeds and cover greater high-speed running distance at the club level, whilst forwards have greater peak average running speeds and greater sprint speed distance, at the International level (Whitehead et al., 2018). Additionally, U18 halves have higher acceleration demands than U16 halves, but U16 hookers have higher demands than U18 hookers (Thornton et al., 2019. Further differences in the physical demands of match-play have also been identified across professional playing pathways (Gabbett, 2013; Hausler et al., 2016; McLellan & Lovell, 2013). The classification of Academy and Super League match-play found that for backs the combination of variables with the highest classification rate was all physical characteristics, indicating that backs complete greater 'global' external workloads (PlayerLoad$_{2D}$), complete either more, or the same amount of high-intensity movements at low locomotor velocities (e.g., change of direction) but whilst carrying more body mass (PlayerLoad$_{SLOW}$kg), and cover greater high-speed running distance than backs during Academy match-play (Whitehead et al., 2020). Such research further supports the need for position-specific consideration in the planning and prescription of training within youth development pathways.

Rugby Union

Technical-Tactical Demands

The research on the technical-tactical demands of youth rugby union typically provides the frequency of technical actions and events (Ashford et al., 2020; Ungureanu et al., 2019). In U18, match-play 86 ± 28 tackles have been reported per team (Ungureanu et al., 2019) and ~6–9 per player (Roe et al., 2016). Additionally, winning teams make less inefficient tackles and lose possession less frequently than losing teams (Ungureanu et al., 2019). Forwards have been found to perform more attacking rucks and tackles than backs, alongside the addition of 14 ± 5 scrums (Roe et al., 2016), indicating the need for the position-specific prescription of contact training practices.

Studies have investigated technical-tactical demands of U16 and U18 rugby union Academy match-play (e.g., Ashford et al., 2020; Read et al., 2018a; Ungureanu et al., 2019), but with no direct comparison between age grades or standards of play. In U16 match-play, 1.54 ± 0.32 passes per minute occur (Ashford et al., 2020), compared to a total of 94 ± 27 passes per game in U18 match-play (Ungureanu et al., 2019). Ball-in-play time as a percentage of the match duration appears similar across age grades, with 27 ± 3 min (~37% of match-play) reported for U18 match-play (Read et al., 2018a), compared to 40 ± 4% of match time reported in U16 match-play (Ashford et al., 2020). Furthermore, it has been found that during ball-in-play time at the U18 age grade, 13 ± 3 minutes is spent in attack and 15 ± 3 minutes in defense, with the longest ball in the play cycle reported as 2.5 minutes (Read et al., 2018a). Information on the phases and cycles of match-play provides the parameters for which the physical demands are performed which should be considered for training practices.

Physical Demands

Across youth rugby union whole match total distances of ~3841–6510 m (Cunningham et al., 2016; Phibbs et al., 2018) and average running speeds of ~59–70 m·min^{-1} (Phibbs et al., 2018; Read et al., 2017) with peak 10-minute average running speeds of ~80–97 m·min^{-1} (Read et al., 2018) have been reported, with positional, age-grade and playing standard differences apparent. The total distance covered and average running speed of match-play have been found to be greater for backs compared to forwards (~5254 *vs.* 4811 m and ~72 *vs.* 69 m·min^{-1}) at the U18 Academy standard (Phibbs et al., 2018; Read et al., 2018b; Roe et al., 2016). Yet, during U16 school match-play the locomotive demands have been reported to be greater for forwards than backs (Read et al., 2017). Across all positions most of the distance covered is at low speeds; however, during U20 International match-play high-speed running (>5 m.s^{-1}) distance covered was found to be greatest in the back three players (728 ± 150 m) and the lowest in front row players (212 ± 113 m; Cunningham et al., 2016). The positional differences suggest that position-specific physical demands become more apparent in older age grades, highlighting the importance in the specialisation of positions at older ages and higher standards of play, which must be considered in training.

Further position-specific demands have been highlighted in different phases-of-play (Read et al., 2018b) and peak average running speeds (Read et al., 2019). In attack, there are unclear differences between forwards and backs, but greater average running speeds have been found for U18 forwards during defense (Read et al., 2018b). Under 18 forwards have been found to have lower peak average running speeds across all durations investigated, with further sub-positional comparisons identifying differences between front row and second and back row players, as well as scrum halves having greater average running speeds than inside and outside backs (Read et al., 2019). These data provide position-specific reference values for coaches preparing academy rugby union players for the most intense periods of play.

Differences in total distance between younger age grades (i.e., U16, U18, U19) are marginal, however, at the U20 age grade the distances are greater, particularly for backs; for example, back three U20 international players (6192 ± 748 m) cover ~1,000 m more than U19 club outside back players (5174 ± 660 m; Cunningham et al., 2016; Flanagan et al., 2017). The increase in the volume of distance is likely due to longer playing durations, with average match speeds appearing similar between age grades. At the school level, backs have been found to cover lower sprint distance at the U16 age grade (165 ± 101 m) compared to the U18 (319 ± 176m m), but with little difference for forwards (Read et al., 2017). Additionally, Academy forwards have been found to cover greater sprint distance than school forwards (Read et al., 2018a), indicating academy rugby to be more physical demanding than school rugby, and given players can play in both standards concurrently they should be conditioned to meet the additional demands.

Summary

In both rugby codes, positional differences are apparent in the demands of match-play, some of which are dependent upon the playing standard, indicating the need for position-specific prescription of training practices. Current research demonstrates differences in technical-tactical demands between standards of competition in rugby league match-play, providing potential focus areas for youth rugby league coaches. However, insufficient research analysing these differences exists in rugby union, and further work is required. The physical demands of match-play in both codes vary depending on the playing standard and age grade of competition, influenced primarily by the match length and duration on field.

Practical Applications

The demands of youth rugby match-play can be used by coaches to enhance and support player development by ensuring appropriate prescription of training practices. During field-based training, a major focus by coaches is to prescribe a variety of drills to holistically develop the technical and tactical skills of players during different phases of the game (e.g., attack, defence, transition). Given the time constraints of youth rugby programmes, there is a need for efficient training practices that provide concurrent development of the physical, technical and tactical elements of the game. Understanding match demands data can assist in both the design of new drills and the evaluation of current drills to ensure players are more consistently exposed to the physical intensities and technical-tactical requirements of their position, for their current age category, future age categories and playing standards. Importantly, the measures (e.g., average speed, collisions) utilised by coaches must be considered to reflect the activity performed and training outcome (Box 6.1).

Box 6.1

The demands of youth rugby match-play quantified through time-motion and performance analysis can be used to prescribe and monitor time-efficient training practices. Training drills can be designed and evaluated to ensure exposure to the position-specific physical intensities and technical-tactical requirements.

Designing and Prescribing Training Drills

Given the intermittent nature of rugby training and matches, coaches should maintain awareness of which variables might best be targeted to reflect the intensity of the activity performed. The average speed (distance/time) of a drill is often used as a measure of intensity, but this does not reflect the regular changes of direction and physical contact players perform during match-specific training and will therefore potentially underestimate the intensity of the activity. As such, for more intensive drills (i.e., those performed in a confined space), such as goal-line defense, measures of changes in speed (acceleration and deceleration) provide a better reflection of drill intensity. On the other hand, for extensive drills (i.e., those performed over a large space), such as small-sided games on a half field or kick chase drills, average speed and high-speed measures may be a suitable variable to reflect intensity. When the drills performed are position specific, different metrics may need to be considered between positional groups. For example, the greater distances covered at high speed by backs, which becomes more of a factor in older age groups (Cunningham et al., 2016; Read et al., 2017), may carry more significance towards the total load performed for backs compared to acceleration and physical contact for forwards (Box 6.2).

Box 6.2

The variables used to monitor and evaluate training drills should be reflective of the activity being performed. For extensive drills (larger space) average speed and high-speed measures may be suitable, whereas for intensive drills (confined space) measures of acceleration and deceleration provide a better reflection of intensity. Collisions should also be quantified alongside the locomotor demands where appropriate.

Coaches can manipulate training drills to influence the physical and technical demands. Figure 6.1 presents several ways to manipulate the demands of any drill

98 Sarah Whitehead et al.

to either increase or decrease the intensity/difficulty and also alter the training focus (Figure 6.1):

1. Size of the playing area. This will largely govern the types of movements and involvements players will perform and should be the first thing to decide upon. Increasing the area will allow for more opportunity for high-speed running, whereas a smaller area constrains the players so they cannot reach high speeds (Gabbett et al., 2012).
2. Area per player. Whilst this may be governed in part by player availability, this is the second aspect that should be decided upon. Increasing the area per player by reducing the player numbers, will result in a more difficult drill with more frequent movements and involvements (Morley et al., 2016).
3. Onside vs. Offside. Offside games will lead to increased running but reduce the specificity of the technical-tactical requirements of the drill (Gabbett et al., 2010).
4. Contact vs. No contact. This may increase the specificity of the drill but will reduce the running demands of the games due to the time spent in contact. This will also alter the fatigue response, inducing more upper-body fatigue and muscle damage (Johnston et al., 2014; Roe et al., 2017).

There are other constraints that can be manipulated regarding the rules of the games to influence physical and technical-tactical demands of game-based

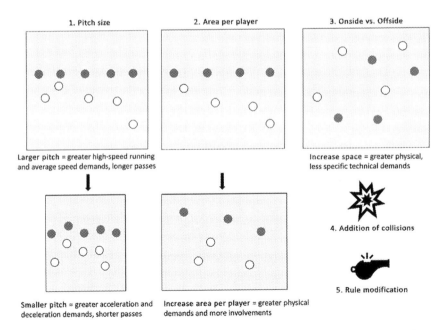

FIGURE 6.1 The Modification of Drill Design to Influence the Physical and Technical Demands

training drills (Zanin et al., 2021). Coaches should be encouraged to monitor the internal (e.g., heart rate, perceived exertion) and external (e.g., acceleration, speed, touches of the ball) demands of the drills as they manipulate the constraints to understand how the intensity of various aspects are impacted.

Positional and Phases-of-Play Specific Design and Prescription

The physical and technical match demands of the rugby codes by position and phases-of-play can be used in the design of training drills to enhance the specificity of training. The greater volume of high-speed and sprint-speed running encountered by backs in both rugby codes (Cunningham et al., 2016; Whitehead et al., 2018) indicates the need for greater exposure and preparation for these demands in training. Similarly, the differences in acceleration and deceleration demands between the playing positions need to be considered. For example, for backs, the pitch area can be made larger to provide greater opportunities to reach and maintain high-speed or sprint-speed efforts more frequently whereas for forwards by reducing the dimensions of a playing area the acceleration and deceleration load would be increased (Figure 6.1).

Designing and selecting drills that achieve these physical differences can be assisted by understanding which phases-of-play elicit greater physical and technical-tactical exposures (Tierney et al., 2017; Whitehead et al., 2021a). For example, Whitehead et al. (2021a) reported higher average speeds and peak high-speed running intensities when transitioning from attack to defense (e.g., chasing kicks) and defense to attack (e.g., returning kicks), as well as the greatest acceleration/deceleration intensity when defending in senior professional rugby league players. Therefore, when considering this within drill design, if the training goal is greater average speeds and high-speed exposure, training drills incorporating constraints that lead to frequent kick chase and kick returns could be a useful approach. This could be achieved by adding specific rule constraints, such as three tackles or rucks then kick to encourage high-speed running. Across both codes, given that backs are generally involved in more transition (i.e., attack to defence, defence to attack) activities than forwards, drills involving frequent kick returns and chases could be useful for the backs positional group. Equally, as forwards are involved in more defensive work than backs, designing and prescribing more frequent defence-specific drills within spatially confined areas could be a useful approach.

As highlighted in Figure 6.1, the addition of collisions will impact the physical demands of a drill by reducing the speed of the game and impacting on the fatigue response. The frequency and type of contact to be used should be guided by the technical-tactical and physical aims of the session. To control the number of collisions, these could be performed in bouts at specific time intervals. To overload collisions, the collisions could be more frequent (e.g., every 1 minute), or more collisions per bout (e.g., 1, 2 or 3). Alternatively, if the aim of the game is to replicate the technical-tactical demands of the game, then including the normal collisions within the context of phase-of-play should be performed. The speed of the game could then either be increased or decreased by constraints around the tackle and ruck contest. For example, in rugby league, reducing the number of players in the tackle and the time it takes for the tackle to be 'completed' would increase the speed of the game. Similarly, in rugby union, having the defending team place a set number of players at each ruck would increase demands for the defending team. Both of these changes would reduce the authenticity of the tackle contest, but increase the running demands, and the associated physical cost. As such, coaches should be mindful of the aims of the session when deciding how to program contact within training drills.

Age Grade and Playing Standard Specific

In both rugby union and league, the relative locomotor demands have been found to be similar across age grades, with increases in match volume due to increased playing duration (Read et al., 2017; Whitehead et al., 2018). Yet, differences in body mass of the players will likely lead to distinct physical demands. Older players are typically heavier and stronger than younger players (Darrall-Jones et al., 2015; Johnston et al., 2014), which also reinforces the need to prioritise player preparation for the contact elements of the game to ensure player safety and performance. Therefore, it is essential that training maximises the contact (e.g., tackle) skill development of rugby players.

Progressing the locomotive or running demands independently of contact may not prepare players for the progression through the age groups. This can be achieved through either the design of drills that prioritise contact skill development (e.g., small-sided games in a constraint space), or contact-specific drills incorporated within this training session. Across the training session, or training week, coaches should ensure that the ball-related skills, contact-related skills, decision-making and physical demands relating to both movement and contact are developed in both isolation and concurrently. This can be through specifically focused drills or small-sided games, whereby the constraints are manipulated to achieve the desired outcome.

Evaluating Training Drills and Match Volumes

As a coaching process, the intensity of any training drill can be evaluated using microtechnology and performance analysis data collected during training. The data collected can be compared to published research data to identify which drills expose players to match intensity for the different physical (e.g., acceleration, high-speed running, collisions) and technical-tactical components (e.g., number of carries/tackles). An example of this is shown in Figure 6.2 where the microtechnology data is exported, analysed and presented visually for coaches to compare the physical demands of each training drill, and the whole session, compared to published match data.

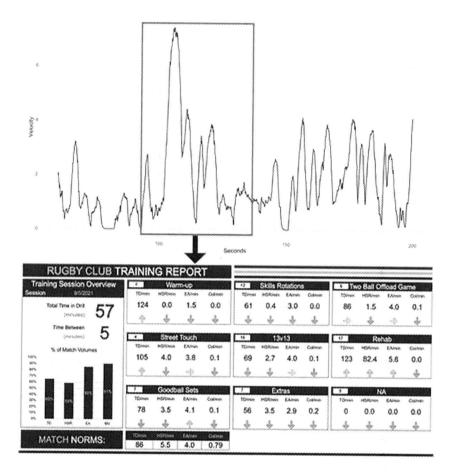

FIGURE 6.2 The Process of Using the Global Navigation Satellite System (GNSS) Raw Velocity Trace to Analyse and Evaluate Training, an Example Report

Note: The box indicates a section of training that is clipped to provide data on a specific drill (e.g., 13 *vs*. 13). The arrows indicate whether the variables within that drill are higher (upward arrow), equal to (sideways arrow) or below (downward arrow) published match data on average running speed (TD/min), high speed running (HSR/min), acceleration (EA/min) and collisions (Col/min).

Such reports provide opportunities for coaches to adapt drills to meet the target physical or technical outcome. For example, if a drill was designed to expose players to the high-speed (i.e., physical) and carry (i.e., technical) intensity of match-play, yet upon review (by comparing to published data) the drill didn't expose players to these intensities, the drill could be amended for future prescription by providing a greater area per player (increasing opportunities to reach high speeds) and reduce the number of players (to allow more opportunities for players to complete greater frequency of carries). Such a process can inform the plan-do-review cycle of the overall coaching process. If microtechnology is not available to the coach, perceptual ratings of perceived exertion can be used as a global approach to understanding the intensity of training drills (McLaren et al., 2017). Using this approach, coaches could collect this measurement during match-play and for individual training drills (and compare) to gauge a global understanding of whether the training drills are reflective of match intensity.

Managing the total volume that a youth rugby player is exposed to across daily, weekly and long-term periods is a key strategy to optimise training adaptation and avoid negative outcomes such as overtraining or underperformance. The match-to-match variation (McLaren et al., 2016) in the physical demands, as well as differences in duration played (e.g., substitutions or selection) poses challenges in the management of weekly load. Coaches can use match data to monitor the volume of activity a player completes during a match to inform the planning of future training weeks. If the match volume has been 'higher than normal' for a player due to playing a different position or playing a longer duration, coaches might consider a reduction in the following weeks training volume leading into the subsequent match for that player. Equally, if match volume has been 'lower than normal' due to an early substitution, coaches might consider an increase in the following weeks training volume for that player. The monitoring of volume (and its changes) can be achieved by using microtechnology variables, such as measuring the total-, high-speed- and acceleration-distances players complete, or if this technology is not accessible, via the use of perceptual ratings of perceived exertion multiplied by match duration to provide a total volume score (Foster et al., 2017). Determining a 'normal' match volume can be achieved via a mean of an individual players data. The variability between matches can be calculated using the coefficient of variation from the mean and standard deviation (standard deviation divided by mean multiplied by 100 [%]). For example, Player A completes 5,000m, 5,500m, 6,000m and 6,500m across four matches, achieving a mean (normal) volume of 5,750m with a standard deviation of 645m. In this example, the coefficient of variation, and therefore typical match variability is 11% (645m divided by 5,750m multiplied by 100). Therefore, changes (increase or decrease) above 11% would constitute a meaningful change in this player's match volume, triggering potential amendments to the coaches planned training programme. Such information could be integrated within players weekly, monthly and seasonal planning.

Key Take Home Messages

- The technical, tactical and physical demands of rugby match-play quantified through time-motion and performance analysis can be used to assist with player preparation through drill design and the evaluation of training practices.
- Training drills should be designed to account for the different match demands, with both intensive (those performed in a confined space) and extensive (those performances over a large space) drills considered.

- Coaches should prescribe training drills based on the position-specific and phase-of-play demands through the manipulation of space and rule constraints.
- Given the differences in the match demands between age grades and playing standards training must be prescribed to help progress players to the older age groups, contact demands should be considered alongside the locomotive.
- Coaches can evaluate training drills through the use of microtechnology, performance analysis data and rating of perceived exertion. Comparisons can be made to published data to assist in the evaluation.
- The plan-do-review process should be used to evaluate a training and which drills expose players to match intensity for the different physical and technical-tactical components.

References

Ashford, M., Burke, K., Barrell, D., Abraham, A., & Poolton, J. (2020). The impact of rule modifications on player behaviour in a talent identification and development environment: A case study of the rugby football union's wellington academy rugby festival. *Journal of Sports Sciences*, 38, 2670–2676. http://doi.org/10.1080/02640414.2020.1795559

Bennett, K. J., Fransen, J., Scott, B. R., Sanctuary, C. E., Gabbett, T. J., & Dascombe, B. J. (2016). Positional group significantly influences the offensive and defensive skill involvements of junior representative rugby league players during match play. *Journal of Sports Sciences*, 34, 1542–1546. http://doi.org/10.1080/02640414.2015.1122206

Cunningham, D. J., Shearer, D. A., Drawer, S., Eager, R., Cook, C. J., & Kilduff, L. P. (2016). Movement demands of elite u20 international rugby union players. *PLoS One*, 110, e0153275. http://doi.org/10.1371/journal.pone.0153275

Dalton-Barron, N., Palczewska, A., McLaren, S.J., Rennie, G., Beggs, C., Roe, G., & Jones, B. (2021). A league-wide investigation into variability of rugby league match running from 322 Super League games. *Science and Medicine in Football*, 5, 225–233. https://doi.org/10.1080/24733938.2020.1844907

Darrall-Jones, J. D., Jones, B., & Till, K. (2015). Anthropometric and physical profiles of English academy rugby union players. *The Journal of Strength & Conditioning Research*, 29, 2086–2096. https://doi.org/10.1519/JSC.0000000000000872

Dempsey, G. M., Gibson, N. V., Sykes, D., Pryjmachuk, B., & Turner, A. P. (2017). Match demands of senior and junior players during international rugby league. *Journal of Strength and Conditioning Research*, 32, 1678–1684. http://doi.org/10.1519/JSC.0000000000002028

Flanagan, E., O'Doherty, P., Piscione, P., & Lacome, M. (2017). The demands of the game – A descriptive analysis of the locomotor demands of Junior International Rugby Union. *Journal of Australian Strength and Conditioning*, 25, 17–24.

Foster, C., Rodriguez-Marroyo, J. A., & de Koning, J. J. (2017). Monitoring training loads: The past, the present, and the future. *International Journal of Sports Physiology and Performance*, 12, S2-2–S2-8. http://doi.org/10.1123/IJSPP.2016-0388

Gabbett, T. J. (2012). Activity cycles of national rugby league and national youth competition matches. *Journal of Strength and Conditioning Research*, 26, 1517–1523. http://doi.org/10.1519/JSC.0b013e318236d050

Gabbett, T. J. (2013). Influence of playing standard on the physical demands of professional rugby league. *Journal of Sports Sciences*, 31, 1125–1138. http://doi.org/10.1080/02640414.2013.773401

Gabbett, T. J. (2014). Influence of playing standard on the physical demands of junior rugby league tournament match-play. *Journal of Science and Medicine in Sport, 17*, 212–217. http://doi.org/10.1016/j.jsams.2013.03.013

Gabbett, T. J., Abernethy, B., & Jenkins, D. G. (2012). Influence of field size on the physiological and skill demands of small-sided games in junior and senior rugby league players. *The Journal of Strength & Conditioning Research, 26*, 487–491. http://doi.org/10.1519/JSC.0b013e318225a371

Gabbett, T. J., Jenkins, D. G., & Abernethy, B. (2010). Physiological and skill demands of 'on-side' and 'off-side' games. *The Journal of Strength & Conditioning Research, 24*, 2979–2983. http://doi.org/10.1519/JSC.0b013e3181e72731

Hausler, J., Halaki, M., & Orr, R. (2016). Player activity profiles in the Australian second-tier rugby league competitions. *International Journal of Sports Physiology and Performance, 11*, 816–823. http://doi.org/10.1123/ijspp.2015-0319

Hulin, B. T., Gabbett, T. J., Johnston, R. D., & Jenkins, D. G. (2017). Wearable microtechnology can accurately identify collision events during professional rugby league match-play. *Journal of Science and Medicine in Sport, 20*, 638–642. http://doi.org/10.1016/j.jsams.2016.11.006

Johnston, R. D., Gabbett, T. J., & Jenkins, D. G. (2014). Applied sport science of rugby league. *Sports Medicine, 44*, 1087–1100. http://doi.org/10.1007/s40279-014-0190-x

Johnston, R. D., Gabbett, T. J., & Jenkins, D. G. (2015). Influence of playing standard and physical fitness on activity profiles and post-match fatigue during intensified junior rugby league competition. *Sports Medicine Open, 1*. http://doi.org/10.1186/s40798-015-0015-y

Johnston, R. D., Gabbett, T. J., Seibold, A. J., & Jenkins, D. G. (2014). Influence of physical contact on neuromuscular fatigue and markers of muscle damage following small-sided games. *Journal of Science and Medicine in Sport, 17*, 535–540. http://doi.org/10.1016/j.jsams.2013.07.018

Kempton, T., Sirotic, A. C., Cameron, M., & Coutts, A. J. (2013). Match-related fatigue reduces physical and technical performance during elite rugby league match-play: A case study. *Journal of Sports Sciences, 31*, 1770–1780. https://doi.org/10.1080/02640414.2013.803583

Kempton, T., Sirotic, A. C., & Coutts, A. J. (2017). A comparison of physical and technical performance profiles between successful and less-successful professional rugby league teams. *International Journal of Sports Physiology and Performance, 12*, 520–526. https://doi.org/10.1123/ijspp.2016-0003

McLaren, S. J., Smith, A., Spears, I. R., & Weston, M. (2017). A detailed quantification of differential ratings of perceived exertion during team-sport training. *Journal of Science and Medicine in Sport, 20*, 290–295. http://doi.org/10.1016/j.jsams.2016.06.011

McLaren, S. J., Weston, M., Smith, A., Cramb, R., & Portas, M. D. (2016). Variability of physical performance and player match loads in professional rugby union. *Journal of Science and Medicine in Sport, 19*, 493–497. http://doi.org/10.1016/j.jsams.2015.05.010

McLellan, C. P., & Lovell, D. I. (2013). Performance analysis of professional, semi-professional, and junior elite rugby league match-play using global positioning systems. *Journal of Strength and Conditioning Research, 27*, 3266–3274. http://doi.org/10.1519/JSC.0b013e31828f1d74

Morley, D., Ogilvie, P., Till, K., Rothwell, M., Cotton, W., O'Connor, D., & McKenna, J. (2016). Does modifying competition affect the frequency of technical skills in junior rugby league? *International Journal of Sports Science & Coaching, 11*, 810–818. http://doi.org/10.1177/1747954116676107

Phibbs, P., Jones, B., Read, D. B., Roe, G., Darrall-Jones, J., Weakley, J., Rock, A., & Till, K. (2018). The appropriateness of training exposures for match-play preparation in adolescent schoolboy and academy rugby union players. *Journal of Sports Sciences, 36,* 704–709. http://doi.org/10.1080/02640414.2017.1332421

Read, D. B., Jones, B., Phibbs, P., Roe, G., Darrall-Jones, J., Weakley, J., & Till, K. (2018a). The physical characteristics of match-play in English schoolboy and academy rugby union. *Journal of Sports Sciences, 36,* 645–650. http://doi.org/10.1080/02640414.2017.1329546

Read, D. B., Jones, B., Williams, S., Phibbs, P. J., Darrall-Jones, J. D., Roe, G. A. B., Weakley, J. J. S., Rock, A., & Till, K. (2018b). The physical characteristics of specific phases of play during rugby union match play. *International Journal of Sports Physiology and Performance, 13,* 1331–1336. http://doi.org/10.1123/ijspp.2017-0625

Read, D. B., Till, K., Beasley, G., Clarkson, M., Heyworth, R., Lee, J., Weakley, J. J., Phibbs, P. J., Roe, G. A., & Darrall-Jones, J. (2019). Maximum running intensities during English academy rugby union match-play. *Science and Medicine in Football, 3,* 43–49. http://doi.org/10.1080/24733938.2018.1464660

Read, D. B., Weaving, D., Phibbs, P., Darrall-Jones, J., Roe, G., Weakley, J., Hendricks, S., Till, K., & Jones, B. (2017). Movement and physical demands of school and university rugby union match-play in England. *BMJ Open Sport and Exercise Medicine, 2,* e000147. http://doi.org/10.1136/bmjsem-2016-000147

Roe, G., Darrall-Jones, J., Till, K., Phibbs, P., Read, D., Weakley, J., Rock, A., & Jones, B. (2017). The effect of physical contact on changes in fatigue markers following rugby union field-based training. *European Journal of Sport Science, 17,* 647–655. http://doi.org/10.1080/17461391.2017.1287960

Roe, G., Halkier, M., Beggs, C., Till, K., & Jones, B. (2016). The use of accelerometers to quantify collisions and running demands of rugby union match-play. *International Journal of Performance Analysis in Sport, 16,* 590–601. http://doi.org/10.1080/24748668.2016.11868911

Thornton, H. R., Smith, M. R., Armstrong, P., Delaney, J. A., Duthie, G. M., Cunneen, H., & Borges, N. R. (2019). Is implementing age and positional specific training drills necessary in elite youth rugby league? *Sports Performance and Science Reports, 1,* 1–3.

Tierney, P., Tobin, D. P., Blake, C., & Delahunt, E. (2017). Attacking 22 entries in rugby union: Running demands and differences between successful and unsuccessful entries. *Scandinavian Journal of Medicine & Science in Sports, 27,* 1934–1941. http://doi.org/10.1111/sms.12816

Ungureanu, A. N., Condello, G., Pistore, S., Conte, D., & Lupo, C. (2019) Technical and tactical aspects in Italian youth rugby union in relation to different academies, regional tournaments, and outcomes. *Journal of Strength & Conditioning Research, 33,* 1557–1569. http://doi.org/10.1519/JSC.0000000000002188

Waldron, M., Worsfold, P. R., Twist, C., & Lamb, K. (2014). A three-season comparison of match performances among selected and unselected elite youth rugby league players. *Journal of Sports Science, 32,* 1110–1119. http://doi.org/10.1080/02640414.2014.889838

Weaving, D., Dalton-Barron, N., McLaren, S., Scantlebury, S., Cummins, C., Roe, G., Jones, B., Beggs, C., & Abt, G. (2020). The relative contribution of training intensity and duration to daily measures of training load in professional rugby league and union. *Journal of Sports Sciences, 38,* 1674–1681. http://doi.org/10.1080/02640414.2020.1754725

Whitehead, S., Dalton Barron, N., Rennie, G., & Jones, B. (2021a). The peak locomotor characteristics of super league (rugby league) match-play. *International Journal of Performance Analysis in Sport, 21,* 981–992. https://doi.org/10.1080/24748668.2021.1968659

Whitehead, S., Till, K., Jones, B., Beggs, C., Dalton-Barron, N., & Weaving, D. (2021b). The use of technical-tactical and physical performance indicators to classify between levels of match-play in elite rugby league. *Science and Medicine in Football*, 5, 121–1277. http://doi.org/10.1080/24733938.2020.1814492

Whitehead, S., Till, K., Weaving, D., Dalton-Barron, N., Ireton, M., & Jones, B. (2020). The duration-specific peak average running speeds of European super league academy rugby league match-play. *Journal of Strength and Conditioning Research*, 35, 1964–1971. http://doi.org/10.1519/JSC.0000000000003016

Whitehead, S., Till, K., Weaving, D., Hunwicks, R., Pacey, R., & Jones, B. (2018) Whole, half and peak running demands during club and international youth rugby league match-play. *Science and Medicine in Football*, 3, 63–69. http://doi.org/10.1080/24733938.2018.1480058

Woods, C. T., Robertson, S., Sinclair, W. H., Till, K., Pearce, L., & Leicht, A. S. (2017a). A comparison of game-play characteristics between elite youth and senior Australian national rugby league competitions. *Journal of Science and Medicine in Sport*, 21, 626–630. http://doi.org/10.1016/j.jsams.2017.10.003

Woods, C. T., Sinclair, W., & Robertson, S. (2017b). Explaining match outcome and ladder position in the national rugby league using team performance indicators. *Journal of Science and Medicine in Sport*, 20, 1107–1111. http://doi.org/10.1016/j.jsams.2017.04.005

Zanin, M., Ranaweera, J., Darrall-Jones, J., Weaving, D., Till, K., & Roe, G. (2021). A systematic review of small sided games within rugby: Acute and chronic effects of constraints manipulation. *Journal of Sports Sciences*, 39, 1633–1660. https://doi.org/10.1080/02640414.2021.1891723

7
PROFILING PHYSICAL QUALITIES IN YOUTH RUGBY

The ProPQ Tool

Jonathon Weakley, Cameron Owen, Ben Jones and Kevin Till

Introduction

It is common knowledge that physical qualities are important for the development of the young rugby player. Well-developed physical qualities can improve on field performance (Cunningham et al., 2018) and support recovery following training and match play (Johnston et al., 2015), alongside reducing the risk of injury (Hislop et al., 2017). However, while physical qualities are widely acknowledged as important, it is essential to pay close attention to *how* these qualities are profiled (i.e., measured, analysed, reported, and evaluated). Such information can inform talent identification, evaluate players strengths and weaknesses, and help monitoring, feedback and goal setting to support the development of the young rugby player.

The measurement, analysis, reporting and evaluation of physical qualities is a process (Figure 7.1; adapted from McGuigan, 2014). Based on the physical demands of a sport; a valid, reliable and appropriate testing battery is designed. This testing battery is then used to collect data on players, which is then analysed (e.g., compared to norms, identify players strengths and weaknesses) and reported back to relevant stakeholders (e.g., players, coaches, academy managers). Based on this information, practitioners can evaluate the data to help make decisions to inform the training programme of their players. The testing battery can then be repeated to inform an ongoing needs analysis process and monitor the development of young players (Till et al., 2018a).

The purpose of this chapter is to summarise the research on the measurement of physical qualities in young rugby players. Whilst this chapter cannot review all assessments it will reflect the most commonly used methods for assessing anthropometrics and body composition, strength, power, linear speed, change of direction and agility, aerobic and anaerobic endurance, and movement skills

DOI: 10.4324/9781003104797-7

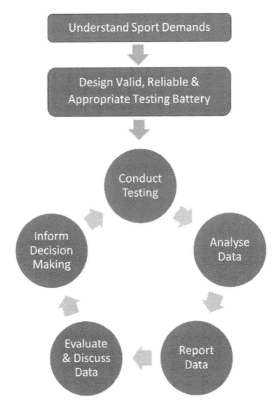

FIGURE 7.1 Process for Profiling Physical Qualities in Team Sports

due to the high physical demands of both rugby codes. The chapter will then showcase a practical application of how physical qualities are profiled within players aged 14–19 years across the United Kingdom that inform the training and development of young players.

Research Overview

Measuring Physical Qualities

A plethora of research studies are available that measure and present the physical qualities of youth rugby players. These are summarised in recent systematic reviews in rugby union (Owen et al., 2020) and league (Till et al., 2017). Traditionally, these studies present the physical qualities into six areas, including:

- Anthropometry, body composition and maturation
- Strength
- Power
- Speed

- Agility and change of direction
- Aerobic/anaerobic capacity

Movement competency is a further physical quality that has been recommended to be assessed (e.g., Ireton et al., 2019) but is lacking in the current literature.

To assess these physical qualities for rugby, researchers and practitioners are often faced with the decision of selecting from a range of available testing methods and protocols. These decisions can be influenced by several factors including the validity and reliability of a test, alongside equipment and resource availability. Therefore, it is worth considering how tests can be classified as field- or laboratory-based measures, when selecting an assessment. However, both have strengths and weaknesses.

Field-based fitness testing protocols involve assessing capacities under 'real-world' conditions (e.g., on the field) and have the advantages of greater specificity, require minimal equipment and have reduced associated costs (Drust & Gregson, 2013; Moore et al., 2022). However, these assessments may also provide less accurate measurements due to contextual factors that are related to the environment within which they are collected (e.g., surface, time of day, environmental conditions; Pyne et al., 2014). Furthermore, field-based methods often do not directly assess the physical quality but utilise proxy measures that are related to a certain physical quality (e.g., jump height and power). Contrasting this, laboratory-based assessments are performed in a controlled environment and generally provide more accurate and reliable results (Drust & Gregson, 2013). However, the access, cost and time constraints of using laboratory-based measures are often high and may have reduced practicality when working with squads of athletes. Finally, when selecting the different tests to form a battery, practitioners must carefully consider the validity and reliability of each test and outcome measure used. This is particularly important for practitioners who utilise testing information to make decisions regarding the selection and subsequent training sessions. Table 7.1 summarises a range of field and laboratory-based tests used within the rugby literature, which are explained in the following sections.

Anthropometrics and Body Composition

In the field, practitioners often measure height and body mass. This is likely due to the relative ease of assessing these characteristics. However, body composition of athletes can also be quantified. Due to the contact nature of the rugby codes,

---

Box 7.1

The validity of a test refers to its ability to measure what it is intended to measure (i.e., accuracy). While the reliability of a test refers to the tests ability to reproduce a given outcome over repeated attempts (i.e., repeatability). These fundamental scientific concepts allow researchers and practitioners to be confident in their monitoring and evaluation processes.

TABLE 7.1 Examples of Testing Methods Used in Youth Rugby and Measures of Reliability Reported in the Literature

Physical Characteristics	Test Type	Test	Reliability	Rugby League	Rugby Union
Anthropometry	Laboratory	Dual X-Ray absorptiometry (DXA)	Fat mass – CV = 0.82% Lean mass – CV = 0.52% Body fat % – CV = 0.82%		Delahunt et al. (2013), Harley et al. (2011)
	Field	Height		Till et al. (2016)	
		Body mass		Till et al. (2016)	Howard et al. (2016)
		Sum of skinfolds (four to nine sites)	Inter-rater – CV = 2.9%	Till et al. (2014)	Darrall-Jones et al. (2015)
		Bioelectrical impedance	Body fat % – CV = ~ 2%		Harries et al. (2016), Walsh et al. (2011), Loenneke et al. (2013)
Speed	Laboratory & Field	Sprint assessments	5m – ICC = 0.85; CV = 2.8% 10m – ICC = 0.94; CV = 1.4% 20m – ICC = 0.90; CV = 1.7% 40m – ICC = 0.96; CV = 1.2%	Till et al. (2014)	Darrall-Jones et al. (2016)
Agility	Lab Laboratory	Reactive agility (Video)		Serpell et al. (2010)	
Change of direction	Field	Agility 505	505 left – ICC = 0.83; CV = 2.1% 505 left – ICC = 0.86; CV = 2.4% 505 – ICC = 0.84; CV = 1.9%	Gabbett et al. (2009)	Darrall-Jones et al. (2015)
		Illinois agility test			Durandt et al. (2018)
		L-Run	ICC = 0.90; CV = 2.50%		Chiwaridzo et al. (2019a)

Strength	Laboratory	Isometric strength	Squat peak force – CV = 4% Isometric mid-thigh pull Peak force - ICC =0.97; CV = 3.5%	Tillin et al. (2013) Darrall-Jones et al. (2015)
	Field	Repetition max (e.g., 1-RM)	3RM back squat – CV = 2.5% 3RM bench press – CV = 1.8% 3RM chin up – CV = 3.7%	Till et al. (2014) Darrall-Jones et al. (2015), Weakley et al. (2017)
		Isometric mid-thigh pull dynamometer	ICC = 0.90; CV = 3.3%	Owen et al., Unpublished
Power	Laboratory	Force plate assessments	Jump height – ICC = 0.92; CV = 3.8% RSImod – ICC = 0.87; CV = 6.5% Peak concentric force – ICC = 0.96; CV = 2.7% Peak concentric power – ICC = 0.96; CV = 2.7% Concentric impulse – ICC = 0.98; CV = 1.9%	Darrall-Jones et al. (2015) McMahon et al. (2016)
		Wingate test		Pienaar and Coetzee (2013)
	Field	Jump tests	Jump mat Height with arms – CV = 6.2% Height without arms – CV= 5.9%	Dobbin et al. (2018) Wood et al. (2018)

(*Continued*)

TABLE 7.1 (Continued)

Physical Characteristics	Test Type	Test	Reliability	Rugby League	Rugby Union
		Medicine Ball Throws	ICC = 0.91; CV = 1.45		Chiwaridzo et al. (2019b), Howard et al. (2016), Argus et al. (2012)
		Watt bike			
		Bench throw			
Aerobic capacity	Field	Multi-stage fitness test	Levels – ICC = 0.90; CV = 3.1%	Till et al. (2013b)	Durandt et al. (2006)
		Yo-Yo intermittent recovery test (level 1)	Total distance – ICC = 0.98; CV = 4.6%	Till et al. (2015)	Darrall-Jones et al. (2016)
		30–15 intermittent fitness test	Final velocity – ICC = 0.96; CV = 1.6%		Darrall-Jones et al. (2015), Darrall-Jones et al. (2016),
Anaerobic endurance	Field	Shuttle tests			Grobler et al. (2017), Wood et al. (2018)
		Repeated sprint tests	ICC = 0.14; TEM = 19.5%	Gabbett (2013)	

ICC Interclass Correlation Coefficient; *CV* Coefficient of Variation; *TEM* Technical Error of Measurement.

the aim for players is to develop lean muscle mass whilst maintaining fat mass (Geeson-Brown et al., 2020). Anthropometry and body composition have been shown to differentiate between positional groups and playing levels in youth rugby (Owen et al., 2020; Till et al., 2017).

Height: Use a stadiometer measured to the nearest 0.1 cm with shoes removed prior to assessment and the head in the Frankfurt plane.

Body Mass: Use calibrated scales measured to the nearest 0.1 kg with the participant wearing minimal clothing (e.g., shorts and bra only). Ideally, measure at the same time of day on each occasion.

Body Composition: Dual-energy x-ray absorptiometry (DXA) is the gold standard assessment when undertaken in standardised conditions (e.g., fasted and euhydrated). Although this assessment method is the most accurate and would be recommended as ideal, the cost and availability of DXA limit its use. To circumvent this issue, alternative field-testing methods may be more applicable and includes the use of skinfold callipers and bioelectrical impedance analysis (BIA). The sum of skinfolds, using skinfold callipers, is the most common assessment within the youth rugby research (Owen et al., 2020; Till et al., 2017). While sum of skinfolds has been shown to positively correlate with DXA, it is important to note that experienced assessors are required to ensure measurements are reliable. Contrasting this, BIA can easily be used to provide an estimate of body composition. BIA has good test re-test reliability (interclass correlation coefficient [ICC]; 0.98; Loenneke et al., 2013), however, some factors (e.g., hydration status) and the prediction equation selected may result in differing outcomes.

When assessing anthropometry and body composition, caution is required due to the variability within and between athletes. Therefore, it is recommended that testing is completed by appropriately trained practitioners.

Strength

Strength testing in youth rugby players can typically be categorised into three groups; external load, body weight and isometric (Owen et al., 2020). External load measures, using isoinertial exercises (e.g., squat, bench press) are the most common in youth rugby research. These assessments allow common testing outcomes (e.g., one repetition [1RM] maximum) to be quantified although concerns can include technical competence for the lift. Instead, submaximal loads have also been used (e.g., 3RM, 5RM; Weakley et al., 2019). With external load assessments, relative strength is also presented, whereby an individual's body mass is considered in relation to the load lifted (i.e., 1RM/body mass [kg·kg^{-1}]; Darrall-Jones et al., 2015). Furthermore, when submaximal and maximal loads have been assessed, load-velocity profiles can be constructed for athletes to help quantify changes in strength and allow improved prescription across the training mesocycle (Orange et al., 2020; Weakley et al., 2021).

Isometric assessments, although less common, have increased in popularity in recent years (Owen et al., 2020). This assessment may be particularly useful for youth athletes due to the lower technical demands compared to an isoinertial test. Such exercises include the isometric mid-thigh pull (IMTP; Darrall-Jones, et al., 2015; Owen et al., 2022) and isometric squat (Tillin et al., 2013) showing reliable measures of strength (ICC > 0.95; coefficient of variation [CV] < 2.0%). However, isometric tests are usually performed on a force platform suggesting the expertise and equipment may be prohibitive in practice (McMaster et al., 2014). More recently, dynamometry IMTP assessments have been validated against force platforms, providing a quick and easier solution when working with larger groups of youth athletes (e.g., Till et al., 2018b).

Power

For the assessment of lower-body power, the countermovement jump (CMJ) has been the most widely implemented test, with a range of outcome measures reported including jump height (cm) and peak power (W; Owen et al., 2020; Till et al., 2017). Other jump variations have included the squat jump, loaded squat jump, horizontal broad jump, and triple hop. Alternatively, lower body power production has occasionally been assessed through a 6 s Watt bike peak power test (Howard et al., 2016).

Testing of upper body power output has been less common within youth rugby research, with power output being assessed during the bench throw at 60% of 1RM (Argus et al., 2012) and the plyometric push up (which demonstrated relatively poor reliability and sensitivity) (Roe et al., 2016). Other studies have utilised medicine ball throws, with distance recorded as the outcome measure (Till et al., 2011).

Linear Speed

The most common measures of linear speed for the youth rugby player are 10, 20, 30 and 40 m (Owen et al., 2020). However, distances as small as 5 m, and as far as 60 m have also been reported. These distances allow acceleration and top speed to be considered, with split times used to derive maximum speed. To enhance the applicability of findings to the practitioner, integrating mass (kg) with average velocity at a set distance to quantify initial and maximal sprint momentum may also be of benefit (Till et al., 2016), as players are often required to develop lean body mass in conjunction with speed. Furthermore, initial sprint momentum may be of interest due to this outcome measure utilising shorter distances (e.g. 10m) that are often completed in rugby. The equation to calculate momentum is: Momentum (kg·s−1) = velocity (m·s−1) × body mass (kg).

When testing speed, an important consideration for the practitioner is the equipment available. Whilst the use of fully automated timing systems, the gold standard, is not common in rugby environments, valid and reliable alternatives include timing gates and video analysis (Haugen & Buchheit, 2016). However, practitioners must use caution when using handheld devices, such as stopwatches, as these may provide inaccurate values, particularly over shorter distances. Finally, it is strongly advised that the starting method during sprint testing is standardised. This is due to the large amount of bias that can be introduced when different methods (e.g., foot switch *vs.* starting 50 cm behind a timing gate) are implemented (Duthie et al., 2006).

Agility and Change of Direction

The most commonly used change of direction tests within youth rugby are the agility 505, Illinois agility test, and L-run, which are all change of direction tests (Owen et al., 2020; Till et al., 2017). While agility assessments are less common, the 'Reactive Agility Test' has been shown to be able to distinguish between players of differing playing levels (Serpell et al., 2010).

Aerobic and Anaerobic Endurance

Aerobic and anaerobic capacities are important considerations for performance in rugby (Duthie et al., 2003; Johnston et al., 2014). Due to the limited practicality of laboratory-based treadmill testing, several different field-based running assessments have been used to quantify the aerobic capacity of youth rugby players. These include continuous (e.g., the multistage fitness-test [MSFT], Yo-Yo Endurance Level 1 [YYE1] and 1500 m time trial) and intermittent (e.g., Yo-Yo Intermittent Recovery Test Level [YYIR1] and 30–15 Intermittent Fitness Test [30–15IFT]) tests (Owen et al., 2020; Till et al., 2017). Data reported can include the number of 'levels', the total distance covered, amount of time and final running velocity have been reported. In recent years, greater sport specificity has been included in an anaerobic capacity test by utilising a prone YYIR1, whereby players start lying on their front (Dobbin et al., 2018).

Despite the importance of anaerobic endurance in rugby, limited information is available assessing this quality. The Wingate anaerobic test has previously been used to assess anaerobic power through peak power, average power, total work and fatigue rate. However, the practicality of this test is limited by specificity, time and resources (Pienaar & Coetzee, 2013). Field running protocols include shuttle tests (250 m, Grobler et al., 2017; 150 m, Wood et al., 2018) and repeated sprint assessments (12 × 20 m sprints; Gabbett, 2013). However, validity and reliability of these tests within adolescent cohorts are still unknown which may reduce the ability for practitioners to accurately detect changes in anaerobic capacity.

Movement Skills

Movement assessments help to evaluate the fundamental actions that underpin training programmes (Ireton et al., 2019). While it may be favourable to use well-established assessments (e.g., the Athletic Ability Assessment; Ireton et al.,

2019), sport-specific assessments have also been used for both rugby league (Morley et al., 2015) and union (Parsonage et al., 2014).

Practical Applications

The above section has summarised the common tests used to quantify the physical qualities of youth rugby players with a wide variety of tests used. One common challenge when reviewing the literature is the lack of consensus of assessment methods which means establishing comparative data is difficult. A recommendation from the research is to develop and use a national standardised fitness testing battery (Owen et al., 2020; Till et al., 2017).

> **Box 7.2**
>
> The benefits of a national standardised fitness testing battery are that it allows players across a nation to be compared and standardised to a large set of comparative data rather than using small, club-based samples alone. In addition, the design and implementation of a national standardised testing battery allow players to be monitored longitudinally, potentially over multiple years, to monitor their physical development, inform their training programmes and establish an ongoing tool to inform the physical development of youth rugby players.

This practical application summarises the national standardised physical qualities testing employed by the Rugby Football League (RFL) for measuring, analysing, evaluating and reporting the physical qualities of youth rugby league players aged 14–19 years within the United Kingdom. Initial work was done by the University of Chester (see Dobbin et al., 2018, 2019) and the project is now led by Leeds Beckett University on behalf of the RFL which has resulted in the ProPQ (Profiling Physical Qualities) Tool. An in depth account of the development of this testing battery and ProPQ Tool has recently been published (Till et al., 2022).

Designing the Assessment

The national standardised fitness testing assessment was designed to be conducted by all 12 RFL academies for players aged 14–19 years. Therefore, this assessment needed to be scientifically designed so that it represented the physical qualities required for rugby league whilst being valid and reliable for measuring physical qualities. In addition to this, the assessment needed to be appropriate and practically designed so that all RFL academies could be tested whilst not affecting their usual training programme. Therefore, this required designing an assessment that could assess up to 30 players within an approximate 90-minute period.

Based on the above, the RFL national standardised fitness testing assessment included:

- Player Information – Date of Birth, Playing Position, Club
- Anthropometry – Height, Sitting Height and Body Mass
- Body Composition – Measured via BIA and reporting body fat percentage.
- Strength – IMTP performed on a custom-built dynamometer reporting Peak Force (N) and relative Peak Force (N·kg^{-1})
- Power – CMJ performed on a force platform reporting jump height (cm) and Peak Power (W)
- Speed – 10, 20 and 40 m sprint performed with Brower Timing Gates from a mark 0.5 m behind the first timing gate. Sprint times were reported to the nearest 0.01 s and momentum was calculated by body mass multiplied by 10 m velocity (k·gs^{-1})
- Aerobic Capacity – Prone YYIR1 test was performed with distance completed reported in metres

This fitness assessment covered the main physical qualities required for rugby league performance using a testing battery that was scientifically valid and reliable but also practically appropriate. It also provided RFL academies the opportunity to conduct their own assessments of other physical qualities where there is more variation in assessment methods in the research literature and which practitioners may prefer in their own practice (e.g., change of direction or agility tests; isoinertial strength tests).

Conducting the Assessments

The national standardised fitness assessment was undertaken by a project lead from Leeds Beckett University. Therefore, all assessments were controlled, supervised and overseen by one individual across all 12 RFL academies to ensure consistency in the way that the tests were conducted. Additional testing support was provided by staff and students from Leeds Beckett University alongside physical development staff from each academy.

Testing was undertaken at three of four time points per season (i.e., Pre-Season, October-November; End of Pre-Season, February-March; Mid-Season, June-July; End of Season, September-October). Players were assessed in their age groups that they trained and competed (i.e., Under 16s; Under 18s; Reserve Players). Testing was conducted in a standardised order, which started indoors whereby players undertook anthropometric and body composition, IMTP and CMJ. Players then undertook the 40 m sprint and prone YYIR1 on an outdoor 3G surface. Prior to all assessments, players undertook a standardised warm up and were fully briefed on all assessment protocols. Height, body mass, body composition was measured once, IMTP, CMJ and 40m sprint was measured twice, and the prone Yo-Yo was measured once. Players best attempt on each assessment was used as their score.

Data Analysis, Reporting and Evaluation

From consultation with key stakeholders (i.e., academy staff including manager, coaches and strength and conditioning coaches) it was identified that for academies to 'buy-in' to the national testing that they needed a reporting function that allowed them to effectively analyse and evaluate their players physical performance. Therefore, this was established by the development of the ProPQ Tool designed in Google Data Studio. The profiling tool allowed all players and teams physical qualities to be compared against all other players. To achieve this, a two-stage interactive online profiling tool was designed and disseminated to all academy staff following all testing protocols. This analysis tool was developed based upon the data collected across all academy players over multiple years. The two-stage reporting process included:

Principal Component Analysis

The first stage of the profiling tool was to provide a simple summary of where an individual players physical performance (and development) was in relation to all academy rugby league players. To achieve this, a principal component analysis (PCA) was undertaken based upon the research in youth rugby players (Till et al., 2016). A PCA simplifies a complex data set (i.e., all data collected) into a simpler data set, known as principal components. Based on the physical qualities data collected in rugby, two principal components were identified; (1) Strength and Mass, and (2) Speed and Power. Such analysis allows a coach to identify where a player is in their overall physical development. Figure 7.2 presents the PCA for one player (player X, red dot) compared to all players (blue dots). From this analysis, it can be deemed that player X performs above average for 'Speed and Power' but is below average for 'Strength and Mass'. Such information could inform coaches that strength development is a key physical focus for this player.

Further analysis can be undertaken with the ProPQ Tool, which allows players to be compared by into further categories including playing position, age group, date of testing and compare specific players. Such analysis allows further interpretation of a player's performance allowing comparisons against smaller cohorts of players. For example, Figure 7.3 presents a comparison of player X with player Y in the Under 16s age group and for 'Backs' positions. This demonstrates a reduced comparative dataset (blue dots). The figure shows player Y has greater 'Power and Speed' and 'Strength and Mass' than player X. When using these graphs, the players should be aiming to move towards the top right quadrant of the graph to represent a greater overall physical performance.

Longitudinal Player Analysis According to Chronological Age

In addition to the PCA, a further function of the profiling tool is the ability to track players physical development longitudinally (i.e., over time) according to each test. Therefore, using the data collected on all players, rolling averages for

Profiling Physical Qualities 119

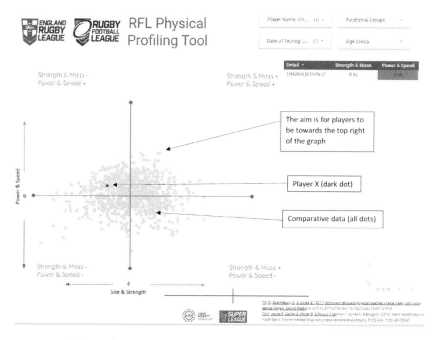

FIGURE 7.2 Principal Component Analysis for Evaluating Physical Performance

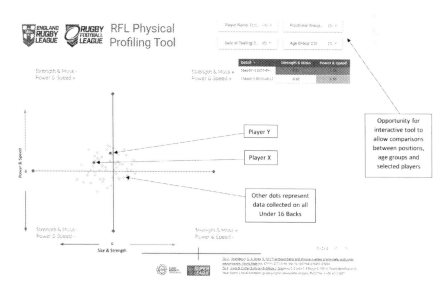

FIGURE 7.3 Principal Component Analysis for Comparison between Two Players Using Interactive Settings

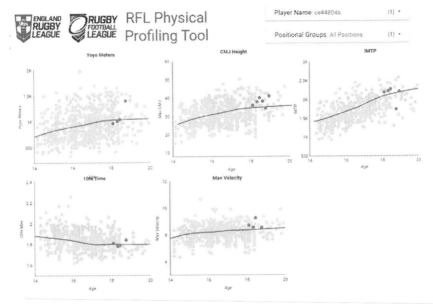

FIGURE 7.4 Longitudinal Analysis according to Chronological Age for Strength, Power, Speed and Aerobic Capacity

each measure for chronological age were established to enhance data interpretation (Till et al., 2018a). This analysis method builds upon previous methods of classifying performance into annual age groups and allows a player to be evaluated according to their specific chronological age (e.g., 15.01 *vs.* 15.99 years rather than Under 16s). Being able to track performance over time relative to the average for age-related gains is also a key aspect of this analysis. Figure 7.4 shows player Z's performance in the prone YYIR1, CMJ, IMTP, 10 m sprint and max velocity according to their chronological age across five timepoints. For YYIR1 performance was on average until the most recent test, whereby a large improvement in aerobic capacity was evident. CMJ performance was above average on most occasions and improved across the timepoints. IMTP and 10 m sprint performance was on average with little change across the period. Max velocity was on or above average across the period. Such analysis provides greater detail and insight into a player's development over time in relation to the comparative data, which can be used by strength and conditioning coaches for specific programme design.

The ProPQ Tool advances on previous data analysis and reporting methods common within sport science (e.g., radar plots, Till et al., 2013b; Total Score of Athleticism, Turner et al., 2019). Its advantages are that it;

1 Allows player comparisons against a large sample of normative data
2 Simplifies an overall physical performance and development of players using PCA analysis

3 Allows individual player tracking over time against a rolling average for chronological age rather than using standardised age group comparisons
4 Allows interactive comparisons between positions, age groups, dates of testing and players, and
5 Provides different 'levels' of data for different staff and stakeholders within clubs.

Such a tool should inform and advance the interpretation of data analysis of the physical qualities of youth rugby players, which in turn would support practitioner decision-making and discussion for enhancing the programmes of youth rugby players as presented in Figure 7.1.

Key Take Home Messages

- Profiling physical qualities provides objective information to inform talent identification, profile strengths and weaknesses, evaluate and prescribe training of youth rugby players.
- The process of profiling physical qualities involves seven steps; (1) understanding the sport demands; (2) designing a valid, reliable and appropriate testing battery; (3) conducting the testing; (4) analysing the data; (5) reporting the data; (6) evaluating and discussing the data; and (7) using the data to inform decision making.
- Designing a testing battery could include field and laboratory measures that are influenced by the validity and reliability of the measures alongside the appropriateness and resources in place to undertake the assessment.
- A testing battery in the youth rugby codes should consider the assessment of anthropometry and body composition, strength, power, speed, agility and change of direction, aerobic and anaerobic capacities and movement skills. Considering absolute and relative measures of each is an important consideration.
- The development of a national standardised fitness assessment is recommended. This allows players to be measured using standardised assessment measures and protocols and allows comparisons against a large sample of normative data rather than club only data.
- The development of an online physical profiling tool (e.g., ProPQ Tool) may have benefits for multiple practitioners within youth rugby. These benefits include (1) the simplification of an overall physical performance score using PCA analysis, (2) longitudinal and individual player tracking against a rolling average, (3) interactive comparisons between subgroups (e.g., position) and (4) provision of different 'levels' of data for different staff and stakeholders within clubs.
- Such information enhances coaching staff to critique, monitor and evaluate player development and inform their decision-making for the physical and holistic development programmes implemented with young rugby players.

References

Argus, C., Gill, N., & Keogh, J. (2012). Characterization of the differences in strength and power between different levels of competition in rugby union athletes. *Journal of Strength and Conditioning Research, 26*, 2698–2704. https://doi.org/10.1519/JSC.0b013e318241382a

Chiwaridzo, M., Ferguson, G., & Smits-Engelsman, B. (2019a). Anthropometric, physiological characteristics and rugby-specific game skills discriminating Zimbabwean under-16 male adolescent rugby players by level of competition. *BMJ Open Sport & Exercise Medicine, 5*, e000576. https://doi.org/10.1136/bmjsem-2019-000576

Chiwaridzo, M., Ferguson, G., & Smits-Engelsman, B. (2019b). Qualities or skills discriminating under 19 rugby players by playing standards: A comparative analysis of elite, sub-elite and non-rugby players using the SCRuM test battery. *BMC Research Notes, 12*, 536. https://doi.org/10.1186/s13104-019-4563-y

Cunningham, D., Shearer, D., Drawer, S., Pollard, B., Cook, C., Bennett, M., Russell, M., & Kilduff, L. (2018). Relationships between physical qualities and key performance indicators during matchplay in senior international rugby union players. *PLoS One, 13*, e0202811. https://doi.org/10.1371/journal.pone.0202811

Darrall-Jones, J., Jones, B., & Till, K. (2015). Anthropometric and physical profiles of English academy rugby union players. *Journal of Strength and Conditioning Research, 29*, 2086–2096. https://doi.org/10.1519/JSC.0000000000000872

Darrall-Jones, J., Jones, B., & Till, K. (2016). Anthropometric, sprint, and high-intensity running profiles of English academy rugby union players by position. *Journal of Strength and Conditioning Research, 30*, 1348–1358. https://doi.org/10.1519/JSC.0000000000001234

Delahunt, E., Byrne, R., Doolin, R., McInerney, R., Ruddock, C., & Green, B. (2013). Anthropometric profile and body composition of Irish adolescent rugby union players aged 16–18. *Journal of Strength and Conditioning Research, 27*, 3252–3258. https://doi.org/10.1519/JSC.0b013e3182915ea6

Dobbin, N., Highton, J., Moss, L., & Twist, C. (2019). The discriminant validity of a standardized testing battery and its ability to differentiate anthropometric and physical characteristics between youth, academy, and senior professional rugby league players. *International Journal of Sports Physiology and Performance, 14*, 1110–1116. https://doi.org/10.1123/ijspp.2018-0519

Dobbin, N., Hunwicks, R., Highton, J., & Twist, C. (2018). A reliable testing battery for assessing physical qualities of elite academy rugby league players. *Journal of Strength and Conditioning Research, 32*, 3232–3238. https://doi.org/10.1519/JSC.0000000000002280

Drust, B., & Gregson, W. (2013). Fitness Testing. In M. Williams, P. Ford, & B Frost (Eds.), *Science and soccer* (pp. 55–76). Routledge.

Durandt, J., du Toit, S., Borresen, J., Hew-Butler, T., Masimla, H., Jakoet, I., & Lambert, M. (2006). Fitness and body composition profiling of elite junior South Africa rugby players. *South African Journal of Sports Medicine, 18*, 38–45. https://doi.org/10.17159/2413-3108/2006/v18i2a242

Durandt, J., Green, M., Masimla, H., & Lambert, M. (2018). Changes in body mass, stature and BMI in South African elite U18 rugby players from different racial groups from 2002–2012. *Journal of Sports Sciences, 36*, 477–484. https://doi.org/10.1080/02640414.2017.1317103

Duthie, G., Pyne, D., & Hooper, S. (2003). Applied physiology and game analysis of rugby union. *Sports Medicine, 33*, 973–991. https://doi.org/10.2165/00007256-200333130-00003

Duthie, G., Pyne, D., Ross, A., Livingstone, S., & Hooper, S. (2006). The reliability of ten-meter sprint time using different starting techniques. *Journal of Strength and Conditioning Research, 20*, 246–251. https://doi.org/10.1519/R-17084.1

Gabbett, T. (2013). Influence of playing standard on the physical demands of professional rugby league. *Journal of Sports Sciences, 31*, 1125–1138. https://doi.org/10.1080/02640414.2013.773401

Gabbett, T., Kelly, J., Ralph, S., & Driscoll, D. (2009). Physiological and anthropometric characteristics of junior elite and sub-elite rugby league players, with special reference to starters and non-starters. *Journal of Science and Medicine in Sport, 12*, 215–222. https://doi.org/10.1016/j.jsams.2007.06.008

Gabbett, T., & Seibold, A. (2013) Relationship between tests of physical qualities, team selection, and physical match performance in semiprofessional rugby league players. *Journal of Strength and Conditioning Research, 27*, 3259–3265. https://doi.org/10.1519/JSC.0b013e31828d6219

Geeson-Brown, T., Jones, B., Till, K., Chantler, S., & Deighton, K. (2020). Body composition differences by age and playing standard in male rugby union and rugby league: A systematic review and meta-analysis. *Journal of Sports Sciences* [Online], Preprint. doi: 10.1080/02640414.2020.1775990

Grobler, T., Shaw, B., & Coopoo, Y. (2017). Influence of physical fitness parameters on relative age effect on amateur secondary school rugby union players. *South African Journal for Research in Sport, Physical Education & Recreation, 39*, 29–39.

Harley, J., Hind, K., & O'Hara, J. (2011). Three-compartment body composition changes in elite rugby league players during a Super League season, measured by dual-energy x-ray absorptiometry. *Journal of Strength and Conditioning Research, 25*, 1024–1029. https://doi.org/10.1519/JSC.0b013e3181cc21fb

Harries, S., Lubans, D., & Callister, R. (2016). Comparison of resistance training progression models on maximal strength in sub-elite adolescent rugby union players. *Journal of Science and Medicine in Sport, 19*, 163–169. https://doi.org/10.1016/j.jsams.2015.01.007

Haugen, T., & Buchheit, M. (2016). Sprint running performance monitoring: methodological and practical considerations. *Sports Medicine, 46*, 641–656. https://doi.org/10.1007/s40279-015-0446-0

Hislop, M., Stokes, K., Williams, S., McKay, C., England, M., Kemp, S., & Trewartha, G. (2017). Reducing musculoskeletal injury and concussion risk in schoolboy rugby players with a pre-activity movement control exercise programme: A cluster randomised controlled trial. *British Journal of Sports Medicine, 51*, 1140–1146. https://doi.org/10.1136/bjsports-2016-097434

Howard, S., Cumming, S., Atkinson, M., & Malina, R. (2016). Biological maturity-associated variance in peak power output and momentum in academy rugby union players. *European Journal of Sport Science, 16*, 972–980. https://doi.org/10.1080/17461391.2016.1205144

Ireton, M., Till, K., Weaving, D., & Jones, B. (2019). Differences in the movement skills and physical qualities of elite senior and academy rugby league players. *Journal of Strength and Conditioning Research, 33*, 1328–1338. https://doi.org/10.1519/JSC.0000000000002016

Johnston, R. D., Gabbett, T. J., & Jenkins, D. G. (2014). Applied sport science of rugby league. *Sports Medicine, 44*, 1087–1100. https://doi.org/10.1007/s40279-014-0190-x

Johnston, R. D., Gabbett, T. J., Jenkins, D. G., & Hulin, B. T. (2015). Influence of physical qualities on post-match fatigue in rugby league players. *Journal of Science and Medicine in Sport, 18*, 209–213.

Loenneke, J., Barnes, J., Wilson, J., Lowery, R., Isaacs, M., & Pujol, T. (2013). Reliability of field methods for estimating body fat. *Clinical Physiology and Functional Imaging*, *33*, 405–408. https://doi.org/10.1111/cpf.12045

McGuigan, M. (2014). Evaluating athletic capacities. In: D. G. Joyce, & D. Lewindon, (Eds.), *High-performance training for sports* (pp. 3–15). Champaign, IL: Human Kinatics.

McMahon, J., Murphy, S., & Comfort, P. (2016). Countermovement jump phase characteristics of senior and academy rugby league players. *International Journal of Sports Physiology and Performance*, *12*, 803–811. https://doi.org/10.1123/ijspp.2016-0467

McMaster, D., Gill, N., Cronin, J., & Mcguigan, M. (2014). A brief review of strength and ballistic assessment methodologies in sport. *Sports Medicine*, *44*, 603–623. https://doi.org/10.1007/s40279-014-0145-2

Moore, D. A., Jones, B., Weakley, J., Whitehead, S., & Till, K. (2022). The field and resistance training loads of academy rugby league players during a preseason: Comparisons across playing positions. *PLoS ONE*, *17*, e0272817. https://doi.org/10.1371/journal.pone.0272817

Morley, D., Pyke, D., & Till, K. (2015). An investigation into the use of a movement assessment protocol for under-14 rugby league players in a talent development environment. *International Journal of Sports Science and Coaching*, *10*, 623–636. https://doi.org/10.1260/2F1747-9541.10.4.623

Orange, S., Metcalfe, J., Robinson, A., Applegarth, M., & Liefeith, A. (2020). Effects of in-season velocity- versus percentage-based training in academy rugby league players. *International Journal of Sports Physiology and Performance*, *15*, 554–561. https://doi.org/10.1123/ijspp.2019-0058

Owen, C., Till, K., Phibbs, P., Read, D.J., Weakley, J., Atkinson, M., Cross, M., Kemp, S., Sawczuk, T., Stokes, K., & Williams, S. (2022). A multidimensional approach to identifying the physical qualities of male English regional academy rugby union players; Considerations of position, chronological age, relative age and maturation. *European Journal of Sport Science*, Preprint, 1–11. https://doi.org/10.1080/17461391.2021.2023658

Owen, C., Till, K., Weakley, J., & Jones, B. (2020). Testing methods and physical qualities of male age grade rugby union players: A systematic review. *PLoS One*, *15*, e0233796. https://doi.org/10.1371/journal.pone.0233796

Parsonage, J., Williams, R., Rainer, P., McKeown, I., & Williams, M. (2014). Assessment of conditioning-specific movement tasks and physical fitness measures in talent identified under 16-year-old rugby union players. *Journal of Strength and Conditioning Research*, *28*, 1497–1506. https://doi.org/10.1519/JSC.0000000000000298

Pienaar, C. & Coetzee, B. (2013). Changes in selected physical, motor performance and anthropometric components of university-level rugby players after one microcycle of a combined rugby conditioning and plyometric training program. *Journal of Strength and Conditioning Research*, *27*, 398–415. https://doi.org/10.1519/JSC.0b013e31825770ea

Pyne, D., Spencer, M., & Mujika, I. (2014). Improving the value of fitness testing for football. *International Journal of Sports Physiology and Performance*, *9*, 511–514. https://doi.org/10.1123/ijspp.2013-0453

Roe, G., Darrall-Jones, J., Till, K., Phibbs, P., Read, D., Weakley, J., & Jones, B. (2016). Between-days reliability and sensitivity of common fatigue measures in rugby players. *International Journal of Sports Physiology and Performance*, *11*, 581–586. https://doi.org/10.1123/ijspp.2015-0413

Serpell, B., Ford, M., & Young, W. (2010). The development of a new test of agility for rugby league. *Journal of Strength and Conditioning Research*, *24*, 3270–3277. https://doi.org/10.1519/JSC.0b013e3181b60430

Till, K., Cobley, S., O'Hara, J., Brightmore, A., Cooke, C., & Chapman, C. (2011). Using anthropometric and performance characteristics to predict selection in junior UK rugby league players. *Journal of Science and Medicine in Sport, 14*, 264–269. https://doi.org/10.1016/j.jsams.2011.01.006

Till, K., Cobley, S., O'Hara, J., Chapman, C., & Cooke, C. (2013a). A longitudinal evaluation of anthropometric and fitness characteristics in junior rugby league players considering playing position and selection level. *Journal of Science and Medicine in Sport, 16*, 438–443. https://doi.org/10.1016/j.jsams.2012.09.002

Till, K., Cobley, S., O'Hara, J., Chapman, C., & Cooke, C. (2013b). An individualized longitudinal approach to monitoring the dynamics of growth and fitness development in adolescent athletes. *Journal of Strength and Conditioning Research, 27*, 1313–1321. https://doi.org/10.1519/JSC.0b013e31828a1ea7

Till, K., Collins, N., McCormack, S., Owen, C., Weaving, D., & Jones, B. (2022). Challenges and solutions for physical testing in sport: The ProPQ (Profiling Physical Qualities) tool. *Strength & Conditioning Journal*. https://doi.org/10.1519/SSC.0000000000000710

Till, K., Jones, B., Darrall-Jones, J., Emmonds, S., & Cooke, C. (2015). Longitudinal development of anthropometric and physical characteristics within academy rugby league players. *Journal of Strength and Conditioning Research, 29*, 1713–1722. https://doi.org/10.1519/JSC.0000000000000792

Till, K., Jones, B., & Geeson-Brown, T. (2016). Do physical qualities influence the attainment of professional status within elite 16–19 year old rugby league players? *Journal of Science and Medicine in Sport, 19*, 585–589. https://doi.org/10.1016/j.jsams.2015.07.001

Till, K., Jones, B., O'Hara, J., Barlow, M., Brightmore, A., Lees, M., & Hind, K. (2016). Three-compartment body composition in academy and senior rugby league players. *International Journal of Sports Physiology and Performance, 11*, 191–196. https://doi.org/10.1123/ijspp.2015-0048

Till, K., Morris, R., Emmonds, S., Jones, B., & Cobley, S. (2018a). Enhancing the evaluation and interpretation of fitness testing data within youth athletes. *Strength and Conditioning Journal, 40*, 24–33. https://doi.org/10.1519/SSC.0000000000000414

Till, K., Morris, R., Stokes, K., Trewartha, G., Twist, C., Dobbin, N., Hunwicks, R., & Jones, B. (2018b). Validity of an isometric midthigh pull dynamometer in male youth athletes. *Journal of Strength and Conditioning Research, 32*, 490–493. https://doi.org/10.1519/JSC.0000000000002324

Till, K., Scantlebury, S., & Jones, B. (2017). Anthropometric and physical qualities of elite male youth rugby league players. *Sports Medicine, 47*, 2171–2186. https://doi.org/10.1007/s40279-017-0745-8

Till, K., Tester, E., Jones, B., Emmonds, S., Fahey, J., & Cooke, C. (2014). Anthropometric and physical characteristics of English academy rugby league players. *Journal of Strength and Conditioning Research, 28*, 319–327. https://doi.org/10.1519/JSC.0b013e3182a73c0e

Tillin, N., Pain, M., & Folland, J. (2013). Explosive force production during isometric squats correlates with athletic performance in rugby union players. *Journal of Sports Sciences, 31*, 66–76. https://doi.org/10.1080/02640414.2012.720704

Turner, A., Jones, B., Stewart, P., Bishop, C., Parmar, N., Chavda, S., & Read, P. (2019). Total score of athleticism: Holistic athlete profiling to enhance decision-making. *Strength and Conditioning Journal, 41*, 91–101. https://doi.org/10.1519/SSC.0000000000000506

Walsh, M., Cartwright, L., Corish, C., Sugrue, S., & Wood-Martin, R. (2011). The body composition, nutritional knowledge, attitudes, behaviors, and future education needs of senior schoolboy rugby players in Ireland. *International Journal of Sport Nutrition and Exercise Metabolism*, *21*, 365–376. https://doi.org/10.1123/ijsnem.21.5.365

Weakley, J., Till, K., Darrall-Jones, J., Roe, G. A. B., Phibbs, P., Read, D., & Jones, B. (2017). The influence of resistance training experience on the between-day reliability of commonly used strength measures in male youth athletes. *Journal of Strength and Conditioning Research*, *31*, 2005–2010. https://doi.org/10.1519/JSC.0000000000001883

Weakley, J., Morrison, M., García-Ramos, A., Johnston, R., James, L., & Cole, M. H. (2021). The validity and reliability of commercially available resistance training monitoring devices: A systematic review. *Sports Medicine*, *51*, 443–502. https://doi.org/10.1007/s40279-020-01382-w

Weakley, J., Till, K., Darrall-Jones, J., Roe, G. A. B., Phibbs, P., Read, D., & Jones, B. (2019). Strength and conditioning practices in adolescent rugby players: Relationship with changes in physical qualities. *Journal of Strength and Conditioning Research*, *33*, 2361–2369. https://doi.org/10.1519/JSC.0000000000001828

Wood, D., Coughlan, G., & Delahunt, E. (2018). Fitness profiles of elite adolescent Irish rugby union players. *Journal of Strength and Conditioning Research*, *32*, 105–112. https://doi.org/10.1519/JSC.0000000000001694

8
STRENGTH AND CONDITIONING TRAINING FOR PHYSICAL DEVELOPMENT

Jonathon Weakley, Josh Darrall-Jones and Nicholas Gill

Introduction

Strength and conditioning training is essential for rugby players of all ages (Coutts et al., 2004; Moore et al., 2022; Till et al., 2015). At the highest level, professional rugby players demonstrate extremely well-developed physical qualities which allow them to evade or physically dominate their opposition (Smart et al., 2014). To enable this to occur, a range of strength and conditioning training methods are used (Jones et al., 2016). These methods are often focussed upon improving fundamental physical qualities including lean body mass, strength, power, speed, change of direction (CoD) ability, and aerobic capacity (Jones et al., 2016; Smart & Gill, 2013). However, when compared to adults, the youth rugby player has different training requirements.

As youth rugby players get older, it is clear that there is an increasing emphasis placed upon their physical development (Darrall-Jones et al., 2015). Consequently, it is important to carefully consider the training methods that are implemented to support this physical development. The most common methods of enhancing physical development include resistance training and aerobic conditioning, which have both been shown to promote favourable improvements in physical qualities (Coutts et al., 2004; Galvin et al., 2013; Smart & Gill, 2013). However, due to the countless combination of acute training variables (e.g., intensity, volume, frequency) and additional considerations (e.g., external supervision, resistance mode), it is important to understand how these factors influence physical development. Furthermore, it is clear that some training methods may result in greater improvements. This chapter will provide an overview of the research literature evaluating strength and conditioning training interventions used within young rugby players and the physical performance outcomes that can be expected by manipulating the acute training variables in youth rugby players.

DOI: 10.4324/9781003104797-8

The chapter will then present strength and conditioning practical applications for working with young rugby players for enhancing physical development.

Research Overview

There has been substantial investigation into the optimal methods to develop physical qualities in youth rugby players. Research has primarily assessed the effects of resistance training and conditioning interventions on these qualities. In the following section, a brief overview of the effects of these two different training methods in youth rugby union and rugby league players is provided.

Resistance Training

Influence on Body Mass

Three studies have investigated the influence of resistance training on changes in body mass and body composition in youth rugby players (Coutts et al., 2004; Harries et al., 2016; Smart & Gill, 2013). Across medium-term training programmes (i.e., 12–15 weeks), both Smart and Gill (2013) and Coutts et al. (2004) have demonstrated that irrespective of supervision, body mass increased by 2–4%. Additionally, Harries et al. (2016) showed that the implementation of different linear and daily undulating periodisation models (see Box 8.1) are associated with slightly smaller changes in body mass of 1–2%. However, it should also be noted that the control group, who completed no resistance training and were approximately one year younger than the intervention group, showed similar changes in body mass compared to both periodised intervention groups (i.e., ~2.4%; Harries et al., 2016). These results suggest resistance training programmes delivered over medium-term durations (~12 weeks) may not cause substantial changes in body mass in youth rugby players beyond what is expected with normal growth and maturation. This is likely due to body mass being influenced by a range of factors including overall training load and calorific intake (Costello et al., 2018). Consequently, while resistance training is widely acknowledged as an important consideration when attempting to increase body mass and improve body composition, it is prudent to account for additional factors (e.g., nutrition) that can also play a substantial role.

> **Box 8.1 Periodisation: What's Best for the Young Rugby Player?**
>
> Periodisation is a fundamental tenet of strength and conditioning and is the logical and systematic sequencing of training factors in order to optimise specific training outcomes at pre-determined time points. Many different forms of periodisation exist, with linear, block and daily undulating methods most commonly used in youth rugby (Coutts et al., 2004; Harries et al., 2016, 2018).

> Linear periodisation often refers to the gradual reduction in volume and increase in relative intensity (as a percentage of one repetition max [1RM]) across a macrocycle. Alternatively, block periodisation involves the strategic targeting of a small set of physical qualities (e.g., strength) in a systematic fashion and is typified by 'blocks' of disparate volume and intensities. Finally, daily undulating periodisation involves the programming of different intensities and volumes within a microcycle and attempts to develop/maintain multiple physical qualities (e.g., strength, power, hypertrophy) at the same time.
>
> While it is undeniable that systematic planning and sequencing of resistance training is of importance, the differences in periodisation methods for youth rugby players appear to be very small. Consequently, greater emphasis should be placed on providing adequate supervision and ensuring appropriate volumes and intensities are completed.

Influence on Strength and Power

Eight studies have investigated the effects of resistance training on upper and lower body strength and power in youth rugby players (Bourgeois et al., 2017; Coutts et al., 2004; Dobbs et al., 2015; Harries et al., 2016; Orange et al., 2019; Rivière et al., 2017; Smart & Gill, 2013; Speirs et al., 2016; see Table 8.1). While a range of different resistance training methods (e.g., auto-regulatory, different periodisation models) have been reported, it is clear that the largest improvements occur when youth rugby players are provided supervision from qualified professionals when compared to no supervision at all (Coutts et al., 2004; Smart & Gill, 2013). Comparisons in both youth rugby union and rugby league have demonstrated changes in strength two–five times greater when supervision is provided (Coutts et al., 2004; Smart & Gill, 2013). These superior adaptations are likely due to the provision of qualified, motivating staff that facilitate the appropriate selection of load and exercise techniques and align with position statements on youth resistance training (e.g., Faigenbaum et al. 2009; Lloyd et al. 2014). Additionally, it should be noted that completing a sufficient amount of training volume each week (measured in total tonnage) is an important consideration for strength and power development and can be a simple method of monitoring training loads (Weakley et al., 2019). Contrasting this, the periodisation model used may play a much smaller role in strength and power development with both linear and daily undulating periodisation strategies inducing similar adaptations over a 12-week period (Harries et al., 2016). Finally, the method of prescription of load likely causes similar outcomes despite differences in acute training fatigue and kinetic and kinematic outputs (Orange et al., 2019). It should be noted though, that the use of maximal strength testing data during prescription (i.e., one repetition maximum; 1RM) may require participants to lift heavier loads

TABLE 8.1 Training Programmes of Studies that have Investigated Resistance Training in Youth Rugby Players

Authors	Subject Description	Study duration, Frequency, & Tempo	Sets	Repetitions	Training Intensity	Exercises Used
Bourgeois et al. (2017)	*All participants:* Age: 15.0 ± 0.9 Height: 1.8 ± 0.1m Mass: 80.2 ± 15.3 kg	**Duration:** 6 weeks Frequency: three sessions per week Repetition tempo: 3:0:X	**Sets:** Weeks 1–6: three for all exercises	**Repetitions:** Main exercises Weeks 1–2: 8–10 Week 3: 6 Week 4–5: 8–10 Week 6: 6–8 Assistant exercises: Weeks 1–2: 5–8 Week 3: 6–8 Week 4–5: 6–10 Week 6: 4–10	**Intensity:?**	**Exercises:** BS, Hexagon-bar squat, BP, Standing overhead press, FS, BB backward lunge, RFESS, KB lateral lunge, Stiff-legged DL, DB incline BP, BB pullover, Unilateral DB BP, BB inverted row, BoR, UR, Prone KB rows, DB shoulder complex
Coutts et al. (2004)	*All participants:* **Age:** 16.7 ± 1.1 y *Supervised group* **Height:** 168.0 ± 6.4 **Mass:** 74.7 ± 8.6 kg **Resistance training history:** 0.26 ± 0.38 y	**Duration:** 12 weeks **Frequency:** three sessions p/w Repetition tempo:?	**Sets:** Number of sets in total: Week 1: 17 Week 2: 17 Week 3: 20 Week 4: 22 Week 5: 22	**Repetitions:** Week 1: 16 Week 2: 14 Week 3: 13 Week 4: 12 Week 5: 11 Week 6: 10 Week 7: 9	**Intensity:** SUP & UNSUP groups: Week 1: 55.0% of 1RM Week 2: 60.0% of 1RM Week 3: 62.5% of 1RM Week 4: 68.5% of 1RM Week 5: 71.0% of 1RM Week 6: 73.5% of 1RM	**Exercises:** *Weeks 1–6* BS, Wide grip pulldown, BP, Military press, Dips, Abdominal crunches, BE *Weeks 7–12*

Study	Participants	Protocol	Sets/Reps/Intensity	Exercises
Dobbs et al. (Ahead of Print)	Unsupervised group: Height: 170.0 ± 5.4 Mass: 77.9 ± 8.7 Resistance training history: 0.28 ± 0.47 y All participants Height: 182 ± 6.0 Mass: 87.4 ± 8.2 kg Resistance training history: >1 year	Duration: 7 weeks Frequency: two sessions p/w Repetition tempo:?	Week 6: 20 Week 7: 18 Week 8: 18 Week 9: 22 Week 10: 22 Week 11: 24 Week 12: 24 **Sets:** *Sets per exercise:* Week 1: 3 Week 2: 3 Week 3: 4 Week 4: 4 Week 5: 4 Week 6: 4 Week 7: 3 Week 8: 8 Week 9: 7 Week 10: 6 Week 11: 5 Week 12: 4 **Repetitions:** Squat and CMJ Week 1: 4 Week 2: 4–6 Week 3: 2–6 Week 4: 2–6 Week 5: 4–6 Week 6: 4–6 Week 7: 4–6 Week 7: 76.0% of 1RM Week 8: 78.5% of 1RM Week 9: 81.0% of 1RM Week 10: 83.5% of 1RM Week 11: 86.0% of 1RM Week 12: 88.5% of 1RM **Intensity:** Week 1–7: Concentric failure	Box Jump, BS, Clean pull to waist, BP, Push Press CU, Abdominal Crunches Ham-glute raise **Exercises:** BS, horizontal and vertical CMJ Upper body:?
Harries et al. (2015)	Linear periodisation group: Age: 16.8 ± 1.0 y Height: 180.4 ± 3.3 cm Mass: 88.7 ± 18.2 kg Undulating periodisation group: Age: 17.0 ± 1.1 y	Duration: 12 weeks Frequency: two sessions p/w	**Sets (session 1 & 2):** Linear Week 1 & 7: 4 Week 2 & 8: 4 Week 3 & 9: 5 Week 4 & 10: 5 Week 5 & 11: 6 Week 6 & 12: 6 **Sets (session 1 & 2):** Linear **Repetitions (session 1 & 2):** Linear Week 1 & 7: 10 Week 2 & 8: 8 Week 3 & 9: 6 Week 4 & 10: 5 Week 5 & 11: 4 Week 6 & 12: 3 **Repetitions (session 1 & 2):** **Intensity (session 1 & 2): Linear Periodised group:** Week 1 & 7: ~75% of 1RM Week 2 & 8: ~78% of 1RM Week 3 & 9: ~83% of 1RM Week 4 & 10: ~86% of 1RM Week 5 & 11: ~88% of 1RM	**Exercises:** BS, BP *Not clarified:* Jump, Upper body pull, Abdominal, Hip-dominant lower body, Loaded carry, Glute/ham/low back

(*Continued*)

TABLE 8.1 (Continued)

Authors	Subject Description	Study duration, Frequency, & Tempo	Sets	Repetitions	Training Intensity	Exercises Used
	Height: 181.3 ± 7.0 cm **Mass:** 82.4 ± 12.6 kg	**Repetition tempo:** 2:0:X	*Undulating periodisation* Week 1–2 & 7–8: 4 & 5 Week 3–4 & 9–10: 4 & 6 Week 5–6 & 11–12: 5 & 6	*Undulating periodisation group* Week 1–2 & 7–8: 10 & 5 Week 3–4 & 9–10: 8 & 4 Week 5–6 & 11–12: 6 & 3	Week 6 & 12: ~90% of 1RM **Intensity (session 1 & 2) Linear Periodised group:** Week 1–2 & 7–8: ~75% & ~86% of 1RM Week 3–4 & 9–10: ~78% & ~88% of 1RM Week 5–6 & 11–12: ~83% & ~90% of 1RM	
Harries et al. (2018)	*Linear periodisation group:* **Age:** 16.8 ± 1.0 y **Height:** 180.4 ± 3.3 cm **Mass:** 88.7 ± 18.2 kg *Undulating periodisation group:* **Age:** 17.0 ± 1.1 y **Height:** 181.3 ± 7.0 cm **Mass:** 82.4 ± 12.6 kg	**Duration:** 12 weeks **Frequency:** two sessions p/w **Repetition tempo:?**	**Sets (session 1 & 2):** *Linear:* Week 1 & 7: 4 Week 2 & 8: 4 Week 3 & 9: 5 Week 4 & 10: 5 Week 5 & 11: 6 Week 6 & 12: 6 *Undulating periodisation group:* Week 1–2 & 7–8: 4 & 5 Week 3–4 & 9–10: 4 & 6 Week 5–6 & 11–12: 5 & 6	**Repetitions (session 1 & 2):** *Linear* Week 1 & 7: 10 Week 2 & 8: 8 Week 3 & 9: 6 Week 4 & 10: 5 Week 5 & 11: 4 Week 6 & 12: 3 *Undulating periodisation group* Week 1–2 & 7–8: 10 & 5 Week 3–4 & 9–10: 8 & 4 Week 5–6 & 11–12: 6 & 3	**Intensity (session 1 & 2) Linear Periodised group:** Week 1 & 7: ~75% of 1RM Week 2 & 8: ~78% of 1RM Week 3 & 9: ~83% of 1RM Week 4 & 10: ~86% of 1RM Week 5 & 11: ~88% of 1RM Week 6 & 12: ~90% of 1RM **Intensity (session 1 & 2) Linear Periodised group:** Week 1–2 & 7–8: ~75% & ~86% of 1RM Week 3–4 & 9–10: ~78% & ~88% of 1RM Week 5–6 & 11–12: ~83% & ~90% of 1RM	**Exercises:** BS, BP *Not clarified:* Jump, Upper body pull, Abdominal, Hip-dominant lower body, Loaded carry, Glute/ham/low back

Strength and Conditioning Training **133**

Orange et al. (2019)	*Percentage-based Training group:* **Age:** 17.0 ± 1.0 y **Height:** 181.0 ± 6.3 cm **Mass:** 84.9 ± 11.9 kg *Velocity-based Training group:* **Age:** 17.0 ± 1.0 y **Height:** 178.0 ± 5.3 cm **Mass:** 81.8 ± 11.9 kg	**Duration:** 7 weeks **Frequency:** two sessions p/w **Repetition tempo:** controlled eccentric/ maximal intent concentric	**Sets (session 1 & 2 total number):** *Percentage-based Training:* Week 1–7: 16 *Velocity-based Training:* Week 1–7: 16	**Repetitions (session 1 & 2 total number):** *Percentage-based Training:* Week 1–7: 94 & 96 *Velocity-based Training:* Week 1–7: 94 & 96	**Intensity** *Percentage-based Training:* Week 1–7: ~60–80% of 1RM *Velocity-based Training:* Week 1–7: ~60–80% of 1RM	**Exercises:** BS, Nordic curl, Incline BP, BoR, SL RDL, DB push press, pull up, front plank, barbell rollout
Riviere et al. (2016)	*All participants:* **Age:** 17.8 ± 0.9 y **Height:** 181.1 ± 8.3 cm **Mass:** 82.6 ± 10.9 kg	**Duration:** 6 weeks **Frequency:** two sessions p/w **Repetition tempo:** 2:0:X	**Sets (session 1 & 2):** Week 1: 3 & 6 Week 2: 3 & 4 Week 3: 3 & 3 Week 4: 3 & 6 Week 5: 3 & 4 Week 6: 3 & 3	**Repetitions (session 1 & 2):** Week 1: 4 & 2 Week 2: 3 & 2 Week 3: 2 & 2 Week 4: 4 & 2 Week 5: 3 & 2 Week 6: 2 & 2	**Intensity (session 1 & 2):** Week 1: 90% & 70% of 1RM Week 2: 85% & 75% of 1RM Week 3: 90% & 80% of 1RM Week 4: 82% & 72% of 1RM Week 5: 87% & 77% of 1RM Week 6: 92% & 82% of 1RM	**Exercises:** BP, Clean, CU, FS, Military press, BS, DL, Incline BP, Hip thrust, High Pull clean, Snatch, Pull up, CMJ, Step up, Bicep Curls, Jerk, Bench Row, One arm rowing, SS, Push Press **Not Clarified:** Human Plank Snatch Force

(*Continued*)

TABLE 8.1 (Continued)

Authors	Subject Description	Study duration, Frequency, & Tempo	Sets	Repetitions	Training Intensity	Exercises Used
Smart et al. (2013)	*Supervised group:* **Age:** 15.4 ± 1.4 y **Height:** 177.9 ± 3.9 cm **Mass:** 79.7 ± 15.2 kg *Unsupervised group:* **Age:** 15.1 ± 1.3 y **Height:** 178.8 ± 2.4 cm **Mass:** 73.9± 12.0 kg	**Duration:** 15 weeks **Frequency:** three sessions p/w **Repetition tempo:** NA	**Sets:** Weeks 1–4: 4 Weeks 5–7: ? Week 8–15: 5	**Repetitions (session 1 & 2):** Weeks 1–4: 10 Weeks 5–7: ? Weeks 8–11: 8–12 Weeks 12–15: 6–10	**Intensity:** Week 1–15: ?	**Exercises:** BxS, DB/BB BP, CU, Seated row, DB shoulder press, Pull down, Single leg step ups, Prone hip extension, DB lateral raise, Seated Hammer row, LP, CR, Bulgarian SS, DB row, UR, DL
Speirs et al. (2016)	*All participants:* **Age:** 18.1 ± 0.5 y *Unilateral group:* **Height:** 183.0 ± 3.4 **Mass:** 96.7 ± 9.3 kg **Resistance training history:** 1.62 ± 0.18 y *Unsupervised group:* **Height:** 185.0 ± 8.9 **Mass:** 98.1 ± 13.4 **Resistance training history:** 1.65 ± 0.18 y	**Duration:** 5 weeks **Frequency:** two sessions per week **Repetition tempo:** 2:0:1	**Sets:** Weeks 1–5: 4 for all exercises	**Repetitions:** RFESS or BS exercises: Week 1: 6 Week 2: 6 Week 3: 5 Week 4: 4 Week 5: 3	**Intensity:** Weeks 1: 75% of 1RM Week 2: 80% of 1RM Week 3: 85% of 1RM Week 4: 90% of 1RM Week 5: 92% of 1RM	**Exercises:** BS or RFESS Upper body: ?

Repetition tempo= eccentric portion: pause: concentric portion;? = Unknown; p/w = per week; RM = repetition maximum; BS = Back squat; BxS = Box Squat; DB = Dumbbell; BB = Barbell; BP = Bench Press; CU = Chin up; FS = Front squat; BoR = Bent-over row; UR = Upright row; SS = Split squat; DL = Deadlift; PC = Power clean; KB = Kettlebell; LP = Leg Press; BE = Back extensions; CR = Calf raise; RFESS = Rear foot elevated split squat and report greater perceived stress. Alternatively, autoregulatory methods (e.g., velocity-based training) can allow for greater accuracy of prescription and enhance velocity and power outputs during training (Orange et al., 2019).

Influence on Sprint and Change of Direction Ability

Six studies have investigated the effects of resistance training on sprint and CoD performance in adolescent rugby players (Bourgeois et al., 2017; Coutts et al., 2004; Harries et al., 2018; Orange et al., 2019; Smart & Gill, 2013; Speirs et al., 2016). While the benefits of supervision during training are again clear, the advantages may be greatest over shorter (e.g., 10 m) sprint distances (Smart & Gill, 2013). When assessing different periodised models, linear and daily undulating methods provide similar benefits (Harries et al., 2018). Additionally, the use of heavy sled training (i.e., loads ~133% of body mass) can provide substantial improvements in 0–20 m sprint performance (effect size: 0.87; Cahill et al., 2020). Finally, lower body exercise selection may also influence sprint and CoD performance outcomes. Speirs et al. (2016) found that unilateral exercises may provide a slightly greater benefit to sprint and CoD performance in comparison to bilateral exercises (Speirs et al., 2016). However, the use of long eccentric contraction durations (i.e., >3 s) during resistance training has shown mixed CoD outcomes (Bourgeois et al., 2017).

Resistance Training Conclusions

It is undeniable that resistance training is a potent and important tool for the development of youth rugby players. However, research suggests that the greatest improvements in physical qualities occur in response to consistent, structured training programmes that have adequate supervision. Furthermore, just like other forms of training, ensuring that an adequate amount of volume completed is an important consideration when trying to enhance physical qualities. On the other hand, it is unlikely that alternative methods of resistance training (e.g., prolonged eccentric tempos) and the periodisation model applied will provide substantial advantage over basic principles of overload. Consequently, this should be remembered by practitioners when developing resistance training programmes and attempting to optimise the long-term development of the youth rugby player.

Training of Aerobic and Anaerobic Capacity

Six studies have investigated the effect of running based conditioning sessions on changes in aerobic and anaerobic capacity (Dobbin et al., 2020; Gabbett, 2006; Gabbett et al., 2008; Galvin et al., 2013; Seitz et al., 2014; Smart & Gill, 2013). It should be acknowledged that across these studies, a range of aerobic fitness assessments have been used (e.g., gas analysis during an incremental fitness and the 30–15 Intermittent Fitness Test [30–15$_{IFT}$]) therefore caution should be made when comparing reported maximal oxygen consumption ($\dot{V}O_2$max) across studies. Gabbett (2006) and Gabbett et al. (2008) examined the effects of a 14-week and 10-week preseason period on aerobic development in youth rugby league players. While the description of the training protocols are vague, Gabbett (2006) and Gabbett et al. (2008) completed two and three field sessions per week, respectively. In both studies the subjects performed repeated sprint training, varying in distances of 10 m to 40 m, with efforts initiated every 15–30 s cycle. While set and repetition details are not provided, the authors stated that intervals of 45–90 s were completed with work-to-rest ratios of 1:1 and 2:1. Furthermore, the study by Gabbett (2006) also used conditioning games. The findings of the studies showed a significant 8.6% improvement in estimated $\dot{V}O_2$max over 14 weeks (Gabbett, 2006), whilst a ten-week preseason resulted in a 11.3% and 4.0% change in estimated $\dot{V}O_2$max in U15 and U18 rugby league players, respectively. These findings suggest that easily implementable work-to-rest ratios (which might be preferable when working with large squads) can be integrated into pre-seasons and induce substantial improvements in aerobic capacity youth rugby players.

In academy rugby union players, Seitz et al. (2014) examined changes in the 30–15$_{IFT}$ and repeated sprint ability following a training intervention that lasted eight weeks. The intervention consisted of two training sessions per week (16 total) of small-sided games (SSGs), with each session including a 10-minute warm-up followed by 4 × 10 min of SSGs. The SSG intervention replaced all speed, repeated sprint training and high-intensity interval training for the eight-week period. Following the intervention, the players showed an ~1% improvement in the final velocity (V_{IFT}) achieved in the 30–15$_{IFT}$ and greater repeated sprint ability. This suggests that practitioners can use SSGs as an efficient method of enhancing high-intensity running capacity while being exercise specific.

Contrasting the 8–14-week intervention periods (Gabbett, 2006; Gabbett et al., 2008; Seitz et al., 2014), Dobbin et al. (2020) examined the effect of a two-week sprint interval training intervention in academy super league players. The intervention consisted of three sessions per week (six total) of either traditional running involving sprint intervals (SIT$_r$) or rugby-specific sprint intervals (SIT$_{r/s}$). Both SIT$_r$ and SIT$_{r/s}$ were matched for volume across the two-week period and showed that short-term training interventions can produce 13–15% positive improvements in the prone Yo-Yo Intermittent Recovery test (Yo-Yo IR-1). Additionally, Galvin et al. (2013) investigated the effect of repeated sprint training during a four-week intervention. The participants completed three sessions per week (12 total) consisting of 10 × 6 s sprints with 30s recovery on a non-motorised treadmill under normoxic (21% F_iO_2) or hypoxic (13% F_iO_2) conditions. Following the interventions, aerobic (Yo-Yo IR-1) performance significantly increased in the normoxic (14% ± 10%) and hypoxic (33% ± 12%) training groups, with the hypoxic training group producing significantly greater improvements. However, changes in $\dot{V}O_2$ within and between groups were not significant with hypoxia and normoxia-inducing changes of 6.9% ± 9.9% and −0.3% ± 8.8%, respectively.

Finally, Smart and Gill (2013) demonstrated that supervision during training has trivial effects on aerobic capacity in adolescent rugby union players. Participants completed a 15-week intervention which consisted of three conditioning sessions in weeks one to four, with the remaining weeks containing two sessions per week. Sessions consisted of the multi-stage fitness test, sprinting, repeated sprints, continuous runs and fartlek-type training sessions. Following the training intervention, changes in 1,500 m time trial were large in both the supervised and unsupervised groups which suggest that, unlike resistance training, conditioning sessions can be equally beneficial irrespective of supervision. Finally, it should be acknowledged that despite supervision not inducing a substantially greater improvement in 1,500 m time, the supervision group did have greater attendance across the training period. This may be important for helping develop a chronic training base and promoting consistent training.

Conditioning Conclusions

The development of aerobic and anaerobic running capacity is important for the youth rugby player. As demonstrated above, there are many ways to do this and the most successful method is likely dependent upon the group of players, training environment and goals of the training session. With this in mind, and considering that youth players are participating in a multifaceted sport that involves technical skills and tactical awareness, if SSGs can be strategically implemented it is likely that this form of conditioning may have the greatest all-round benefit. The exposure to different skills (e.g., catching, passing, marking/tracking other players) while participating in an enjoyable form of training is an important consideration. Furthermore, the volumes and intensities of these types of games can be manipulated and game-specific movements (e.g., starting in a prone position; Dobbin et al., 2020) can be introduced to alter the physiological load.

Practical Applications

The first half of this chapter has summarised the scientific evidence base that has evaluated the physical development of youth rugby players following strength and conditioning training interventions. While there are many different methods that can efficiently improve physical qualities in youth, there are also issues that can occur from trying to replicate what well-trained and professional athletes complete within youth populations. Therefore, to mitigate risk and ensure long-term athlete development, the following recommendations for youth players are based upon an 'earn the right' philosophy. This approach promotes the idea that before a young player progresses to more complex movements or taxing exercises, first they must be able to demonstrate good technique and be able to tolerate sufficient training load and volume. By using this approach alongside a logical progression of exercises, the strength and conditioning practitioner can ensure that all fundamental movement patterns are developed and that progressive overload can help promote training adaptations.

This practical application section provides a framework and general recommendations that have been implemented in professional rugby union academies in both the United Kingdom and Australasia. Furthermore, due to the general nature of these methods, recommendations can be beneficial for both youth rugby union and rugby league players.

Developing the Strength and Conditioning Programme

All strength and conditioning programmes are underpinned by acute training variables that promote progressive overload and subsequent adaptation. These variables include the mode of exercise, intensity and volume applied, recovery provided, exercise selection and order, and the frequency of exercise completed. By appropriately applying these fundamental variables, training programmes can be highly specific and individualised. However, it is important to also consider several factors so that training is suitable. These include the training age of the athlete, movement competency, training background, current and competing training demands, and facilities/equipment available (Lloyd & Oliver, 2012). Once this information has been established, training can be implemented throughout the micro- or meso-cycle and periodised into the annual plan.

Designing the Resistance Training Programme

At the most basic level, most resistance training exercises can be broken down into one of the below categories:

- Bilateral lower body (e.g., squat)
- Unilateral lower body (e.g., lunge)
- Hinge (e.g., Romanian deadlift)
- Horizontal pull (e.g., prone row)
- Horizontal push (e.g., push up)
- Vertical pull (e.g., chin-up)
- Vertical push (e.g., shoulder press)
- Core (e.g., sit ups)

Within each of these categories, exercises can then be placed onto a continuum of competency that progresses over time (see Figure 8.1). With each exercise, changes in range of motion, degrees of freedom, and placement of external load can alter the stimulus and help support the attainment of later exercises. An example of this could be completing a body weight squat prior to a goblet squat.

Strength and Conditioning Training 139

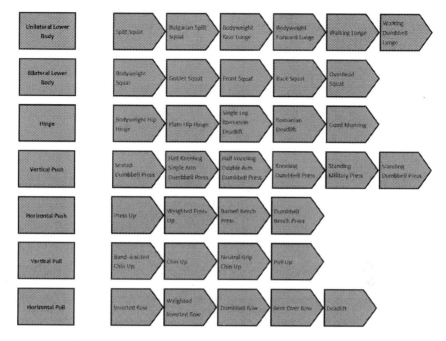

FIGURE 8.1 Resistance Training Progressions to Guide Exercise Prescription.

As the body weight squat uses the same movement patterns as a goblet squat, although without the external load, it is important to be able to complete this movement first. Within each exercise, it is recommended that six to eight weeks of practice is completed prior to progressing (Lloyd et al., 2014). While this could vary, this length is recommended as it provides enough time to become familiar with an exercise, have sufficient exposure, and accumulate adequate time and volume with the exercise before moving on. Additionally, before progressing, form should be able to be maintained across all sets and repetitions with sufficient external load. Two examples of training programmes (beginner, Table 8.2; more advanced, Table 8.3) are provided to help illustrate the progression of training for an U16-year-old rugby player.

Periodisation and planning are fundamental to the development of a training programme. Considering the attention that periodisation receives in the adult strength and conditioning literature, for youth rugby players, it is unlikely that one style of periodisation provides substantially better adaptations than another (see Harries et al., 2016). Of greater importance is the support, supervision, and guidance that is provided to the young athlete. Thus, to enhance adaptations, decreasing the player-to-coach ratio and providing frequent feedback so that consistent training is achieved with appropriate volumes and intensity should be of greatest priority. Thereafter, the periodisation method that best meets the players needs and their current training loads should be considered.

TABLE 8.2 Example of a Beginner's Resistance Training Programme

Beginners Resistance Training Session

Phase	Exercise	Movement Pattern Emphasis	Volume (Sets and Reps)	Intensity	Rest
Warm up	Foam roller complex	Lower body myofascial release therapy	5 minutes	–	–
	Miniband walk	Gluteal and pelvis activation	2 × 10	Self-selected band	2 minutes
	Hip bridge	Gluteal and pelvis activation	2 × 12	Unweighted	1 minute
	Countermovement jump	Jumping and landing mechanics	3 × 3	Maximal unweighted	2 minutes
Main Resistance Training Exercises	1A Goblet squat	Bilateral lower body	3 × 12	3 Repetitions-in-reserve	–
	1B Supine row	Horizontal pull	3 × Max	Body weight	2 minutes
	2A Plate hip hinge	Hinge	3 × 12	Self-selected	–
	2B Seated shoulder press	Vertical push	3 × 12	3 Repetitions-in-reserve	2 minutes
	3A Split squat	Unilateral lower body	3 × 8 Each leg	3 Repetitions-in-reserve	–
Auxiliary Exercises	3B Dead bugs	Core	3 × 10	Body weight	2 minutes
	Core exercise of choice	Core	2 × 12	–	2 minutes
	Prescribed rehabilitation or prehabilitation exercises	Rehab/prehab	–	–	–

TABLE 8.3 Example of an Advanced Resistance Training Programm

Advanced Resistance Training Session

Phase	Exercise	Movement Pattern Emphasis	Volume (Sets and Reps)	Intensity	Rest
Warm up	Foam roller complex	Lower body myofascial release therapy	5 minutes	–	–
	Miniband walk	Gluteal and pelvis activation	2 × 10	Self-selected band	2 minutes
	Rear lunge	Gluteal and pelvis activation	2 × 15 Each leg	Unweighted	2 minute
	Rope jump	Repeated jumping and landing mechanics	3 × 50	Unweighted	3 minutes
Main Resistance Training Exercises	1A Back squat	Bilateral lower body	4 × 6	Two repetitions-in-reserve	–
	1B Broad jumps	Bilateral lower body	4 × 2	Maximal intent with body weight	3 minutes
	2A Bench press	Horizontal push	4 × 8	Two repetitions-in-reserve	–
	2B Step downs	Unilateral lower body	4 × 8	Body weight	3 minutes
	3A Romanian deadlift	Bilateral lower body	4 × 8 Each leg	Four repetitions-in-reserve	–
	3B Plank walkout	Core	4 × 8	Body weight	3 minutes
Auxiliary Exercises	Prescribed rehabilitation or prehabilitation exercises	Rehab/prehab	–	–	–

Within the training programme, the frequency and placement of training sessions throughout the microcycle should be carefully planned. With too frequent training, unwarranted fatigue and maladaptations can occur. With training that is sporadic or infrequent, physical capacity can be lost through detraining (Lloyd et al., 2014). Thus, accounting for, and individualising the frequency of training based on the competing demands of the adolescent player is likely the best method for mitigating the risk of overtraining and enhancing physical development. However, as a general rule, one to two resistance training sessions per week in novice trainers will likely suffice. As the youth player ages and their training base grows, the frequency then may increase to two to four sessions per week. Although it should be noted that this may fluctuate across the year and based upon the other training that is occurring, training frequency may be increased or decreased to improve adaptations or mitigate fatigue (Lloyd et al., 2014).

The correct selection of training intensity can be difficult when designing the youth rugby player's resistance training programme due to the rapid gains in strength that often occur during adolescence. While maximal strength testing can be reliably completed after only several months of training, frequent completion of this form of testing can be impractical. Therefore, at least initially, it is suggested that ratings of perceived exertion and repetitions-in-reserve are used to guide the selection of the external load. As the youth rugby player becomes more familiar with resistance training, it is then suggested that prescription as a percentage of maximal strength becomes integrated into the training cycle. However, it should be noted that these different methods of training prescription are not mutually exclusive and that auto-regulatory methods (e.g., repetitions-in-reserve, rating of perceived exertion) can still be used throughout the training cycle to ensure appropriate load and proximity to failure is achieved.

Box 8.2 Fixed Prescription *vs* Autoregulatory Prescription

Resistance training is traditionally prescribed weeks in advance using a percentage of maximum strength (e.g., 75% of 1RM). However, maximal strength testing can be time-consuming and there can be rapid and substantial improvements in strength development in relatively inexperienced athletes. Therefore, it can sometimes be difficult to prescribe the appropriate load for an adolescent. To counter these issues, autoregulatory prescriptive methods, such as repetitions-in-reserve, rating of perceived exertion and velocity-based training have been developed to help the accurate prescription of load and volume. It should be noted, fixed prescriptive and autoregulatory methods can be used in conjunction and may help provide greater day-to-day context to training. A brief description of these methods is detailed below.

Repetitions-in-reserve: Athletes are required to subjectively assess when they feel that they cannot complete more than a certain number of repetitions.

> This signifies the termination of a set. For example, a young rugby player may be programmed to complete repetitions until they deem they have 'two repetitions-in-reserve'. In this example, if a player could complete ten repetitions with a load, they would terminate the set following the eighth repetition.
>
> *Rating of perceived exertion*: Athletes are required to subjectively assess when they feel that they are exercising at a given rating of perceived exertion from 0 to 10. When they feel that they are exercising at this value, the set is terminated. For example, a youth rugby player may be programmed to complete repetitions until they deem they are exercising at an 'eight out of 10'. In this example, the individual would finish the set when they feel the set is at an eight out of ten intensity.
>
> *Velocity-based training*: Velocity-based training is a method that 'uses velocity to inform or enhance training practice' (Weakley et al., 2021). While many different methods of velocity-based training can be applied, the load that is used by an athlete can be moderated by assessing the speed of the exercise. Additionally, volume can be moderated by terminating sets when exercise becomes too slow.

Resistance training volume is one of the most important variables, as it has been shown to have strong relationships with strength and power development in youth rugby players (Weakley et al., 2019). Volume, measured as the sum of total tonnage lifted, can be influenced by a range of factors and the 'optimal' stimulus is likely dictated by the training background of the athlete. However, during early adolescence, it is suggested that approximately two to three sets that consist of approximately eight to twelve repetitions are implemented. As exercise competency improves and the young rugby player matures, it could be recommended that a greater number of sets (e.g., three to five) and a decrease in repetitions (e.g., four to eight) with a corresponding increase in relative external load be introduced into the training plan. To increase the amount of volume that can be completed within a training session, alternative resistance training structures such as supersets (i.e., the completion of two exercises consecutively) and tri-sets (i.e., the completion of three exercises consecutively) can be implemented. In Tables 8.2 and 8.3, supersets are being integrated into the training session, with this able to be seen by the pairing of 'A' and 'B' exercises (e.g., 1A Goblet Squat; 1B Supine Row). If these methods are included within the training programme though, it is strongly recommended that antagonist-agonist and upper-lower body combinations are used with young athletes as these reduce the fatigue response and maintain training quality (Weakley et al., 2017, 2020). If training exercises of a similar body part (e.g., lower peripheries), it is recommended that they are used in a potentiating complex which involves heavier and then lighter exercises (e.g., 1A – Back Squat; 1B – Broad Jumps; Dobbs et al., 2015). Finally, it should be noted that the intensity and volume should fluctuate throughout the annual training cycle and these changes should be considered in conjunction with any additional training that the young player is undertaking.

Finally, resistance training can be completed through a range of methods. Initially, emphasis should be placed on body weight exercises and, as competency is developed, greater external loads through barbells and dumbbells should be used. Once these exercises are mastered, the inclusion of accommodating resistance can be implemented with particular benefits observed when used with heavier (i.e., >80% of 1RM) loads. However, alternative methods of applying external loads that are not confined to the gym can also be applied. An example of this is the inclusion of pushing/pulling weighted (i.e., a load that causes a reduction of ~75% of maximal velocity) sleds. This method of training has been shown to augment force development when running and may allow a relatively efficient method of resistance training in a 'sport specific' manner.

Designing the Conditioning Session

While resistance training sessions often require a range of specialised equipment, conditioning sessions often are implemented without these constraints. However, a considerable range of different methods and strategies can still be used to develop aerobic and anaerobic physical qualities. Therefore, there is a need to understand the role of frequency, intensity, time and type during programme development and how these acute variables can influence training outcomes.

It is recommended that youth rugby players complete two to three conditioning sessions per week. This is to ensure that the athletes are exposed regularly to a training stimulus, whilst also allowing sufficient time to recover between sessions. However, it should be noted that for youth rugby players who train and compete for multiple teams, they may not require additional conditioning sessions as long as the sessions they participate in occur at a relatively high intensity. This is due to the overall load accumulated across a training week when participating for multiple teams. In contrast to this, the youth rugby player contracted to a single team or professional club is more likely to require targeted conditioning sessions as part of a periodised plan. Therefore, for these athletes, a greater emphasis may need to be placed on scheduling two to three sessions across a week that can be implemented alongside technical and tactical training.

It is recommended that the intensity of conditioning sessions is high enough to allow youth rugby players to spend several minutes above 90% $\dot{V}O_{2max}$ (Buchheit & Laursen, 2013). Whilst this is difficult to assess in the field when coaching a large group of youth athletes, evidence suggests that this can be attained by completing multiple repetitions of short duration (e.g., 4–6 s) maximal effort sprints, and short (e.g., 10–30 s at 140% maximal aerobic speed [MAS]) and long (e.g., >60 seconds at 100% MAS) intervals. Additionally, practitioners may wish to use mixed-intensity SSGs that have intervals greater than 60 s. While monitoring the intensity of SSGs can be difficult compared to interval-based training, the use of rule and constraint manipulation can increase or decrease training intensity depending on the goal of the session.

For the youth rugby player involved with multiple programmes, they may not be able to tolerate sessions that would be classed as 'high-intensity' due to the number of sessions they complete within a week hindering their recovery. Therefore, this should be considered when planning for these players. In contrast, a contracted youth rugby player, who exclusively trains in a professional environment is likely to be able to tolerate and complete high-intensity sessions, as the club will likely have greater control of training and rest days. This may allow greater recovery between sessions, and therefore a higher output when training.

The duration of conditioning sessions is naturally determined by the intensity and type of session being implemented. With increases in intensity, there are natural reductions in the volume of total work that can be completed and vice-versa. Sessions that are maximal in nature (e.g., 10–30 s maximal repeats) require a greater period of passive recovery (e.g., 3 min) between repetitions. In contrast, interval sessions require a greater amount of time due to the reduced intensity of exercise. Short interval duration sessions can last approximately 20 minutes in length based on 30 s intervals (e.g., 120% MAS) that provide 30 s to 1 min recovery between repetitions and 2 min between sets. Additionally, long interval duration sessions can last approximately 25 min when 3–5 minute intervals with 1.5–2.5 minutes recovery periods between repetitions at intensities of 90–100% MAS are used. While these methods require either maximal effort, or working at a fixed intensity for specific durations, the inclusion of mixed intensity, long-duration SSGs has also been shown to be an effective method of improving aerobic fitness in youth rugby players. Similar to interval training, SSGs generally consist of multiple bouts with incomplete recovery periods but SSGs have the advantage of concurrently developing sport-specific skills alongside fitness qualities, and therefore may be the most efficient use of training time. While the amount of time spent completing SSGs is dependent on the constraints of the game (e.g., number of players), for the development of aerobic and anaerobic qualities it is recommended that intervals should be greater than 60 s in duration, and last up to 5 min.

Box 8.3 Small-Sided Games for Rugby

Both rugby union and rugby league are multifaceted sports that require the development of physical, technical and tactical qualities. Therefore, integrating all these aspects into training may be beneficial. But, based on the aims of the session, the physiological load can be manipulated. Below are some examples of altering the constraints of small-sided games and their possible effects on physiological load.

> *Altering the size of the playing area:* Increasing the size of the playing area can increase the external running load (Gabbett et al., 2012) while increasing blood lactate concentrations and ratings of perceived exertion (Kennett et al., 2012).
>
> *Altering the number of players per team:* When holding the total size of the playing area constant, it has been shown that decreasing the number of players per team (i.e., increasing the amount of 'free space') can significantly increase the external workload of players (Kennett et al., 2012).
>
> *Removal of collisions (i.e., 'touch'):* By altering the rules of the game so that collisions are removed, a greater number of technical skills, such as passing, may be executed. This may be due to a faster pace of the game and more opportunities for technical actions (Morley et al., 2016).
>
> *Removal of 'off-side':* By allowing the ball to be passed in any direction, players complete greater external loads. However, cognitive ratings of perceived exertion may decrease (Gabbett et al., 2010).

It is generally recommended that running-based conditioning sessions are used as these have the greatest similarity to rugby union and league. The form of running-based conditioning does depend on the amount of time available and the physiological qualities targeted (e.g., greater aerobic or anaerobic contributions). Following general recommendations of periodisation, it is suggested that longer intervals that have greater aerobic contribution be implemented earlier in the season when more time is available (e.g., pre-season). Furthermore, as the pre-season period continues and greater emphasis is placed upon match-play, practitioners may wish to implement shorter intervals that have greater intensities but also require less time. Also, small additions to each interval (e.g., players must touch their chest on the ground prior to each interval) may support the specificity of training and break the monotony of intervals for players. The systematic introduction of collision-based conditioning should also be considered, as the need to adequately prepare players for collisions is important and the integration of this form of training can be made possible during a range of technical, tactical, and physical drills. Finally, throughout the playing season, it is recommended that the majority of conditioning is achieved through SSGs. The benefit of this form of training is that it can be used to develop certain skills or emphasise tactical decision-making that occurs throughout match-play. However, it should be acknowledged that the intensity of SSGs may not allow each player to receive the required conditioning stimulus, thus small additional amounts of conditioning (e.g., short intervals) may be required to 'top up' players.

Key Take Home Messages

- Improvements in physical development can be achieved through strength and conditioning training. However, all exercise that an athlete undertakes should be considered when designing the training cycle.

- Exercises implemented should follow a logical progression that allows for potentiation of exercises in the following training phase. Furthermore, it is strongly recommended that when completing resistance training, technique should be able to be maintained with external load throughout all repetitions and sets before progression occurs.
- The provision of supervision allows athletes to achieve greater adaptations than when it is not provided. Thus, suitably qualified practitioners should be available during training sessions to ensure exercises are performed correctly and the appropriate loads and volumes are used.
- The use of autoregulatory prescriptive methods such as ratings of perceived exertion and repetitions-in-reserve can be used to guide training prescription. However, these methods must be explained prior to use to ensure that the athlete understands how they can be applied.
- The use of SSGs is an efficient method of training prescription that can enhance aerobic and anaerobic qualities while also exposing players to rugby-specific skills. The training intensity can easily be altered through rule modification and the manipulation of game constraints.
- Depending on the number of training sessions and teams a player participates in each week, the need for additional conditioning sessions may be reduced. Practitioners should carefully consider the total volume of training a youth athlete undertakes and whether additional conditioning is required.

References

Bourgeois, F. A., Gamble, P., Gill, N. D., & Mcguigan, M. R. (2017). Effects of a six-week strength training programme on change of direction performance in youth team sport athletes. *Sports, 5*, 83–100. https://doi.org/10.3390/sports5040083

Buchheit, M., & Laursen, P. B. (2013). High-intensity interval training, solutions to the programming puzzle. *Sports Medicine, 43*, 313–338. https://doi.org/10.1007/s40279-013-0029-x

Cahill, M. J., Oliver, J. L., Cronin, J. B., Clark, K. P., Cross, M. R., & Lloyd, R. S. (2020). Influence of resisted sled-push training on the sprint force-velocity profile of male high school athletes. *Scandinavian Journal of Medicine & Science in Sports, 30*, 442–449. https://doi.org/10.1111/sms.13600

Costello, N., McKenna, J., Sutton, L., Deighton, K., & Jones, B. (2018). Using contemporary behavior change science to design and implement an effective nutritional intervention within professional rugby league. *International Journal of Sport Nutrition and Exercise Metabolism, 28*, 553–557.

Coutts, A. J., Murphy, A. J., & Dascombe, B. J. (2004). Effect of direct supervision of a strength coach on measures of muscular strength and power in young rugby league players. *Journal of Strength & Conditioning Research, 18*, 316–323. https://doi.org/10.1519/R-12972.1

Darrall-Jones, J. D., Jones, B., & Till, K. (2015). Anthropometric and physical profiles of English academy rugby union players. *Journal of Strength & Conditioning Research, 29*, 2086–2096. https://doi.org/10.1519/JSC.0000000000000872

Dobbin, N., Highton, J., Moss, S. L., & Twist, C. (2020). The effects of in-season, low-volume sprint interval training with and without sport-specific actions on the physical characteristics of elite academy rugby league players. *International Journal of Sports Physiology & Performance, 15,* 705–713. https://doi.org/10.1123/ijspp.2019-0165

Dobbs, C. W., Gill, N. D., Smart, D. J., & Mcguigan, M. R. (2015). The training effect of short term enhancement from complex pairing on horizontal and vertical countermovement and drop jump performance. *Journal of Strength &Conditioning Research,* Ahead of Print. https://doi.org/10.1519/JSC.0000000000000874

Faigenbaum, A. D., Kraemer, W. J., Blimkie, C. J. R., Jeffreys, I., Micheli, L. J., Nitka, M., & Rowland, T. W. (2009). Youth resistance training: Updated position statement paper from the national strength and conditioning association. *Journal of Strength & Conditioning Research, 23,* S60–S79. https://doi.org/10.1519/JSC.0b013e31819df407

Gabbett, T. J. (2006). Performance changes following a field conditioning program in junior and senior rugby league players. *Journal of Strength &Conditioning Research, 20,* 215–221. https://doi.org/10.1519/R-16554.1

Gabbett, T. J., Abernethy, B., & Jenkins, D. G. (2012). Influence of field size on the physiological and skill demands of small-sided games in junior and senior rugby league players. *Journal of Strength & Conditioning Research, 26,* 487–491. https://doi.org/10.1519/JSC.0b013e318225a371

Gabbett, T. J., Jenkins, D. G., & Abernethy, B. (2010). Physiological and skill demands of 'on-side' and 'off-side' games. *Journal of Strength & Conditioning Research, 24,* 2979–2983. https://doi.org/10.1519/JSC.0b013e3181e72731

Gabbett, T. J., Johns, J., & Riemann, M. (2008). Performance changes following training in junior rugby league players. *Journal of Strength & Conditioning Research, 22,* 910–917. https://doi.org/10.1519/JSC.0b013e31816a5fa5

Galvin, H. M., Cooke, K., Sumners, D. P., Mileva, K. N., & Bowtell, J. L. (2013). Repeated sprint training in normobaric hypoxia. *British Journal of Sports Medicine, 47* (Suppl 1), i74–i79. https://doi.org/10.1136/bjsports-2013-092826

Harries, S. K., Lubans, D. R., Buxton, A., Macdougall, T. H. J., & Callister, R. (2018). Effects of 12-week resistance training on sprint and jump performances in competitive adolescent rugby union players. *Journal of Strength & Conditioning Research, 32,* 2762–2769. https://doi.org/10.1519/JSC.0000000000002119

Harries, S. K., Lubans, D. R., & Callister, R. (2016). Comparison of resistance training progression models on maximal strength in sub-elite adolescent rugby union players. *Journal of Science & Medicine in Sport, 19,* 163–169. https://doi.org/10.1016/j.jsams.2015.01.007

Jones, T. W., Smith, A., Macnaughton, L. S., & French, D. N. (2016). Strength and conditioning and concurrent training practices in elite rugby union. *Journal of Strength & Conditioning Research, 30,* 3354–3366. https://doi.org/10.1519/JSC.0000000000001445

Kennett, D. C., Kempton, T., & Coutts, A. J. (2012). Factors affecting exercise intensity in rugby-specific small-sided games. *The Journal of Strength & Conditioning Research, 26,* 2037–2042. https://doi.org/10.1519/JSC.0b013e31823a3b26

Lloyd, R. S., Faigenbaum, A. D., Stone, M. H., Oliver, J. L., Jeffreys, I., Moody, J. A., Brewer, C., Pierce, K. C., Mccambridge, T. M., Howard, R., Herrington, L., Hainline, B., Micheli, L. J., Jaques, R., Kraemer, W. J., Mcbride, M. G., Best, T. M., Chu, D. A., Alvar, B. A., & Myer, G. D. (2014). Position statement on youth resistance training: The 2014 international consensus. *British Journal of Sports Medicine, 48,* 498–505. https://doi.org/10.1136/bjsports-2013-092952

Lloyd, R. S., & Oliver, J. L. (2012). The youth physical development model: A new approach to long-term athletic development. *Strength & Conditioning Journal, 34,* 61–72. https://doi.org/10.1519/SSC.0b013e31825760ea

Moore, D. A., Jones, B., Weakley, J., Whitehead, S., & Till, K. (2022). The field and resistance training loads of academy rugby league players during a preseason: Comparisons across playing positions. *PLoS ONE, 17*, e0272817. https://doi.org/10.1371/journal.pone.0272817

Morley, D., Ogilvie, P., Till, K., Rothwell, M., Cotton, W., O'Connor, D., & Mckenna, J. (2016). Does modifying competition affect the frequency of technical skills in junior rugby league? *International Journal of Sports Science & Coaching, 11*, 810–818. https://doi.org/10.1177/1747954116676107

Orange, S. T., Metcalfe, J. W., Robinson, A., Applegarth, M. J., & Liefeith, A. (2019). Effects of in-season velocity-versus percentage-based training in academy rugby league players. *International Journal of Sports Physiology & Performance, 15*, 554–561. https://doi.org/10.1123/ijspp.2019-0058

Rivière, M., Louit, L., Strokosch, A., & Seitz, L. B. (2017). Variable resistance training promotes greater strength and power adaptations than traditional resistance training in elite youth rugby league players. *Journal of Strength & Conditioning Research, 31*, 947–955. https://doi.org/10.1519/JSC.0000000000001574

Seitz, L. B., Rivière, M., De Villarreal, E. S., & Haff, G. G. (2014). The athletic performance of elite rugby league players is improved after an 8-week small-sided game training intervention. *Journal of Strength & Conditioning Research, 28*, 971–975. https://doi.org/10.1519/JSC.0b013e3182a1f24a

Smart, D. J., & Gill, N. D. (2013). Effects of an off-season conditioning program on the physical characteristics of adolescent rugby union players. *Journal of Strength & Conditioning Research, 27*, 708–717. https://doi.org/10.1519/JSC.0b013e31825d99b0

Smart, D. J., Hopkins, W. G., & Gill, N. D. (2013). Differences and changes in the physical characteristics of professional and amateur rugby union players. *Journal of Strength & Conditioning Research, 27*, 3033–3044. https://doi.org/10.1519/JSC.0b013e31828c26d3

Smart, D. J., Hopkins, W. G., Quarrie, K. L., & Gill, N. (2014). The relationship between physical fitness and game behaviours in rugby union players. *European Journal of Sport Science, 14*, S8–S17. https://doi.org/10.1080/17461391.2011.635812

Speirs, D. E., Bennett, M. A., Finn, C. V., & Turner, A. P. (2016). Unilateral vs. bilateral squat training for strength, sprints, and agility in academy rugby players. *Journal of Strength & Conditioning Research, 30*, 386–392. https://doi.org/10.1519/JSC.0000000000001096

Till, K., Cobley, S., O'Hara, J., Morley, D., Chapman, C., & Cooke, C. (2015). Retrospective analysis of anthropometric and fitness characteristics associated with long-term career progression in Rugby League. *Journal of Science and Medicine in Sport, 18*, 310–314. https://doi.org/10.1016/j.jsams.2014.05.003

Weakley, J., Mann, B., Banyard, H., Mclaren, S., Scott, T., & Garcia-Ramos, A. (2021). Velocity-based training: From theory to application. *Strength & Conditioning Journal, 43*, 31–49. https://doi.org/10.1519/ssc.0000000000000560

Weakley, J. J., Till, K., Darrall-Jones, J., Roe, G. A., Phibbs, P. J., Read, D. B., & Jones, B. L. (2019a). Strength and conditioning practices in adolescent rugby players: Relationship with changes in physical qualities. *Journal of Strength & Conditioning Research, 33*, 2361–2369. https://doi.org/10.1519/JSC.0000000000001828

Weakley, J., Till, K., Read, D., Phibbs, P., Roe, G., Darrall-Jones, J., & Jones, B. (2020). The effects of superset configuration on kinetic, kinematic, and perceived exertion in the barbell bench press. *Journal of Strength & Conditioning Research, 34*, 65–72. https://doi.org/10.1519/JSC.0000000000002179

Weakley, J. J. S., Till, K., Read, D. B., Roe, G. a. B., Darrall-Jones, J., Phibbs, P. J., & Jones, B. (2017). The effects of traditional, superset, and tri-set resistance training structures on perceived intensity and physiological responses. *European Journal of Applied Physiology, 117*, 1877–1889. https://doi.org/10.1007/s00421-017-3680-3

9
THE PSYCHOSOCIAL DEVELOPMENT OF YOUTH RUGBY PLAYERS

Ross A. Shand, Lea-Cathrin Dohme and Stephen D. Mellalieu

Introduction

Psychosocial development reflects the interaction between an individual and their environment, leading to the attainment of intrapersonal (psychological) and interpersonal (social) skills and characteristics (Shand et al., 2022). When working with young players, it is important to consider their psychosocial development given that its associated outcomes enhance the likelihood of healthy maturation and the fulfilment of athletic and personal potential (Rongen et al., 2020). Furthermore, the development of psychosocial skills and characteristics (PSCs) plays an important role in supporting the successful transition of young rugby players to senior elite environments (Hill et al., 2015; Jones et al., 2014). Indeed, a lack of development of PSCs has been associated with rugby union players' failure to progress to the senior level (Taylor & Collins, 2019). The development of PSCs is therefore integral for both health and performance.

Sports, including rugby, are excellent vehicles for the development of PSCs, as the training undertaken and social influences experienced within these environments provide ideal opportunities for the intentional and systematic practice of PSCs (Holt et al., 2017). Additionally, talented young rugby players commonly engage in talent development pathways during adolescence (12–25 years), a time characterised by significant psychological and social change (Blakemore, 2018). Talent development environments (TDE) are structured pathways designed to support the development, progression and performance of young players (Abbott & Collins, 2004; Martindale et al., 2007). The characteristics of these environments and the timing at which young players engage within them significantly influence their psychosocial development, therefore organisations have a responsibility to support young players. Within these environments, coaches and practitioners have been identified as influencing the psychosocial development of players (Holt et al., 2017). To create and maintain TDEs that support players' psychosocial development, coaches and practitioners can promote learning, foster relationships and support PSC development and transfer (Bloom et al., 2020).

To outline how these principles can be embedded into young rugby players' everyday development, the purpose of this chapter is twofold. First, the chapter summarises the research investigating the psychosocial development of young rugby players, which is influenced by their stage of maturation and the characteristics of the TDE they inhabit. Second, informed by the work of Bloom et al. (2020) and our experiences working within applied rugby settings, we provide recommendations for coaches and practitioners that aim to support their efforts in developing and maintaining TDEs that deliberately foster the psychosocial development of their players.

Research Overview

What is Psychosocial Development?

'Psychosocial development' refers to the interaction between a player's individual (e.g., their level of maturation) and environmental (e.g., the characteristics of the sporting environment) factors that facilitate the development of intrapersonal (e.g., emotional control and self-confidence) and interpersonal skills and characteristics (e.g., communication skills, team cohesion; Shand et al., 2022). The definition refers to psychosocial development as a *process* that leads to associated *outcomes*, whereby the interaction between players and their environment shapes their development of PSCs (Shand et al., 2022). Psychosocial characteristics (e.g., emotional control or resilience) refer to players' trait-like dispositions that are influenced by individual, social and environmental factors; while psychosocial skills refer to players' abilities to use learned methods (e.g., relaxation techniques or positive self-talk), to regulate or enhance their psychosocial characteristics (Dohme et al., 2017, 2019). A recent systematic review of the talent development literature identified 11 psychosocial characteristics (Table 9.1) and eight psychosocial skills (Table 9.2) as facilitative of young players' development (Dohme et al., 2019). Optimally developed PSCs are suggested to facilitate the attainment and maintenance of elite athletic performance by allowing players to maximise developmental opportunities and more readily overcome the demands faced within high-level sport as well as within other life domains (MacNamara et al., 2010a).

Psychosocial Development within Rugby

Research investigating the psychosocial development of rugby players has mainly focused on two areas. First, exploring the differences in PSCs between groups, such as elite and non-elite players; and second, to identify which PSCs support the effective development of young players and how they facilitate this process.

TABLE 9.1 Psychosocial Characteristics Facilitative of Young Players' Development (adapted from Dohme et al., 2019)

Psychosocial Characteristic	Description
Hard work ethic	A player's commitment to consistently invest significant amounts of time and effort into training and competition, even if success is not immediate. Players with a hard work ethic balance the various responsibilities of their lives effectively, demand high standards of themselves and persist in the face of adversity.
Emotional control	A player's ability to manage emotions and associated behaviours arising from stressors of development (e.g., transitions), adversity (e.g., injury) or performance (e.g., competition pressure).
(Self-) Confidence	A player's belief that they have the ability to execute behaviours required to achieve desired outcomes successfully.
Interpersonal competencies	A player's ability to interact effectively with others using social skills, such as respecting and expressing appreciation for others, that allow them to get along with and function well in groups.
Motivation	An intrinsic (e.g., love of the game) or extrinsic (e.g., renewal of playing contract) desire that drives and directs a player's behaviour towards the achievement of specific goals.
Focus	A player's ability to maintain attention on relevant environmental cues in the presence of distractions.
Competitiveness	A player's desire to outperform or beat others during training and competition. Competitive players enjoy getting immersed in challenges and investing maximum effort.
Positivity	The frequent experience of pleasant emotions allowing players to interpret adversity in an optimistic manner and perceiving challenging situations as opportunities for personal growth.
Resilience	A player's ability to 'bounce back' from setbacks without suffering negative impact, allowing them to continue their goal directed trajectory.
Independence	A player's willingness and ability to take responsibility for their learning and development. Independent players are able to manage themselves and their behaviour without constant input from managers, coaches, or support staff.
Sport intelligence	A player's ability to understand the nature and demands of their sport allowing them to implement knowledge into practice and support correct decision making in response to a dynamic training or competitive environment.

TABLE 9.2 Psychosocial Skills Facilitative of Young Players' Development (adapted from Dohme et al., 2019)

Psychosocial Skill	Description
Goal setting	A motivational technique allowing players to select desired and specific objectives that can be achieved in a timely and systematic manner.
Social support seeking	A player's ability to ask for and willingness to accept help and advice from others such as coaches, parents, teammates or teachers.
Realistic self-evaluation	The conscious process of players assessing their performance during or after training and competition to identify strengths and areas of improvement, commonly informing the development or adaptation of goals.
Imagery	A technique used to acquire, maintain, review, or rehearse skills through the production of vivid, controllable and realistic images in players' minds using all senses. In addition to physical training, imagery allows players to practice, honing their focus and confidence.
Relaxation	A collection of strategies that reduce cognitive, somatic and behavioural signs of tension, worry, stress or anxiety. These may include deep breathing, progressive muscular relaxation or mindfulness.
Maintaining a sense of balance	A player's ability to recognise the importance of having interests beyond sport. This may include academic studies, vocational activities, social encounters or other hobbies.
(Pre–) Performance routine	A considered sequence of thoughts and behaviours engaged in prior to, or during, the performance of a skill helping players to focus on task-relevant information. (Pre–) Performance routines may also help players to achieve their individual optimal activation state prior to competition.
Self-talk	An (un–)intentional spoken word or internal thought that is directed at the self. The intentional regulating of players' self-talk can help to reduce negative statements and promote positive ones.

In relation to the former, Neil et al. (2006) found senior elite rugby players displayed higher levels of confidence; a greater use of psychosocial skills, and more facilitative interpretations of anxiety (i.e., symptoms of anxiety being perceived as helpful to performance) when compared to their non-elite counterparts. In relation to the latter, the development and deployment of PSCs, as outlined in Dohme et al.'s (2019) review, support young players with engaging in and maximising developmental opportunities; navigating transitions to senior rugby; and overcoming setbacks (Hill et al., 2015; Jones et al., 2014; McCarthy et al., 2016).

While some PSCs can positively influence the development of young rugby players (see Tables 9.1 and 9.2), others can have a negative or dual effect (Hill et al., 2015; Taylor & Collins, 2019). For instance, Taylor and Collins (2019) reported that negative PSCs, such as shyness and avoidance-based coping, had the potential to reduce players' engagement in developmental opportunities and impede their progress. In comparison, dual-effect PSCs can negatively affect players' development, yet if managed appropriately by practitioners and coaches can foster positive outcomes (Hill et al., 2015). For example, a degree of perfectionism can enhance youth rugby players' hard work ethic, while inappropriate deployment can increase risk of burnout and injury (Hill & Appleton; 2011; Madigan et al., 2018). Therefore, coaches and practitioners should support young players in the appropriate development and deployment of PSCs. In fact, it is important to consider every player's individual needs and characteristics when aiming to support their psychosocial development, as numerous internal (e.g., maturation) and external (the characteristics of the environment) factors can influence this development.

Factors Influencing Rugby Players' Psychosocial Development

Rugby Players as Adolescents

Adolescence is a transitional stage of development between childhood and adulthood, with young people experiencing physical and psychosocial changes as they develop into independent adults (Blakemore, 2018). During adolescence, the brain continues to develop, allowing for more complex and abstract thought along with an improving self-regulatory capacity (Diamond, 2013). Adolescents also experience significant relational changes, their relationships with parents become less prominent and the importance of peer relationships increases, as adolescents are drawn to those who share similar interests, values and beliefs (Van Norden & Burkowski, 2017). The increased importance of peers means that adolescents are likely to engage in behaviours that maintain or enhance their group membership, increasing their willingness to engage in high-risk activities if necessary (Gardner & Steinberg, 2005).

It is important to consider how adolescence may influence the acquirement and utilisation of PSCs in young rugby players. Commonly, the possession of well-developed PSCs infers a player's ability to self-regulate their thoughts, feelings and behaviours, yet effective self-regulation has been identified as a key challenge during adolescence (Steinberg, 2010). For example, Di Corrado et al.

(2014) found that senior rugby players were much better at maintaining concentration during competition than their junior counterparts. This may reflect younger players inability to regulate their focus in response to distractions. Dual effect PSCs (e.g., perfectionism or obsessive passion) may reflect these regulatory challenges whereby young players struggle to recognise when helpful behaviours become unhelpful (Winter et al., 2019). When working with young rugby players, it is therefore important to recognise they are not miniature adults and their stage of maturation will impact their psychosocial competencies.

Talent Development Environments

In addition to adolescence, the characteristics of TDEs also play a fundamental role in players' development. TDEs are structured pathways designed to support the development, progression and performance of young players (Abbot & Collins, 2004; Martindale et al., 2007). Effective TDEs are those which consistently develop senior players from their junior squads, whilst also supporting development in other life domains including education or work (Larsen et al., 2020). Characteristics of effective TDEs include: (1) the provision of individualised support; (2) a focus on long-term aims; (3) clearly defined organisational values; and (4) an intentional effort to holistic player development (i.e., physically and psychosocially; Larsen et al., 2020; MacNamara et al., 2010b). Facilitating these characteristics helps players to navigate the complex, nonlinear process of talent development and promotes the importance of players' development across multiple life domains (Henriksen et al., 2010a; Martindale et al., 2007; Rongen et al., 2020). The characteristics of TDEs determine their overall effectiveness at supporting the development of young players (Henriksen et al., 2010). It is important to recognise that the structured, selective and intensive nature of TDEs can give rise to several challenges which may influence the psychosocial development of young players and, with this, their progress and health. For instance, overly prescriptive and highly demanding TDEs are commonly associated with several physical and psychosocial consequences including reduced wellbeing and relatedness with others (Bergeron et al., 2015). These negative effects can impact players' mental health and overall development (Bergeron et al., 2015; Rongen et al., 2018). It is therefore important that TDE managers, coaches and practitioners consider the development of environments that support the long-term, holistic and individualised development of young players systematically.

Practical Applications

Recommendations for the Psychosocial Development of Young Rugby Players

To develop effective TDEs, coaches and practitioners can use coaching frameworks to guide their thinking and practices. Bloom et al. (2020) reviewed four coaching frameworks (i.e., the Mastery Approach to Coaching; Positive Youth Development in Sport; the Life Skills Development Model; and Humanistic Coaching) and synthesised recommendations that empower coaches and practitioners to build learning environments structured to meet the psychosocial needs and desires of youth players. In line with the characteristics of effective TDEs, Bloom and colleagues found ideal youth sports environments: (1) promoted learning and development over winning; (2) created supportive environments; (3) intentionally planned and promoted players' psychosocial development; (4) facilitated players with opportunities to practice PSCs; (5) promoted and facilitated the transfer of PSCs to other life domains; and (6) considered athletes' individual differences and wider social environments. In the next part of this chapter, we will draw upon our applied experiences to outline how these recommendations can be embedded by coaches and practitioners to systematically support young rugby players' psychosocial development. Before outlining how these recommendations can be embedded into the rugby context it is important to highlight that all six recommendations are interconnected in some way. For example, promoting learning and development over winning is also likely to create a more supportive environment. Considering this connectedness, along with the complexity of psychosocial development, can help coaches and practitioners navigate the multifaceted and non-linear process. Further, coaches and practitioners should consider how the six recommendations related to their own context, which will influence how they may be implemented.

Recommendation 1: Promoting Learning and Development Over Winning

As established, coaches and practitioners play an important role in supporting players' psychosocial development through quality interactions and relationships. Central to these positive relationships is the prioritisation of long-term, developmentally focused processes (e.g., creating connection amongst peers) over short-term outcomes (e.g., winning). Achieving this balance can be difficult (Preston et al., 2021), but adherence to it will likely be influenced by coaches' and practitioners' core beliefs and values. Coaches and practitioners should therefore consider their underpinning beliefs and how these influence their approach to working with athletes (Grecic & Collins, 2013). Engaging in critical reflection can raise both coaches and practitioner awareness as to why they work in the way they do and the potential impact this has on their athletes' development (See Box 9.1 for example questions to assist with engaging in critical reflection). Incongruence between core beliefs and values and a willingness to promote learning and development over winning can lead to ineffective TDEs (Henriksen et al., 2014).

Box 9.1 Questions to reflect on your core beliefs and values

'What are my core beliefs and values?'
'How do these influence my coaching?'
'Why do I coach?'
'How does the development of young people occur?'
'What role do I play in this?'
'Other than physical, technical and tactical skills, what do I want the player to develop from their engagement in this environment?'
'How will this be achieved?'

To promote learning and development, coaches and practitioners should also consider the use of individual development plans. Ubiquitous throughout TDEs, individual development plans should promote the setting of goals that support long-term development, these may be self-referenced or related to developmental benchmarks. Adopting goals that focus on long-term development rather than short-term outcomes will help facilitate an environment where players focus on skill and performance accomplishments, such as improving lower body strength or enhancing on field decision making, rather than showing ability in relation to others.

Recommendation 2: Creating Supportive Environments

The creation of a supportive environment is underpinned by positive relationships between players, coaches, practitioners, teammates and parents (Henriksen et al., 2010a, 2010b). Techniques such as Personal Disclosure Mutual Sharing (PDMS; Windsor et al., 2011) can facilitate supportive and cohesive relationships through the sharing of personal stories which give insight into an individual's values, beliefs, attitudes and personal motives (for full guidance see Holt & Dunn, 2006). PDMS can also support players' ability to communicate effectively and seek social support when needed. For example, players can be asked to share a personal story providing insight into their aspirations, achievements, as well as the challenges faced and overcome (see Box 9.2 for examples). This activity could be conducted at training or within identified sessions (e.g., team building days) and should also include coaches and practitioners.

Box 9.2 Examples of PDMS activities

Example 1: Using three photos describe why they are meaningful to you.

> **Example 2:** Tell the group about your biggest achievement to date, a time of adversity and your reason for being here.
>
> **Example 3:** Tell a personal story that will help the team understand you better, a story you would like others to know about you which gives an insight into your character, motives and desires.

The provision of balanced training and playing time can also help foster positive relationships between youth players, their peers and adults (Dohme et al., 2020). This provision allows all players to practice their technical, tactical, as well as psychosocial skills. Within TDEs, older, earlier developing players are often given more opportunities to perform in matches and training, whereas younger, later developing players are afforded fewer opportunities (Preston et al., 2021). The provision of balanced playing and training time can limit the formation of cliques and, instead, enhance feelings of team cohesion, ultimately bringing the team closer together (Dohme et al., 2020).

Finally, coaches and practitioners are urged to consider how their behaviour and language may influence the environment. Specifically, it is important to: (a) offer positive reinforcement through verbal feedback and positive body language; (b) focus on players' strengths, talents and interests rather than just weaknesses; (c) limit judgemental comments; (d) model positive behaviours such as respect, empathy and patience; (e) show interest in players' lives beyond the sport context; and (f) acknowledge players' perspectives and opinions (Bloom et al., 2020). Engaging in these practices will likely minimise potential perfectionistic environments which may impede development. It is worth noting that language which promotes the need to achieve short-term outcomes (e.g., winning the next match) can increase pressure on young players, having a detrimental impact on their performance and potentially health (Preston et al., 2021). Therefore, coaches and practitioners should consider how their behaviour and language may influence levels of challenge and support within the environment (Fletcher & Sarkar, 2016).

Recommendation 3: Intentionally Plan and Promote Players' Psychosocial Development

Even when TDEs emphasise learning and personal growth along with providing supportive environments, the development of players' PSCs is not guaranteed (Camiré et al., 2011; Smith & Smoll, 2002). Coaches and practitioners should therefore explicitly plan and systematically integrate players' psychosocial development into their everyday practices (Bean & Forneris, 2016). To make this possible, coaches and practitioners should engage in 'nested planning' that allows for the integration of PSCs development across the short-, medium- and long-term cycles of the TDE (Abraham & Collins, 2011; See chapter 17 for in depth description). Coaches and practitioners should first identify and define the PSCs, along with clarifying associated behaviours across different age groups. For example, a

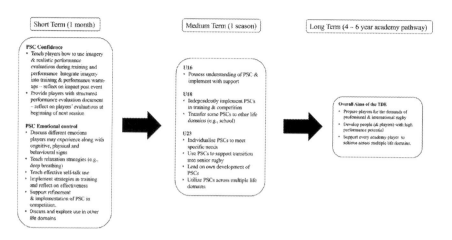

FIGURE 9.1 The Planning for Psychosocial Skills and Characteristics Development across Short, Medium and Long-Term in a Rugby Talent Development Environment.

14-year-old player may be expected to control emotions in training, whereas an 18-year-old player may be expected to do this in competition as well. To support the development of emotional control, appropriate psychosocial skills should be developed such as self-talk. Engaging in this process facilitates shared knowledge and understanding among the TDE staff, allowing for clear and consistent support to be provided to players (Alfano & Collins, 2021). PSCs may be identified that are deemed relevant to the specific context (e.g., a club may prioritise the development of self-awareness), or pre-existing frameworks can be utilised (i.e., the 5Cs, Harwood, 2008; or PCDEs, MacNamara et al., 2010a, 2010b). Following this, it is important to plan for their systematic development. This should occur at the short-, medium- and long-term level. Adopting such an approach allows for alignment between long-term outcomes (i.e., the successful development of players) and short-term decisions (i.e., the content of specific training sessions; Abraham & Collins 2011). Figure 9.1 provides an example of how PSC development may be planned across short-, medium- and long-term cycles within a TDE.

Recommendation 4: Facilitating Players with Opportunities to Practice PSCs

Once planned for, coaches and practitioners should actively support PSCs development by providing players with opportunities to practice them. To best support, the development of PSCs, coaches and practitioners should take advantage of pre and post-session conversations as key teachable moments. Collins and MacNamara (2017) proposed the *'teach – test – tweak - repeat'* which in addition to the repetitive practice of PSCs highlights the timeframes before, after and between activities as central to the development of PSCs. The importance of the pre and post-time points are reflected within Harwood et al.'s (2015) 'PROGRESS' framework.

This encourages eight behaviours within sessions to support PSCs development: (1) Promote the PSCs; (2) Role model the PSCs; (3) Provide ownership of PSCs; (4) Grow each PSC; (5) Reinforce PSCs; (6) Empower peer support; (7) Support the supporter; and (8) Self-review and responsiveness (see Harwood et al., 2015 for further information regarding how to implement these principles). The use of questioning by coaches and practitioners at these time points can enhance players use and development of PSCs within and between sessions (see Box 9.3 for example questions). In addition to facilitating players' development and PSCs use within session, other activities can also be used to support their development, such as asking players to present a review of training or a match to their teammates, which may in turn facilitate both communication skills and sporting intelligence.

Recommendation 5: Promoting and Facilitating Players' Transfer of PSCs to Other Life Domains

Once PSCs have been developed within a sporting context, they can be transferred to other life domains to facilitate the holistic development of young players. For example, the development of effective goal-setting principles and a hard work ethic within a rugby environment can be transferred to support learning and attainment in education (Bean et al., 2018). To promote transfer coaches and practitioners can discuss this process with players. Such discussion can raise players' awareness of potential transferability. To facilitate transfer, coaches should plan for and provide players with the opportunity to practice (see Box 9.3 for examples). Other examples of transfer opportunities may include players engaging in off-field duties on behalf of their club or team whereby they attend commercial events and meet and interact with sponsors, supporters or members of the general public.

Box 9.3 Example questions

Pre-session questions

'How might confidence to perform successfully be developed?'
'What is going to help us build confidence in this session?'
'What skills can we use to maintain/develop confidence in this session?'
'What might confidence look like in this session?'

Post-session questions – reflecting on the session

'How would you rate your confidence in that session?'
'What did you do to maintain your confidence in that session?'
'How successful was this?'
'What impact did I have on your confidence in that session?'

Post-session questions – looking forward

'What will you do the same/differently next time?'
'What could I (coach) do the same/different next time?'
'What other areas could you apply these skills in before the next session?'
'What would help you in transferring these skills?'

Recommendation 6: Considering Players' Individual Differences and Wider Social Environments

To support players' psychosocial development effectively, coaches and practitioners need to consider players' individual internal (e.g., personal and physical attributes) and external (e.g., family and coaching background) differences. Coaches and practitioners are encouraged to invest time into getting to know their players as people, not just athletes. Through conversations with players, coaches and practitioners can get an insight into their life at home and in education/work, their subsequent aims and aspirations, and hobbies outside of sport. Where possible, abiding by the players' right to confidentiality, information should be shared with staff within the TDE to facilitate shared understanding and more effective support for the players.

When transferring psychosocial skills, it is important to collaborate with parents and teachers, who play an important role within players' lives (Knight & Newport, 2017). Working in collaboration with these individuals can significantly increase the power and effectiveness of coach and practitioner efforts, as well as player perceptions of the importance of the development and transfer of psychosocial skills. To work effectively with the parents and teachers of players, coaches are encouraged to communicate with these individuals regularly at parent evenings, school or college visits, or events that are open to the players' support network. During conversations with parents and teachers, coaches are encouraged to share and discuss their underpinning philosophy and intended psychosocial outcomes for the development of the players (Camiré et al., 2011). Doing so increases the likelihood of everyone close to the player reinforcing the same values and offering appropriate practice and transfer opportunities.

To summarise, the development of PSCs is best achieved through creating alignment throughout the TDE. This is underpinned by coaches and practitioners holding congruent philosophies which prioritise and plan for the development of PSCs through intentional and explicit approaches within a supportive environment. Further, transfer of PSCs is encouraged and supported by considering and engaging with the player's wider social environments.

Key Take Home Messages

- Coaches and practitioners should consider their own philosophies and the congruence with supporting players' long-term psychosocial development.
- The prioritisation of individualised, long-term player development over short-term outcomes (e.g., winning) will support positive psychosocial development.
- Coaches and practitioners play an important role in creating a supportive environment that facilitates the development of meaningful relationships between players, peers and adults.
- Psychosocial development should be consciously and explicitly planned for.
- Coaches and practitioners should plan and provide opportunities for players to practice PSCs.
- Pre- and post-activity are key teachable moments to discuss, reflect on and refine PSCs.
- PSCs can be transferred from sport to other life domains with coaches and practitioners playing an important role in supporting this process.
- Getting to know the individual and their wider social context is imperative to successfully supporting their psychosocial development.

References

Abbott, A., & Collins, D. (2004). Eliminating the dichotomy between theory and practice in talent identification and development: Considering the role of psychology. *Journal of Sports Sciences*, 22, 395–408. https://doi.org/10.1080/02640410410001675324

Abraham, A., & Collins, D. (2011). Taking the next step: Ways forward for coaching science. *Quest*, 63, 366–384. https://doi.org/10.1080/00336297.2011.10483687

Alfano, H., & Collins, D. (2021). Good practice delivery in sport science and medicine support: Perceptions of experienced sport leaders and practitioners. *Managing Sport and Leisure*, 26, 145–160. https://doi.org/10.1080/23750472.2020.1727768

Bean, C., & Forneris, T. (2016). Examining the importance of intentionally structuring the youth sport context to facilitate positive youth development. *Journal of Applied Sport Psychology*, 28, 410–425. https://doi.org/10.1080/10413200.2016.1164764

Bean, C., Kramers, S., Forneris, T., & Camiré, M. (2018). The implicit/explicit continuum of life skills development and transfer. *Quest*, 70, 456–470. https://doi.org/10.1080/00336297.2018.1451348

Bergeron, M. F., Mountjoy, M., Armstrong, N., Chia, M., Cote, J., Emery, C. A., Faigenbaum, A., Hall, G., Jr., Kriemler, S., Leglise, M., Malina, R. M., Pensgaard, A. M., Sanchez, A., Soligard, T., Sundgot-Borgen, J., van Mechelen, W., Weissensteiner, J. R., & Engebretsen, L. (2015). International Olympic Committee consensus statement on youth athletic development. *British Journal of Sports Medicine*, 49, 843–851. https://doi.org/10.1136/bjsports-2015-094962

Blakemore, S. J. (2018). *Inventing ourselves: The secret life of the teenage brain*. Penguin.

Bloom, G. A., Dohme, L-C., & Falcão, W. R. (2020). Coaching youth athletes. In R. Resende & A. R. Gomes (Eds.), *Coaching for human development and performance in sports* (pp. 143–169). Springer.

Camiré, M., Forneris, T., Trudel, P., & Bernard, D. (2011). Strategies for helping coaches facilitate positive youth development through sport. *Journal of Sport Psychology in Action*, 2, 92–99. https://doi.org/10.1080/21520704.2011.584246

Collins, D., & MacNamara, Á. (2017). *Talent development: A practitioner guide.* Routledge.

Diamond, A. (2013). Executive functions. *Annual Review of Psychology, 64,* 135–168. https://doi.org/10.1146/annurev-psych-113011-143750

Di Corrado, D., Murgia, M., & Freda, A. (2014). Attentional focus and mental skills in senior and junior professional rugby union players. *Sport Sciences for Health, 10,* 79–83. https://doi.org/10.1007/s11332-014-0177-x

Dohme, L.-C., Backhouse, S., Piggott, D., & Morgan, G. (2017). Categorising and defining popular psychological terms used within the youth athlete talent development literature: A systematic review. *International Review of Sport and Exercise Psychology, 10,* 134–163. https://doi.org/10.1080/1750984X.2016.1185451

Dohme, L.-C., Lefebvre, J. S., & Bloom, G. A. (2020). Team building in youth sport. In M. W. Bruner, M. Eys, & L. J. Martin (Eds.), *Exploring the power of groups in youth sport* (pp. 165–183). Elsevier.

Dohme, L.-C., Piggott, D., Backhouse, S., & Morgan, G. (2019). Psychological skills and characteristics facilitative of youth athletes' development: A systematic review. *The Sport Psychologist, 33,* 261–275. https://doi.org/10.1123/tsp.2018-0014

Fletcher, D., & Sarkar, M. (2016). Mental fortitude training: An evidence-based approach to developing psychological resilience for sustained success. *Journal of Sport Psychology in Action, 7,* 135–157. https://doi.org/10.1080/21520704.2016.1255496

Gardner, M., & Steinberg, L. (2005). Peer influence on risk taking, risk preference, and risky decision making in adolescence and adulthood: An experimental study. *Developmental Psychology, 41,* 625–635. https://doi.org/10.1037/0012-1649.41.4.625

Grecic, D., & Collins, D. (2013). The epistemological chain: Practical applications in sports. *Quest, 65,* 151–168. https://doi.org/10.1080/00336297.2013.773525

Harwood, C. (2008). Developmental consulting in a professional football academy: The 5Cs coaching efficacy program. *The Sport Psychologist, 22,* 109–133. https://doi.org/10.1123/tsp.22.1.109

Harwood, C. G., Barker, J. B., & Anderson, R. (2015). Psychosocial development in youth soccer players: Assessing the effectiveness of the 5Cs intervention program. *The Sport Psychologist, 29,* 319–334. https://doi.org/10.1123/tsp.2014-0161

Henriksen, K., Larsen, C. H., & Christensen, M. K. (2014). Looking at success from its opposite pole: The case of a talent development golf environment in Denmark. *International Journal of Sport and Exercise Psychology, 12,* 134–149. https://doi.org/10.1080/1612197X.2013.853473

Henriksen, K., Stambulova, N., & Roessler, K. K. (2010a). Holistic approach to athletic talent development environments: A successful sailing milieu. *Psychology of Sport and Exercise, 11,* 212–222. https://doi.org/10.1016/j.psychsport.2009.10.005

Henriksen, K., Stambulova, N., & Roessler, K. K. (2010b). Successful talent development in track and field: Considering the role of environment. *Scandinavian Journal of Medicine & Science in Sports, 20,* 122–132. https://doi.org/10.1111/j.1600-0838.2010.01187

Hill, A. P., & Appleton, P. R. (2011). The predictive ability of the frequency of perfectionistic cognitions, self-oriented perfectionism, and socially prescribed perfectionism in relation to symptoms of burnout in youth rugby players. *Journal of Sports Sciences, 29,* 695–703. https://doi.org/10.1080/02640414.2010.551216

Hill, A., MacNamara, Á., & Collins, D. (2015). Psychobehaviourally based features of effective talent development in rugby union: A coach's perspective. *The Sport Psychologist, 29,* 201–212. https://doi.org/10.1123/tsp.2014-0103

Holt, N. L., & Dunn, J. G. (2006). Guidelines for delivering personal-disclosure mutual-sharing team building interventions. *The Sport Psychologist, 20,* 348–367. https://doi.org/10.1123/tsp.20.3.348

Holt, N. L., Neely, K. C., Slater, L. G., Camiré, M., Côté, J., Fraser-Thomas, J., MacDonald, D., Strachan, L., & Tamminen, K. A. (2017). A grounded theory of positive youth development through sport based on results from a qualitative meta-study. *International Review of Sport and Exercise Psychology*, 10, 1–49. https://doi.org/10.1080/1750984X.2016.1180704

Jones, R. A., Mahoney, J. W., & Gucciardi, D. F. (2014). On the transition into elite rugby league: Perceptions of players and coaching staff. *Sport, Exercise, and Performance Psychology*, 3, 28–45. https://doi.org/10.1037/spy0000013

Knight, C. J., & Newport, R. A. (2017). Understanding and working with parents of young athletes. In C. J. Knight, C. G. Harwood, & D. Gould (Eds.), *Sport psychology for young athletes* (pp. 303–314). Routledge.

Larsen, C. H., Storm, L. K., Sæther, S. A., Pyrdol, N., & Henriksen, K. (2020). A world class academy in professional football. *Scandinavian Journal of Sport and Exercise Psychology*, 2, 33–43. https://doi.org/10.7146/sjsep.v2i0.119746

MacNamara, Á., Button, A., & Collins, D. (2010a). The role of psychological characteristics in facilitating the pathway to elite performance part 1: Identifying mental skills and behaviours. *The Sport Psychologist*, 24, 52–73. https://doi.org/10.1123/tsp.24.1.52

MacNamara, Á., Button, A., & Collins, D. (2010b). The role of psychological characteristics in facilitating the pathway to elite performance part 2: Examining environmental and stage-related differences in skills and behaviours. *The Sport Psychologist*, 24, 74–96. https://doi.org/10.1123/tsp.24.1.74

Madigan, D. J., Stoeber, J., Forsdyke, D., Dayson, M., & Passfield, L. (2018). Perfectionism predicts injury in junior athletes: Preliminary evidence from a prospective study. *Journal of Sports Sciences*, 36, 545–550. https://doi.org/10.1080/02640414.2017.1322709

Martindale, R. J., Collins, D., & Abraham, A. (2007). Effective talent development: The elite coach perspective in UK sport. *Journal of Applied Sport Psychology*, 19, 187–206. https://doi.org/10.1080/10413200701188944

McCarthy, N., Collins, D., & Court, D. (2016). Start hard, finish better: Further evidence for the reversal of the RAE advantage. *Journal of Sports Sciences*, 34, 1461–1465. https://doi.org/10.1080/02640414.2015.1119297

Neil, R., Mellalieu, S. D., & Hanton, S. (2006). Psychological skills usage and the competitive anxiety response as a function of skill level in rugby union. *Journal of Sports Science & Medicine*, 5, 415–423.

Preston, C., Allan, V., & Fraser-Thomas, J. (2021). Facilitating positive youth development in elite youth hockey: Exploring coaches' capabilities, opportunities, and motivations. *Journal of Applied Sport Psychology*, 33, 1–19. https://doi.org/10.1080/10413200.2019.1648327

Rongen, F., McKenna, J., Cobley, S., Tee, J. C., & Till, K. (2020). Psychosocial outcomes associated with soccer academy involvement: Longitudinal comparisons against aged matched school pupils. *Journal of Sports Sciences*, 38, 1387–1398. https://doi.org/10.1080/02640414.2020.1778354

Rongen, F., McKenna, J., Cobley, S., & Till, K. (2018). Are youth sport talent identification and development systems necessary and healthy? *Sports Medicine-Open*, 4, 2–4. https://doi.org/10.1186/s40798-018-0135-2

Shand, R., Dohme, L. C., & Mellalieu, S. (2022). The psychosocial development of the youth rugby player. In K. Till, J. Weakley, S. Whitehead, & B. Jones (Eds.), *Youth rugby* (pp. 169–181). Routledge.

Smith, R. E., & Smoll, F. L. (2002). Youth sports as a behaviour setting for psychosocial interventions. In J. L. Van Raalte & B. W. Brewer (Eds.), *Exploring sport and exercise psychology* (pp. 341–371). American Psychological Association. https://doi.org/10.1037/10465-017

Steinberg, L. (2010). A dual systems model of adolescent risk-taking. *Developmental Psychobiology, 52*, 216–224. https://doi.org/10.1002/dev.20445

Taylor, J., & Collins, D. (2019). Shoulda, coulda, didnae—why don't high-potential players make it? *The Sport Psychologist, 33*, 85–96. https://doi.org/10.1123/tsp.2017-0153

Van Norden T. H. J., & Burkowski, W. M. (2017). Social development. In A. Slater & G. Bremner (Eds.), *An introduction to developmental psychology* (3rd ed., pp. 579–610). Wiley.

Windsor, P. M., Barker, J., & McCarthy, P. (2011). Doing sport psychology: Personal-disclosure mutual-sharing in professional soccer. *The Sport Psychologist, 25*, 94–114. https://doi.org/0.1123/tsp.25.1.94

Winter, S., O'Brien, F., & Collins, D. (2019). Things ain't what they used to be? Coaches' perceptions of commitment in developing athletes. *Journal of Applied Sport Psychology*, 1–20. https://doi.org/10.1080/10413200.2019.1646839

10
TECHNICAL AND TACTICAL DEVELOPMENT IN YOUTH RUGBY

Michael Ashford and Jamie Taylor

Introduction

Rugby union and rugby league are intermittent team invasion games, where two teams attempt to technically and tactically outwit and outscore their opponent (Ashford et al., 2020; Tee et al., 2018). The laws of both codes create complex games that pose numerous technical and tactical problems that players and teams must solve (Ashford et al., 2022). Due to the physical and combative nature of both codes, the technical proficiency of a player's actions in overcoming these problems is essential for safety and enjoyment, especially in younger age groups. Recently, the Rugby Football Union released their Talent Development Framework (RFU, 2021), where they adopted the work of Ashford and colleagues (2020, 2022) to separate the game of rugby union into three distinct moments; attack, defence and contest. For each of these game moments, base technical and tactical requirements have been offered for players at all levels of the game (RFU, 2021). Rugby league can also be segmented into attack, defence and contest moments yet the technical and tactical solutions produced in the game are clearly different due to the different set of laws. The two codes of rugby present two different games which differ in the internal logic of the game, nonetheless the types of passing, tackling, evasive movement, agility, ground skills and kicking remain constant across both codes.

Whilst common sense indicates that technical and tactical qualities are essential for the development of the young rugby player, research has suggested that game intelligence, decision-making and skill play a key role in differentiating between the best from the rest (Ashford et al., 2021a; O'Connor & Larkin, 2015). Yet, from a practical perspective, whilst coaches will spend significant time considering how to develop technical and tactical qualities (hopefully along with other dimensions of performance; Collins et al., 2011) there remains limited practical use of analysis, measurement and evaluation of this through a player's career. This is surprising given that so much attention has been paid to analysis of team performance and tracking of individual physical load (e.g., Malone et al., 2017). Such information would be useful as a means of understanding player development, effectiveness of technical refinement (Carson & Collins, 2011) and essentially, if we are to be truly evidence informed in our practice, provide a marker to evaluate the effectiveness of various coaching methods in a nested plan (see Chapter 17).

Therefore, the purpose of this chapter is to summarise the research investigating the technical and tactical development of young rugby players and provide practical recommendations. The research overview will address three clear areas, where authors have (1) measured technical and tactical qualities; (2) developed technical and tactical qualities; and (3) modified competition formats for enhancing technical and tactical qualities in young rugby players. Following, applied recommendations will be offered for each of these research areas. Unfortunately, the wider literature in youth rugby is limited and much of it descriptive in nature. Therefore, specific studies exploring technical and tactical development in other populations, such as professional, university or amateur playing groups have been included and applied where appropriate. Finally, clear practical applications are offered for the measurement and development of technical and tactical qualities for those supporting the development of young rugby players.

Research Overview

Measurement of Technical and Tactical Qualities

Testing Batteries

A breadth of research exploring technical and tactical qualities of players has focussed on the identification of 'talent' through measurement (see Table 10.1). This work has typically aimed to measure player's current technical proficiency as an indicator of potential to perform at higher levels of the game. Pienaar et al. (1998) first measured a group of ten-year-old rugby union players game-specific skills, using a testing battery that included passing for distance, passing for accuracy at 4 m and 7 m targets, running and catching, kicking for distance and kick off for distance. Their results indicated that those who scored highly were more likely to be selected for their district team. Building on their original testing battery Van Gent and Spamer (2005) and Spamer et al. (2009) extended Pienaar and colleagues (1998) work to include a score out of ten for ground skills (e.g., landing, work on the floor or in contact), side steps and air and ground kicks. Within Van Gent and Spamer's (2005) study, game-specific skills of young players were compared by age group and position (see Table 10.1 for a breakdown of age groups). Significant differences were found within age groups, between positions and between age groups. The authors suggested that testing batteries

TABLE 10.1 Summary of the Research Studies Measuring Technical and Tactical Qualities

Authors	Purpose of Study	Participants	Code	Topic	Method
Pienaar et al. (1998)	Identify motor skill variables that will enable coaches to identify 10-year-old boys who could become successful rugby players.	10-year-old boys $n = 173$.	Union	Testing batteries	Passing for distance (m) Passing for accuracy, 7 m (score) Passing for accuracy, 4 m (score) Running and catching (n) Kick for distance (m) Kick-oV for distance (m)
Van Gent & Spamer (2005)	To compare rugby-specific skills among different age groups of elite rugby players within positional groups (tight forwards, loose forwards, halves and backline).	U13 $n = 21$ U16 $n = 22$ U18 $n = 18$ U19 $n = 19$	Union	Testing batteries	Group skills, side steps, aerial and ground kicks, passing for distance (m), passing for accuracy (4 m), passing for accuracy (7 m), kicking for distance, kick-off for distance and catching while running.
Spamer, et al. (2009)	Comparison of U16 players game-specific skills concerning a group of elite South African and New Zealand players.	U16 South African players $n = 64$, New Zealand players $n = 24$	Union	Testing batteries	Ground skills, side steps (/10), air and ground kicks (/10), passing distance (m). passing accuracy over 4 m (/10), passing accuracy over 7 m (/30), kicking distance (m) and kick-off distance (m)
Gabbett et al. (2011)	Importance of skill qualities e.g. technical skill (tackling proficiency, draw and pass proficiency) and perceptual skill (reactive agility, pattern recall, pattern prediction) to team selection.	High-performance rugby league players competing for selection for an NRL club $n = 86$	League	Testing batteries	Testing battery made up of a 1 vs 1 tackling assessment, 2 vs 1 draw and pass assessment, reactive agility test, pattern recall assessment and pattern predication assessment.

Chiwaridzo et al. (2019a)	Explore the differences between different levels of playing competition for U16 players in Zimbabwe, listed as elite, sub elite and non-rugby.	U16 participants Elite $n = 41$ Subelite = 30 29 = non-rugby players	Union	Testing batteries	The School Clinical Rugby Measure (SCRuM) test battery was used to compare rugby-specific game skills tackling proficiency test, passing ability skills test and running and catching ability skills test.
Chiwaridzo (2019b)	Explore the differences between different levels of playing competition in Zimbabwe for U19 players, listed as elite, sub-elite and non-rugby	U19 participants Elite $n = 41$ Sub-elite $n = 46$ Non-rugby $n = 26$	Union	Testing batteries	The School Clinical Rugby Measure (SCRuM) test battery was used to compare rugby-specific game skills tackling proficiency test, passing ability skills test and running and catching ability skills test.
Hendricks et al. (2015)	Review the strengths and limitations of skill assessments that have been employed in a rugby team setting previously.	Seven skill assessments have been employed across 12 studies in a rugby team setting.	Union & league	Testing batteries	Spamer and colleagues (2009) Rugby Union skill assessment battery. Gabbett's (2007, 2008, 2011, 2012) skill assessments. Serpell and colleagues (2010) agility test for rugby league. Gabbett and Abernethy (2013) rugby league anticipation test. Pavely et al. (2009) passing the ball on the run-in reaction to a signal. Wheeler and Sayers (2010, 2011) agility and carrying the ball into contact drill. Jackson et al. (2006) movement recall and anticipation.

(*Continued*)

TABLE 10.1 (Continued)

Authors	Purpose of Study	Participants	Code	Topic	Method
Oorschot et al. (2017)	(1) Give an overview of commonly used game-specific skills tests in rugby. (2) Evaluate available psychometric information of these tests.	10 papers (union n = 3; league n = 7). Four studies explored youth age groups.	Union & league	Testing batteries	Reactive agility (Gabbett et al., 2008; Green et al., 2011; Serpell et al., 2010) Technical and perceptual skills (Gabbett et al., 2011) Catching & passing (Pienaar et al., 1998). Game-specific skills during match (Bennett at al., 2016; Gabbett et al., 2007; Kempton et al., 2013; Sirotic et al., 2009).
Bennett et al. (2016)	Explore the positional characteristics on technical and tactical outcomes in rugby league	Australian junior representative rugby league players n = 46	League	Performance analysis	Frequency of offensive involvements (ball carry, support run, offensive miss, line break and line break assist) and defensive involvements (tackle completed & tackle not completed) by playing position.
Den Hollander et al. (2016)	The purpose of this study was to analyse line breaks within elite southern hemisphere rugby union and identify key skills and playing characteristics leading to them.	Footage of n = 125 Super Rugby games	Union	Performance analysis	12 operational variables were collected from the game footage, including the type of pass, number of passes, pick & go, running speed, running angle, change in speed, change in angle, evasion, deception, field position, possession and tries.

Den Hollander et al. (2019)	Examine the validity of a tool that assesses ruck technique in training.	Senior mens rugby players $n = 37$; 16 forwards & 21 backs. First Academy players $n = 51$; 21 forwards & 21 backs. Second Academy players $n = 43$; 19 forwards & 24 backs.	Union	Performance analysis	Contact drill proficiency was examined using a 2 vs 2 contact drill. All drills were filmed from a side angle and players were awarded 1 point for successful technique and 0 points if they failed to perform the criterion. Criterion were broken down into pre-contact, contact and post-contact for the ball carrier and in the ruck.
Gabbett et al. (2010)	Skill demands of on-side and off-side small-sided games.	U19 elite male rugby league players. Playing members of an NRL team $n = 16$	League	Performance analysis	Comparison of on-side (only permitted to pass backwards) and on-side (can pass forwards and backwards) small-sided games regarding the number of involvements for players. Involvements included touches, passes and effective passes.
Ungureanu et al. (2019)	Analyse the technical and tactical aspects of the Italian under-18 Academy Rugby Union in relation to different academies, regional tournaments and game outcomes.	U18 Italian Academy Rugby games $n = 16$	Union	Performance analysis	The games were measured using post-facto notational analysis of 44 performance indicators. They included the frequency and effectiveness of, attacking behaviour (breakdown, passes, possession, phases), defensive behaviour (breakdown, tackles), contest (set piece) and ball in play.
Wheeler et al. (2010)	Explore the attributes of agility skill execution related to attacking strategies in rugby union.	All carries made $n = 1372$ across Super 14 Rugby games $n = 7$	Union	Technical and tactical – offensive play	Notational analysis was conducted on game footage for nine attacking performance indicators, two defensive pattern indicators and two attacking outcome indicators.

should be made specific to the demands of the age group in question. Comparatively, Spamer et al. (2009) compared two groups of U16 South African rugby players with a group of New Zealand rugby players. Findings indicated that the New Zealand playing group outscored the South African group in six of the eight tests, but only two of these measures were significantly different (i.e., ground skills and kicks). The South African group performed significantly better in passing for accuracy over 4 m.

In contrast to this work, Gabbett and colleagues (2011) devised a testing battery that measured players technical proficiency under opposed conditions, to correlate the relationship between game-specific skills and team selection. Eighty-six professional rugby league players competing in the National Rugby League (NRL) conducted a 1 vs 1 tackling assessment, 2 vs 1 draw and pass assessment, a reactive agility test, and a pattern recall and predication assessment. The findings indicated that players who were selected in the first NRL game of the season were older, had more years of experience, superior tackling and draw and pass proficiency.

Chiwaridzo and colleagues (2018, 2019a, 2019b) have validated the School Clinical Rugby Measure (SCRuM) test battery. This tool was then employed to measure the technical ability of U16 (2019a) and U19 (2019b) rugby union players. The SCRuM test battery measures game skills which include a tackling proficiency test (% of successful tackles), a passing ability test (accuracy over 4 and 7 m) and a running and catching ability test (accuracy). Using these measures, Chiwaridzo et al. (2019a), with the unfortunate label of 'elite', explored the differences between elite, sub-elite and non-playing U16 rugby union players game skills. Findings indicated that the 'elite' group outscored the other two populations across all three measures. However, significant differences were only found for tackling. Similarly, Chiwaridzo and colleagues (2019b) explored the differences between U19 elite and sub-elite playing competitions. The elite playing group outscored the other two populations on all game skills, whilst significant differences were found for the passing ability test.

Two review articles have evaluated the strengths and limitations of testing batteries commonly used to measure game-skills in a rugby team setting (Hendricks et al., 2015; Oorschot et al., 2017). Hendricks et al. (2015) reviewed testing batteries that measured game-specific skills (Gabbett et al., 2007, 2008, 2011, 2012; Pienaar et al., 1998; Spamer et al., 2009), agility (Serpell et al., 2010; Wheeler & Sayers, 2011, 2010), anticipation (Gabbett & Abernethy, 2013; Jackson et al., 2006), passing on the run (Pavely et al., 2009) and ball carrying (Wheeler & Sayers, 2010, 2011). Similarly, Oorschot et al. (2017) reviewed ten studies, five of which were also included in Hendricks et al.'s (2015) paper. This review evaluated measures of reactive agility (Gabbett et al., 2008; Green et al., 2011; Serpell et al., 2010), technical and perceptual skills (Gabbett et al., 2011), catching and passing (Pienaar et al., 1998) and game-specific skills during matches (Bennett et al., 2016; Gabbett et al., 2007; Kempton et al., 2013; Sirotic et al., 2009). The findings of both review articles suggested that these studies lacked methodological quality and failed to represent the complex realities of the game. Hendricks et al. (2015) concluded that Gabbett and colleagues' employment of the 1 vs 1 testing battery, whilst not without limitations, was most appropriate as the measurements employed opposed activities between an attacker and defender.

Studies measuring technical and tactical qualities have often employed testing batteries as a vehicle to identify talented individuals or compare talented individuals across varying contexts (Chiwaridzo et al., 2019a, 2019b; Gabbett et al., 2011; Pienaar et al., 1998; Spamer et al., 2009; Van Gent and Spamer, 2005). Across the studies included in this overview, such approaches have aimed to validate the identification of 'talented' players across multiple age groups and playing contexts, including U10 (Pienaar et al., 1998) and U13 (Van Gent & Spamer, 2005) age groups. A detailed explanation of the inappropriateness of such approaches is beyond the scope of this chapter, but identifying U10 players on the basis of their current ability in discreet technical tests, is on a number of levels a completely incoherent approach (see Box 10.1; Abbott & Collins, 2004). Furthermore, most testing batteries used across this body of research have measured players technical and tactical qualities in conditions withdrawn from the true complexities of the game (Oorschot et al., 2017). These approaches may hold some sort of validity for the tracking of performance improvement in a limited subset of technical skills. Yet, much like the use of unidimensional testing in any sport, they represent a fool's errand for those who believe that high potential players can be identified at an early stage (or indeed any level) based on technical skill alone (Abbott et al., 2005).

Box 10.1 Reflection Box – Applied Considerations

The Use of Testing Batteries – Why We Shouldn't Identify High Potential Players at Such a Young Age

- First, much of the studies that have used testing batteries have often labelled children as young as ten as **elite** participants. First, Swann et al. (2015) conducted a systematic review aimed at defining elite athletes and considering their working definition, these studies have inappropriately labelled players as *elite*.
- Second, the use of these testing batteries largely assesses technical competence in rugby-specific skills, without contextual interference from the game (Williams & Hodges, 2005), such as opponents, consequences and affective factors (pressure, anxiety, fatigue). They test **isolated technique**, rather than skill and limited transfer is noted in performance.
- Third, the notion that players should be (de)selected at the age of 10–13 is concerning. Furthermore, using isolated, unopposed tasks, without need for decision-making or sense making provides young players with tasks that are not representative of the game and therefore may present an illusion of competence (Hodges & Lohse, 2022).

Performance Analysis

To measure the technical and tactical qualities of rugby players in game contexts, authors have employed performance analysis methods to capture and measure key performance indicators (Bennett et al., 2016; Den Hollander et al., 2016, 2019; Gabbett et al., 2010; Ungureanu et al., 2019). Bennett et al. (2016) explored the relationship between positional characteristics and game involvements for U17 youth representative rugby league players. Specifically, the authors collected the frequency of offensive involvements, including ball carries, support runs, offensive misses, line breaks and line break assists. Additionally, defensive involvements including tackles completed and tackles not completed were recorded. Their findings indicated that hit-up forwards (props and second rows) performed a significantly greater number of offensive, defensive and overall skill involvements compared with all other positional groups. The outside backs (wingers and full back) demonstrated the least attacking involvements, although the authors suggest that this was due to the limited opportunities to receive the ball.

Den Hollander et al. (2016) conducted post-facto performance analysis on 125 Super Rugby games to identify key game skills and playing characteristics that led to line breaks. Their analysis was made up of 12 operational variables (see Table 10.2). Findings indicated that running speed when receiving the ball and fast passing between offensive players created line break opportunities. Interestingly, the authors inferred that an attacker's awareness of the defender's line speed and depth was a key discriminator in the event of a line break. We would argue that this assumption is unwarranted given the sole use of observational methods in den Hollander et al. (2016) study. To offer such an inference regarding the perceptual strategies of players, authors would need to investigate players perceptual strategies through eye tracking methodologies or valid verbalisation methods. Wheeler and Sayers (2010) employed a similar approach to explore effective attacking strategies in elite rugby union. 1,372 carries were analysed from seven Super Rugby games where performance indicators were collected for attacking indicators, attacking outcomes and defensive pattern indicators. The findings suggested that tackle-breaks and line-breaks were positively associated with a try scored on the next phase and offloading was positively associated with scoring tries within two phases. In both cases, it is likely that the findings are unsurprising to coaches of the game.

Den Hollander et al. (2019) explored rugby union players technical execution of a clear out in senior and academy rugby union players. This study examined the validity of a measurement tool that was developed to assess technical proficiency in the attacking breakdown within training environments. Den Hollander and colleagues (2019) also developed a contact drill that included two attackers vs. two defenders, with specific criterion attached to execution in the contact and breakdown phases. This criterion was used to analyse and score players performance pre-contact, in contact and post-contact. Findings indicated that this contact drill was a valid method of measuring proficiency in

TABLE 10.2 Definitions for Measures of Technical and Tactical Qualities Offered within the Research Literature as Key Game Skills (Definitions Derived Directly from; Bennett et al., 2016; Den Hollander et al., 2016, 2019; Gabbett et al., 2010; Ungureanu et al., 2019)

Measure	Definition (Criteria)
Measurement of technical qualities	
Ball carry	An attacking player makes a genuine run (greater than two steps) with the ball in hand
Support run	An attacking player runs in support of the ballcarrier and pushes through the defensive line
Offensive miss	An attacking player makes a defending player miss a genuine tackle using evasion skills
Line break	An attacking player breaks through the defensive line while in possession of the ball and makes an advancement towards the opposition's try line
Line break assist	An attacking player moves a defending player away from a support runner and delivers a pass that results in a line break
Tackle completed	The defending player(s) makes physical contact with a ball carrier halting their progress and as a result, the ball carrier is required to play the ball
Tackle not completed	The defending player(s) makes physical contact with a ball carrier, but fails to prevent an offload or the ball carrier is able to break free
Short lateral pass	Standard pass to the next player in the attacking line, within a 5 m radius
Long lateral pass	Standard pass to the next player in the attacking line, further than a 5 m radius
Skip pass	Ball is transferred past the closest player to another further away
Flat pass	Ball is transferred horizontally, so that the receiving player runs onto the ball when catching it
Double around	Ball is passed to a player who moved from the inside of the passer to their outside channel
Inside ball	Ball is passed to a player running on the inside channel of the passer
Lob pass	High looping pass
Pop pass	Short pass initiated from the wrists, rather than the arms, to a player in the immediate proximity of the ball-carrier
Quick-hands	Ball is received and passed in one rapid movement
Switch pass	Ball is transferred in the opposite direction of the previous pass
Straight running angle	Ball-carrier runs straight at defence
Arcing running angle	Ball-carrier runs in a wavy line at defence

(Continued)

TABLE 10.2 (Continued)

Measure	Definition (Criteria)
Lateral running angle	Ball-carrier runs laterally, from touchline to touchline
Diagonal running angle	Ball-carrier runs in a straight angled line at defence
Measurement of Tactical qualities	
Set pieces won/regained	All own and opponents' scrums, lineouts, starts and restarts won or regained, respectively. Indicates the number of own possession useful to start attacking.
Set pieces lost	All own and opponents' scrums, lineouts, starts and restarts won by the opponents. Indicates the opponents' number of possession useful to start attacking.
Offensive breakdown 'v++' (%)	An offensive breakdown when the ball is used quickly (=3 s) using maximum two attacking supports.
Offensive breakdown 'v+' (%)	An offensive breakdown when the ball is used quickly (=3 s) with maximum three attacking supports.
Offensive breakdown 'v-' (%)	An offensive breakdown when the ball is used quickly (=3 s) with more than three attacking supports.
Offensive breakdown 'I' (%)	An offensive breakdown when the ball is not used quickly (>3 s) regardless the number of attacking supports.
Offensive breakdown '−' (%)	An offensive breakdown that results in a turnover or penalty/free kick against.
Defensive breakdown '>>' (%)	A defensive breakdown where the defending support is much numerous than the attacking support.
Defensive breakdown '=' (%)	A defensive breakdown where the defending support is as numerous as the attacking support.
Defensive breakdown '<<' (%)	A defensive breakdown where the defending support is less numerous than the attacking support.
Tackle '++' (%)	Dominant tackle that stops the opponent and the ball (stops the ball carrier from making a pass) and drives opposition player one or more steps backward.
Tackle '+' (%)	Tackle that stops the opponent and the ball (stops the ball carrier from making a pass) and the event happens on the collision point
Tackle '−' (%)	Tackle that stops the opponent and the ball (stops the ball carrier from making a pass) and the tackler is driven backwards one or more steps by the ball carrier)
Tackle '2 off' (%)	Tackle that stops the opponent but not the ball (allows the ball carrier to recycle the ball).
Missed tackle (%)	Tackle that does not stop the opponent.
Pass '+' (%)	Pass that centres the target (receiver's hands) and allows receiver to maintain speed and acceleration.
Pass '−' (%)	Pass forward or which does not center the target (receiver's hands) or which does not allow to maintain speed and acceleration.

contact whilst the senior players scored significantly higher than both groups of academy players in terms of their technique. Drills such as this are an excellent coaching method to assess, acquire, refine and develop players technical proficiency in the clear out. Furthermore, they offer a sound alternative to more game-like practices when coaches need to reduce the physical demands of a training session.

Gabbett et al. (2010) measured the use of onside and offside small-sided games (see Table 10.1 for descriptions) on the frequency of key performance indicators (KPIs; touches, passes and effective passes). The findings indicated that offside small-sided games had a significantly greater number of involvements, passes and effective passes. Interestingly, the authors offered clear implications regarding the use of both methods, where offside games may be employed to increase players involvement and skill attempts, whilst onside games may be used to support recovery or focus more on tactical understanding and perceptual development. Finally, Ungureanu et al. (2019) employed 44 performance indicators to analyse the playing behaviour of U18 Italian Academy players. Indicators were broken up into attacking behaviour, defensive behaviour, the contest and ball in play. Whilst the findings of the study were largely inconclusive the purpose of the study was to prioritise and measure the technical and tactical development of players, which the authors expressed was evident to see from the analysis data.

The use of post-facto performance analysis methods has allowed these authors to explore the technical and tactical qualities of players in the game context. We would suggest that this approach, in contrast with 'lab like', low fidelity testing batteries, appears to hold significant potential for both research and practice in assessing and tracking tactical and technical qualities over time. Therefore, coaches and performance analysis staff could make use of a similar approach to understand the technical and tactical development of their players in high-fidelity conditions. This is not, however, to suggest the need to adopt the same approach. From a pragmatic perspective, there is a need to carefully select which performance measures are appropriate given the needs of the players. Thus, we have provided Table 10.2, as a point of reference to consider what a coach would choose to analyse and why.

Developing Technical and Tactical Qualities

Table 10.3 summarises the studies evaluating the development of technical and tactical qualities.

Passing

Hooper et al. (2008) investigated the influence of a training programme, where players either used weighted rugby balls or regular rugby balls on players spin

TABLE 10.3 Summary of the Research Studies Developing Technical and Tactical Qualities in Youth Rugby

Authors	Purpose of Study	Participants	Code	Topic	Method
Hooper et al. (2008)	The purpose of this study was to investigate the influence of training with heavy rugby balls on selected spin pass variables in youth rugby union players.	U19 youth rugby players $n = 14$	Union	Technical – passing	Spin passing development ranging between 5 and 12 metres with each hand. Participants split into a heavy ball group or normal weighted ball group to train twice weekly for eight weeks. Participants assessed pre- and post-intervention.
Worsfold and Page (2014)	Comparison of two types of spin passes of the dominant and non-dominant hand.	Male competitive rugby players $n = 30$	Union	Technical – passing	Three 8 m long running channels away from a 4 m, 8 m and 12 m distance from a passing target. From the start the player received the ball at 5 m from 1 m away and had 3 m to adjust and pass towards the target. Trials were repeated on the dominant, non-dominant, including body drop and excluding body drop conditions at each distance.
Ashford et al. (2022)	The purpose of this study was to monitor the impact of a modified scoring system created by the Rugby Football Union as a vehicle to shape desired cognitive, affective and behavioural outcomes whilst players carried the rugby ball into contact.	U16 English Regional Academy players. Scoring and psychometrics $n = 87$. Interviews $n = 9$.	Union	Technical and tactical – carrying	Key performance indicators (Total Carries, Total Points & Points Per Carry) were collected to monitor player effectiveness across three competitive games. Semi-structured interviews and psychometric scales were used to gain insight into the players learning experiences, feelings, decision-making and declarative knowledge.
Parrant and Martin (2010)	For teachers and coaches to better understand how the players learn to make better decisions in game-based situations.	U15 rugby players from an independent boys school in Christchurch, NZ $n = 6$	Union	Tactical	Semi-structured interviews conducted pre- during and post-intervention. Intervention was seven sessions in duration and incorporated variable practice, random practice, bandwidth feedback, questioning, video feedback, direct instruction and modelling.

Ashford et al. (2021b)	(i) to consider how game situations influence players perception of information; (ii) how game situations influence the application of cognitive mechanisms whilst making decisions; and (iii) the influence of tactics and/or strategy on player decision-making.	English professional rugby union players $n = 8$ and university rugby players $n = 8$ Number of games $n = 32$	Union	Technical & tactical – game decision making	Players conducted two procedures within 48 hours of the final whistle twice. Step one involved a decision classification task (slow, fast & no thought). Step two involved a verbalisation task through self-confrontation interviews.
Collins et al. (2022)	Explore the role and development of cognition, understanding and knowledge as it relates to contextual information in elite rugby players decision-making. Examine player perceptions of contextual information as understood by those making decisions.	Top-tier professional rugby players $n = 9$	Union	Technical and tactical – game decision-making	Semi-structured interviews were conducted with questions on players pre-performance process, in performance process and around cognitively primed understanding.
Sherwood et al. (2019)	This study aimed to understand whether accuracy when recalling rugby union patterns is a valid measure of on-field decision-making performance.	Study 1: Elite male rugby union players $n = 57$ Study 2: University students $n = 41$ & Under 18 Super Rugby team $n = 47$	Union	Tactical	Study 1: Recall of structured patterns of play from still images viewed for 5 s. Study 2: Recall of unstructured semi-structured and structured patterns from still images viewed for 5 s.

passing proficiency with U19 players. The participants were assessed before, during and following the eight-week intervention which required players to engage in 50–90 passes twice a week, exploring their accuracy of passes between 5 and 12 metres with each hand. Notably, both groups improved significantly following the training intervention. Unsurprisingly, the authors offered the implication that deliberate and intensive practice resulted in an increase in technical proficiency. Additionally, they suggested that heavy rugby balls could be useful for spin pass training in players who are already proficient in that skill. Worsfold and Page (2014) compared two types of spin pass with adult rugby players. Within a passing accuracy task, players were required to run, receive and spin pass the ball to a target at 4, 8 and 12 m. They were required to repeat the trial twice, first with a body drop at the point of catching the ball (bend at the knees) and second without the body drop. Findings suggested that the body drop technique resulted in higher ball velocities and improved accuracy from both the dominant and non-dominant passing hands. In comparison, the more upright passing technique resulted in a faster passing movement but was compromised by lower ball velocity and accuracy. The ecological validity of this method can be questioned as passing in both conditions took place in contexts unrepresentative of the true competitive environment (i.e., no defenders initiating the pass). Studies of this nature should employ the use of a transfer test under competitive conditions or incorporate experimental designs which are high in task and action fidelity (Barnett et al., 1973).

Carrying

Ashford et al. (2022) examined the influence of a modified scoring system that was introduced to the English Rugby Football Union's U16 Academy Festival. The modified scoring system was used by each of the Regional Academy performance analysts, with players scoring between one and four points for each carry. Scores would be awarded depending on the use of footwork before contact, a fend (handoff), or fighting to stay on their feet in contact and whether this ultimately led to a line break. Post-hoc performance analysis of the player scores and reflexive thematic analysis derived from semi-structured interviews suggested that performance was largely shaped by their learning experiences leading into the festival. Themes demonstrated that players from Regional Academies who were supported to gain an understanding of the scoring system, experiment with technical solutions in training, and reflect on successful/unsuccessful performance before the festival held significantly higher points per carry scores. Conversely, players who received limited to no support from coaches had significantly lower points per carry scores, described negative affect, such as feelings of confusion, fear and nervousness before competition. Therefore, coaches working with young players should aim to promote player understanding at all time, not only of what to do and how to do it, but *why* a technique is appropriate in light of new technical challenges (Abraham & Collins, 2011b).

Decision-making

Out of the studies included in this research overview, only one explicitly investigated the decision-making of youth rugby players. Parrant and Martin (2010) conducted semi-structured interviews pre, during and post a seven-session intervention designed to support the development of six U15 rugby union players decision-making. The intervention included coaching strategies such as variable practice, random practice, bandwidth feedback, questioning, video analysis, use of video feedback, direct instruction and positive/negative modelling (see Box 10.2). Although using non-stimulated retrospective recall, semi-structured interviews suggested improvements in perception, motor skill development and tactical understanding. Collectively, a consequence of these improvements was greater intra-team communication supportive of team decision-making.

Box 10.2 Definitions for Coaching Strategies Offered by Parrant and Martin (2010)

Variable practice – *One technique/tactic practised in a variety of ways.*
Random practice – Several techniques/tactics practised randomly in one practice.
Bandwidth feedback – Only offering feedback when a players has performed extremely well or below an acceptable level of performance.
Questioning – Asking players to share their knowledge and beliefs around a technique/tactic.
Video analysis – Asking players to watch footage of technical/tactical qualities and engaging in reflection on what this would mean for the players.
Video feedback – Using video footage of the player(s) or teammate(s) to offer feedback to a player regarding effective technical/tactical performance
Direct instruction – Using verbal information to guide the players change in behaviour towards the optimal technique/tactic.
Positive/negative modelling – Demonstrating the right OR wrong way to do something, building a player's ability to develop that quality themselves.

Ashford et al. (2021b) and Collins et al. (2022) have investigated the processes underlying professional and university rugby union players decision-making. Using a decision-classification task, stimulated recall (Ashford et al., 2021b) and semi-structured interviews (Collins et al., 2022), findings from both studies suggested that player decision-making is driven by perception and interaction with dynamic (e.g., score board, refereeing decisions, patterns in opponent behaviour) and static (e.g., preparation for the game, coach instruction, physical state) contextual priors, whereby players collect and make sense of game information with the intention of influencing individual and collective decision-making. Additionally, Ashford et al. (2021b) found that a player's decision-making process is highly contextual. That is the time, complexity of information, typicality of information and available contextual priors, would demand no-, slow- or fast-thought decision-making. The implications offered by both sets of authors suggest that the methods used by Parrant and Martin (2010) should form part of a broader coaching toolbox, to be used depending on the player and the nature of the decision being developed.

Pattern Recall

Sherwood et al. (2019) explored elite, university, and U18 rugby union players pattern recall, to investigate whether it was a valid measure of their on-field decision-making performance. Using still pictures taken from game footage, which were removed after a five-second duration, players recall accuracy of structured and unstructured moments of play was measured. The findings suggested that only the total number of years playing rugby union was correlated with recall accuracy. Furthermore, the elite playing group was significantly more accurate in their recall within the structure condition, whilst no differences were found in the unstructured condition.

Use of Competition to Address Technical and Tactical Development

Table 10.4 summarises the studies that have used rule modifications within competition to address technical and tactical development within rugby (Ashford et al., 2020; Morley et al., 2016; Thomas & Wilson, 2015). Ashford et al. (2020) explored the influence of the 'Wellington rules' enforced during the 2017 U16 Regional Academy Wellington Rugby festival. The modifications were designed to increase the ball in play time during games and the frequency of passes and offloads, decrease the frequency kicks out of hand, whilst increasing the total frequency of decision-making opportunities. The results identified that the modifications had a desired influence, however significant differences between pre- and post-rule modification were mainly found in shortened durations of the game (30–40 minutes). Similarly, Thomas and Wilson (2015) examined the effect of rule changes on skill involvements of U9 rugby union players. The pilot modifications were found to result in 25% more ball-in-play time, 55% increase in runs with the ball, more than twice as many successful passes and nearly twice as many tries scored. Finally, Morley et al. (2016) examined the frequency of skill involvements between the traditional and modified versions of the U7, U8 and U9 formats. The findings indicated that the modified rules, intended to increase skill involvements had the desired effect across all age groups.

Practical Application

There is significant variance in approaches to research exploring technical and tactical development in youth rugby settings. Therefore, findings provide

TABLE 10.4 Summary of the Research Studies Using Competition to Address Technical and Tactical Development

Authors	Purpose of Study	Participants	Code	Topic	Method
Ashford et al. (2020)	The purpose of this study was to monitor the impact of rule modifications on player behaviour within a talent identification and development system in rugby union.	English Regional Academy games during the Wellington Rugby Festival n = 105 between 2016 & 2019.	Union	Competition	Post-facto notational analysis was conducted on each game to measure ball in play percentage, passes per minute, offloads per minute and kicks per minute between full length (70 minutes) and shortened durations (30–42 minutes) of these competitive matches.
Morley et al. (2016)	Compared the frequency of technical skills between traditional and modified game of primary rugby league.	472 children, U7's n = 108, U8's n = 223 and U9's n = 144. Traditional games n = 49. Modified games n = 249.	League	Competition	Notational analysis examined the frequency and effectiveness of technical skills (e.g. number of involvements, passes, catches, tackles, kicks, knock on's, line breaks, tackle count, completed sets and tries) within 'traditional' and 'modified' games.
Thomas and Wilson (2015)	The current study examined the effect of rules changes on game behaviours and opinions of under-nine rugby union players.	U9 Age group. Games n = 89	Union	Competition	Measured the percentage of ball in play, tries, runs, open play passes, tackles, breakdown (rucks and mauls), set pieces (scrums and lineouts).

an ambiguous picture to coaches seeking to adopt evidence-informed approach to practice. Nonetheless, using the findings and implications derived from the research overview, the practical applications have been divided into three distinct sections, *measurement*, *technical* and *tactical development* and *competition*.

Measurement

There has been a substantial amount of research employing and evaluating the use of testing batteries to examine the technical qualities of young rugby players. Whilst the validity of such methods has gradually improved over time (Hendricks et al., 2015; Oorschot et al., 2017), testing batteries have not been able to measure the technical proficiency of players under high fidelity (i.e., open phase play in attack vs. defence or kicking to compete for possession) conditions. Similar issues with the validity of testing to those identified above have been levelled at the battery of tests used in the American Football National Football League (NFL) combine. Comparatively, the tests reviewed in this sample fail to adequately create a picture of the current performance level, let alone act as a predictor of future performance (Kuzmits & Adams, 2008; Robbins, 2010). Indeed, further challenges are posed by the nature of technical and tactical skilled performance. This is not necessarily the result of the idea that *all* technique is completely unique to the individual athlete (Rudd et al., 2021), a cursory observation of any game of elite rugby will demonstrate a series of parameters that need to be met in skill execution. Instead, we need to consider the contextual appropriateness of given techniques in specific settings, both as a feature of the shared mental model of the team and also based on changing approaches to the game.

Given the substantial limitations of the use of testing batteries, in its place we offer three recommendations to coaches. First, we suggest that coaches generate a *mental model* of the game of rugby union (see Figure 10.1 for an example),

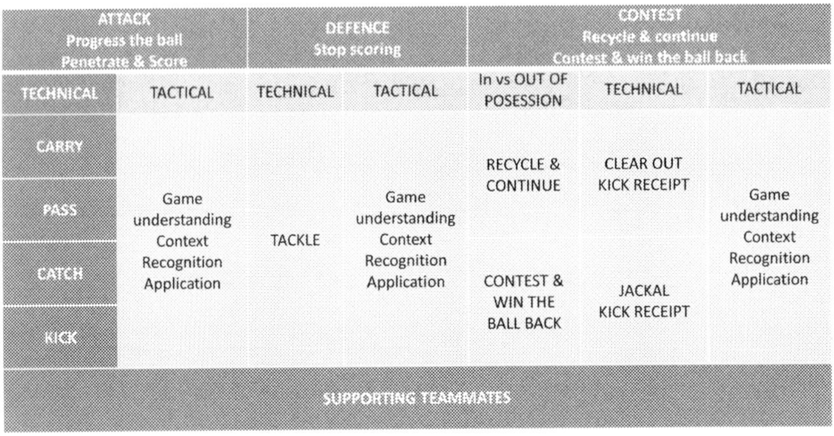

ATTACK Progress the ball Penetrate & Score		DEFENCE Stop scoring		CONTEST Recycle & continue Contest & win the ball back		
TECHNICAL	TACTICAL	TECHNICAL	TACTICAL	In vs OUT OF POSESSION	TECHNICAL	TACTICAL
CARRY	Game understanding Context Recognition Application		TACKLE	RECYCLE & CONTINUE	CLEAR OUT KICK RECEIPT	Game understanding Context Recognition Application
PASS		Game understanding Context Recognition Application				
CATCH				CONTEST & WIN THE BALL BACK	JACKAL KICK RECEIPT	
KICK						
SUPPORTING TEAMMATES						

FIGURE 10.1 An Example Mental Model of Rugby Union.

inclusive of the technical and tactical qualities that need developing. The development of a mental model of a sport can serve as a mechanism to simplify the complexities created by the laws/rules. From here, the model will act as a reference point of problems to solve, to consider what technical and tactical solutions should be implemented, when and why (Richards et al., 2017).

Second, we have offered Table 10.2 as a resource where coaches can make use of clear definitions regarding technical and tactical key performance indicators to execute notation performance analysis in both training and games.

Third and final, we suggest that in addition to producing frequencies of attempts, coaches should also seek to assess the quality of the movement and/or decision by the player. From this data, coaches assess and diagnose technical/tactical strengths/deficiencies, plan their coaching intentions for impact and implement appropriate interventions to support their player's development (Martindale & Collins, 2005).

Technical and Tactical Development

At the centre of a young rugby player's technical and tactical development is the role of the coach. Part of a coach's role is largely, but not exclusively, to design effective learning environments that best support a player's development in alignment to their wants and needs (Abraham & Collins, 2011a, 2011b). Coaches should be aware that human development is a biopsychosocial phenomenon. As a result, there are a myriad of complex and interacting factors that influence the development of technical and tactical qualities (Collins et al., 2012).

In many cases, the findings presented in this chapter will be unsurprising for coaches of either code. Despite limitations, there appear similar coaching implications on the technical side of player development (see Figure 1 for summary; Ashford et al., 2022; den Hollander et al., 2019). First, coaches should consider the end in mind, what are they aiming to achieve and how this shapes their intentions for impact over the duration of the session and/or period of time (Martindale & Collins, 2005; Muir et al., 2011). This end in mind should include a technical model, or model of expert performance that a player can work towards. This point in itself seems somewhat controversial in the literature (Rudd et al., 2021), yet it would appear that these factors do matter when it comes to the development of athletes. We would then suggest that coaches use a Professional Judgment and Decision Making approach to deploy the most optimal practice design and coaching behaviours to best meet the needs of their players (Abraham & Collins, 2011a, 2011b; Cruickshank & Collins, 2013; for more on this please read Chapter 17).

Second, certainly in lieu of any evidence to suggest otherwise, for the most part we would suggest that coaches need to deploy highly deliberate approaches to player's technical development. Amongst other options (e.g., 5As – Carson & Collins, 2011), the findings of these studies suggest that deliberate practice of a particular technique in a variety of practice types (i.e., opposed, unopposed,

TABLE 10.5 The Seven Key Principles When Applying Deliberate Practice in Your Coaching (adapted from Eccles et al., 2022, p. 3)

Principles of Deliberate Practice – EXPERTS	Description of Principle
Established training techniques	Deliberate practice develops skills for which established and effective training techniques have been developed
e**X**isting skills as building blocks	Deliberate practice involves building step-by-step on, and modifying prior skills
Pushing the envelope	Deliberate practice involves constant attempts at skills just beyond one's current ability level
Enhancing mental representations	Improved performance depends on more sophisticated mental representations
Responding to feedback	Getting better requires obtaining and responding to feedback from informed instructors
Total application & focus	Deliberate practice requires full attention and conscious actions
Specific goals	Deliberate practice involves setting and focusing on specific goals for improvement

small-sided games, blocked, constant, random or variable) can result in effective outcomes. The concept of deliberate practice has been largely misinterpreted in sporting literature in recent times, often being promoted as the idea that young athletes should aim to achieve 10,000 hours of practice. Instead, Eccles et al. (2022) dismiss this idea and instead offer seven key principles under the acronym **EXPERTS**' (see Table 10.5) for applying the method of deliberate practice within coaching.

Eccles et al. (2022) suggest that coaches should make use of established training techniques that have worked overtime to support the development of their players technical and tactical qualities. To consider what qualities requires development, player's *needs* should be assessed and identified as building blocks for future development within their context. Additionally, coaches should set the difficulty of practices at a desirable level for the performer, which should reach above their current capabilities (Hodges & Lohse, 2022). Finally, Eccles et al. (2022) idea of total application connects suggests that coaches should consistently encourage players game understanding in light of the development of technical and tactical qualities (Ashford et al., 2020, 2021, 2022; Collins et al., 2022; Green et al., 2019; Parrant & Martin, 2010; Sherwood et al., 2018). This is perhaps even more important in rugby as collision sports, where at least one team will always be aiming to physically impose on the other. As such, more 'self-discovery' or 'self-organising' approaches to skill development may pose a significant risk to the progression and indeed, the safety of players. Therefore, players should, regardless of the technique or skill being employed, such as tackling, scrummaging or a clear out in the ruck, be supported to understand *when* and *why* an appropriate skill and technique should be used.

Competition

Within the research overview, the concept of competitive engineering was introduced which suggests that those in charge of organising competition formats should begin with the end goal in mind and reverse engineer to the type of game they want to create, rather than simply scale competition down from the adult format (Burton et al., 2011). The evidence supporting this approach is substantial, therefore competition formats should have the players needs at the centre. For example, modified rule 7 of the Wellington rules prohibits players from kicking the ball directly out of play without the ball bouncing before crossing the touchline. Players are therefore required to execute the technique of a kick with more accuracy given the increase of difficulty (Ashford et al., 2020). However, these approaches are not without limitations as rule and law changes often result in unintended consequences. For instance, the effect of the Wellington rules (see Table 10.6) was only evident in shortened versions of the game, as players were less likely to employ pacing strategies and there was a large influence of fatigue during longer games that were played on the final day of the festival (Ashford et al., 2020). Furthermore, the Wellington rules largely negated players opportunities to develop technical and tactical qualities within the scrum and lineout. Given the prevalence of set piece proficiency in the elite levels of the game (see Collins et al., 2022) it is important to ensure these game moments are still considered as skill involvements for players. One of the main implications from this body of research is that laws constrain players actions, cognitions and behaviours and therefore serve as evidence-informed methods of coaching that can be used in training situations (Ashford et al., 2020, 2022). However, alongside the use of constraints and conditions, we also promote that coaches consistently support players to understand why these laws shape the technical and tactical qualities of players (Abraham & Collins, 2011).

Key Take Home Messages

- Testing batteries may provide reliable measures of player's technical qualities, but they currently lack task fidelity and therefore validity. As such, we suggest that the use of technical batteries for the purpose of talent 'identification' is a fool's errand.
- Notational analysis of performance indicators that examine the (1) number of skills attempts, (2) the execution of attempts and (3) the technical quality of each attempt is a more appropriate method for formative assessment.
- When supporting a player's technical development in physical areas of 'contest' (i.e., tackle, scrummage, clear-out or maul), safe and efficient

TABLE 10.6 List of the Wellington Rules Introduced in 2017 (Ashford et al., 2020, p. 2672)

Match Situation	Standard U16 Rule	Modified Wellington Rule
Scrum	1 Infringements at the scrum can be penalised.	1 For all infringements at the scrum the sanction is a free kick – apart from foul play
Lineout	2 Unlimited time to perform a lineout (to the referee's discretion).	2 20 secs to throw the ball in from the assistant referee marking the line out – the sanction is a free kick.
	3 Infringements at the lineout can be penalised.	3 The sanction for all infringements at the lineout is a free kick – apart from foul play.
	4 Unlimited number of mauls allowed per game.	4 1 maul per half on Matchday one and two per half on Matchday two – the sanction is a free kick if a team exceeds this.
Restarts	5 The team who concedes a try kicks off to their opponent and can land anywhere in field.	5 Team that has just conceded a try has the choice to kick or receive. All kick offs to land between 10 and 22 m line, if it lands elsewhere the sanction is a free kick.
Open Play	6 1 minute to play from a penalty or free kick – the sanction is a penalty or free kick is reversed.	6 10 secs to play from a penalty or free kick – the sanction is the penalty or free kick if reversed.
	7 Can kick out on the full if the kick is conducted within own 22 – the sanction is lineout to the opposition in line with where the kick was taken.	7 No open field kicks to land directly out of touch on the full – the sanction is lineout to the opposition in line with where the kick was taken.
	8 A quick throw cannot be taken with a different ball.	8 Quick throws can be taken with a different ball, if the ball hits the crowd/stand etc.
	9 No constraints on selection.	9 All players start at least one game

execution of movements is essential. In these moments, technique should be acquired (or refined) *before* the execution of skill in an opposed setting.
- For this purpose, player engagement in deliberate practice offers a strong evidence-informed framework for the acquisition, or refinement of new techniques/skills.
- Promote players understanding of **where** and **why** skills should be employed, not simply the what and the how.
- Competition environments in youth rugby should not be scaled-down versions of the adult game, but instead promote the frequency and quality of skill involvements under high fidelity conditions.
- More empirical and longitudinal research is needed to understand how different coaching strategies impact technical and tactical development over time. In the meantime, caution is urged to all suggesting that there is *a way* to coach.

References

Abbott, A., Button, C., Pepping, G. J., & Collins, D. (2005). Unnatural selection: Talent identification and development in sport. *Nonlinear Dynamics, Psychology, and Life Sciences*, 9, 61–88. http://europepmc.org/abstract/MED/15629068

Abbott, A., & Collins, D. (2004). Eliminating the dichotomy between theory and practice in talent identification and development: Considering the role of psychology. *Journal of Sports Sciences*, 22, 395–408. https://doi.org/10.1080/02640410410001675324

Abraham, A., & Collins, D. (2011a). Taking the next step: Ways forward for coaching science. *Quest*, 63, 366–384. https://doi.org/10.1080/00336297.2011.10483687

Abraham, A., & Collins, D. (2011b). Effective skill development: How should athletes' skills be developed. In D. Collins, A. Button, & H. Richards (Eds.), *Performance Psychology: A Practitioner's Guide* (pp. 207–230): Churchill Livingstone, Elsevier.

Ashford, M., Abraham, A. K., & Poolton, J. (2021a). A communal language for decision-making in team invasion sports. *International Sport Coaching Journal*, 8(1). https://doi.org/10.1123/iscj.2019-0062

Ashford, M., Abraham, A. K., & Poolton, J. (2021b). What cognitive mechanism, when, where and why? Exploring the decision making of university and professional rugby union players during competitive matches. *Frontiers in Psychology*, 12(609127), 1–25, https://doi.org/10.3389/fpsyg.2021.609127

Ashford, M., Burke, K., Barrell, D., Abraham, A. K., & Poolton, J. (2020). The impact of rule modifications on player behaviour in a talent identification and development environment: A case study of the Rugby Football Union's Wellington Academy Rugby Festival. *Journal of Sports Sciences*, 38, 2670–2676, https://doi.org10.1080/02640414.2020.1795559

Ashford, M., Burke, K., Barrell, D., Abraham, A. K., & Poolton, J. (2022). The impact of a player scoring system on cognitive, affective and behavioural outcomes of players in a talent identification and development environment. *Journal of Sport & Exercise Science*, 6(1), 42–57, https://jses.net/the-impact-of-a-player-scoring-system-on-cognitive-affective-and-behavioural-outcomes-of-players-in-a-talent-identification-and-development-environment/

Barnett, M. L., Ross, D., Schmidt, R. A., & Todd, B. (1973). Motor skills learning and the specificity of training principle. *Research Quarterly*, 44, 440–447.

Bennett, K. J., Fransen, J., Scott, B. R., Sanctuary, C. E., Gabbett, T. J., & Dascombe, B. J. (2016). Positional group significantly influences the offensive and defensive skill involvements of junior representative rugby league players during match play. *Journal of Sports Sciences, 34*, 1542–1546. https://doi.org/10.1080/02640414.2015.1122206

Burton, D., Gillham, A. D., & Hammermeister, J. (2011). Competitive engineering: Structural climate modifications to enhance youth athletes' competitive experience. *International Journal of Sports Science & Coaching, 6*, 201–217. https://doi.org/10.1260/1747-9541.6.2.201

Carson, H. J., & Collins, D. (2011). Refining and regaining skills in fixation/diversification stage performers: The five-a model. *International Review of Sport and Exercise Psychology, 4*, 146–167. https://doi.org/10.1080/1750984X.2011.613682

Chiwaridzo, M., Chandahwa, D., Oorschot, S., Tadyanemhandu, C., Dambi, J. M., Ferguson, G., & Smits-Engelsman, B. C. (2018). Logical validation and evaluation of practical feasibility for the SCRuM (School Clinical Rugby Measure) test battery developed for young adolescent rugby players in a resource-constrained environment. *PLoS One, 13*(11), e0207307. https://doi.org/10.1371/journal.pone.0207307

Chiwaridzo, M., Ferguson, G. D., & Smits-Engelsman, B. C. (2019a). Anthropometric, physiological characteristics and rugby-specific game skills discriminating Zimbabwean under-16 male adolescent rugby players by level of competition. *BMJ Open Sport & Exercise Medicine, 5*, e000576. https://doi.org/10.1136/bmjsem-2019-000576

Chiwaridzo, M., Ferguson, G. D., & Smits-Engelsman, B. C. M. (2019b). Qualities or skills discriminating under 19 rugby players by playing standards: A comparative analysis of elite, sub-elite and non-rugby players using the SCRuM test battery. *BMC Research Notes, 12*, 1–8. https://doi.org/10.1186/s13104-019-4563-y

Collins, D., Abbott, A., & Richards, H. (2011). *Performance psychology: A practitioner's guide*. Churchill Livingstone.

Collins, D., Bailey, R., Ford, P. A., MacNamara, Á., Toms, M., & Pearce, G. (2012). Three worlds: New directions in participant development in sport and physical activity. *Sport, Education and Society, 17*, 225–243. https://doi.org/10.1080/13573322.2011.607951

Collins, R., Collins, D., & Carson, H.J. (2022) Muscular collision chess: a qualitative exploration of the role and development of cognition, understanding and knowledge in elite-level decision making, *International Journal of Sport and Exercise Psychology, 20*(3), 828-848, DOI: 10.1080/1612197X.2021.1907768

Cruickshank, A., & Collins, D. (2013). Culture change in elite sport performance teams: Outlining an important and unique construct. *Sport & Exercise Psychology Review, 9*, 6–21. https://doi.org/10.1080/10413200.2011.650819

den Hollander, S., Brown, J., Lambert, M., Treu, P., & Hendricks, S. (2016). Skills associated with line breaks in Elite Rugby Union. *Journal of Sports Science and Medicine, 15*, 501–508.

den Hollander, S., Lambert, M., Jones, B., & Hendricks, S. (2019). Tackle and ruck technique proficiency within academy and senior club rugby union. *Journal of Sports Sciences, 37*, 2578–2587. https://doi.org/10.1080/02640414.2019.1648121

Eccles, D.W., Leone, E.J., & Williams, A.M., (2022) Deliberate Practice: What Is It and How Can I Use It?, *Journal of Sport Psychology in Action, 13*(1), 16-26, DOI: 10.1080/21520704.2020.1850577

Gabbett, T. J., & Abernethy, B. (2012). Dual-task assessment of a sporting skill: Influence of task complexity and relationship with competitive performances. *Journal of Sports Sciences, 30*, 1735–1745. https://doi.org/10.1080/02640414.2012.713979

Gabbett, T. J., & Abernethy, B. (2013). Expert–novice differences in the anticipatory skill of rugby league players. *Sport, Exercise, and Performance Psychology*, *2*, 138–155. https://doi.org/10.1037/a0031221

Gabbett, T. J., Jenkins, D. G., & Abernethy, B. (2010). Physiological and skill demands of 'on-side' and 'off-side'games. *The Journal of Strength & Conditioning Research*, *24*, 2979–2983. https://doi.org/10.1519/JSC.0b013e3181e72731

Gabbett, T. J., Jenkins, D. G., & Abernethy, B. (2011). Relative importance of physiological, anthropometric, and skill qualities to team selection in professional rugby league. *Journal of Sports Sciences*, *29*, 1453–1461. https://doi.org/10.1080/02640414.2011.603348

Gabbett, T., Kelly, J., & Pezet, T. (2007). Relationship between physical fitness and playing ability in rugby league players. *The Journal of Strength Conditioning Research*, *21*(4), 1126–1133. https://doi.org/10.1519/R-20936.1

Gabbett, T., Kelly, J., & Pezet, T. (2008). A comparison of fitness and skill among playing positions in Sub-Elite Rugby League Players. *Journal of Science and Medicine in Sport*, *11*, 585–592. https://doi.org/10.1016/j.jsams.2007.07.004

Gabbett, T. J., Ullah, S., & Jenkins, D. (2012). Skill qualities as risk factors for contact injury in professional rugby league players. *Journal of Sports Science*, *30*(1), 1421–1427. https://doi.org/10.1080/02640414.2012.710760

Green, B. S., Blake, C., & Caulfield, B. M. (2011). A valid field test protocol of linear speed and agility in rugby union. *The Journal of Strength & Conditioning Research*, *25*, 1256–1262. https://doi.org/10.1519/JSC.0b013e3181d8598b

Hendricks, S., Lambert, M., Masimla, H., & Durandt, J. (2015). Measuring skill in rugby union and rugby league as part of the standard team testing battery. *International Journal of Sports Science & Coaching*, *10*, 949–965. https://doi.org/10.1260/1747-9541.10.5.949

Hodges, N. J., & Lohse, K. R. (2022). An extended challenge-based framework for practice design in sports coaching. *Journal of Sports Sciences*, *40*(7), 754–768. https://doi.org/10.1080/02640414.2021.2015917

Hooper, J. J., James, S. D., Jones, D. C., Lee, D. M., & Gál, J. M. (2008). The influence of training with heavy rugby balls on selected spin pass variables in youth rugby union players. *Journal of Science and Medicine in Sport*, *11*, 209–213. https://doi.org/10.1016/j.jsams.2006.09.005.

Jackson, R. C., Warren, S., & Abernethy, B. (2006). Anticipation skill and susceptibility to deceptive movement. *Acta Psychologica*, *123*, 355–371.

Kempton, T., Sirotic, A. C., Cameron, M., & Coutts, A. J. (2013). Match-related fatigue reduces physical and technical performance during elite rugby league match-play: A case study. *Journal of Sports Sciences*, *31*, 1770–1780. https://doi.org/10.1080/02640414.2013.803583

Kuzmits, F. E., & Adams, A. J. (2008). The NFL combine: Does it predict performance in the National Football League? *The Journal of Strength & Conditioning Research*, *22*, 1721–1727. https://doi.org/10.1519/JSC.0b013e318185f09d

Malone, J. J., Lovell, R., Varley, M. C., & Coutts, A. J. (2017). Unpacking the black box: Applications and considerations for using GPS devices in sport. *International Journal of Sports Physiology and Performance*, *12*, S2-18–S12-26. https://doi.org/10.1123/ijspp.2016-0236

Martindale, A., & Collins, D. (2005). Professional judgment and decision making: The role of intention for impact. *The Sport Psychologist*, *19*, 303–317. https://doi.org/10.1123/tsp.19.3.303

Muir, B., Morgan, G., Abraham, A., & Morley, D. (2011). Developmentally appropriate approaches to coaching children. In I. Stafford (Ed.), *Coaching Children in Sport* (pp. 17–37): Routledge.

Morley, D., Ogilvie, P., Till, K., Rothwell, M., Cotton, W., O'Connor, D., & McKenna, J. (2016). Does modifying competition affect the frequency of technical skills in junior rugby league? *International Journal of Sports Science & Coaching*, 11, 810–818. https://doi.org/10.1177/1747954116676107

O'Connor, D., & Larkin, P. (2015). Decision-making for Rugby. In K. Till, & B. Jones (Eds.), *The science of sport: Rugby* (pp. 102–112). Marlborough: Crowood Press.

Oorschot, S., Chiwaridzo, M. C. M., & Smits-Engelsman, B. P. (2017). Sychometric evaluation of commonly used game-specific skills tests in rugby: A systematic review. *BMJ Open Sport & Exercise Medicine*, 3, 1–11. https://doi.org/10.1136/bmjsem-2017-000281

Parrant, D., & Martin, A. (2010). Developing decision-making in rugby. *Waikato Journal of Education*, 15(3), 69–86. https://doi.org/10.15663/wje.v15i3.82

Pavely, S., Adams, R. D., Di Francesco, T., Larkham, S., & Maher, C. G. (2009). Execution and outcome differences between passes to the left and right made by First-Grade Rugby Union Players. *Physical Therapy in Sport*, 10, 136–141. https://doi.org/10.1016/j.ptsp.2009.05.006

Pienaar, A. E., Spamer, E. J., & Steyn Jr, H. (1998). Identifying and developing rugby talent among 10-year-old boys: A practical model. *Journal of Sports Sciences*, 16, 691–699. https://doi.org/10.1080/026404198366326

RFU (2021). *England rugby development framework – The future England Rugby Player*. Twickenham: Rugby Football Union.

Richards, P., Collins, D., & Mascarenhas, D. R. D. (2017). Developing team decision-making: A holistic framework integrating both on-field and off-field pedagogical coaching processes. *Sports Coaching Review*, 6, 57–75. https://doi.org/10.1080/21640629.2016.1200819

Robbins, D. W. (2010) The National Football League (NFL) combine: Does normalized data better predict performance in the NFL draft? *Journal of Strength & Conditioning Research*, 24, 2888–2899. https://doi.org/10.1519/JSC.0b013e3181f927cc

Rudd, J. R., Fouls, J., O'Sullivan, M., & Woods, C. T. (2021). A 'fundamental' myth of movement with a 'functional' solution. In A. Whitehead, & J. Coe (Ed.), *Myths of sports coaching* (pp. 36–52). Sequoia Books.

Serpell, B. G., Ford, M., & Young, W. B. (2010). The development of a new test of agility for rugby league. *Journal of Strength & Conditioning Research*, 24, 3270–3277. https://doi.org/10.1519/JSC.0b013e3181b60430

Sherwood, S., Smith, T., & Masters, R. S. (2019). Pattern recall, decision making and talent identification in rugby union. *European Journal of Sport Science*, 19(6), 834–841. https://doi.org/10.1080/17461391.2018.1545051

Sirotic, A. C., Coutts, A. J., Knowles, H., & Catterick, C. (2009). A comparison of match demands between elite and semi-elite rugby league competition. *Journal of Sports Sciences*, 27, 203–211. https://doi.org/10.1080/02640410802520802

Spamer, E. J., du Plessis, D. J., & Kruger, E. H. (2009). Comparative characteristics of elite New Zealand and South African u/16 rugby players with reference to game specific skills, physical abilities and anthropometric data. *South African Journal of Sports Medicine*, 21, 53–57. https://doi.org/10.17159/2078-516X/2009/v21i2a298

Swann, C., Moran, A., & Piggott, D. (2015). Defining elite athletes: Issues in the study of expert performance in sport psychology. *Psychology of Sport and Exercise*, 16, 3–14. https://doi.org/https://doi.org/10.1016/j.psychsport.2014.07.004

Tee, J. C., Ashford, M., & Piggott, D. (2018). A tactical periodization approach for rugby union. *Strength and Conditioning Journal, 40*, 1–13. https://doi.org/10.1519/SSC.0000000000000390

Thomas, G. L., & Wilson, M. R. (2015). Playing by the rules: A developmentally appropriate introduction to rugby union. *International Journal of Sports Science & Coaching, 10*(2–3), 413–423. https://doi.org/10.1260/1747-9541.10.2-3.413

Ungureanu, A. N., Condello, G., Pistore, S., Conte, D., & Lupo, C. (2019). Technical and tactical aspects in Italian Youth Rugby Union in Relation to Different Academies, regional tournaments, and outcomes. *Journal of Strength and Conditioning Research, 33*, 1557–1569. https://doi.org/10.1519/JSC.0000000000002188.

Van Gent, M. M., & Spamer, E.J. (2005). Comparisons of positional groups in terms of anthropometric, rugby-specific skills, physical and motor components among, U13, U16, U18 and U19 elite rugby players. *Kinesiology, 37*(1), 50–63.

Williams, A. M., & Hodges, N. J. (2005). Practice, instruction and skill acquisition in soccer: Challenging tradition. *Journal of Sports Sciences, 23*(6), 637–650.

Wheeler, K. W., Askew, C. D., & Sayers, M. G. (2010). Effective attacking strategies in Rugby Union. *European Journal of Sport Science, 10*, 237–242. https://doi.org/10.1080/17461391.2010.482595

Wheeler, K. W., & Sayers, M. G. L. (2010). Modification of agility running technique in reaction to a defender in Rugby Union. *Journal of Sports Science and Medicine, 9*, 445–451.

Wheeler, K. W., & Sayers, M. G. L. (2011). Rugby union contact skills alter evasive agility performance during attacking ball carries. *International Journal of Sports Science & Coaching, 6*(3), 419–432. https://doi.org/10.1260/1747-9541.6.3.419

Worsfold, P. & Page, M. (2014). The influences of rugby spin pass technique on movement time, ball velocity and passing accuracy. *International Journal of Performance Analysis in Sport, 14*(1), 296–306. https://doi.org/10.1080/24748668.2014.11868722.

11
IMPROVING YOUNG RUGBY PLAYER'S TACKLE ABILITY

Sharief Hendricks, Gregory Tierney and Steven den Hollander

Introduction

The tackle is a physical, dynamic and technically challenging contest between two or more opposing players in rugby. The defending player(s), known as the tackler(s), attempt to impede the attacker's (the ball-carrier) progression towards the try-line and regain possession of the ball – this action is called tackling. The ability to win the tackle contest is a key performance indicator for players and teams and is associated with positive match outcomes (Hendricks & Lambert, 2010; Hendricks et al., 2014). However, the dynamic, physical and frequent nature of the tackle renders it a high-risk injury event (Quarrie & Hopkins, 2008). Accordingly, the ability to tackle and carry the ball into contact are two of the most essential contact skills required for safe and successful participation in rugby, particularly within young players. Over the last decade, measures to reduce tackle-related injury risk, whilst maintaining effective tackle performance have been a key area of research. Therefore, the purpose of this chapter is to (1) highlight the key findings of this tackle-related research, and (2) subsequently offer practical applications for coaches and practitioners to minimise the risk of tackle injuries while maximising performance.

Research Overview

Tackle Injury Risk in Youth Rugby

In youth rugby union, tackle injuries account for 39%–62% of all injuries, with the frequency of injury between the ball-carrier and tackler not dissimilar (Burger et al., 2020). In youth rugby league, tackle injuries account for 61% of all injuries, with an injury rate of 29.3 tackle injuries per 1,000 players hours

(Burger et al., 2021). One of the major risk factors for sports injuries is technique (Meeuwisse, 1994) and this holds true for the tackle in youth rugby. To date, from both a tackle performance and injury prevention perspective, understanding how we can improve players tackling and ball-carrying technique has been a focal point of research in youth rugby. Tables 11.1 and 11.2 summarise studies evaluating the tackle in youth rugby union and rugby league, respectively.

Improving Knowledge, Attitudes and Behaviours

For the tackle, proper technique has been shown to reduce the risk of injury for both the ball-carrier and tackler (Burger et al., 2016b; Hendricks et al., 2015c, 2016). Therefore, promoting the use of safe technique in contact, is crucial to protect the health and wellbeing of players. Several national injury prevention programmes have provided players, coaches and other stakeholders in the sport, with resources on safe and effective tackle techniques (Brown et al., 2016; Gianotti et al., 2009; Quarrie et al., 2020; Viljoen & Patricios, 2012). These programmes aim to improve players' and coaches' knowledge on safe tackle technique, and subsequently, influence their attitudes and behaviours.

There are two types of knowledge – declarative and procedural (Kim et al., 2013). Declarative knowledge is factual (Kim et al., 2013). It emphasises what to do to perform a skill (Thomas & Thomas, 1994). If a player has declarative knowledge of how to tackle safely, they can describe to you, step by step, each technical movement they would need to perform. Procedural knowledge is the knowledge of how to perform those movements (Kim et al., 2013). Gaining declarative knowledge is often described as the first stage of knowledge (Kim et al., 2013). This knowledge needs to then be developed into procedural knowledge, through practice and repetition (Kim et al., 2013). To test this, researchers showed 50 collegiate and high-school rugby players an educational video on safe tackling technique (Kerr et al., 2018). The educational video was based on World Rugby's RugbyReady injury prevention initiative (World Rugby, 2007). They assessed the players' biomechanics before and after watching the video to determine if watching the video of how to tackle safely could alter their tackle biomechanics. The players' performed six tackles, three before and three after watching the video. This allowed the researchers to determine the effect of repetition on the players' technique. They found that for the younger players, repeating the tackles had more of an effect on improving their technique proficiency than the educational video, suggesting that repetition may be more important, than instructional information alone, for younger players to learn to tackle safely and effectively (Kerr et al., 2018).

Along with knowledge, a player's attitude and behaviours towards safety are key determinants in their execution of safe tackle technique (Hendricks et al., 2012). Attitude can be defined as a person's knowledge concerning the consequences of a certain behaviour (Van Mechelen et al., 1992). In this case, whether a person believes that performing proper tackle technique is important to improve

TABLE 11.1 Summary of Studies Evaluating the Tackle in Youth Rugby Union

Author (Year)	Sample Size	Age Group	Level	Analysis Environment	Technique Analysed	Analysis Model	Outcome(s) or Factor(s) Variables	Key Findings
Burger et al. (2016b)	297 tackles	U18	Elite	Match	Tackle Ball-carry	Technical Criteria	Injury	Higher total technique scores were associated with non-injury tackle events.
Burger et al. (2016a)	297 tackles	U18	Elite	Match	Tackle Ball-carry	Technical Descriptors	Injury	Awareness of contact and fending were likely to reduce the risk of injury for the ball-carrier. Shoulder tacklers were likely to reduce the risk of injury for the tackler.
Chiwaridzo et al. (2019a)	87 players	U19	Educational	Training	Tackle	Technical Criteria	Level of play	Tackling proficiency did not discriminate between levels of play.
Chiwaridzo et al. (2019b)	71 players	U16	Educational	Training	Tackle	Technical Criteria	Level of play	Players who competed at a higher level of play had higher tackle technique scores, compared to players who competed at a lower level.
Chiwaridzo et al. (2020)	158 players	U16 U19	Educational	Training	Tackle	Technical Criteria	Age group & level of play	U19 players scored better in tackle technique assessment than U16 players. Players who competed at a higher level of play had higher tackle technique scores, compared to players who competed at a lower level.

den Hollander et al. (2019)	131 players	U21	Amateur	Training	Tackle Ball-carry Ruck	Technical Criteria	Level of play	Senior-level players scored significantly higher than the academy level players in the tackle, ball-carry and ruck technique assessments.
Hendricks et al. (2015c)	24 tackles 65 rucks	U18	Elite	Match	Tackle Ball-carry Ruck	Technical Criteria	Injury	Higher total technique scores were associated with non-injury tackle and ruck events.
Hendricks et al. (2016)	24 tackles	U18	Elite	Match	Tackle Ball-carry	Technical Descriptors	Injury	In 72% of tackles that lead to concussions the tacklers head was not 'up and forward.
Mcintosh et al. (2010)	6,618 tackles	U15 U18 U20 Senior	Educational Amateur Elite International	Match	Tackle Ball-carry	Technical Descriptors	Injury	No specific tackle technique was observed to be associated with a significantly increased risk of injury.
Sobue et al. (2018)	3,970 tackles	U21	International	Match	Tackle	Technical Descriptors	Injury	The injury incidence for head incorrectly positioned was 69.4/1000 tacklers, compared to 2.7/1000 tackles for correct head positioning.

TABLE 11.2 Summary of Studies Evaluating the Tackle in Youth Rugby League

Author(s)	Sample Size	Age Group	Level	Analysis Environment	Technique Analysed	Analysis Model	Outcome(s) or Factor(s)	Key Findings
Gabbett et al. (2010)	41 players	U15	Amateur Elite	Training	Tackle	Technical Criteria	Level of play & physical measures	Fast acceleration and lower body power contributed positively to effective tackling ability.
Pearce et al. (2019)	88 players	U18 U20 Senior	Amateur	Training	Tackle	Technical Criteria	Level of play	Senior level players demonstrated greater tackle proficiency, compared to u18 & u20 level players
Speranza et al. (2016)	36 players	U20 Senior	Amateur	Training	Tackle	Technical Criteria	Level of play & physical measures	Tackling ability was associated with squats, bench press, relative squats, and plyometric push ups.

their safety. Examples of behaviour are a player's training habits, on-field actions, or their interactions with teammates, opponents, coaches, or referees. In a number of studies, Hendricks and colleagues have assessed the attitudes and behaviours (reported and observed) of youth rugby players and coaches regarding safe tackle technique (Hendricks et al., 2012, 2015a, 2020a; Hendricks & Sarembock, 2013). They found that although players rated winning the tackle contest as more important than injury prevention (Hendricks et al., 2012), the importance of injury prevention, and time spent on technique, was associated with behaviours that reduce the risk of injuries in matches (Hendricks et al., 2015a). Interestingly, national intervention programmes advocate that safe technique is also effective in winning the tackle contest. This claim is supported by research, where 11 tackle techniques and five ball-carrier techniques associated with reduced injury risks have also been associated with winning the tackle contest (Tables 11.3 and 11.4; den Hollander et al., 2021). There is, therefore, no need for a trade-off between safety and performance in the tackle. Hendricks and colleagues (2017a) also found that although coaches were aware of the risk of injury and rated coaching proper technique as important, their reported knowledge and attitude did not translate to time spent coaching tackle technique. These findings are not unique to this study. In a study examining trends in training volume over 11 seasons of English Professional rugby, out of a total of 6 hours 48 minutes/player/week of training, only 24 minutes was spent in full-contact rugby skills training, and one hour in semi-contact skills training (West et al., 2020). Improving a coach's confidence in their ability to coach tackle technique, and providing them with the tools to do so, is therefore, important to allow young players the opportunity to practice tackling safely and effectively.

Tackle Height

Related to tackle technique is the height where the tackler makes initial contact with the ball-carrier. Within senior-level rugby union, Tierney et al. (2016) originally found that tacklers sustained most head impacts and that intending to contact the ball carrier at the upper body region was the main cause of head impacts for the tackler. Tierney and colleagues (Tierney et al., 2016; Tierney & Simms, 2017) conducted further analysis on tackle height and found that tackles to the upper trunk region (chest and shoulder area) of the ball carrier were the main cause of tackler-related head injury assessments (the protocol that players undergo in rugby union if suspected of a concussion). The study also found that tackling at the lower trunk (roughly at the hips) of the ball carrier is the optimal location. Tackling around the upper trunk or upper legs leaves the head vulnerable to being impacted by moving limbs such as the arms and legs, respectively. However, the lower trunk tends to follow the bulk movement of the player, making safe head placement more achievable for the tackler (Simms, 2018). Additionally, tackling lower down on the ball carrier's body can reduce inertial head loading for the ball carrier during a tackle event (Tierney et al.,

TABLE 11.3 Tackle Techniques Associated with Injury Prevention and Performance in Rugby Union (Hollander et al., 2021)

Tackle Technique	Studies (N)	Injury Prevention	Performance
Pre-contact			
Identify ball-carrier onto shoulder	4	✓	–
Body position – upright to low (dipping)	6	✓	✓
Back straight, centre of gravity ahead of support base	4	✓	✓
Alignment square to ball-carrier	5	✓	–
Head up and face forward	6	✓	✓
Boxer stance – elbows low and close, hands up	5	✓	–
Shortening steps	5	✓	✓
Approach from front/oblique	5	✓	–
Contact			
Explosiveness on contact	4	–	✓
Contact with shoulder	8	✓	✓
Contact in centre of gravity	5	✓	✓
Head placement on the correct side of ball-carrier	8	✓	✓
Post contact			
Shoulder drive upon first contact	4	✓	✓
Leg drive upon contact	7	✓	✓
Punch arms forward, wrap and pull (hit and stick)	5	✓	✓
Release ball-carrier and compete for possession	4	✓	✓

Note, studies include junior and senior cohorts.

n: number of studies describing the relationship between the technique and outcome.

✓ positive association; – no association.

2018; Tierney & Simms, 2017). Inertial head loading is an acceleration of the head due to an impact on the body (i.e., no direct contact to the head). Reducing inertial head loading in the tackle would likely reduce the overall repetitive sub-concussive head loading environment in the game (Tierney et al., 2018; Tierney & Simms, 2017). At the senior elite level, these data have contributed to law modifications, with stricter rulings around high-tackles, and law trials to lower the height of a legal tackle to below the nipple line (Raftery et al., 2021; Stokes et al., 2021). No doubt, stricter rulings around high tackles should also be applied at the youth level. Also, although the findings are at the senior level, such findings provide strong support for the current coaching instructions at the youth level in terms of where to target the ball carrier to make a safe and effective tackle.

TABLE 11.4 Ball-Carry Techniques Associated with Injury Prevention and Performance in Rugby Union (Hollander et al., 2021)

Ball-Carry Technique	Studies (n)	Injury Prevention	Performance
Pre-contact			
Focus on tackler	7	✓	–
Body position – upright to low (dipping)	4	✓	✓
Back straight, centre of gravity ahead of support base	4	✓	–
Shift ball away from contact to correct arm	4	–	–
Head up, face forward	4	✓	–
Shuffle or evasive manoeuvre	5	–	✓
Contact			
Fend into contact	6	✓	✓
Side-on into contact	4	✓	–
Explosiveness on contact	4	✓	✓
Body position – from low up into contact	4	✓	–
Ball in correct arm and protected	4	–	✓
Post contact			
Use of arm and/or shoulder to push tackler	4	✓	–
Leg drive upon contact	4	✓	✓
Go to ground and present ball	5	✓	✓

Studies include junior and senior cohorts.

n: number of studies describing the relationship between the technique and outcome.

✓ positive association; – no association

Physical Conditioning for the Tackle

In 2014, Hendricks and Lambert proposed a theoretical model describing the relationship between tackle load (acute and chronic load), tackle injury risk and tackle performance (Hendricks & Lambert, 2014). In brief, the model postulated that players who are physically conditioned (see Chapters 7 and 8) and have high technical proficiency can repeatedly engage in tackles with high loads, without negatively changing their injury risk and performance profile (Hendricks & Lambert, 2014). Evidence to support this theoretical model can be found in senior rugby union and rugby league studies (Gabbett et al., 2011b ; Tierney et al., 2017a). For example, in rugby league, players involved in the most tackle contests exhibit the lowest contact injury incidence Gabbett et al., 2011b. In rugby league and rugby union, physical fatigue has shown to decrease tackling technique (Gabbett et al., 2011b). While these studies have been conducted in senior-level players, the findings apply to young rugby players. For safe and successful participation, players need to be technically proficient and have the technical capacity to maintain proper tackling technique through-out a match. Therefore, youth players need to develop technical capacity for the tackle. To build youth players technical capacity, players need to train the tackle technique (tackling and ball-carrying into contact) in a fatigued state (Hendricks et al., 2018).

Specific physical qualities have also been shown to improve the skill of tackling and ball-carrying itself. In academy players, den Hollander et al. (2022) showed that muscular strength, lower body muscle power, agility and mobility were associated with tackling, while only upper body power was associated with carrying the ball into contact (den Hollander et al., 2022). The physical qualities associated with each contact skill performed in the contact drill are indicative of the physical-technical demands to optimally perform each skill. In rugby league, similar studies have shown that physical qualities that correlate with tackling ability seem to differ by playing level. For example, in junior elite and professional rugby league, acceleration and lower body muscle power have been associated with tackling ability (Gabbett et al., 2010, 2011a). In contrast, lower body strength, upper body strength and upper-body power have been associated with tackling ability in semi-professional rugby league (Speranza et al., 2015a). The associations between the physical qualities and tackler and ball-carrier techniques provide strength and conditioning trainers, clinicians and coaches with insight into the specific physical requirements to optimally contest in the tackle. Strength and conditioning trainers may be able to use these results to design contact-specific physical training programmes to enhance training adaptation; clinicians can monitor these physical qualities to return players back to contact safely after an injury; and coaches can use the information presented here to set the optimum physical-technical challenge during contact training sessions.

Monitoring the Tackle in Matches and Training

Video analysis is one of the most common tools used to monitor the tackle. Video analysis software allows us to identify any tackle that occurs in a game, differentiate those tackles by measures of performance or injury outcomes, and describe the tackles using a set of descriptor variables. One of the main purposes of video analysis research is to provide players and coaches with objective and reliable information which can be used to inform practice (den Hollander et al., 2018, O'Donoghue, 2009). Therefore, to be useful, research should not only inform on what happens in a game (the number of tackles and injuries) but also how those events occurred (how a player got injured in a tackle; den Hollander et al., 2018).

A number of studies have described the 'what' and 'how' of tackle-related injuries at an annual U18 tournament in South Africa (Brown et al., 2017; Burger et al., 2014, 2016a, 2016b; Hendricks et al., 2015c, 2016). On average, there were 123 tackles a game (Brown et al., 2017), with a tackle-related injury incidence of 27 injuries per 1,000 playing hours (Burger et al., 2014). Tacklers were less likely to get injured when performing a shoulder tackle, compared to an arm tackle, and ball-carriers were less likely to get injured when they were aware of the impending contact (Burger et al., 2016a). For both the ball-carrier and tackler, poor overall technique proficiency increased the risk of injury (Burger et al., 2016b; Hendricks et al., 2015c). The researchers scored the players technique based on a list of observable actions that represent the ideal form of the technique (Hendricks et al., 2020b). The list of technical criteria was standardised across the studies and was based on technique prescribed by national rugby unions and used by coaches in training (Hendricks et al., 2015b). One point was awarded when a prescribed technique was performed and zero if the technique was not performed. The points were then summed to determine the technical proficiency score of the player. This standardised list of criteria has subsequently been used to compare the technique proficiency of injured and non-injured senior international players, dominant and non-dominant tackles in matches and different levels of play in training (Davidow et al., 2018; den Hollander et al., 2019; Tierney et al., 2017b).

To assess the tackle technique of different levels of play, den Hollander et al. (2019) developed a tool that evaluates tackle and ruck technique in a two-on-two contact drill. The drill was based on research in rugby league (e.g., Gabbett, 2008; Speranza et al., 2015b, 2018a, 2018b) and designed to have a high degree of ecological validity and representativeness. The standardised contact drill and method of scoring players' technique have shown encouraging construct validity by differentiating between levels of play (den Hollander et al., 2019; Gabbett et al., 2010; Speranza et al., 2015a) and associated with better tackle performance outcomes (e.g., higher proportion of dominant tackles) in matches (Gabbett & Ryan, 2009; Speranza et al., 2015b, 2018a). The contact drill is filmed and includes a phase of play before the tackle and is performed in the corner of the field where the touchline and try-line meet, and the ball-carrier is instructed to aim to score the try and the tackler to aim to prevent the try from being scored. Two different levels of players (senior and academy) participated in the drill, and the players technique was assessed using standardised criteria (Table 11.5). The study showed that senior-level players scored higher than the academy players during the tackler, ball-carrier and ruck technique assessments. The findings from this study illustrate the importance of developing contact technique for progression to higher levels of play and provide validity of an assessment tool to facilitate this process (den Hollander et al., 2019).

Are We Training the Tackle Enough?

Research has also suggested we may not be training the tackle adequately enough; and there may be a mismatch between tackle contact training and tackle contact match demands (Campbell et al., 2017; Hendricks, 2017a, Hendricks et al., 2017b; West et al., 2020). Coaches at the youth level have also reported to rely mainly on informal, anecdotal resources (e.g., playing experience, watching rugby matches)

TABLE 11.5 Criteria to Assess Tackler and Ball-Carrier Technical Skills (Adapted from Hendricks et al., 2018)

Tackler	Ball-Carrier
Pre-contact	*Pre-contact*
1 Identify ball-carrier onto shoulder	1 Focus on tackler
2 Body position – upright to low (dipping movement)	2 Shift ball away from contact to correct arm
3 Keep back straight, and centre of gravity ahead of base of support	3 Body position – upright to low (dipping movement)
4 Alignment square to ball-carrier	4 Keep back straight, and centre of gravity ahead of base of support
5 Assume 'boxer stance' – elbows low and close, hands up	5 Head up and face forward
6 Head up and face forward	6 Shuffle or evasive manoeuvre
7 Shortening steps	
8 Approach from front/oblique	
Contact	*Contact*
9 Explosiveness (rapid movement) on contact	7 Fending into contact
10 Contact with shoulder	8 Side-on into contact
11 Contact in centre of gravity	9 Explosiveness (rapid movement) on contact
12 Head placement on the correct side of ball-carrier	10 Body position - from low up into contact (airplane movement)
	11 Ball in correct arm and protected
Post contact	*Post contact*
13 Shoulder drive upon first contact	12 Leg drive upon contact
14 Leg drive upon contact	13 Arm usage - use arm and shoulder to push tackler
15 Arm usage - punch arms forward, wrap and pull (hit and stick)	14 Go to ground and present ball/break tackle/offload
16 Release ball-carrier and compete for possession	

to inform their tackle training (Hendricks, 2017a; Hendricks & Sarembock, 2013). Coaches at the youth level acknowledge the high risk of injury in the tackle and the importance of proper technical preparation, but also recognise that they may not fully understand the technical components of contact skill training, which may influence their ability to coach the tackle for both safety and performance (Hendricks, 2017a). Youth players also report that identifying specific technique deficiencies and fixing them as the most influential form of feedback when being coached the tackle (Hendricks et al., 2012). This learning approach positively influences their attitude and behaviour towards injury prevention and performance in training and matches (Hendricks et al., 2020a). Additionally, coaches seek and are receptive towards novel tackle training approaches that may improve player performance and reduce players' risk of injury (Hendricks, 2017a).

Summary

The tackle is the major cause of injury in youth rugby. These tackle injuries are largely a result of poor tackle technique, both when tackling and carrying the ball into contact. Improving tackling and ball-carrying technique requires an understanding and change in players attitude and knowledge of tackle techniques, regularly assessing players techniques and building the player's physical and technical capacities. We may not be training the tackle adequately enough and different approach to coaching the tackle is required. In the next section, we will discuss how some of the research outlined above has been used to develop a tackle training framework and programme to help develop young rugby players tackle skills.

Practical Application: A Tackle Skill Training Framework

Tackling and Carrying the Ball into Contact are Movement Skills

The first realisation that needs to be is that tackling and carrying the ball into contact are fundamentally highly technical and physical movement skills. As such, they can be acquired, developed and mastered. Based on this realisation and the available evidence at the time, Hendricks et al. (2018) developed a technical skill training framework for the tackle. Over the last 10–15 years, knowledge of the dynamic nature of the tackle, the physical demands of tackle, the fitness conditioning requirements, the technical requirements, and how tackle injuries occur have been gained to minimise tackle injury risk while maximising tackle performance. In addition, our understanding of how to effectively design and plan training to optimise skill learning and transfer (to competition) has grown.

Models of Skill Training for the Tackle

The tackle training framework is based on three skill training models; (1) the constraints-based framework for skilled performance (Davids et al., 2008); (2) the challenge point framework (Guadagnoli & Lee, 2004); and (3) the skill acquisition periodisation framework (Farrow & Robertson, 2017). These skill training frameworks can also be used to model other fundamental contact (e.g., rucking) and non-contact (e.g., passing) skills in rugby. The constraints-based framework for skilled performance explains how coordination patterns emerge during goal-oriented behaviour and views movement as a functionality of the player (physical and psychological characteristics), the task and the environment (Davids et al., 2008). The challenge point framework describes the interaction between the difficulty of the task (i.e., dependent on the skill level of the player) and potential available information to the player (i.e., too much or too little information). By understanding this relationship, the framework describes how the optimal challenge point can be achieved to ensure successful skill learning and transfer (Guadagnoli & Lee, 2004). The skill acquisition periodisation framework reconceptualised the principles of physical training and focuses on specificity, progression, overload, reversibility and tedium to describe how sport skill training can be periodised (Farrow & Robertson, 2017).

When and How to Use the Tackle Skill Framework

The tackle skill training framework can be used to develop players' tackle contact skills, build contact readiness (when introducing players to rugby), contact readiness as part of match warm-up, return to contact (for players returning from injury), contact capacity (maintaining proper technique while fatigued) and contact efficiency (highly proficient contact technique with minimal physical effort). Using the tackle skill training framework, Hendricks et al. (2018) proposed a detailed training plan for coaches, strength and conditioning coaches, and trainers to help design and monitor tackle training, with the goal of reducing players' risk of injury while improving their tackle performance in matches (Hendricks et al., 2018).

Before applying the tackle training framework, the skill level of the player(s) should be determined, along with the main training goals for each session (and how these goals fit into the overall training plan; Table 11.6). The skill of the player(s) can be determined using the tackle contact drill and technical proficiency scoring described above (Table 11.5). Training purposes can be divided into (1) learning proper tackle contact technique(s); (2) developing and refining technical proficiency; (3) building technical capacity (i.e., the maintaining quality technique under a fatigued state); (4) developing and refining tackle contact skill proficiency (quality); and (5) building skill capacity (i.e., the ability to maintain quality skill under a fatigued state). A distinction is made here between technique and skill, where technique is considered the execution of a set of co-ordinated movement patterns and skill as the proficiency of execution of the correct actions in response to the demand of the situation. As such, technique proficiency and technique capacity act as pre-requisites for skill proficiency.

Once the purpose of the training session has been determined, the optimal conditions can be set to achieve the training session goals. The training conditions are set by determining the difficulty of task, which can either be nominal (the amount of difficulty is constant, regardless of who is performing the task, the level of the athlete and conditions) or functional (how challenging the task is relative to the skill level of the individual performing the task and to the conditions under which it is being performed), and by setting the amount of available information in the environment. The environment could be highly structured, blocked and become progressively more representative of match-play. The relationship between task difficulty and the availability of information can be used

TABLE 11.6 Tackle Contact Skill Training Variables (adapted from Hendricks et al., 2018)

	Variable	Description
Training Purpose	• Technique Proficiency • Technique Capacity • Skill Proficiency • Skill Capacity	• Execution of proper contact techniques • Maintain technique proficiency under a fatigued state • Execution of correct actions determined by the demand of the situation • Maintain skill proficiency under a fatigued state
Skill Training Variables	**External Skill Load** • Available Information • Task Difficulty • Challenge Point **Internal Skill Load** • Rating of Perceived Challenge (RPC) • Skill Load	• Amount of potential information in the environment available to the player (1–10 rating scale) • How hard the task is for the player to perform (player skill level dependent) (1–10 rating scale) • Sum of the available information and task difficulty divided by two • Player's rating of perceived challenge (RPC, rating scale, 1 = Not very challenging, 10 = Maximal) • Rate of contacts per session multiplied by RPC
Physical Training Variables	**External Load** • Number of Contact Repetitions • Duration • Rate **Internal Load** • Intensity • Physical Load • Mental Effort	• Number of contacts (ball-carrying and tackling) per session • Length of the session (minutes) • Number of contacts (ball-carrying and tackling) divided by session duration (contacts per minute) • Rating of perceived exertion (RPE, 0–10 rating scale) • Duration of session multiplied by RPE • Rating of perceived mental effort (0–10 rating scale)

(Continued)

TABLE 11.6 (Continued)

	Variable	Description
Training Conditions	• Highly Structured, Blocked, Low Representativeness • Semi-structured, Moderate Representativeness • Unstructured, High Representativeness • Practice Match	• 1 vs. 1 drills, limited space, static, low impact • 2+ vs. 2+ drills, more space, dynamic, moderate-high impact • Small sided games
Coaching Style	• Prescriptive • Descriptive • Guided-discovery	• Instructing the player to perform the required actions and movements • Informing the player that an error has been committed and that improvements can made • Players self-learn unique solutions to movement challenges through exploration and discovery

Improving Young Rugby Player's Tackle Ability 209

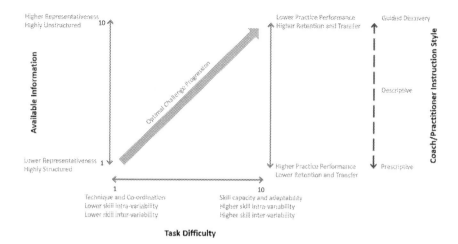

FIGURE 11.1 Technical Skill Training Framework (adapted from Hendricks et al., 2019).

to determine the optimal challenge point of the training session (Figure 11.1). Knowing the aim of the training session will also guide how the coach instructs the players.

From a technical-tactical skill training perspective, the challenge point can be used to quantify skill load (Farrow & Robertson, 2017; Guadagnoli & Lee, 2004; Hendricks et al., 2019). The task difficulty and the availability of information are usually set by the coach and serve as an external quantification of skill load. For practical purposes, coaches, strength and conditioning coaches and trainers could use a visual analogue scale from 1 to 10 (Figure 11.1) to rate the difficulty of the task (1 = technique and co-ordination; 10 = skill capacity and adaptability) and the level of information available to the players (1 = highly structured, lower representativeness; 10 = highly unstructured, higher representativeness). The resulting values from these two ratings would indicate the challenge point set out by the coach. To determine whether the player experiences this challenge and works around the optimal challenge point, the player could be asked to rate how challenging they perceived the skill session to be (rating of perceived challenge [RPC], 1 = not very challenging, 10 = maximal). The players' RPC of the skill session would represent a measure of internal skill load. A further measurement of internal skill load would be to multiply the RPC by the amount of tackles a player performs within a given time (i.e., tackle rate).

When training the tackle, it is also important to consider the performance-learning paradox (Davids et al., 2008). A training session with a low challenge point (highly structured and blocked) will potentially lead to high levels of skill performance in practice and low levels of skill learning (retention and transfer), whereas a session that is high in task difficulty and highly representative (e.g., match practice and high challenge point) may lead to lower levels of skill performance in practice but have a higher potential for skill learning. These relationships are dependent on the skill level of the player, and the optimal challenge point is when the potential for skill retention and transfer is high and decrements in practice performance are kept to a minimum (Farrow & Robertson, 2017). For a progressive tackle contact skill training plan, it is recommended to start the plan with a low challenge point (high levels of performance in practice) and build toward a higher challenge point.

Tackle Programme Example

To show an example of a tackle skill training programme, we present a three week plan for an experienced junior player for both tackling and ball carrying (Table 11.7). The proposed plan is adaptable and should be modified based on the team setting, the technical ability and skill level of each player, and the phase of the season. A description is provided below.

- The objective of week 1 is to develop the player's technical proficiency for the front-on and side-on tackle. Because the focus is technique, the first couple of days is highly structured using a 1 vs. 1 static drill that is low impact and does not require the attacker and defender to accelerate toward each other.
- Week 2 starts with another highly structured 1 vs. 1 drill; however, the ball-carrier and tackler move toward each other (no direction change from ball-carrier). For each shoulder (right and left) and type of tackle (front-on and side-on), the player engages in a set of eight contact events (players engage in 10–15 contact events during a match). Once players are technically proficient and able to maintain good technique under fatigue, players can start developing their skill proficiency – that is, execute the correct actions based on the demands of the situation.
- This occurs during week 3 by increasing the task difficulty and the available information to players during drills. For skill proficiency, drills are semi-structured with more space and players work in mini-units of two or more attackers vs. two or more defenders.
- Future planning could include skill refinement including small-sided contact games leading towards a practice match.

Progression

Increasing the skill loads and progression through the training plan would vary based on the age and skill level of the player (Hendricks et al., 2018). For example, the rate of progression for a younger, less-experienced player will be more gradual than the rate of progression described in Table 11.7. The younger, less-experienced player may require extra or repeat sessions under lighter skill loads before progressing to more challenging sessions. The training plan could

TABLE 11.7 An Example Tackle Contact Training Program

Week 1	Day 1	Day 2	Day 3	Day 4	Day 5, 6 and 7	Week 1 Workloads
Training Purpose	Technique Proficiency (Front-on)	Technique Proficiency (Side-on)	No Tackle Contact Training	Technique Proficiency (Front on and Side-on)	No Tackle Contact Training	
Skill Training Workload						
External Skill Load						
Task Difficulty	3	3		5		3.7
Available Information	1	1		3		1.7
Internal Skill Load						
Rating of Perceived Challenge (RPC)	2	2		4		2.7
Skill Load (Rate × RPC, AU)	1	1		3.2		5.2
Physical Workload						
External Load						
Number of Contact Reps	4 each shoulder	4 each shoulder		3 each shoulder × 2 types tackles		28
Duration (minutes)	15	15		15		45
Rate (contacts per minute)	0.5	0.5		0.8		0.6
Internal Workload						
Intensity (RPE)	2	2		5		3
Physical Load (RPE × duration, AU)	30	30		75		135

(*Continued*)

TABLE 11.7 (Continued)

Week 1	Day 1	Day 2	Day 3	Day 4	Day 5, 6 and 7	Week 1 Workloads
Mental Effort (rating 1–10)	2	2		5		3
Training Description	Highly structured, blocked, low impact, technique focus, 1v1 drill, static, no attacker-defender run up	Highly structured, blocked, low impact, technique focus, 1v1 drill, static, no attacker-defender run up		Semi-structured, moderate impact, 1v1 drill, dynamic, players run-up, attacker side-steps left or right		
Coaching Style Description	Prescriptive, focus on technical points	Prescriptive, focus on technical points		Prescriptive, focus on technical points		

Week 2	Day 1	Day 2	Day 3	Day 4	Day 5, 6 and 7	Week 2 Workloads
Training Purpose	Technique Capacity	Technique Refinement/ Remediate	No Tackle Contact Training	Technique Capacity	No Tackle Contact Training	
Skill Training Workload						
External Skill Load						
Task Difficulty	5	4		5		4.7
Available Information	3	3		3		3
Internal Skill Load						
Rating of Perceived Challenge (RPC)	4	3.5		4		3.8

Improving Young Rugby Player's Tackle Ability 213

Skill Load (Rate × RPC, AU)	6.4	2.8	8.4	17.6
Physical Workload				
External Load				
Number of Contact Repetitions	8 each shoulder X 2 types of tackles with physical conditioning block	4 each shoulder X 2 types tackles	8 each shoulder X 2 types of tackles (close contact, wrestling)	80
Duration (minutes)	20	15	15	50
Rate (contacts per minute)	1.6	0.8	2.1	1.5
Internal Workload				
Intensity (RPE)	6	3	6.5	5.2
Physical Load (RPE × duration, AU)	120	45	97.5	262.5
Mental Effort (rating 1–10)	3	4	4	3.7
Training Description	Highly structured, moderate impact, technique focus, 1v1 drill, attacker-defender run up, no direction change, physical conditioning block (e.g. running/repeated sprints between sets, high-intensity non-contact skill drill, A-frames etc.), before and between sets	Highly structured, blocked, low impact, technique focus, 1v1 drill, static, attacker-defender run up	Highly structured, moderate impact, 1v1 drill, dynamic, no run-up, attacker and defender wrestle in contact	
Coaching Style Description	Prescriptive and descriptive, focus on maintaining technique	Prescriptive, focus on technical points	Prescriptive and descriptive, focus on maintaining technique	

(*Continued*)

TABLE 11.7 (Continued)

Week 3	Day 1	Day 2	Day 3	Day 4	Day 5, 6 and 7	Week 3 Workloads
Training Variable Training Purpose	Skill Proficiency	Skill Proficiency	No Tackle Contact Training	Skill Capacity	No Tackle Contact Training	
Skill Training Workload						
External Skill Load						
Task Difficulty	5	7		6		6
Available Information	7	8		7		7.3
Internal Skill Load						
Rating of Perceived Challenge (RPC)	6	7.5		6.5		6.7
Skill Load (Rate × RPC, AU)	6.6	8.3		13.7		28.6
Physical Workload						
External Load						
Number of Contact Repetitions	4 each shoulder X 2 types tackles	4 each shoulder X 2 types tackles		8 each shoulder X 2 types of tackles with physical conditioning block		64
Duration (minutes)	15	15		15		45
Rate (contacts per minute)	1.1	1.1		2.1		1.4

Internal Workload			
Intensity (RPE)	6	7.5	8
Physical Load (RPE × duration, AU)	90	112.5	120
Mental Effort (rating 1–10)	6	7	7
Training Description	Semi-structured, more space, mini-units, 2+ vs 2+ drills, attackers decide play, defender needs to identify ball-carrier, fast attacker-defender run up speed, high impact, work within team context	Semi-structured, more space, mini-units, 2+ vs 2+ drills, attackers decide play, defender needs to identify ball-carrier, fast attacker-defender run up speed, high impact, work within team context, tactical awareness, double tackles, post-tackle actions (jackal for tackler, ball placement for ball-carrier)	Semi-structured, mini-units, more space, 2+ vs 2+ drills, attackers decide play, defender needs to identify ball-carrier, fast attacker-defender run up speed, high impact, work within team context, tactical awareness, post-tackle actions (jackal for tackler, ball placement for ball-carrier), physical conditioning block (e.g. running/repeated sprints between sets, high-intensity non-contact skill drill, A-frames etc.) before and between sets
			7.2
			322.5
			6.7
Coaching Style Description	Descriptive and guided-discovery	Descriptive and guided-discovery	Descriptive and guided-discovery

be adapted to include extra or repeat sessions. Progression through the plan should be determined on an individual basis; however, this may not always be possible in a team or squad setting. The best method to determine the rate of progression of players is through observation, assessment, and the players' response to the session (Hendricks et al., 2018). Using the tackle skill framework, assessments and technical skill variables, practitioners and coaches can determine if a young player is ready for full tackle contact during competition, and subsequently building tackle contact readiness. The assessments and progressive loading of tackle skill variables can also be used during warm-up and during the return to play process following an injury (i.e., return to contact; Burger et al., 2020). For example, once a player who has suffered a shoulder injury is pain-free and completed the rehabilitation phase of the return to sport process, players can undergo a low-impact static tackling technique assessment. Thereafter, progressively increase the skill and physical variables, as well as the demands of the training conditions.

Key Take Home Messages

- In youth rugby union, tackle injuries account for 39%–62% of all injuries, with the frequency of injury between the ball-carrier and tackler not dissimilar and in youth rugby league, tackle injuries account for 61% of all injuries.
- Proper contact technique when tackling and carrying the ball into contact reduces players' risk of injury and increases their likelihood of winning the tackle.
- Improving players' and coaches' knowledge and attitudes about safe and effective tackle contact techniques may modify players' tackle training and match behaviours.
- Coaches and practitioners should use video analysis to monitor the tackle in both training and matches. Video analysis of the tackle allows us to understand what happens in a game (for example, tackle frequency and number of tackler injuries), how tackle injuries occur, and how to win the tackle contest.
- Tackling and carrying the ball into contact are fundamentally highly technical and physical movement skills. As such, skill training literature and models can be applied to training the tackle. Also, specific physical qualities are required to perform optimally during the tackle.
- The tackle skill training framework uses skill literature and models to outline the training purpose (technique proficiency, technique capacity, skill proficiency and skill capacity), skill workload measurements (available information, task difficulty, rating of perceived challenge and skill load), as well as the training conditions and coaching style for the tackle.
- The tackle skill training framework can be used to develop players' tackle contact skills, build contact readiness (when introducing players to rugby), contact readiness as part of match warm-up, return to contact (for players

returning from injury), contact capacity (maintaining proper technique while fatigued) and contact efficiency (highly proficient contact technique with minimal physical effort

References

Brown, J., Boucher, S., Lambert, M., Viljoen, W., Readhead, C., Hendricks, S., & Kraak, W. (2017). Non-sanctioning of illegal tackles in South African youth community rugby. *Journal of Science and Medicine in Sport, 21*, 631–634. https://doi.org/10.1016/j.jsams.2017.10.016

Brown, J., Verhagen, E., Knol, D., Van Mechelen, W., & Lambert, M. I. (2016). The effectiveness of the nationwide b ok s mart rugby injury prevention program on catastrophic injury rates. *Scandinavian Journal of Medicine & Science in Sports, 26*, 221–225. https://doi.org/10.1111/sms.12414

Burger, N., Jones, B., & Hendricks, S. (2021). Tackle injury epidemiology and performance in rugby league–narrative synthesis. *South African Journal of Sports Medicine, 33*, 1–8. https://doi.org/10.17159/2078-516x/2021/v33i1a9313

Burger, N., Lambert, M., & Hendricks, S. (2020). Lay of the land: Narrative synthesis of tackle research in rugby union and rugby sevens. *BMJ Open Sport and Exercise Medicine, 6*, e000645. https://doi.org/10.1136/bmjsem-2019-000645

Burger, N., Lambert, M. I., Viljoen, W., Brown, J. C., Readhead, C., den Hollander, S., & Hendricks, S. (2016a). Mechanisms and factors associated with tackle-related injuries in South African youth rugby union players. *The American Journal of Sports Medicine*, 0363546516677548. https://doi.org/10.1136/bmjsem-2019-000645

Burger, N., Lambert, M. I., Viljoen, W., Brown, J. C., Readhead, C., & Hendricks, S. (2014). Tackle-related injury rates and nature of injuries in South African youth week tournament rugby union players (under-13 to under-18): An observational cohort study. *BMJ Open, 4*, e005556. https://doi.org/10.1136/bmjopen-2014-005556

Burger, N., Lambert, M. I., Viljoen, W., Brown, J. C., Readhead, C., & Hendricks, S. (2016b). Tackle technique and tackle-related injuries in high-level South African rugby union under-18 players: Real-match video analysis. *British Journal of Sports Medicine*, bjsports-2015–095295. https://doi.org/10.1136/bjsports-2015-095295

Campbell, P. G., Peake, J. M., & Minett, G. M. (2017). The specificity of rugby union training sessions in preparation for match demands. *International Journal of Sports Physiology and Performance*, 1–23. https://doi.org/10.1123/ijspp.2017-0082

Chiwaridzo, M., Ferguson, G. D., & Smits-Engelsman, B. (2019a). Qualities or skills discriminating under 19 rugby players by playing standards: A comparative analysis of elite, sub-elite and non-rugby players using the scrum test battery. *BMC Research Notes, 12*, 1–8. https://doi.org/10.1186/s13104-019-4563-y

Chiwaridzo, M., Ferguson, G. D., & Smits-Engelsman, B. (2019b). Anthropometric, physiological characteristics and rugby-specific game skills discriminating zimbabwean under-16 male adolescent rugby players by level of competition. *BMJ Open Sport & Exercise Medicine, 5*, e000576. https://doi.org/10.1136/bmjsem-2019-000576

Chiwaridzo, M., Ferguson, G. D., & Smits-Engelsman, B. (2020). Anthropometric, physiological characteristics and rugby-specific game skills of schoolboy players of different age categories and playing standards. *BMC Sports Science, Medicine and Rehabilitation, 12*, 1–15. https://doi.org/10.1186/s13102-019-0155-3

Davidow, D., Quarrie, K., Viljoen, W., Burger, N., Readhead, C., Lambert, M., Jones, B., & Hendricks, S. (2018). Tackle technique of rugby union players during head impact tackles compared to injury free tackles. *Journal of Science and Medicine in Sport, 21*, 1025–1031. https://doi.org/10.1016/j.jsams.2018.04.003

Davids, K. W., Button, C., & Bennett, S. J. (2008). *Dynamics of skill acquisition: A constraints-led approach*, Champaign, IL: Human Kinetics.

den Hollander, S., Lambert, M., Jones, B., & Hendricks, S. (2018). The what and how of video analysis research in rugby union: A critical review. *Sports Medicine Open.* https://doi.org/10.1186/s40798-018-0142-3

den Hollander, S., Lambert, M., Jones, B., & Hendricks, S. (2019). Tackle and ruck technique proficiency within academy and senior club rugby union. *Journal of Sports Sciences, 37*, 2578–2587. https://doi.org/10.1080/02640414.2019.1648121

den Hollander, S., Ponce, C., Lambert, M., Jones, B., & Hendricks, S. (2021). Tackle and ruck technical proficiency in rugby union and rugby league: A systematic scoping review. *International Journal of Sports Science & Coaching, 16*, 421–434.

den Hollander, S., Lambert, M., Jones, B., & Hendricks, S. (2022). The relationship between physical qualities and contact technique in academy rugby union players. *International Journal of Sports Science & Coaching,* 17479541221076297. https://doi.org/10.1177/17479541221076297

Farrow, D., & Robertson, S. (2017). Development of a skill acquisition periodisation framework for high-performance sport. *Sports Medicine,* 1–12. https://doi.org/10.1007/s40279-016-0646-2

Gabbett, T. J. (2008). Influence of fatigue on tackling technique in rugby league players. *The Journal of Strength & Conditioning Research, 22*, 625–632. https://doi.org/10.1519/JSC.0b013e3181635a6a

Gabbett, T. J., Jenkins, D. G., & Abernethy, B. (2010). Physiological and anthropometric correlates of tackling ability in junior elite and subelite rugby league players. *The Journal of Strength & Conditioning Research, 24*, 2989–2995. https://doi.org/10.1519/JSC.0b013e3181f00d22

Gabbett, T. J., Jenkins, D. G., & Abernethy, B. (2011a). Correlates of tackling ability in high-performance rugby league players. *The Journal of Strength & Conditioning Research, 25*, 72–79. https://doi.org/10.1519/JSC.0b013e3181ff506f

Gabbett, T. J., Jenkins, D. G., & Abernethy, B. (2011b). Physical collisions and injury in professional rugby league match-play. *Journal of Science and Medicine in Sport, 14*, 210–215. https://doi.org/10.1016/j.jsams.2011.01.002

Gabbett, T. J., & Ryan, P. (2009). Tackling technique, injury risk, and playing performance in high-performance collision sport athletes. *International Journal of Sports Science & Coaching, 4*, 521–533. https://doi.org/10.1260/174795409790291402

Gianotti, S. M., Quarrie, K. L., & Hume, P. A. (2009). Evaluation of rugbysmart: A rugby union community injury prevention programme. *Journal of Science and Medicine in Sport, 12*, 371–375. https://doi.org/10.1016/j.jsams.2008.01.002

Guadagnoli, M. A., & Lee, T. D. (2004). Challenge point: A framework for conceptualizing the effects of various practice conditions in motor learning. *Journal of Motor Behavior, 36*, 212–224. https://doi.org/10.3200/JMBR.36.2.212-224

Hendricks, S., den Hollander, S., & Lambert, M. (2020a). Coaching behaviours and learning resources; influence on rugby players' attitudes towards injury prevention and performance in the tackle. *Science and Medicine in Football, 4*, 10–14. https://doi.org/10.1080/24733938.2019.1633470

Hendricks, S., den Hollander, S., Tam, N., Brown, J., & Lambert, M. 2015a. The relationships between rugby players' tackle training attitudes and behaviour and their match tackle attitudes and behaviour. *BMJ Open Sport & Exercise Medicine, 1*, e000046. https://doi.org/10.1136/bmjsem-2015-000046

Hendricks, S., Jordaan, E., & Lambert, M. (2012). Attitude and behaviour of junior rugby union players towards tackling during training and match play. *Safety Science, 50*, 266–284. https://doi.org/10.1016/j.ssci.2011.08.061

Hendricks, S., & Lambert, M. (2010). Tackling in rugby: Coaching strategies for effective technique and injury prevention. *International Journal of Sports Science and Coaching, 5*, 117–136. https://doi.org/10.1260/1747-9541.5.1.117

Hendricks, S., & Lambert, M. (2014). Theoretical model describing the relationship between the number of tackles in which a player engages, tackle injury risk and tackle performance. *Journal of Sports Science & Medicine, 13*, 715. PMC4126314

Hendricks, S., Lambert, M., Masimla, H., & Durandt, J. (2015b). Measuring skill in rugby union and rugby league as part of the standard team testing battery. *International Journal of Sports Science & Coaching, 10*, 949–965. https://doi.org/10.1260/1747-9541.10.5.949

Hendricks, S., Matthews, B., Roode, B., & Lambert, M. (2014). Tackler characteristics associated with tackle performance in rugby union. *European Journal of Sport Science, 14*, 753–762. https://doi.org/10.1080/17461391.2014.905982

Hendricks, S., O'Connor, S., Lambert, M., Brown, J., C. Burger, N., Mc Fie, S., Readhead, C., & Viljoen, W. (2015c). Contact technique and concussions in the South African under-18 Coca-Cola Craven week rugby tournament. *European Journal of Sport Science, 15*, 557–564. https://doi.org/10.1080/17461391.2015.1046192

Hendricks, S., O'Connor, S., Lambert, M., Brown, J. C., Burger, N., Mc Fie, S., Readhead, C., & Viljoen, W. (2016). Video analysis of concussion injury mechanism in under-18 rugby. *BMJ Open Sport & Exercise Medicine, 2*, e000053. https://doi.org/10.1136/bmjsem-2015-000053

Hendricks, S., & Sarembock, M. (2013). Attitudes and behaviours of top-level junior rugby union coaches towards the coaching of proper contact technique in the tackle – A pilot study. *South African Journal of Sports Medicine, 25*. https://doi.org/10.17159/SAJSM.459

Hendricks, S., Sarembock, M., Jones, B., Till, K., & Lambert, M. (2017a). The tackle in youth rugby union – gap between coaches' knowledge and training behaviour. *International Journal of Sport Science and Coaching, 12*, 708–715. https://doi.org/10.1177/1747954117738880

Hendricks, S., Till, K., Brown, J. C., & Jones, B. (2017b). Rugby union needs a contact skill-training programme. *British Journal of Sports Medicine, 51*, 829–830. https://doi.org/10.1136/bjsports-2016-096347

Hendricks, S., Till, K., den Hollander, S., Savage, T. N., Roberts, S. P., Tierney, G., Burger, N., Kerr, H., Kemp, S., Cross, M., Patricios, J., Mckune, A. J., Bennet, M., Rock, A., Stokes, K. A., Ross, A., Readhead, C., Quarrie, K. L., Tucker, R., & Jones, B. (2020b). Consensus on a video analysis framework of descriptors and definitions by the rugby union video analysis consensus group. *British Journal of Sports Medicine, 54*, 566–572. https://doi.org/10.1136/bjsports-2019-101293

Hendricks, S., Till, K., Oliver, J. L., Johnston, R. D., Attwood, M. J., Brown, J. C., Drake, D., Macleod, S., Mellalieu, S. D., & Jones, B. (2019). Rating of perceived challenge as a measure of internal load for technical skill performance. *British Journal of Sports Medicine, 53*, 611–613. https://doi.org/10.1136/bjsports-2018-099871

Hendricks, S., Till, K., Oliver, J. L., Johnston, R. D., Attwood, M. J., Brown, J. C., Drake, D., Macleod, S., Mellalieu, S. D., & Treu, P. (2018). Technical skill training framework and skill load measurements for the rugby union tackle. *Strength & Conditioning Journal, 40*, 44–59. https://doi.org/10.1519/SSC.0000000000000400

Hollander, S. D., Ponce, C., Lambert, M., Jones, B., & Hendricks, S. (2021). Tackle and ruck technical proficiency in rugby union and rugby league: A systematic scoping

review. *International Journal of Sports Science & Coaching, 16*, 421–434. https://doi.org/10.1177/1747954120976943
Kerr, H. A., Ledet, E. H., Ata, A., Newitt, J. L., Santa Barbara, M., Kahanda, M., & Sperry Schlueter, E. (2018). Does instructional video footage improve tackle technique? *International Journal of Sports Science & Coaching, 13*, 3–15. https://doi.org/10.1177/1747954117711867
Kim, J. W., Ritter, F. E., & Koubek, R. J. (2013). An integrated theory for improved skill acquisition and retention in the three stages of learning. *Theoretical Issues in Ergonomics Science, 14*, 22–37. https://doi.org/10.1080/1464536X.2011.573008
Mcintosh, A. S., Savage, T. N., Mccrory, P., Frechede, B. O., & Wolfe, R. (2010). Tackle characteristics and injury in a cross section of rugby union football. *Medicine and Science in Sports and Exercise, 42*, 977–984. https://doi.org/10.1249/MSS.0b013e3181c07b5b
Meeuwisse, W. H. (1994). Assessing causation in sport injury: A multifactorial model. *Clinical Journal of Sport Medicine, 4*(3), 166–170. https://doi.org/10.1097/00042752-199407000-00004
O'Donoghue, P. (2009). *Research methods for sports performance analysis*. Oxford: Routledge.
Pearce, L. A., Sinclair, W. H., Leicht, A. S., & Woods, C. T. (2019). Passing and tackling qualities discriminate developmental level in a rugby league talent pathway. *International Journal of Performance Analysis in Sport, 19*, 985–998. https://doi.org/10.1080/24748668.2019.1689750
Quarrie, K., Gianotti, S., Murphy, I., Harold, P., Salmon, D., & Harawira, J. (2020). Rugbysmart: Challenges and lessons from the implementation of a nationwide sports injury prevention partnership programme. *Sports Medicine, 50*, 227–230. https://doi.org/10.1007/s40279-019-01177-8
Quarrie, K. L., & Hopkins, W. G. (2008). Tackle injuries in professional rugby union. *The American Journal of Sports Medicine, 36*, 1705–1716. https://doi.org/10.1177/0363546508316768
Raftery, M., Tucker, R., & Falvey, É. C. (2021). Getting tough on concussion: How welfare-driven law change may improve player safety—a rugby union experience. *British Journal of Sports Medicine, 55*, 527–529. https://doi.org/10.1136/bjsports-2019-101885
Simms, C. (2018). *A biomechanical assessment of direct and inertial head loading in rugby union*. Trinity College.
Sobue, S., Kawasaki, T., Hasegawa, Y., Shiota, Y., Ota, C., Yoneda, T., Tahara, S., Maki, N., Matsuura, T., & Sekiguchi, M. (2018). Tackler's head position relative to the ball carrier is highly correlated with head and neck injuries in rugby. *British Journal of Sports Medicine, 52*, 353–358. https://doi.org/10.1136/bjsports-2017-098135
Speranza, M. J., Gabbett, T. J., Greene, D. A., Johnston, R. D., & Townshend, A. D. (2018a). Relationship between 2 standardized tackling proficiency tests and rugby league match-play tackle performance. *International Journal of Sports Physiology and Performance, 13*, 770–776. https://doi.org/10.1123/ijspp.2017-0593
Speranza, M. J., Gabbett, T. J., Greene, D. A., Johnston, R. D., Townshend, A. D., & O'Farrell, B. (2018b). An alternative test of tackling ability in rugby league players. *International Journal of Sports Physiology and Performance, 13*, 347–352. https://doi.org/10.1123/ijspp.2016-0701
Speranza, M. J., Gabbett, T. J., Johnston, R. D., & Sheppard, J. M. (2015a). Muscular strength and power correlates of tackling ability in semiprofessional rugby league players. *The Journal of Strength & Conditioning Research, 29*, 2071–2078. https://doi.org/10.1519/JSC.0000000000000897

Speranza, M. J., Gabbett, T. J., Johnston, R. D., & Sheppard, J. M. (2015b). Relationship between a standardized tackling proficiency test and match-play tackle performance in semiprofessional rugby league players. *International Journal of Sports Physiology and Performance, 10*, 754–760. https://doi.org/10.1123/ijspp.2015-0044

Speranza, M. J., Gabbett, T. J., Johnston, R. D., & Sheppard, J. M. (2016). Effect of strength and power training on tackling ability in semiprofessional rugby league players. *The Journal of Strength & Conditioning Research, 30*, 336–343. https://doi.org/10.1519/JSC.0000000000001058

Stokes, K. A., Locke, D., Roberts, S., Henderson, L., Tucker, R., Ryan, D., & Kemp, S. (2021). Does reducing the height of the tackle through law change in elite men's rugby union (the championship, england) reduce the incidence of concussion? A controlled study in 126 games. *British Journal of Sports Medicine, 55*, 220–225. https://doi.org/10.1136/bjsports-2019-101557

Thomas, K. T., & Thomas, J. R. (1994). Developing expertise in sport: The relation of knowledge and performance. *International Journal of Sport Psychology, 25*, 295-295.

Tierney, G. J., Denvir, K., Farrell, G., & Simms, C. K. (2017a). Does player time-in-game affect tackle technique in elite level rugby union? *Journal of Science and Medicine in Sport, 21*, 221–225. https://doi.org/10.1016/j.jsams.2017.06.023

Tierney, G. J., Denvir, K., Farrell, G., & Simms, C. K. (2017b). The effect of technique on tackle gainline success outcomes in elite level rugby union. *International Journal of Sports Science & Coaching, 13*, 16–25. https://doi.org/10.1177/1747954117711866

Tierney, G. J., Lawler, J., Denvir, K., Mcquilkin, K., & Simms, C. K. (2016). Risks associated with significant head impact events in elite rugby union. *Brain Injury, 30*, 1350–1361. https://doi.org/10.1080/02699052.2016.1193630

Tierney, G. J., Richter, C., Denvir, K., & Simms, C. K. (2018). Could lowering the tackle height in rugby union reduce ball carrier inertial head kinematics? *Journal of Biomechanics, 72*, 29–36. https://doi.org/10.1016/j.jbiomech.2018.02.023

Tierney, G. J., & Simms, C. K. (2017). The effects of tackle height on inertial loading of the head and neck in rugby union: A multibody model analysis. *Brain Injury, 31*, 1925–1931. https://doi.org/10.1080/02699052.2017.1385853

Van Mechelen, W., Hlobil, H., & Kemper, H. C. (1992). Incidence, severity, aetiology and prevention of sports injuries. A review of concepts. *Sports Medicine, 14*, 82–99. https://doi.org/10.2165/00007256-199214020-00002

Viljoen, W., & Patricios, J. (2012). Boksmart–implementing a national rugby safety programme. *British Journal of Sports Medicine, 46*, 692–693. https://doi.org/10.1136/bjsports-2012-091278

West, S. W., Williams, S., Kemp, S. P., Cross, M. J., Mckay, C., Fuller, C. W., Taylor, A., Brooks, J. H., & Stokes, K. A. (2020). Patterns of training volume and injury risk in elite rugby union: An analysis of 1.5 million hours of training exposure over eleven seasons. *Journal of Sports Sciences, 38*, 238–247. https://doi.org/10.1080/02640414.2019.1692415

World Rugby. (2007). *Rugby ready*. Available: https://passport.world.rugby/injury-prevention-and-risk-management/rugby-ready/the-tackle/

12
TRAINING PRACTICES IN YOUTH RUGBY PLAYERS

Padraic Phibbs, Timothy Hartwig and Sarah Whitehead

Introduction

Athlete development can be optimised within a framework that carefully manages the amount and type of training and recovery (i.e., training practices). The training load, which includes the volume and intensity of training and competition, and the distribution of these loads within a periodised program, typically lead to favourable adaptations that result in improved player health and performance (Smith, 2003). On the other hand, some training practices, including inappropriately prescribed training and competition loads, can result in negative outcomes including increasing the risk of injury, illness, overtraining and burnout (Gabbett et al., 2014).

Although training is known to produce positive adaptations in youth athletes (see Chapter 8), youth athlete participation patterns in sport vary considerably from adult athletes and youth respond differently than adults to a given training stimulus. For example, youth rugby players accumulate training and competition loads (collectively referred to as 'training load') through participation in on- and off-field rugby training sessions and competitions but also frequently participate in other sports and can play rugby for more than one team. This pattern of multi-sport and multi-team participation has been described as 'organised chaos' (Phibbs et al. 2018b) and highlights the importance of quantifying and evaluating youth training practices, including monitoring exposure to overall training loads.

Load monitoring can be achieved by measuring the external workloads performed (e.g., duration in minutes, distance covered) or the internal response to a given load (e.g., heart rate, session rating of perceived exertion [sRPE]). Monitoring load is common practice in most elite sports, but advances in technologies and methods have made it easier than ever before in a wide range of 'non-elite' athletic populations. Microtechnology devices, housing global positioning system (GPS) receivers and triaxial accelerometers, and training diaries are frequently used to measure external training loads in rugby. Alongside internal load measures such as sRPE and heart rate, coaches and trainers at most playing standards typically have a range of options available for monitoring player load in multiple environments to maximise health and support player development.

The purpose of this chapter is to summarise the research on training practices, including training load in youth rugby players, and demonstrate how this knowledge can be used to help guide decisions around appropriate load management by stakeholders (e.g., coaches, sport scientists, parents) responsible for the development of young rugby players.

Research Overview

Seasonal Load

Studies have assessed typical training loads and practices of young rugby players as well as the distribution of these loads within a periodised program. It has been reported that the average English Premiership Youth Academy U18 player is reported to complete around 2.5 times more training than a school player (190 *vs.* 72 training hours per season) with relatively more time spent on resistance training (27% *vs.* 13% training activity) but less relative time on rugby specific training (37% *vs.* 58% of training activity) (Palmer-Green et al., 2015). In English regional rugby academies, U15 and U16 players had a higher volume of rugby matches and training in September to April than May to August with players completing an average of 10–11 sessions per week in this period, equating to ~12 hours of activity per week (Hendricks et al., 2019).

In rugby league, training loads in non-elite junior players have been reported to progressively increase in the pre-season period followed by reductions as the competitive season progresses (Gabbett, 2005). The training practices of nine academies in England have been described at the U16 and U19 age groups (McCormack et al., 2020). U16 players trained less than U19 players with U19s showing greater rugby and strength and conditioning training volume across all phases of the season. However, this study was reported by coaches and may not take into account the training players did away from the professional club. Additionally, both age groups spent the greatest proportion of pre-season training activities on resistance training (pre-season U16s: 40% gym, 32% skills, U19s: 29% gym, 25% skills).

Weekly Load

Youth rugby players accumulate weekly load via on and off-field rugby training and competitive rugby matches but may also accumulate load by engaging in other sports and exercise. Youth rugby union players' weekly loads have previously been assessed using minutes of participation, GPS and computer-based tracking, or combinations of these methods along with subjective internal load measures, including sRPE. Some studies have specifically aimed to measure all sport and exercise youth rugby players participate in while others have limited this to only rugby and rugby-related training practices. Australian 14–18-year-old rugby union players representing three playing standards (schoolboy, representative level, elite talent squad) reported time spent participating in all sport and exercise (Hartwig et al., 2008) showing the representative squad players participated in the greatest number of training minutes per week, equivalent of eight to nine hours. Similar findings were reported when this study was repeated in a subsequent rugby season (Hartwig et al., 2009). A striking finding from these studies was the weekly volumes experienced by some individual players. For example, individual players from these teams reported average weekly durations of between 730 and 804 minutes (equivalent to 12 and 13 hours) per week with the duration in some weeks as high as 1,591 minutes (equivalent to nearly 27 hours). These high weekly training loads are likely accrued as a result of concurrently participating with multiple teams and sometimes in multiple sports. For example, a study of Australian 14–16-year-old schoolboy and representative rugby union players found that 21% of athletes participated in rugby league and rugby union at the same time and 80% of athletes regularly played rugby union for more than one team each week (Hartwig et al., 2019). Clearly, some individual players experience excessive weekly training loads and could benefit from load monitoring and better load management.

Players aged 16–18 years from four school rugby union teams in the United Kingdom reported weekly duration of rugby training and matches, gym sessions and extracurricular activities over a 12-week season (Weakley et al., 2019). Players spent on average 78 minutes per week training in the gym (range: 13.8–177 min) and 120 minutes on-field (range: 3–637 min). Academy U18 players in England who also concurrently played rugby union for their schools and clubs reported an average weekly duration of 301 minutes (range: 200–578) consisting of an average of 214 minutes spent in rugby-related training and matches, 72 minutes spent in gym training and 15 minutes spent in 'other' extracurricular training activities (Phibbs et al., 2018b). These studies highlight the highly individual nature of weekly training loads experienced by youth rugby players with some individual players experiencing weekly loads that are considerably higher than the team average.

Several studies (Hartwig et al., 2009, 2011; Phibbs et al., 2018c; Taylor et al., 2018) have used GPS or computer-based tracking systems to measure the external loads of youth rugby union players. English U18 players reported mean weekly in-season running loads of ~11,500 m during rugby training, which were higher than values previously reported in senior professional players during the in-season and preseason (Phibbs et al., 2018c). Australian age-grade players covered an average distance per hour of 4,000±500 m during matches and 2,710±770 m during training (Hartwig et al., 2011). Combining weekly duration and distance covered measures can help coaches and trainers better understand players' weekly training loads. Similarly, using sRPE, a measure that incorporates a relative perceived intensity score, can improve the overall picture of a player's weekly load. Mean weekly workload during rugby training and matches ranges from 877 ± 273 AU in U18 Academy players in the United Kingdom (Taylor et al., 2018) to 3,645 ± 1,588 AU in U18 Representative players in Australia (Hartwig et al., 2009). Despite inconsistencies in the methods used to measure loads and the fact that some previous studies recorded all sports and exercise while others only recorded rugby-related activities, there is evidence of highly variable training practices and loads with some individual players participating in very high weekly loads. These players may be at greater risk of negative outcomes associated with high training and competition loading, insufficient recovery and high competition-to-training ratios.

Session Load

Research into the physical loads of youth rugby training sessions has identified differences in training volumes and intensities between age categories, playing standards and geographical regions. However, direct comparisons between studies are difficult due to methodological differences. In Australia, Hartwig et al. (2008) investigated the volume and intensity of rugby union training sessions across three playing standards (i.e., schoolboy, representative and talent squad). Despite being the highest playing standard, talent squad players had the lowest total distance and maximum heart rate (2,208±637 m and 189±15 b·min^{-1}) compared to schoolboy (3,511 ± 836 m and 200 ± 13 b·min^{-1}) and representative players (3,576 ± 956 m and 196 ± 12 b·min^{-1}). Average session durations ranged from 58 to 93 minutes, with no substantial differences in mean heart rate or sRPE between playing standards (136–141 b·min^{-1} and 6.4–6.8 AU, respectively). In England, differences between playing standards during training sessions have been shown to be more predictable (Phibbs et al. 2017a). The frequency and duration of training sessions increased with age (i.e., U16–U18), with increases in training intensity observed with playing standard (i.e., school, club and academy). Session durations were lower in England compared to Australia (range: 50–70 minutes), although mean heart rates (134–151 b·min^{-1}) and sRPE descriptors (moderate-hard) were similar between regions. However, the average speed of training sessions in adolescent rugby union players has been shown to be higher in England compared to Australia (range: 55–60 m·min^{-1} vs. 38–50 m·min^{-1}, respectively). Research in South African age-grade rugby union sessions is limited to a single school cohort, where a high training session volume (86 ± 34 min) and subjective intensity (6.3 ± 1.7 AU) have been reported (Barnard et al., 2020). Although the volume and intensity of youth rugby training sessions appear to be influenced by age category, playing standard and region, the appropriateness of training session loads should be determined by the specific match demands of each group and the long-term athletic development aims of the players within the group.

Match-Play Preparation

To be prepared for the physical and movement demands of match-play, it is important to simulate and exceed those characteristics during training. Hartwig et al. (2011) compared the average external loads of training to match-play in U18 rugby union players. During matches, players covered greater total distance (4,000 ± 500 *vs.* 2,720 ± 770 m), with more time jogging, striding and sprinting compared to the average training exposure. However, it might be unsurprising that the average match values would be greater than the average of multiple training exposures during the training week (which might have different individual focuses on running, collisions, technical-tactical preparation, etc. in each session). Another study in English age-grade rugby union investigated the physical and movement characteristics of U18 training and match-play by comparing the peak match values to the peak training value observed throughout the entire training week (Phibbs et al., 2018a). This study found that U18 Academy rugby union players were exposed to similar or higher external loads during training compared to match-play in the forwards and backs positional groups. However, at a lower playing standard, school-level forwards were exposed to lower PlayerLoad^{TM} and low-speed distance (<61% maximum sprint speed [MSS]) in training compared to matches. School level backs were also underprepared for total distance, low-speed distance, high speed running (>61% MSS), very high speed running (>90% MSS) and peak speed during training compared to matches. These findings suggest that the training exposures of school rugby union players observed in this study were suboptimal for position-specific match-play preparation. Additionally, peak speeds achieved during either training or matches rarely exceeded 90% of maximum sprint speed in academy and school groups (range: 83–91% MSS), demonstrating the need for supplementary speed exposures to increase physical output and reduce associated injury risk.

Summary

Previous research has described the training practices of youth rugby players. These studies have assessed training and match characteristics, how effectively training activities might prepare players for the demands of matches, how training and competition contribute to weekly loads, as well as how training loads are distributed within periodised approaches. This research has highlighted that youth training and competition practices tend to be chaotic with regards to periodisation, sometimes lack specificity in training that would help prepare players for match demands and exhibit weekly training loads that could be excessive for many players. Examples of individual youth players engaging in very high training and competition workloads suggest some youth athletes are at risks that could be mitigated by monitoring training practices and the careful management of player loads.

Practical Applications

Monitoring Player Loads

It is clear from previous research that rugby players could benefit from having their training loads monitored and managed appropriately. Ideally, measures such as GPS, heart rate or accelerometery would be included when quantifying training loads. Whilst these training load measures provide objective data, youth rugby players often train at various locations (i.e., school, club, academy), are supervised by different coaches, participate in multiple sports and despite advances in affordable technologies, may have limited access to technologies that allow objective load monitoring. If training load technology is available for some, but not all training and competition, this can result in missing data that limits the ability for coaches and trainers to assess the accumulation of load over time and monitor changes in load exposures. Therefore, more practical methods of monitoring youth player loads may be required to adequately capture the full spectrum of load exposures in youth players.

Self-reported training load measures (e.g., questionnaires and diaries) are a practical approach for training load monitoring in youth athletes. These could be used in conjunction with external load measures when available or they can be used on their own. Self-reported training load can be recorded conveniently with the use of smartphone applications or online forms which can be administered instantaneously with minimal burden on coaches and athletes. In addition to obtaining weekly duration of training and matches, internal training load can be monitored using sRPE. Players can be asked to give a global rating of the perceived intensity of a training session or match on a scale from 0 (rest) to 10 (maximal; Foster et al., 2017). Even if it is not possible to collect sRPE data immediately after a session, sRPE load 24–48 hours post-training has been shown to be valid in adolescent athletic populations (Phibbs et al., 2017b; Scantlebury et al., 2018). Although sRPE is a simple method to determine the internal load, caution must be taken to ensure that validated sRPE scales are used and external factors are controlled (e.g., presence of peers or not, verbal, written, or digital rating collection) to ensure accuracy of the data collected.

Box 12.1

Self-reported training load can be used to monitor internal training load in youth rugby players. sRPE is a simple measure of internal load and can be collected easily with free online resources such as Microsoft or Google Forms. However, caution must be taken to ensure the validated sRPE scales are used, external factors are controlled, and data is collected within 48 hours to ensure accuracy of data.

For a more holistic representation of training loads experienced in rugby, it would be ideal to use a combination of internal and external training loads (Weaving et al., 2014). However, combining a wide variety of internal and external load measures can add complexity to making decisions about player load management and risk. Some studies have explored ways of simplifying this process. For example, a recent study showed the number of load monitoring variables could be reduced while retaining the overall accuracy of the information (Weaving et al., 2018). In this study either sRPE (internal load measure), or total distance, or PlayerLoad^{TM} (measurements provided by GPS monitors) could explain 60–70% of variance in professional rugby union skills training. Interestingly, because all three variables provided similar information, the study authors suggested that only one of these variables need to be monitored (Weaving et al., 2018). Combining internal and external measurements of load provides the most comprehensive analysis of training loads (Quarrie et al., 2017). However, even if it is only practical to monitor load in youth rugby using a limited number of methods (e.g., time and sRPE), practitioners will be able to use this information to help make important decisions around load management.

Box 12.2

When external training load quantification tools (e.g., GPS) are available, they should be combined with internal load measures (e.g., sRPE) to provide a more comprehensive analysis of training loads.

Analysis and Communication of Training Load Data

Once valid and reliable data has been collected, various analytical approaches can be used to make evidence-based decisions on player readiness to train/play, ideally in combination with recovery or wellness markers. The athlete monitoring cycle should account for the external load applied, the internal load exerted and the fatigue response before making decisions on appropriate future match or training involvements for players (Figure 12.1; Gabbett et al., 2017). In rugby union, a combination of measures of cumulative load (e.g., one- to four-week cumulative load, exponentially weighted moving averages or training strain), change in load (e.g., week-to-week change or acute:chronic workload ratios) and daily training load have been identified as important variables to monitor for load management and injury risk reduction (Williams et al., 2017). Once a baseline for these variables has been established, it is important to consider the typical error of the measure to help identify 'real' change. For example, if the typical error of sRPE load is 4.3% in age-grade rugby players, then any week-to-week variation below this threshold may not be considered substantial in this context. It is also important for coaches and trainers to be aware of what

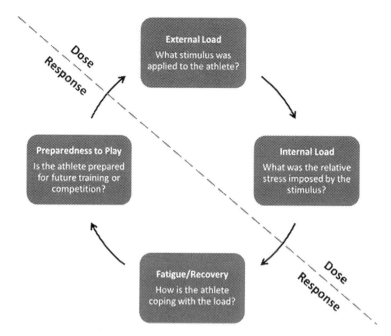

FIGURE 12.1 The Athlete Monitoring Cycle.

constitutes a 'meaningful' change in their athletes. Different statistical methods can be used to identify meaningful change such as standard deviation, Z-scores, effect size, smallest worthwhile change, coefficient of variation or risk ratios, although each will provide different outputs that will ultimately affect interpretation (Figure 12.2; Robertson et al., 2017).

It is important to note that the effectiveness of load monitoring data relies on the ability of practitioners to communicate findings to relevant stakeholders (Thornton et al., 2019). The target audience (e.g., coaches, medical staff, athletes, parents) should be considered when developing feedback reporting tools, including relevant knowledge, experience and personal preference (e.g., numbers/tables or figures/charts; Figures 12.3 and 12.4).

Challenges

In youth rugby, where many athletes are concurrently participating with multiple teams and sometimes in multiple sports, clear communication between all stakeholders on training and match schedules is key to protecting the welfare and long-term development of players (Scantlebury et al., 2020). This can be challenging in practice due to each team's perception on the importance of their own training sessions and matches, however, the long-term development of the player must be the primary consideration on what is best for the athlete at their specific stage of development. Additionally, as youth rugby players are generally full-time academic students, the effect of academic stress on sports performance and,

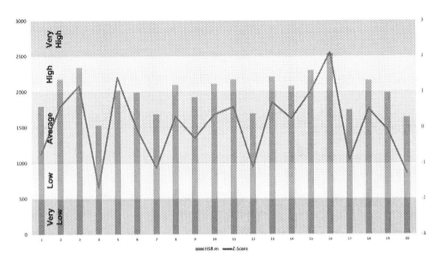

FIGURE 12.2 Longitudinal Analysis of Weekly High-Speed Running Exposures Using Z-Scores.

Player Name	sRPE Load AU	sRPE Load Z	High Speed Running m	High Speed Running Z	Perceived Recovery AU	Perceived Recovery Z
Player 1	1800	-0.7	2561	2.5	3	-2.1
Player 2	2179	0.6	1998	0.4	5	0.7
Player 3	2342	1.2	1866	0.0	3	-1.5
Player 4	1529	-1.7	2366	1.8	6	-0.3
Player 5	2024	1.4	1971	0.3	3	-1.6
Player 6	1996	0.0	1599	-1.0	7	0.3
Player 7	1687	-1.1	1921	0.2	5	-0.6
Player 8	2097	0.3	1666	-0.8	8	1.2
Player 9	1925	-0.3	2010	0.5	6	-0.2
Player 10	2113	0.4	2051	1.4	5	-0.5
Player 11	2174	0.6	2151	1.0	7	0.3
Player 12	1696	-1.1	1961	0.3	6	0.0
Player 13	2213	0.7	1620	-0.9	7	0.6
Player 14	2081	0.2	1925	0.2	7	0.6
Player 15	2301	1.0	1462	-1.5	9	1.7

FIGURE 12.3 Squad Load and Recovery Summary Table Including Weekly High-Speed Running, sRPE Load and Subsequent Daily Perceived Recovery Scale Scores.

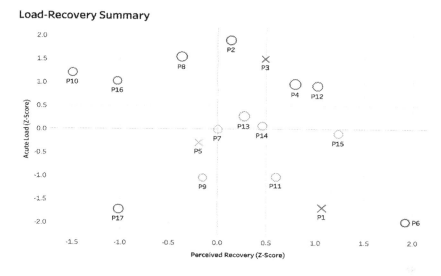

FIGURE 12.4 Visualisation of Squad Load and Recovery Interactions from Rolling Weekly sRPE Load and Daily Perceived Recovery Scale Z-scores.

conversely, the effect of post-training fatigue on academic performance, must be incorporated into load management decisions. An athlete-centred approach is required from practitioners when trying to balance sporting and academic stressors, by identifying periods of high academic stress (e.g., exams and assignment deadlines) to modify training/competition schedules. When communication and collaboration between stakeholders are poor or non-existent, the training and match exposures of adolescent rugby players have been described as 'organised chaos' (Phibbs et al., 2018b). Therefore, education of athletes and parents on training stress, recovery and athletic development can empower those individuals to take ownership of the decision-making process and work with coaches on determining appropriate training and competition loads.

Competition to Training Ratios

In addition to considering the overall training and competition load, competition-to-training ratios should be monitored. One of the earliest models of long-term athlete development recommended that youth athletes progress from a competition-to-training ratio of 25:75 during early adolescence to a 50:50 ratio in late adolescence (Balyi et al., 2013). Importantly, competition-specific training was intended to be included in the proportion of time spent in competition. For example, minutes of time spent in game-based training drills should be included as competition minutes. Other widely implemented youth athlete development frameworks (Côté and Fraser-Thomas, 2007; Gulbin et al., 2013) and consensus statements (Bergeron et al., 2015) do not make specific recommendations for competition-to-training ratios. However, they do generally advocate that youth athletes focus on training in order to develop the competencies required to perform in higher levels of competition. This means that exposing young athletes to a higher competition load, or competition at higher levels without first accomplishing the goals of focused, intensified training should be discouraged. Practically, coaches and trainers can easily calculate competition-to-training ratios by determining the number of minutes spent in these activities each week. While there are no clear guidelines for prescribing optimal ratios, practitioners will likely be able to determine when competition is being disproportionately prioritised over training.

> **Box 12.3**
>
> Exposing young athletes to a higher competition load, or competition at higher levels without first accomplishing the goals of focused, intensified training should be discouraged.

Key Take Home Messages

- The quantification of training and competition practices helps inform overall training load which needs to be managed to elicit favourable adaptations and reduce the risk of overtraining and injury.
- Particularly for youth players, it is important to understand that rugby and non-rugby loads contribute to overall load. These loads fluctuate over the pre-season and in-season periods and weekly loads typically vary substantially from week-to-week and between different players within any given age or playing standard.
- Some youth rugby players have very high weekly loads, sometimes exceeding the loads experienced by professional adult rugby players. These weekly loads sometimes also exhibit high competition-to-training ratios.
- Monitoring rugby and non-rugby loads is possible at all levels of play and could include the use of simple tools like training diaries and sRPE or, if resources permit, modern technologies like GPS trackers.
- Online or smartphone applications can also be used to conveniently obtain and track individual player loads. Ideally, this information should be integrated into a player load management system capable of monitoring longitudinal and individual player loading against rolling averages.
- The training dose-response is of importance to coaches and practitioners in order to determine the optimum training load to maximise positive outcomes (i.e., fitness, performance), while minimising negative outcomes (i.e., fatigue, burnout, injury).
- Consistent monitoring of workloads, growth, and maturity, and minimising high competition to training ratios is recommended to decrease injury risk.

- Coaches, players and parents all play a role in managing load including decisions on acceptable overall weekly loads, preferably within a youth development framework that prioritises preparation (i.e., training) over competition.
- The competition-to-training ratio should be considered to prevent competition being prioritised over training.

References

Balyi, I., Way, R., & Higgs, C. (2013). *Long-term athlete development*. Human Kinetics.

Barnard, D., Pote, L., & Christie, C. J. (2020). Workloads of forward and backline adolescent rugby players: A pilot study. *South African Journal of Sports Medicine, 32*, 1–5. http://doi.org/10.17159/2078-516x/2020/v32i1a7427

Bergeron, M. F., Mountjoy, M., Armstrong, N., Chia, M., Côté, J., Emery, C.A., Faigenbaum, A., Hall, G., Kriemler, S., Léglise, M., & Malina, R. M. (2015). International Olympic Committee consensus statement on youth athletic development. *British Journal of Sports Medicine, 49*, 843–851. http://doi.org/10.1136/bjsports-2015-094962

Côté, J., & Fraser-Thomas, J. (2007). Youth involvement in sport. In: P. Crocker, (Ed.). *Sport psychology: A Canadian perspective* (3rd ed., pp. 256–287). Pearson Prentice Hall.

Foster, C., Rodriguez-Marroyo, J. A., & de Koning, J. J. (2017). Monitoring training loads: The past, the present, and the future. *International Journal of Sports Physiology and Performance, 12*, S2-2–S2-8. http://doi.org/10.1123/IJSPP.2016-0388

Gabbett, T. J. (2005). Physiological and anthropometric characteristics of junior rugby league players over a competitive season. *Journal of Strength and Conditioning Research, 19*, 764. http://doi.org/10.1519/R-16804.1

Gabbett, T. J., Nassis, G.P., Oetter, E., Pretorius, J., Johnston, N., Medina, D., Rodas, G., Myslinksi, T., Howells, D., Beard, A., & Ryan, A. (2017) The athlete monitoring cycle: A practical guide to interpreting and applying training monitoring data. *British Journal of Sports Medicine, 51*, 1451–1452. http://doi.org/10.1136/bjsports-2016-097298

Gabbett, T. J., Whyte, D. G., Hartwig, T. B., Wescombe, H., & Naughton, G.A. (2014). The relationship between workloads, physical performance, injury and illness in adolescent male football players. *Sports Medicine, 44*, 989–1003. http://doi.org/10.1007/s40279-014-0179-5

Gulbin, J.P., Croser, M. J., Morley, E. J., & Weissensteiner, J. R. (2013). An integrated framework for the optimisation of sport and athlete development: A practitioner approach. *Journal of Sports Science, 31*, 1319–1331. http://doi.org/10.1080/02640414.2013.781661

Hartwig, T. B., Gabbett, T. J., Naughton, G., Duncan, C., Harries, S., & Perry, N. (2019). Training and match volume and injury in adolescents playing multiple contact team sports: A prospective cohort study. *Scandinavian Journal of Medicine and Science in Sports, 29*, 469–475. http://doi.org/10.1111/sms.13343

Hartwig, T. B., Naughton, G., & Searl, J. (2008). Defining the volume and intensity of sport participation in adolescent rugby union players. *International Journal of Sports Physiology and Performance, 3*, 94–106. http://doi.org/10.1123/ijspp.3.1.94

Hartwig, T. B., Naughton, G., & Searl, J. (2009). Load, stress, and recovery in adolescent rugby union players during a competitive season. *Journal of Sports Sciences, 27*, 1087–1094. http://doi.org/10.1080/02640410903096611

Hartwig, T. B., Naughton, G., & Searl, J. (2011). Motion analyses of adolescent rugby union players: A comparison of training and game demands. *Journal of Strength and Conditioning Research, 25*, 966–972. http://doi.org/10.1519/JSC.0b013e3181d09e24

Hendricks, S., Till, K., Weaving, D., Powell, A., Kemp, S., Stokes, K., & Jones, B. (2019). Training, match and non-rugby activities in elite male youth rugby union players in England. *International Journal of Sports Science and Coaching*, *14*, 336–343. http://doi.org/10.1177/1747954119829289

McCormack, S., Jones, B., & Till, K. (2020). Training practices of academy rugby league and their alignment to physical qualities deemed important for current and future performance. *International Journal of Sports Science and Coaching*, *15*, 512–525. http://doi.org/10.1177/1747954120924905

Palmer-Green, D. S., Stokes, K. A., Fuller, C. W., England, M., Kemp, S. P., & Trewartha, G. (2015). Training activities and injuries in English youth academy and schools rugby union. *The American Journal of Sports Medicine*, *43*, 475–481. http://doi.org/10.1177/0363546514560337

Phibbs, P. J., Jones, B., Read, D. B., Roe, G. A., Darrall-Jones, J., Weakley, J. J., Rock, A., & Till, K. (2018a). The appropriateness of training exposures for match-play preparation in adolescent schoolboy and academy rugby union players. *Journal of Sports Sciences*, *36*, 704–709. http://doi.org/10.1080/02640414.2017.1332421

Phibbs, P. J., Jones, B., Roe, G. A., Read, D. B., Darrall-Jones, J., Weakley, J. J., Rock, A., & Till, K. (2018b). Organized chaos in late specialization team sports: Weekly training loads of elite adolescent rugby union players. *Journal of Strength and Conditioning Research*, *32*, 1316–1323. http://doi.org/10.1519/JSC.0000000000001965

Phibbs, P. J., Jones, B., Roe, G. A., Read, D. B., Darrall-Jones, J., Weakley, J. J., Rock, A., & Till, K. (2018c). The organised chaos of English adolescent rugby union: Influence of weekly match frequency on the variability of match and training loads. *European Journal of Sport Science*, *18*, 341–348. http://doi.org/10.1080/17461391.2017.1418026

Phibbs, P. J., Jones, B., Roe, G. A., Read, D. B., Darrall-Jones, J., Weakley, J. J., & Till, K. (2017a). We know they train, but what do they do? Implications for coaches working with adolescent rugby union players. *International Journal of Sports Science & Coaching*, *12*, 175–182. http://doi.org/10.1177/1747954117694734

Phibbs, P. J., Roe, G. A., Jones, B., Read, D. B., Weakley, J. J., Darrall-Jones, J., & Till, K. (2017b). Validity of daily and weekly self-reported training load measures in adolescent athletes. *Journal of Strength Conditioning Research*, *31*, 1121–1126. http://doi.org/10.1519/JSC/0000000000001708

Quarrie, K. L., Raferty, M., Blackie, J., Cook, C.J., Fuller, C. W., Gabbett, T. J., Gray, A. J., Gill, N., Hennessy, L., Kemp, S., Lambert, M., Nichol, R., Mellalieu, S.D., Piscione, J., Stadelmann, J., & Tucker, R. (2017). Managing player load in professional rugby union: A review of current knowledge and practices. *British Journal of Sports Medicine*, *51*, 421–427. http://doi.org/10.1136/bjsports-2016-096191

Robertson, S., Bartlett, J. D., & Gastin, P. B. (2017). Red, amber, or green? Athlete monitoring in team sports: the need for decision-support systems. *International Journal of Sports Physiology and Performance*, *12*, S273–S279. http://doi.org/10.1123/ijspp.2016-0541

Scantlebury, S., Till, K., Sawczuk, T., Phibbs, P., & Jones, B. (2018). Validity of retrospective session rating of perceived exertion to quantify training load in youth athletes. *Journal of Strength and Conditioning Research*, *32*, 1975–1980. http://doi.org/10.1519/JSC.0000000000002099

Scantlebury, S., Till, K., Sawczuk, T., Phibbs, P., & Jones, B. (2020). Navigating the complex pathway of youth athletic development: Challenges and solutions to managing the training load of youth team sport athletes. *Strength and Conditioning Journal*, *42*, 100–108. http://doi.org/10.1519/SSC.0000000000000564

Smith, J. (2003). A framework for understanding the training process leading to elite performance. *Sports Medicine*, 33, 1103–1126. http://doi.org/10.2165/00007256-200333150-00003

Taylor, R. J., Sanders, D., Myers, T., Abt, G., Taylor, C. A., & Akubat, I. (2018). The dose-response relationship between training load and aerobic fitness in academy rugby union players. *International Journal of Sports Physiology and Performance*, 13, 163–169. http://doi.org/10.1123/ijspp.2017-0121

Thornton, H. R., Delaney, J. A., Duthie, G. M., & Dascombe, B. J. (2019). Developing athlete monitoring systems in team-sports: Data analysis and visualisation. *International Journal of Sports Physiology and Performance*, 14, 698–705. http://doi.org/10.1123/ijspp.2018-0169

Weakley, J. J., Till, K., Darrall-Jones, J., Roe, G. A., Phibbs, P. J., Read, D. B., & Jones, B. L. (2019). Strength and conditioning practices in adolescent rugby players: Relationship with changes in physical qualities. *Journal of Strength and Conditioning Research*, 33, 2361–2369. http://doi.org/10.1519/JSC.0000000000001828

Weaving, D., Dalton, N. E., Black, C., Darrall-Jones, J., Phibbs, P. J., Gray, M., Jones, B., & Roe, G. A. (2018). The same story or a unique novel? Within-participant principal-component analysis of measures of training load in professional rugby union skills training. *International Journal of Sports Physiology and Performance*, 13, 1175–1181. http://doi.org/10.1123/ijspp.2017-0565

Weaving, D., Marshall, P., Earle, K., Nevill, A., & Abt, G. (2014). Combining internal- and external-training-load measures in professional rugby league. *International Journal of Sports Physiology and Performance*, 9, 905–912. http://doi.org/10.1123/ijspp.2013-0444

Williams, S., Trewartha, G., Cross, M. J., Kemp, S. P. T., & Stokes, K. A. (2017). Monitoring what matters: A systematic process for selecting training-load measures. *International Journal of Sports Physiology and Performance*, 12, S2-101-S2-106. http://doi.org/10.1123/ijspp.2016-0337

13
MONITORING FATIGUE AND RECOVERY IN YOUTH RUGBY

Carlos Ramírez-López, Cédric Leduc, Mathieu Lacome and Ben Jones

Introduction

Because of the physical demands of rugby training and match-play, players experience an acute fatigue response that can last for up to 72 hours after training or competition (Johnston et al., 2013a; Lacome et al., 2018; Ramírez-López et al., 2020; Roe et al., 2016c). Researchers in youth rugby have shown that fatigue manifests as changes in neuromuscular performance (Johnston et al., 2013a; Lacome et al., 2018; Ramírez-López et al., 2020; Roe et al., 2016c), elevations in biomarkers of muscle damage (Johnston et al., 2013b; Lacome et al., 2018; Roe et al., 2016c) and changes in psychophysiological status (Lacome et al., 2018; Ramírez-López et al., 2020; Roe et al., 2016c). As such, youth rugby players need to adequately recover from the demands of the sport to avoid negative health outcomes (Meeusen et al., 2013), to enable safe completion of training and to be ready to perform in ensuing games (Halson, 2014). At the senior level, games are typically played once a week which often allows sufficient time for players to completely recover from match-play. However, young rugby players are regularly exposed to a greater frequency of matches, with variable turnaround times (e.g., tournament-style match-play). This is particularly concerning for youth athletes with already congested training and academic commitments as it is accepted that excessively high competition loads coupled with incomplete recovery can put athletes at undue risk (Meeusen et al., 2013). This in turn may lead to non-functional overreaching and a greater risk of injury (Meeusen et al., 2013). It is therefore important for practitioners to understand the typical time course of recovery following training and match-play and what markers can be used for quantifying player's fatigue status.

Researchers have used a number of surrogate measures and methods to investigate the fatigue response to youth rugby training (Noon et al., 2018; Roe et al., 2017), single games (Roe et al., 2016c) and periods of congested fixtures (Johnston et al., 2013a, 2013b; Lacome et al., 2018; Ramírez-López et al., 2020; Tee et al., 2017). These investigations have provided insightful information for the monitoring and management of fatigue in the real world. Therefore, this chapter aims to summarise the research on fatigue and recovery in youth rugby including an overview of commonly used measures of fatigue, and a description of fatigue following training, match-play and congested fixtures. The chapter will then showcase practical considerations for the implementation of a fatigue monitoring system and will conclude by providing implications and recommendations for practice.

Research Overview

Measuring and Monitoring Fatigue

Fatigue is a complex and multidimensional phenomenon with a variety of underlying psycho-physiological mechanisms (Enoka & Duchateau, 2016). Because of a lack of consensus, several definitions for fatigue exist. However, it is generally accepted that fatigue is a state associated with an inability to complete a task that was once achievable within a recent timeframe and is often associated with altered perceptions of effort and feelings of tiredness (Halson, 2014). Whilst the psychological and physiological mechanisms of fatigue are not yet fully understood, its adequate monitoring is paramount for protecting players' health and their ability to perform (Tavares et al., 2017). Furthermore, monitoring and understanding the fatigue response has become vital to determine appropriate training periodisation and to provide insights into whether the players are adapting positively or negatively to the stressors of training and competition (Halson, 2014). Below some of the most widely used assessments are discussed, considering their strengths and limitations.

Neuromuscular Performance

Assessments of lower- and upper-body neuromuscular performance have been commonly used by researchers in youth rugby as surrogate measures of fatigue (Johnston et al., 2013a; Lacome et al., 2018; Ramírez-López et al., 2020; Roe et al., 2016c). Due to its relative ease of administration and reliability, the countermovement jump (CMJ) test has been favoured by practitioners as the preferred method for assessing lower-body neuromuscular performance (Starling & Lambert, 2018). The CMJ is commonly assessed using force platforms, which are typically considered the 'gold standard' as they provide valid and reliable information related to the time-force characteristics of the effort (Duncan et al., 2008). However, alternatives to force platforms exist, including jump mats, optical systems and mobile applications (Rago et al., 2018), all of which have their own set of advantages and disadvantages (Table 13.1). When conducting the

TABLE 13.1 Commonly Used Methods and Tools for Measuring Fatigue

Neuromuscular Performance	Advantages	Disadvantages
Force platforms	• Gold standard for measuring force–time characteristics of the tests • Widely documented validity and reliability of different metrics	• Cost • Portability • Need for specific software • Must be operated over a specific type of surface
Optical systems	• Portable • Less expensive than force platforms • Can be operated over different surfaces	• Cost • Need for specific software • No information about force-time characteristics • Jump height is indirectly measured through flight time
Jump mats	• Portable • Less expensive than optical systems	• No information about force-time characteristics • Jump height is indirectly measured through flight time
Mobile applications	• Most affordable option for assessing neuromuscular performance • Available on most mobile application stores	• No information about force-time characteristics • Jump height is indirectly measured through flight time

Athlete Self-Reported Measures

	Advantages	Disadvantages
Empirical measures (e.g., POMS, BAM)	• Widely documented validity and reliability of specific questionnaires • Minimal to no equipment required	• Lengthy • Often not available on the public domain
Customised wellness questionnaires	• Quick and easy to administer • Minimal to no equipment required	• Unknown validity

Biochemical and Hormonal Markers

	Advantages	Disadvantages
Creatine kinase	• Can provide information related to fatigue and health status	• High inter-individual variability • Poor temporal relationship with performance • Cost • Invasiveness • Not suitable for routine use in team sports
Testosterone and cortisol	• Can provide information related to fatigue and health status	• Cost • Invasiveness • Not suitable for routine use in team sports

CMJ test, players should first undergo a standardised warm-up which can be designed by practitioners in their own environment. Following, and starting from an upright position with their hands on their hips, players are asked to lower themselves to a self-selected depth before jumping for maximal height. Players perform two or more jumps, and the best attempt is recorded. The reliability of this method has been tested in youth rugby players (Roe et al., 2016b), with outcome variables demonstrating acceptable to poor levels of reliability and sensitivity.

Given the collision demands of youth rugby match-play, assessment of upper-body neuromuscular performance can provide additional information regarding players' fatigue status. One commonly used method for this assessment is the plyometric push-up on a force platform (Johnston et al., 2013b; Roe et al., 2016c). For assessing the plyometric push-up, players start in a push-up position with hands on the force platform and elbows extended to a self-selected position. Players then perform a push-up as quickly and explosively as possible with the aim of their hands leaving the platform after the concentric phase of the movement. Two or three efforts are typically performed, and the best trial is recorded. The reliability of this method has been assessed in academy rugby union players (Roe et al., 2016b) and much like the CMJ, depends on the selected variables with mean force displaying the lowest CV (2.6%).

Athlete Self-Reported Measures

Athlete self-reported measures (ASRM) are a set of tools that have been widely used for the assessment of player fatigue and include empirical questionnaires such as the Profile of Mood States (POMS; Raglin & Morgan, 1994) and the Brief Assessment of Mood (BAM; Shearer et al., 2015). However, such questionnaires can be time-consuming, limiting their use for routinely monitoring players, especially youths (Halson, 2014). As such, shorter and easier to implement customised wellness questionnaires have emerged as the most widely used fatigue monitoring tool (Saw et al., 2016; Taylor et al., 2012). In addition to their ease of implementation, wellness questionnaires have been shown to indicate fatigue prevalence for longer than neuromuscular and biochemical measures after youth rugby match-play (Ramírez-López et al., 2020; Roe et al., 2016c). However, it should be acknowledged that these customised questionnaires have not gone through a validation process, which questions their use in practice and research (Jeffries et al., 2020). Furthermore, researchers have recently demonstrated unclear associations between customised wellness questionnaires and technical-tactical match performance in youth rugby players (Ramírez-López et al., 2021), adding to the criticism that ASRM have previously faced (Jeffries et al., 2020; Saw et al., 2016). Consequently, ASRM can be valuable tools for routine monitoring of fatigue, but practitioners should be aware of these limitations.

Biochemical and Hormonal Markers

Biochemical markers have also been used to monitor the fatigue response after youth rugby training and competition. Researchers have reported that plasmatic concentrations of creatine kinase ([CK]) can provide useful information related to muscle damage which is typically associated to blunt trauma and eccentric contractions (Takarada, 2003). However, given their invasiveness, time required for collecting and analyse samples, and need for specialised equipment, the use of biochemical markers is more suitable for research than practical environments. Hormonal markers such as testosterone and cortisol can also be used to monitor fatigue and recovery as they can provide information about the systemic metabolic balance (West et al., 2014), although these have not been investigated in youth cohorts and are often not suitable for routine use.

Fatigue Responses in Youth Rugby

Training

Given the complex multi-sport and multi-environment training that youth rugby players are typically exposed to (Phibbs et al., 2018), practitioners must consider the structure of the training week and the overall fatigue response to multiple sessions. Adequate management of fatigue arising from an already congested training week is essential as limited time for recovery has been associated with decreased performance and can lead to a greater risk of injury (Quarrie et al., 2017).

The volume, intensity and content of training sessions can have a direct effect on the subsequent fatigue response. Thus, to provide empirical guidance to adequately periodise training programmes, researchers have investigated the fatigue response to different configurations of training in youth rugby players. For instance, Noon et al. (2018) identified greater deteriorations of self-reported wellness following higher volumes of training. Moreover, Roe et al. (2017) assessed the effects of the inclusion of contact during training and reported a greater deterioration in upper body neuromuscular performance and self-reported wellness, and a greater increase in markers of muscle damage following training inclusive of contact. Conversely, non-contact training resulted in a substantial reduction in lower-body neuromuscular performance, which was attributed to the resulting greater running volumes (Roe et al., 2017). Johnston et al. (2017) reported no effect of session order (i.e., weights then speed vs. speed then weights) on fatigue markers immediately and 24 hours after training. However, 10 m sprint time was significantly faster when speed was sequenced second which can have important implications for training session design depending on the desired outcomes. Finally, Roe et al. (2016a) assessed changes in surrogate measures of fatigue during an 11-week pre-season training block. The authors reported decreases in CMJ performance for most of the training blocks, which were associated with periods of higher training volume. However, improvements in lower body strength and speed occurred over the course of the investigated pre-season suggesting that physical performance can still be enhanced in the presence of lower-body neuromuscular fatigue.

Match-Play

Following match-play, decrements in neuromuscular performance along with perceptions of tiredness occur. Thereby, post-match fatigue has been assessed by researchers via different methodologies and in different cohorts. For instance, Johnston et al. (2015) reported significant impairments in lower body neuromuscular performance which recovered at 48 hours post-match, while upper body fatigue and markers of muscle damage remained elevated at the 48-hour mark in youth rugby league players. Similarly, a study in youth rugby union identified that upper- and lower-body neuromuscular performance, perceptions of wellness, and [CK] display peak changes in the first 24 hours after a game (Roe et al., 2016c). Within the same investigation, lower-body neuromuscular performance recovered at 48 hours, whilst [CK] and perceived wellness remained altered at 72 hours post-match. However, there is substantial variability observed within individual recovery profiles (Roe et al., 2016c).

Congested Fixtures

Young rugby players are often exposed to congested periods of match-play (e.g., tournaments). These congested periods may place youth players at risk of fatigue accumulation and potential negative consequences on health and performance (Johnston et al., 2013b; Lacome et al., 2018; Ramírez-López et al., 2020; Tee et al., 2017). However, the current evidence for fatigue accumulation during congested periods is conflicting and may depend on player- and context-related factors. Moreover, no evidence of progressive accumulation of fatigue has been reported in international-level youth players when match turnarounds were between 94 and 120 hours (Lacome et al., 2018; Ramírez-López et al., 2020). However, it must be noted that players in these studies were investigated over international competitions, in controlled camp environments, and away from academic and other training stressors. Similarly, Tee et al. (2017) reported no evidence for fatigue accumulation in a group of school rugby union players who played three games over five days. However, the authors limited their assessment to lower-body neuromuscular performance as their only surrogate measure of fatigue. Alternatively, in youth rugby league players, progressive deterioration of upper- and lower-body neuromuscular performance, [CK], wellness and running performance has been reported when exposed to periods of congested fixtures with very short turnarounds (i.e., 48 hours or less; Johnston et al., 2013a, 2013b). In a different investigation, Oliver et al. (2015) monitored short- and long-term neuromuscular and perceptual fatigue during a seven-week in-season mesocycle in which games were played in weeks 1, 4 and 7. Despite having long turnarounds between matches (i.e., three weeks) the authors reported fatigue accumulation during the investigated period. This was likely a result of the training demands of the block and some players being involved with multiple teams in different environments, which is not uncommon in youth rugby (Phibbs et al., 2018).

Based on the current evidence, practitioners must consider multiple factors including the content of the training session, the turnaround time between fixtures, player characteristics, playing level and the management of environmental stressors (e.g., academic, social, multi-sport) to be able to understand and adequately manage the fatigue response to training and competition. Given the highly individual nature of this response, the need for valid, reliable and individualised monitoring protocols that can be easily implemented in practice is warranted.

Practical Applications

Practical Considerations for Monitoring of Fatigue

Monitoring fatigue status can provide insightful information on whether players are adapting to and recovering from the demands of training and competition. However, a structured stepped approach should be considered to increase the chances of successfully implementing an efficient fatigue monitoring system (Figure 13.1).

There are several reasons for implementing a fatigue monitoring system including to support the planning of training loads and attempting to reduce the risk of injury, illness and non-functional overreaching (Halson, 2014). Furthermore, collected data may be useful for team selection and determining if players are recovered and prepared for the demands of competition. Whatever the purpose might be, it should be clearly outlined as it will have an impact on other important factors that can relate to the success of the fatigue monitoring system such as the frequency of the assessments and formatting of the gathered data. The logistical and financial capabilities of the environment should also be considered before proceeding with its development and implementation. Factors such as time, money, equipment availability or the human resources needed to collect and analyse the data will impact the selection of tests and key metrics which should be valid, reliable and sensitive to changes induced by fatigue (Thorpe et al., 2017). Further, testing and metric selection should also be guided by the training content or match activities. For instance, practitioners may wish to monitor upper-body neuromuscular performance the days following heavy contact sessions but might find it less valuable following non-contact training. As such, a battery inclusive of different tests and metrics that can adapt to the training and competition cycle would be beneficial. The frequency of monitoring (e.g.,

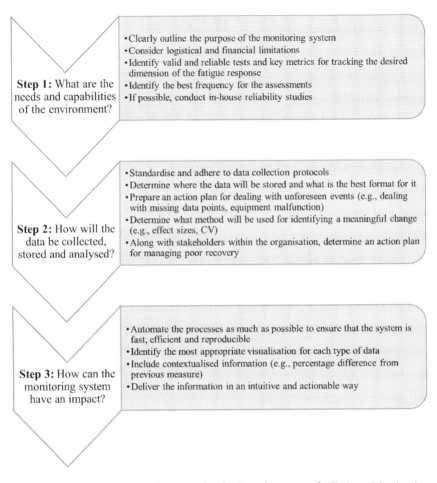

FIGURE 13.1 Practical Considerations for the Development of a Fatigue Monitoring System.

weekly, multiple times per week, daily) will often depend on training and competition schedules but should be standardised in relation to the day of the week or the day relative to a game (e.g., game +2). As a minimum, surrogate markers of fatigue should be monitored weekly within two to three days post-match (Twist & Highton, 2013).

Factors related to the testing protocols including time of the day, warm-up structure and verbal cues should be considered and standardised as they all may influence the results of the assessments (Chtourou et al., 2013; Kershner et al., 2019). Decisions about where the data is stored and who will have access to it are important from a data protection perspective but also for conserving its structure to facilitate analysis. It must also be considered that missing data points are undesirable but often inevitable when monitoring fatigue. These missing data may result from multiple reasons including data being recorded but not being stored or being deleted, data not being recorded due to time constraints, poor athlete adherence, injury or equipment malfunction.

After the appropriate tests and key metrics have been selected, it will be critical to identify what changes in players' fatigue status are meaningful, above and beyond what's considered 'normal' or simply a product of random variation. Different approaches have been proposed in the literature to identify what a meaningful change is (Robertson et al., 2017). Examples of these metrics include standard deviation (SD), effect size (ES), smallest worthwhile change (SWC) and coefficient of variation (CV), all of which may be useful in practice. However, practitioners are advised to be consistent with their selected approach as different statistics can result in different outputs for the same dataset (Robertson et al., 2017). Much like the test and metric selection, the choice of statistics aimed to identify meaningful changes will greatly depend on resources, time availability and expertise within the environment where they will be applied. Irrespective of the selected statistic, researchers have discouraged the use of arbitrary cut-off points (e.g., change of 5%) to identify a meaningful change in fatigue status as this may fall within the typical variation of certain test variables but not others. For instance, an arbitrary cut-off point at 5% may fall outside the CV of ~4.6% for CMJ height, but within the CV of ~8.5% of plyometric push-up height. Therefore, practitioners are encouraged to conduct in-house reliability assessments to aid in detecting a meaningful change for the metric they have selected for monitoring. If this is not possible, reliability data from the literature may be used, but careful consideration of the subject characteristics (e.g., rugby code, age group, level) and protocols (e.g., technical specifications of the measuring tool, experimental design) is required.

Meaningful changes in fatigue measures can be expected following matches, some types of training sessions, and periods of high training and competition loads. However, a successful fatigue monitoring system should be able to identify players that are diverging from the expected time course of recovery. When this occurs, an action plan for when poor recovery is identified must be available, with this involving different stakeholders including sports scientists, coaches and medics. The purpose of the group should be to discuss possible interventions such as conversations with players, recovery modalities, training modifications and team selection.

To be actionable, information related to players' fatigue status must be delivered in an easy to interpret and clear manner. For this, data should be communicated in a language that is understandable by everyone involved in the decision-making process (e.g., avoiding the excessive use of scientific jargon) and visualised in a simple and interpretable form. The method for presenting information may depend on the collected data (e.g., tables for displaying multiple variables, line charts for visualising trends over a period of time) but certain considerations should be followed to ensure the content is delivered accurately (Buchheit, 2017). For instance, extra decimal points should be removed, and labels may be added to provide additional context to a datapoint (e.g., percentage of previous performance). Also, traffic-light systems which are intuitive and often used in sport may be used for clear data presentation (Robertson et al., 2017). Developing skills in advanced data visualisation tools, such as Tableau or Power BI, can help to create impactful representations of the data.

Key Take Home Messages

- The physical demands of youth rugby lead to a highly individual and multidimensional fatigue response that can last for 72 hours and varies according to the content of the activity (e.g., training content, configuration, competition demands).
- A variety of surrogate methods for measuring fatigue exist, although neuromuscular assessments and athlete self-reported measures are the most widely used in practice. This results from their ease of implementation, non-invasiveness and validity and reliability of some of their metrics.
- The successful implementation of an actionable fatigue monitoring system should consider (1) the needs and capabilities of the environment, (2) data collection, storing and analysis processes and (3) the visualisation and delivery of the information.
- Actionable information gathered through a fatigue monitoring system may aid in planning for training loads, reducing the risk of injury, illness, and non-functional overreaching, and determining how well players have recovered to face the demands of competition.

References

Buchheit, M. (2017). Want to see my report, coach? *Aspetar Sports Medicine Journal, 6*, 36–43.

Chtourou, H., Aloui, A., Hammouda, O., Chaouachi, A., Chamari, K., & Souissi, N. (2013). Effect of static and dynamic stretching on the diurnal variations of jump performance in soccer players. *PLoS One, 8*, e70534. https://doi.org/10.1371/journal.pone.0070534

Duncan, M. J., Lyons, M., & Nevill, A. M. (2008). Evaluation of peak power prediction equations in male basketball players. *Journal of Strength and Conditioning Research, 22*, 1379–1381. https://doi.org/10.1519/JSC.0b013e31816a6337

Enoka, R. M., & Duchateau, J. (2016). Translating fatigue to human performance. *Medicine and Science in Sport and Exercise, 48*, 2228–2238. https://doi.org/10.1249/MSS.0000000000000929

Halson, S. L. (2014). Monitoring training load to understand fatigue in athletes. *Sports Medicine, 44*, 139–147. https://doi.org/10.1007/s40279-014-0253-z

Jeffries, A. C., Wallace, L., Coutts, A. J., McLaren, S. J., McCall, A., & Impellizzeri, F. M. (2020). Athlete-reported outcome measures for monitoring training responses: A systematic review of risk of bias and measurement property quality according to the COSMIN guidelines. *International Journal of Sports Physiology and Performance, 15*, 1203–1215. https://doi.org/10.1123/ijspp.2020-0386

Johnston, M., Johnston, J., Cook, C. J., Costley, L., Kilgallon, M., & Kilduff, L. P. (2017). The effect of session order on the physiological, neuromuscular, and endocrine responses to maximal speed and weight training sessions over a 24-h period. *Journal of Science and Medicine in Sport, 20,* 502–506. https://doi.org/10.1016/j.jsams.2016.03.007

Johnston, R. D., Gabbett, T. J., & Jenkins, D. G. (2013a). Influence of an intensified competition on fatigue and match performance in junior rugby league players. *Journal of Science and Medicine in Sport, 16,* 460–465. https://doi.org/10.1016/j.jsams.2012.10.009

Johnston, R. D., Gabbett, T. J., Jenkins, D. G., & Hulin, B. T. (2015). Influence of physical qualities on post-match fatigue in rugby league players. *Journal of Science and Medicine in Sport, 18,* 209–213. https://doi.org/10.1016/j.jsams.2014.01.009

Johnston, R. D., Gibson, N. V., Twist, C., Gabbett, T. J., MacNay, S. A., & MacFarlane, N. G. (2013b). Physiological responses to an intensified period of rugby league competition. *Journal of Strength & Conditioning Research, 27,* 643–654. https://doi.org/10.1519/JSC.0b013e31825bb469

Kershner, A. L., Fry, A. C., & Cabarkapa, D. (2019). Effect of internal vs. external focus of attention instructions on countermovement jump variables in NCAA division I student-athletes. *Journal of Strength & Conditioning Research, 33,* 1467–1473. https://doi.org/10.1519/JSC.0000000000003129

Lacome, M., Carling, C., Hager, J.-P., Dine, G., & Piscione, J. (2018). Workload, fatigue, and muscle damage in an under-20 rugby union team over an intensified international tournament. *International Journal of Sports Physiology and Performance, 13,* 1059–1066. https://doi.org/10.1123/ijspp.2017-0464

Meeusen, R., Duclos, M., Foster, C., Fry, A., Gleeson, M., Nieman, D., Raglin, J., Rietjens, G., Steinacker, J., & Urhausen, A. (2013). Prevention, diagnosis, and treatment of the overtraining syndrome: Joint consensus statement of the European College of Sport Science and the American College of Sports Medicine. *Medicine and Science in Sport and Exercise, 45,* 186–205. https://doi.org/10.1249/MSS.0b013e318279a10a

Noon, M. R., James, R. S., Clarke, N. D., Taylor, R. J., & Thake, C. D. (2018). Next day subjective and objective recovery indices following acute low and high training loads in academy rugby union players. *Sports (Basel), 6,* 56–66. https://doi.org/10.3390/sports6020056

Oliver, J. L., Lloyd, R. S., & Whitney, A. (2015). Monitoring of in-season neuromuscular and perceptual fatigue in youth rugby players. *European Journal of Sports Science, 15,* 514–522. https://doi.org/10.1080/17461391.2015.1063700

Phibbs, P. J., Jones, B., Roe, G., Read, D., Darrall-Jones, J., Weakley, J. J. S., Rock, A., & Till, K. (2018). The organised chaos of English adolescent rugby union: Influence of weekly match frequency on the variability of match and training loads. *European Journal of Sports Science, 18,* 341–348. https://doi.org/10.1080/17461391.2017.1418026

Quarrie, K. L., Raftery, M., Blackie, J., Cook, C. J., Fuller, C. W., Gabbett, T. J., Gray, A. J., Gill, N., Hennessy, L., Kemp, S., Lambert, M., Nichol, R., Mellalieu, S. D., Piscione, J., Stadelmann, J., & Tucker, R. (2017). Managing player load in professional rugby union: A review of current knowledge and practices. *British Journal of Sports Medicine, 51,* 421–427. https://doi.org/10.1136/bjsports-2016-096191

Raglin, J., & Morgan, W. (1994). Development of a scale for use in monitoring training-induced distress in athletes. *International Journal of Sports Medicine, 15,* 84–88. https://doi.org/10.1055/s-2007-1021025

Rago, V., Brito, J., Figueiredo, P., Carvalho, T., Fernandes, T., Fonseca, P., & Rebelo, A. (2018). Countermovement jump analysis using different portable devices: Implications for field testing. *Sports, 6,* 91–105. https://doi.org/10.3390/sports6030091

Ramírez-López, C., Till, K., Pledger, S., & Jones, B. (2020). A multi-nation examination of the neuromuscular and perceptual fatigue responses during the inaugural under-18 Six Nations rugby union competition. *Journal of Sports Sciences, 38*, 644–651. https://doi.org/10.1080/02640414.2020.1722589

Ramírez-López, C., Till, K., Weaving, D., Boyd, A., Peeters, A., Beasley, G., Bradley, S., Giuliano, P., Venables, C., & Jones, B. (2021). Does perceived wellness influence technical-tactical match performance? A study in youth international rugby using partial least squares correlation analysis. *European Journal of Sports Science, 22*, 1085–1093. https://doi.org/10.1080/17461391.2021.1936195

Robertson, S., Bartlett, J. D., & Gastin, P. B. (2017). Red, amber, or green? Athlete monitoring in team sport: The need for decision-support systems validating the decision not to train. *International Journal of Sports Physiology and Performance, 12*, 73–79. https://doi.org/10.1123/ijspp.2016-0541

Roe, G., Darrall-Jones, J. D., Till, K., & Jones, B. (2016a). Preseason changes in markers of lower body fatigue and performance in young professional rugby union players. *European Journal of Sport Science, 16*, 981–988. https://doi.org/10.1080/17461391.2016.1175510

Roe, G., Darrall-Jones, J. D., Till, K., Phibbs, P., Read, D., Weakley, J., & Jones, B. (2016b). Between-days reliability and sensitivity of common fatigue measures in rugby players. *International Journal of Sports Physiology and Performance, 11*, 581–586. https://doi.org/10.1123/ijspp.2015-0413

Roe, G., Darrall-Jones, J. D., Till, K., Phibbs, P., Read, D., Weakley, J., Rock, A., & Jones, B. (2017). The effect of physical contact on changes in fatigue markers following rugby union field-based training. *European Journal of Sport Science, 17*, 647–655. https://doi.org/10.1080/17461391.2017.1287960

Roe, G., Till, K., Darrall-Jones, J., Phibbs, P., Weakley, J., Read, D., & Jones, B. (2016c). Changes in markers of fatigue following a competitive match in elite academy rugby union players. *South African Journal of Sports Medicine, 28*, 3–5. https://doi.org/10.17159/2078-516X/2016/V28I1A1411

Saw, A. E., Main, L. C., & Gastin, P. B. (2016). Monitoring the athlete training response: Subjective self-reported measures trump commonly used objective measures: A systematic review. *British Journal of Sports Medicine, 50*, 281–291. https://doi.org/10.1136/bjsports-2015-094758

Shearer, D. A., Kilduff, L. P., Finn, C., Jones, R. M., Bracken, R. M., Mellalieu, S. D., Owen, N., Crewther, B. T., & Cook, C. J. (2015). Measuring recovery in elite rugby players: The brief assessment of mood, endocrine changes, and power. *Research Quarterly for Exercise & Sport, 86*, 379–386. https://doi.org/10.1080/02701367.2015.1066927

Starling, L. T., & Lambert, M. I. (2018). Monitoring rugby players for fitness and fatigue: What do coaches want? *International Journal of Sports Physiology and Performance, 13*, 777–782. https://doi.org/10.1123/ijspp.2017-0416

Takarada, Y. (2003). Evaluation of muscle damage after a rugby match with special reference to tackle plays. *British Journal of Sports Medicine, 37*, 416–419. https://doi.org/10.1136/bjsm.37.5.416

Tavares, F., Smith, T. B., & Driller, M. (2017). Fatigue and recovery in rugby: A review. *Sports Medicine, 47*, 1515–1530. https://doi.org/10.1007/s40279-017-0679-1

Taylor, K.-L., Chapman, D. W., Cronin, J. B., Newton, M. J., & Gill, N. (2012). Fatigue monitoring in high performance sport: A survey of current trends. *Journal of Australian Strength and Conditioning, 20*, 12–23.

Tee, J. C., Till, K., & Jones, B. (2017). Effects of an intensified competition period on neuromuscular function in youth rugby union players. *Sport Performance and Science Reports, 1,* 1–3.

Thorpe, R. T., Atkinson, G., Drust, B., & Gregson, W. (2017). Monitoring fatigue status in elite team-sport athletes: Implications for practice. *International Journal of Sports Physiology and Performance, 12,* S227–S234. https://doi.org/10.1123/ijspp.2016-0434

Twist, C., & Highton, J. (2013). Monitoring fatigue and recovery in rugby league players. *International Journal of Sports Physiology and Performance, 8,* 467–474. https://doi.org/10.1123/ijspp.8.5.467

West, D. J., Finn, C. V., Cunningham, D. J., Shearer, D. A., Jones, M. R., Harrington, B. J., Crewther, B. T., Cook, C. J., & Kilduff, L. P. (2014). Neuromuscular function, hormonal, and mood responses to a professional rugby union match. *Journal of Strength and Conditioning Research, 28,* 194–200. https://doi.org/10.1519/JSC.0b013e318291b726

14
NUTRITION FOR THE YOUNG RUGBY PLAYER

Marcus Hannon, Sarah Chantler and Nessan Costello

Introduction

As a youth rugby player progresses from childhood (timeframe up until the onset of adolescence) through adolescence (identified with the onset of sexual maturation) and into adulthood (achieved once fully mature), they undergo many anatomical, physiological and metabolic changes because of biological growth and maturation. Growth and maturation are complex processes that are influenced by many factors including the nutritional intake of an individual. As such, ensuring an appropriate nutritional intake throughout this important period in a youth rugby players life is not only necessary to optimise growth, maturation and physical development but to also maximise sporting performance. Importantly, the role of nutrition extends further to support psychosocial wellbeing. Therefore, developing a positive life-long relationship with food is critical for the holistic development of youth rugby players.

This chapter aims to review the nutritional requirements of youth rugby players, while also discussing the safe assessment of anthropometrics and body composition (a role that often falls to sports nutritionists in practice). The authors have highlighted some common questions that are often asked by players, parents and/or or coaches that can illustrate the confusion or misinformation that can exist around nutritional practices for growing rugby players.

Energy Requirements – 'How much should they eat?'

One of the key goals for maximising the health and performance of a youth rugby player is to increase fat-free mass (FFM) and overall body mass (BM) as they progress into adulthood (Geeson-Brown et al., 2020). To achieve this, it is essential that a youth player *at least* matches their energy intake to their energy expenditure, ideally achieving a consistently positive daily energy balance that meets the requirements of the individual.

Before evaluating the energy requirements of a youth rugby player (i.e., how much should they eat), it is essential to first understand energy expenditure (and its sub-components). Resting metabolic rate (RMR; the amount of energy required to sustain homeostatic physiology in a rested state), the thermic effect of food/diet-induced thermogenesis (the amount of energy required for digestion, absorption and transport of nutrients) and activity energy expenditure are the three major components that contribute towards total energy expenditure (TEE). In growing individuals, such as youth rugby players, there is also a small amount of energy required for tissue growth (~5 kcal per gram of weight gain), both to synthesise new tissue and for deposition into this new tissue (Torun, 2005). The highly variable rates of growth amongst youth rugby players, particularly around peak height velocity (the maximum rate of growth in stature during adolescence), will influence an individual's energy requirements, and in particular their RMR.

Recently, RMR was quantified in professional academy and senior male rugby players. RMR was similar between players at U16 (2168 ± 353 kcal•day^{-1}), U20 (2318 ± 335 kcal•day^{-1}) and U24 age groups (2232 ± 221 kcal•day^{-1}), despite the U24 players having a greater average BM (U16s; +~17 kg, U20s; +~13 kg) and FFM (U16s; +~15 kg, U20s; +~12 kg; Smith et al., 2018). Consequently, the U16 (33 ± 4 kcal•kg•FFM•day^{-1}) and U20 (35 ± 5 kcal•kg•FFM•day^{-1}) players had a greater relative RMR than the U24 (28 ± 2 kcal•kg•FFM•day^{-1}) players, when accounting for differences in body size (Smith et al., 2018). This trend corresponds with recent observations from a large data set of over 6,000 participants, inclusive of professional rugby players, where absolute RMR continued to increase with biological (i.e., FFM, BM and stature) and chronological age until 20.5 years, despite steady decreases of −2.8 ± 0.1% per year in body size-adjusted RMR (Pontzer et al., 2021). Collectively, current evidence suggests that once adulthood has been achieved (a fully ossified skeletal system, a fully functioning reproductive system and the attainment of adult stature), there is no further increase in the RMR of youth rugby players.

The TEE of a youth rugby player appears to increase as players get older, although it is highly variable between individuals. Smith et al. (2018) quantified TEE in professional academy and senior male rugby players using the gold-standard 'doubly labelled water' technique; TEE increased in a hierarchal manner across U16 (4,010 ± 744 kcal•day^{-1}), U20 (4,414 ± 688 kcal•day^{-1}) and U24 (4,761 ± 1,523 kcal•day^{-1}) age groups. However, when adjusted to player body size, TEE was similar between age groups (~50 kcal•kg^{-1}•day^{-1}; ~60 kcal•kg•FFM•day^{-1}). Importantly, there was a large inter-individual variability between players, with absolute TEEs varying by up to ~4000 kcal•day^{-1}, even amongst players competing within the same rugby code (Smith et al., 2018). This may be the result of differences in player anthropometric profile, playing position and/or load. These data highlight the necessity of adopting an individual approach when prescribing energy intakes for youth rugby players.

The energy expenditure of a youth rugby player is likely influenced by the number and magnitude of collisions. Research has shown an increase in the RMR and TEE of youth rugby players in the days following competitive match-play and collision-based training. Costello et al. (2019a) reported an increase of 569 ± 244 kcal•day^{-1} (~23%), 344 ± 222 kcal•day^{-1} (~14%) and 224 ± 186 kcal•day^{-1} (~9%) in RMR (from baseline) in the 24, 48 and 72 hours following academy male rugby league match-play, respectively. Moreover, in the same population, Costello et al. (2018) reported that collision-based training (10 tackles and 10 hit-ups) significantly increased TEE (1,185 ± 232 kcal; 5%) when compared to matched non-collision-based training. Similar elevations in RMR have been observed in professional adult male rugby union players following competitive match-play (~231 kcal; 10%; Hudson et al., 2020). These data highlight the increased energy cost of recovery in rugby, over and above calculation-based requirements (i.e., prediction equations), which typically under-estimate resting energy requirements in rugby populations (MacKenzie-Shalders et al., 2019; Smith et al., 2018).

Physical activity level (PAL) represents activity energy expenditure, which is expressed as a magnitude of RMR (PAL = TEE/RMR). This value enables direct comparison between athletes competing in different sports; it also permits estimation of TEE if RMR is known. Smith et al. (2018) reported slightly greater PALs for senior (U24: 2.1 ± 0.6 arbitrary units [AU]) in comparison to academy (U16: 1.9 ± 0.2 AU; U20: 1.9 ± 0.3 AU) mixed male rugby league and union players (Smith et al., 2018). These values are slightly higher than values observed for academy (U19) male rugby league players (1.6 ± 0.2 AU; range: 1.4 – 2.0 AU; Costello et al., 2019). The PAL values of youth rugby players are slightly higher than those of academy male soccer players (~1.5 AU; Hannon et al., 2021), but substantially lower than those of U18 national team male (2.9 ± 0.5 AU) and female (2.6 ± 0.3 AU) basketball players (Silva et al., 2013). Interestingly, the PALs of professional adult male rugby players range from 2.1 to 2.9 AU (Morehen et al., 2016; Smith et al., 2018), demonstrating a marked increase in activity energy expenditure.

Macronutrient and Fluid Requirements – 'What should they eat and drink?'

Carbohydrate

Carbohydrate (CHO) is the primary fuel for high-intensity activities; it is therefore a key macronutrient when preparing youth rugby players for both training and match-play. On the day prior to a match (MD-1), CHO intakes should be at least 6–8 g•kg^{-1}•day^{-1} (i.e., 480–640 g for an 80 kg player) to saturate both muscle and liver glycogen stores (Table 14.1). Due to potential differences in the BM of youth rugby players, an absolute upper CHO intake of ~600 g can be targeted. It is important to acknowledge that every gram of glycogen is stored

Nutrition 253

TABLE 14.1 Dietary Carbohydrate Recommendations for Young Rugby Players across Training and Match Days. Values Represent a Guide, Which Should Be Individually Tailored to the Requirements of Each Player.

Time Period	Dietary Aim	Guideline	Supporting Scientific Evidence in Youth Rugby Players
Match day–1	Elevate both muscle and liver glycogen stores	6–8 g•kg^{-1}•day^{-1} (~600 g)	**Academy male RL**: 6 g•kg^{-1}•day^{-1} CHO resulted in more homogenous pre-match muscle glycogen stores than 3 g•kg^{-1}•day^{-1} in the 36 hours prior to competition (449 ± 51 vs. 444 ± 81 mmol•kg dry mass^{-1} (dm); Bradley et al., 2015b).
Match day	Support optimal preparation, performance and recovery from match-play	6–8 g•kg^{-1}•day^{-1} (~600 g)	**Academy male RL**: 6 g•kg^{-1}•day^{-1} CHO resulted in a lower reduction in high-speed meters than 3 g•kg^{-1}•day^{-1} in the second half of a competitive match (effect size ± 90% confidence limits: −0.55 ± 0.36 vs. −1.42 ± 0.69; Bradley et al., 2017).
Pre-match meal	Top up liver glycogen stores	1–3 g•kg^{-1}•day^{-1}	*No youth rugby-specific research*: Guidelines drawn from the American College of Sports Medicine (Thomas et al., 2016).
During match-play	Maintain blood glucose concentration and endogenous CHO stores	30–60 g of CHO per hour	*No youth rugby specific research*: Guidelines drawn from the American College of Sports Medicine (Thomas et al., 2016).
Immediate post-match recovery period (four hours)	Replenish depleted muscle and liver glycogen stores	1–1.2 g•kg^{-1}•day^{-1} of CHO or 0.8 g•kg^{-1}•day^{-1} CHO and 0.3 g•kg^{-1}•day^{-1} protein, for the first four hours following match-play	**University male RL**: Immediate refeed (90 g Maltodextrin and 30 g protein. +1 hour: 90 g Maltodextrin) resulted in enhanced muscle glycogen resynthesis than delayed refeed (immediate: 30 g protein. +1 hour: zero carbohydrate placebo hypotonic sports drink, 51 ± 47% vs. 24 ± 49%; Bradley et al., 2017).

(*Continued*)

TABLE 14.1 (Continued)

Time Period	Dietary Aim	Guideline	Supporting Scientific Evidence in Youth Rugby Players
Muscle glycogen cost of youth rugby match-play		–	**Academy male RL**: 45.0 ± 9.5% reduction in muscle glycogen. Post-match muscle glycogen concentration of 243 ± 43 mmol·kg·dm^{-1} (6 g·kg^{-1}·day^{-1} CHO). 38.2 ± 17.5% reduction in muscle glycogen. Post-match muscle glycogen concentration of 298 ± 130 mmol·kg·dm^{-1} (3 g·kg^{-1}·day^{-1} CHO; Bradley et al., 2016).
Match day +1 (typical rest day)	Replenish depleted muscle and liver glycogen stores	6–8 g·kg^{-1}·day^{-1} (~600 g) for at least 24 hours after competition	**No youth rugby specific research**: Guidelines drawn from the American College of Sports Medicine (Thomas et al., 2016).
Training days (single)	Support achievement of overall energy demands	6 g·kg^{-1}·day^{-1}	**Academy male RL & RU**: Guidelines drawn from doubly labelled water determined TEE in English academy male rugby players (Smith et al., 2018).
Training days (double)	Replenish depleted muscle and liver glycogen stores	1–1.2 g·kg^{-1}·day^{-1} of CHO or 0.8 g·kg^{-1}·day^{-1} CHO and 0.3 g·kg^{-1}·day^{-1} protein, in-between training sessions	**Academy male RU**: Performance maintained across the second of two small-sided games (60 min each), when optimal glycogen resynthesis protocols followed in the three hours between sessions. There was no additional benefit of combining fructose with glucose-based CHOs (Hengist et al., 2021)

CHO = carbohydrate, RL = rugby league, RU = rugby union.

Box 14.1

PARENT: Isn't there too much sugar in sports drinks and fruit juices?

Carbohydrate (and therefore sugar) is the primary fuel for rugby – so carbohydrate fluid like fruit juice or sports drink can be a great choice to delay fatigue during training and games.

Sports drinks, diluted fruit juice, sugar-based cordial or even diluted coca cola are all appropriate. However, ensure your child practices good oral hygiene.

PLAYER: Won't too much carbohydrate make me fat?

Increases in body fat are caused by excessive energy intakes for prolonged periods. This can be from excessive amounts of fat, protein and/or carbohydrate.

Carbohydrate has a high turnover/usage in the body (brain, muscles, liver, etc.). Therefore, it is not naturally stored as body fat.

---

with approximately three grams of water (Kreitzman et al., 1992). Therefore, an acute increase in BM is a noticeable response to glycogen super-compensation and should not be alarming to either the player or coach.

On match-day, CHO intakes should again target at least 6–8 g•kg^{-1}•day^{-1} (Table 14.1). The distribution of this daily CHO target will be practically dictated by the timing of kick-off. The pre-match meal should achieve 1–3 g•kg^{-1}•day^{-1} of CHO (Thomas et al., 2016) with the predominant aim of topping up liver glycogen stores (Chryssanthopoulos et al., 2004; Wee et al., 2005), which are depleted by ~50% after an overnight fast (Nilsson et al., 1973). Three hours is insufficient for the complete digestion and absorption of a CHO-rich meal, highlighting the importance of CHO intakes on MD-1 for the youth rugby player. Considering the limited relevance of the glycaemic index within practice (i.e., players consume mixed meals rather than isolated CHOs), and the high variability in glycaemic responses to the same CHOs between individuals (Schenk et al., 2003), youth rugby players are advised to consume a range of CHO rich foods and fluids that they can tolerate and enjoy.

During match-play, players should consume ~30–60 g of CHO per hour to maintain blood glucose concentration, CHO oxidation and exercise performance (Table 14.1). Therefore, it is practically recommended that players consume ~30–60 g of CHO after the warmup and again at half-time. This can come from foods (e.g., sweets, fruits, banana bread) or drinks (e.g., fruit juice, non-dairy smoothie, sports drinks). Match-play CHO intakes should be practiced during high-intensity training, inclusive of collisions, to reduce the risk of gastrointestinal symptoms on MD itself. Players prone to symptoms of rebound hypoglycaemia (i.e., weakness, dizziness or nausea), should ensure CHO is consumed 5–15 minutes prior to exercise (e.g., a banana; Jeukendrup & Killer, 2011).

A primary objective following match-play is to reduce the time required to fully recover (i.e., rapidly replenish depleted CHO stores). After exercise, glycogen synthesis is rapid, highlighting the importance of CHO intakes in the immediate post-match period (Bradley et al., 2017). Therefore, youth rugby players are recommended to follow optimal glycogen resynthesis protocols (1–1.2 g•kg•h^{-1} of CHO or 0.8 g•kg•h^{-1} CHO and 0.3 g•kg•h^{-1} of protein) for each of the four hours after match-play (Table 14.1). Appetite is typically decreased in the immediate post-match period. Therefore, players might benefit from prioritising CHO drinks (e.g., fruit juices, fizzy drinks). Finally, muscle damage can significantly retard the resynthesis of muscle glycogen following exercise (Costill et al., 1990). Therefore, youth rugby players are advised to maintain high CHO intakes of 6–8 g•kg^{-1}•day^{-1} (~600 g) for at least 24 hours after competition (i.e., MD + 1).

On training and rest days it is important that the dietary CHO intakes of a youth rugby player are not purposefully decreased. Current sports nutrition literature advocates the manipulation of dietary energy (via CHO) to support the achievement of player BM and composition goals. To this end, professional senior male rugby union players have self-reported low CHO intakes of approximately 3 g·kg^{-1}·day^{-1} across both pre-season and in-season training days (Bradley et al., 2015a; 2015b). However, a similar application of dietary CHO periodisation within youth rugby populations is ***not recommended***. As previously stated, youth rugby players are still growing and maturing, while also attempting to increase FFM and strength in line with senior populations (Geeson-Brown et al., 2020). Therefore, the CHO intakes of youth rugby players should not fall below 6 g·kg^{-1}·day^{-1}.

Protein

Based on current evidence, a high daily total protein intake of between 1.6 and 2.2 g·kg^{-1}·day^{-1} may be appropriate to maximise the anabolic response of injury-free and hypercaloric youth rugby players (e.g., 130–175 g per day for an 80 kg youth rugby player; Phillips, 2012). A protein intake of ~1.6 g·kg^{-1}·day^{-1} has been shown to meet protein requirements in 15-year-old male soccer players (Boisseau et al., 2002), while protein intakes of 1.4 and 1.5 g·kg^{-1}·day^{-1} exceeded protein requirements for junior elite male and female sprinters, respectively (Aerenhouts et al., 2013). However, two participants (one girl and one boy) failed to achieve their protein requirements with a protein intake of nearly 2 g·kg^{-1}·day^{-1} (Aerenhouts et al., 2013). Importantly, youth athletes do not appear to have increased protein requirements during peak height velocity (Aerenhouts et al., 2013).

Practically, protein intakes should be spilt evenly across the day (0.4–0.55 g·kg^{-1} every three to four hours; e.g., 30–45 g per meal for an 80 kg youth rugby player; Phillips, 2012). Sufficient intakes of high-quality protein should be prioritised at breakfast and pre-bed, where self-reported intakes are typically suboptimal in youth athletes. Finally, youth rugby players are advised to achieve this protein target through real foods rather than through supplementation.

Box 14.2 PARENT: Should my son or daughter be taking protein shakes?

- No, the supplement industry/media has left a skewed representation with regards to how much protein is required to optimise the growth and physical development of young athletes. Your son or daughter can obtain sufficient protein from real foods and drinks (e.g., eggs, meat, fish, dairy or certain plant-based alternatives).
- Your child should focus on an adequate frequency of meals and snacks with a varied combination of foods. This holds true for those who are growing or who are aiming to increase muscle mass.
- Foods such as pasta, rice, noodles and bread also contain amino acids that contribute to overall protein intakes.
- The supplement industry is poorly regulated. Therefore, there is always a risk of contamination and an anti-doping violation when you take any supplement.

Fat

Dietary fat recommendations for athletes replicate public health guidelines, which should not fall below or exceed 20–35% of total energy intake, respectively (Thomas et al., 2016). Currently, there is no evidence to suggest that these recommendations should be altered for youth rugby players. The maximum 35% target is based on limiting saturated fat intake and possible weight gain within the general population. Therefore, it is recommended that the dietary fat intake of a youth rugby player is ~30–35% of TEE, to support the achievement of sufficient energy intake. Importantly, there is no Tolerable Upper Intake Level for total fat intake (i.e., highest daily intake without adverse health outcomes; Trumbo et al., 2002). Consequently, higher fat intakes might be warranted for youth rugby players struggling to achieve a positive daily energy balance.

Regarding dietary fat composition, youth rugby players are advised to limit the consumption of industrial trans fats from partially hydrogenated oils (e.g., fried foods, commercial baked pastries and packaged snack foods). Instead, prioritising greater consumption of omega-6 (e.g., nuts, seeds and vegetable oils) and omega-3 (e.g., oily fish, nuts and seeds) fatty acids. Overall consumption of

> **Box 14.3 PLAYER: Are takeaways 'bad'?**
>
> - First, there are no 'good' or 'bad' foods – just consistently better or worse dietary patterns and behaviours.
> - Take aways are typically high in unhealthy fats (e.g., trans fats), salts, sugars, and a poor source of micronutrients. However, this does not mean you can never eat them.
> - Take aways can be a gateway to exciting new foods and flavours. Moreover, they can be a great source of energy and psycho-social enjoyment. Enjoying them as part of a varied and balanced diet is fine.

saturated fat (e.g., fatty cuts of meat, butter, pastries and cakes) should be limited to <10% of total energy intake (Trumbo et al., 2002). Although, slightly higher intakes are suitable when consumed from appropriate sources (e.g., full-fat dairy). Finally, the consumption of a very high fat and low CHO ketogenic diet (i.e., 75–80% of total energy intake from dietary fat) is not recommended for youth rugby players (Burke, 2020).

Fluid

There is limited research investigating the dietary fluid intakes of youth rugby players, especially in warmer climates. Although there are no fluid guidelines specific to youth rugby players, dietary fluid recommendations for athletes range from 30 to 35 ml·kg^{-1} (Thomas et al., 2016). Youth male U16 and U19 mixed rugby union and rugby league players have self-reported consuming 3.1 ± 1.0 and 4.2 ± 1.3 L of fluid per day across a four-day pre-season period, inclusive of a weekend, respectively (Smith et al., 2016). Although there are limited comparative fluid intakes for youth rugby players, reported intakes were within recommendations and likely adequate to maintain fluid balance given losses were similar to those previously reported in senior rugby union (Jones et al., 2016; Smith et al., 2016) in the northern hemisphere. Irish school rugby players had good knowledge of correct hydration practices (mean score: 76.3%), with 99% of players following recommendations to consume fluid during exercise (Walsh et al., 2011).

Whilst the hydration requirements (in addition to fluid and electrolyte balance) of adult rugby players in both training and match-play scenarios are well documented, there is limited research in youth rugby players. Bargh et al. (2016) investigated fluid losses and intake in ten academy male rugby league players (17 ± 1 years old) during rugby training, which consisted of 6 × 6-minute bouts of intermittent non-contact small-sided games (interspersed with two mins passive rest; ~46 minutes in total). During training *ad libitum* drinking of fluids was permitted. Interestingly, 50% of players arrived for training in a hypohydrated state (>295 mOsmol·kg^{-1}) and these players consumed significantly less fluid during training compared to players who arrived in a euhydrated state. During training players consumed 0.88 ± 0.38 kg of fluid (range: 0.41–1.38 kg) and had net fluid losses of 1.02 ± 0.31 kg (range: 0.49–1.51 kg). Players sweat rate was 1.15 ± 0.35 L•h^{-1} which resulted in a decrease of −0.17 ± 0.59% in BM. It should be noted that there was a large range in both sweat rate and fluid intake between players, highlighting the need for an individualised approach to hydration strategies. To conclude, youth rugby players are encouraged to *avoid* excessive fluid intakes during exercise (e.g., that cause weight gain). Players can determine their sweat rate by weighing themselves before and after training sessions and/or match-play, consuming 125–150% of the BM loss in fluids to rehydrate (e.g., 1.25–1.5 L for an 80 kg player, who lost one kg during exercise).

Evaluation of Practice – 'What do they currently eat?'

Dietary assessment can be an important tool to educate youth rugby players about recommended sport nutrition practices. However, it is important to acknowledge that all forms of dietary assessment are subject to measurement error; therefore, should be interpreted carefully. Youth rugby players typically under consume dietary CHO, while overconsuming protein and saturated fat. Moreover, intakes of fruits, vegetables, dairy and starchy CHOs do not meet recommendations (Smith et al., 2016). Alcohol intakes are rarely reported in youth rugby populations, although concentrated intakes have been reported following match-play (~7 units•person^{-1}; Potgieter et al., 2014) and in youth cohorts in Ireland (i.e., U16s; Walsh et al., 2011). These dietary behaviours might negatively impact the health and wellbeing of youth rugby players, alongside post-match recovery (e.g., muscle protein synthesis, glycogen synthesis, hydration status and food choices).

Sport Foods and Supplements – 'Is there need for supplementation?'

Across youth rugby populations, the use of supplements (as defined by the International Olympic Committee position stand; Maughan et al., 2018) to improve performance is questionable. While common nutritional ergogenics like caffeine, creatine and beta-alanine are generally thought to be safe, there is no robust data on the impact of various supplements on growth, muscle mass accrual, recovery, or performance in youth rugby age-groups. Moreover, due to ethical and safeguarding concerns, there are limited opportunities to conduct primary research. As a result, all current position stands advocate a food-first approach, with only clinically necessitated (i.e. a nutritional deficiency) supplementation provided under professional supervision (e.g., iron, calcium, vitamin D; Desbrow et al., 2019).

Importantly for practitioners, supplement usage has been shown to be as high as 68% and 92% in junior (U16) and academy (U19) male rugby populations, respectively (Smith et al., 2016). Consequently, the risks of unwarranted or poor supplementation practices are high. Consideration is required for unwarranted supplementation being a potential additional risk factor towards doping behaviours, especially within a sport that prioritises rapid increases in size particularly FFM. This includes using common sports foods (e.g., isotonic gels and sports drinks) with caution. An example dietary intake for a youth rugby player is shared in Table 14.2. This example is not appropriate for all players and does not represent a concrete plan. Instead, it is hoped to guide what a typical day might look like for a youth player.

Anthropometric Assessment – 'How do we know if players are eating enough?'

One way to infer if energy intake is sufficient is to monitor the progression of growth (e.g., stature and BM) and somatic maturation (e.g., maturity offset/percentage of predicted adult stature), in addition to being alert to symptoms of low energy availability (e.g., chronic fatigue, low mood, reduced performance, poor concentration, impaired immune system, and in females, absence of menarche). This is of particular importance considering the inherent difficulty in accurately measuring both energy expenditure and energy intake in practice. Considering that energy and macronutrient requirements are prescribed per kilogram of BM, regular monitoring of growth (particularly BM) during adolescence can be a useful tool (when conducted appropriately) to subsequently adjust the nutritional requirements of an individual and prevent chronic under-fuelling.

Box 14.4 PLAYER: You want me to eat more but I don't want to get fat?

- Growing, training, building muscle, brain development and general day to day activities 'cost' a lot of energy. We are encouraging you to eat more so that you can create an energy surplus, allowing for all these normal physiological processes, including increasing muscle mass and strength, to occur.
- It is helpful to understand that developing muscle mass, strength and power is a critical contributor to your performance. Therefore, any associated increase in body fat is normal, important for your development and should not be seen as a negative.
- Increasing your snacks and portion sizes, while not missing meals/snacks, is a simple and practical way to help you eat more. Making sure you're never hungry is also important. Finally, try to avoid long periods (e.g., three to four hours) without eating or drinking something.

TABLE 14.2 Example Dietary Energy, Macronutrient, and Fluid Intake on a Training Day for a Young Rugby Player. Dietary Energy and Macronutrient Distribution Targets and Coaching Points are Examples for Practitioners Working with Young Rugby Players

Meal/Snack	Foods and Fluids	Nutritional Target	Coaching Points
Breakfast (07:30)	**Example 1:** Weetabix (x4) with full fat milk, banana (x1) and honey (1 tbsp). Buttered toast (x1), avocado (½), poached egg (x1). Water (500 ml). **Example 2:** Ham and cheese omelette (x3 eggs) with baked beans (½ tin). American pancakes (x3), berries (80 g), honey (2 tbsp). Water (500 ml).	**Energy:** 970 kcal CHO: 120 g (1.5 g·kg^{-1}) Pro: 32 g (0.4 g·kg^{-1}) Fat: 40 g (0.5 g·kg^{-1})	**Don't skip breakfast** - Prioritise CHO - x1 high quality protein source (eggs, dairy) - *Minimum* of x1 fruit or veg - *Minimum* x1 fluid
Snack 1 (10:30)	**Example 1:** Cereal bar, portioned cheese (20 g), orange **Example 2:** Flavoured milk (250 ml), snack popcorn (30 g), pear	**Energy:** 280 kcal CHO: 40 g (0.5 g·kg^{-1}) Pro: 8 g (0.1 g·kg^{-1}) Fat: 10 g (0.1 g·kg^{-1})	**Always pack snacks** - Add x1 fruit
Lunch (13:00)	**Example 1:** Ham and cheese paninis (x2) with ketchup (2 tbsp), chocolate bar (20 g), apple. Water with squash (500 ml). **Example 2:** Chicken fajitas (½ chicken breast, ×2 tortilla wraps, ½ pepper, 2 tbsp guacamole, 1 tbsp sour cream, 1 tbsp sweet chilli), with spicy rice (½ bag of microwave rice). Water with squash (500 ml).	**Energy:** 1000 kcal CHO: 120 g (1.5 g·kg^{-1}) Pro: 40 g (0.5 g·kg^{-1}) Fat: 40 g (0.5 g·kg^{-1})	**Have a meal for lunch** - Prioritise CHO - Have x1 high quality protein source (meat, fish, alternatives) - *Minimum* of x1 fruit or veg - *Minimum* x1 fluid
Snack 2 (Pre-Training) (15:30)	**Example 1:** Soreen (30 g), mixed nuts and raisins (handful). Water (500 ml). **Example 2:** Fruit winder, cereal bar, grapes (handful).Water (500 ml).	**Energy:** 280 kcal CHO: 40 g (0.5 g·kg^{-1}) Pro: 8 g (0.1 g·kg^{-1}) Fat: 10 g (0.1 g·kg^{-1})	**Always pack snacks** - Add x1 fruit - Start training hydrated

(*Continued*)

TABLE 14.2 (Continued)

Meal/Snack	Foods and Fluids	Nutritional Target	Coaching Points
During Training (17:00–18:30)	**Example 1:** Fruit juice (350 ml) and water **Example 2:** Sports drink (500 ml) and water	**Energy:** 120 kcal CHO: 30 g (0.3 g·kg^{-1})	***Bring fluids*** - Make one CHO based
Dinner (Post-Training) (19:30)	**Example 1:** Chicken pasta (½ chicken breast, 260 g pasta, 1 tbsp pesto, 20 g cheese), with garlic bread (×4 slices) and steamed veg (85 g). Apple juice (300 ml). **Example 2:** Chilli nachos (100 g Quorn, 300 g rice, 50 g tortilla chips, 30 g cheese, tomatoes, peppers, kidney beans, seasoning). Orange juice (300 ml).	**Energy:** 1160 kcal CHO: 160 g (2.0 g·kg^{-1}) Pro: 40 g (0.5 g·kg^{-1}) Fat: 40 g (0.5 g·kg^{-1})	***Try and eat within one hour of training*** - Prioritise CHO (large plate, full) - Have x1 high quality protein source (meat, fish, alternatives) - *Minimum* of x1 veg - *Minimum* x1 fluid (CHO-based)
Pre-Bed (21:00)	**Example 1:** Homemade smoothie (300 ml full fat milk, 80 g frozen blueberries, 10 g spinach, ½ banana, 200 g 0% fat Greek yoghurt). **Example 2:** Flavoured quark yoghurt (200 g), honey (1 tbsp), granola (1 tbsp). Glass of full fat milk (250 ml).	**Energy:** 380 kcal CHO: 40 g (0.5 g·kg^{-1}) Pro: 32 g (0.4 g·kg^{-1}) Fat: 10 g (0.1 g·kg^{-1})	***Don't forget pre-bed*** - Prioritise high quality protein (dairy)
Daily Totals	**Energy:** 4,200 kcal (53 kcal·kg^{-1}) – represents a small (~200 kcal) energy surplus **CHO:** 560 g (7 g·kg^{-1}) **Pro:** 160 g (2.0 g·kg^{-1}) **Fat:** 150 g (33% of TER or 1.8 g·kg^{-1})		- Aim for three main meals and three snacks each day - Eat every ~3 hours - Avoid being hungry

CHO = Carbohydrate.

Body Composition Assessment – 'What should be measured and how?'

The main physical development goal of a youth rugby player is to *increase FFM* as they progress into adulthood. Therefore, practitioners should prioritise monitoring changes in FFM over changes in body fat. Since absolute fat mass in young rugby players is similar between age groups and FFM increases as a player increases in both biological and chronological age, younger players present with a higher percent body fat compared to older players (Geeson-Brown et al., 2020). These higher percent body fat values observed in younger players are therefore a product of them possessing lower FFM and not actually due to higher amounts of absolute fat mass. Therefore, when a youth rugby player presents with what is perceived as a high body fat percentage, the most appropriate strategies may be interventions that promote increases in FFM, growth and development (e.g., optimal energy and protein intakes, exposure to a safe resistance training program), as opposed to strategies designed to reduce body fat *per se* (e.g., energy restriction and/or increased energy expenditure). In this way, youth players are more likely to achieve a body composition that is more representative of professional adult players, and therefore potentially cope with the increased physical demands of senior match-play.

To date, body composition assessments in young rugby players (in both scientific research and applied practice) have typically been measured via skinfold callipers to determine the sum of skinfold thickness (Gavarry et al., 2018; Till et al., 2017). Whilst this method is cheap, quick and generally reliable, it only provides an indication of fat mass rather than FFM, and as such *should not be used* in growing and maturing youth rugby players. Skinfold thickness has also been used to estimate percent body fat and percent FFM using different available prediction equations (Gavarry et al., 2018). However, these equations have been developed on specific populations (e.g., general population adolescents) and when applied to different populations from which they were developed (e.g., youth rugby players), often have a high degree of error.

Dual-energy X-ray absorptiometry (DXA) is another method that is used to determine body composition in youth rugby players (Till et al., 2017). Dual-energy X-ray absorptiometry is a three-compartmental method (i.e., fat mass, FFM and bone mineral content), which provides body composition at both whole body and regional level (i.e., arms, trunk, legs). Dual-energy X-ray absorptiometry is often considered the reference method for assessing body composition (Nana et al., 2015). However, whilst DXA is a quick and reliable method its use in applied practice is limited due to the availability of necessary equipment and expertise, alongside exposure to radiation (albeit a small and generally safe dose). Moreover, body composition assessment by DXA (in particular FFM) is influenced by the nutritional status (e.g., hydration, glycogen and creatine content) of the individual being scanned. Therefore, it is important that scans are completed under standardised conditions, typically in a fasted and euhydrated state, following a day of minimal physical activity (Nana et al., 2015).

To summarise, it is important that any body composition assessments performed in youth rugby populations follow a standardised approach, have a clear rationale for use (e.g., are supporting increases in FFM) and are completed by an accredited professional. It is very important that players and associated support personnel, coaches and parents are educated as to why the chosen test is being performed, and what the results mean in practice (e.g., how can this information be used to improve the health and wellbeing of the player). If appropriate assessment tools or personnel are not available, then it is *strongly recommended* that body composition assessments are *not performed* in youth rugby populations. Instead, practitioners can prioritise tracking changes in anthropometrics (i.e., BM and stature) across the season (e.g., quarterly or bi-annually) to ensure that increases in both growth and maturation are achieved. In the case that a youth player is expected of under-fuelling (e.g., tracked anthropometric data and/or symptoms of low energy availability), then the player and associated care giver(s) should be alerted and signposted to a registered health care professional (e.g., doctor and/or dietician).

Box 14.5 COACH: I think we should be measuring player body fat?

- Young people have bodies that are changing rapidly. They typically want to 'look good' and conform to their view of 'normal'. As a result, they are susceptible to insecurities that might manifest into body image issues, body dysmorphia and disordered eating habits. Therefore, we should not be measuring the body fat of youth rugby players.
- Research shows that youth players have less muscle mass than senior players. Therefore, any assessment of body composition should practically support increases in fat-free mass. If the tools available are not valid or reliable, then we can track changes in height and BM, alongside strength or capacity on the field.
- Ultimately, we are responsible for the health and wellbeing of our players first and foremost. Our job is to help them grow, develop, and have fun. Assessments of body fat are unlikely to achieve this.

Summary

The nutritional requirements of a youth rugby player are influenced by biological growth and maturation, the demands of training and competition, alongside a requirement to significantly increase fat-free and overall BM towards those of senior players. Therefore, it is inappropriate to simply apply the nutrition guidelines and dietary practices of senior rugby players within youth populations. Current evidence outlines the large resting and total energy requirements of youth male rugby players, necessitating equally large energy intakes, especially in the days following competitive match-play and training-based collisions. A consistently positive energy and protein balance is required to ensure targeted physical developments are achieved. Sufficient intakes of dietary CHO, fat and fluid are essential to meet the demands of training and match-play, alongside overall health and wellbeing. A varied and balanced diet that meets these requirements should provide sufficient intakes of essential micronutrients. Supplement intakes should be overseen by a nutrition professional and only prioritised in periods of clinical necessity (i.e., iron, vitamin D). Care is required around the assessment of anthropometric and body composition variables, emphasising appropriate fuelling for FFM development. Future research is required to establish the dietary requirements and practices of youth female rugby players. To conclude, developing a positive life-long relationship with food is critical for the holistic development of youth rugby players.

Key Take Home Messages

- Youth rugby players should target a positive daily energy balance.
- The average TEE of youth rugby players is ~50 kcal·kg^{-1}·day^{-1} (e.g., ~4,000 kcal·day^{-1} for an 80 kg player). Therefore, they are required to consume a calorie intake in excess of this each day.
- Training-based collisions and competitive match-play likely increase the energy costs of recovery. Therefore, players should eat more after such sessions.
- Youth rugby players should target 6–8 g·kg^{-1}·day^{-1} of dietary CHO on match days (–1/+1), with a minimum intake of 6 g·kg^{-1}·day^{-1} achieved daily (e.g., 480–640 g for an 80 kg player). Importantly, youth rugby players *should not* periodise purposeful decreases in dietary CHO.
- Youth rugby players should target a high meal-by-meal or daily protein intake of between 0.4 and 0.55 or 1.6 and 2.2 g·kg^{-1}·day^{-1} (e.g., meal: 30–45 g; daily: 130–175 g for an 80 kg player). Practically, this should be spilt evenly across main meals and snacks, particularly the pre-bed snack each day.
- Youth rugby players should target 30–35% of TEE from dietary fat (e.g., 130–155 g for an 80 kg player), with higher intakes potentially warranted in individuals struggling to achieve energy balance. Players should limit consumption of trans fats and prioritise greater intakes of unsaturated fats.
- Youth rugby players should consume 5–10 mL·kg^{-1} of fluid in the two to four hours prior to exercise to achieve euhydration. Players should avoid excessive fluid intakes (i.e., finishing exercise heavier than they started) and replace 125–150% of BM lost (e.g., 1.25–1.5 L for an 80 kg player, who lost 1 kg during exercise).
- Youth rugby players typically under consume starchy CHOs, fruits and vegetables, while overconsuming proteins and saturated fats.

- A food-first approach should be practically encouraged, with only clinically necessitated supplementation provided under professional supervision.
- Youth rugby players should get heavier and taller as they progress through adolescence. Tracking changes in BM and stature can help identify players who are potentially under-fuelling. Practically, this could be completed quarterly or bi-annually.
- Research shows that young rugby players have less FFM than senior players, but similar levels of absolute fat mass. Therefore, any assessments of body composition should practically support increases in FFM. The assessment of fat mass is not recommended in youth rugby players.

References

Aerenhouts, D., Cauwenberg, J. Van, Poortmans, J. R., Hauspie, R., & Clarys, P. (2013). Influence of growth rate on nitrogen balance in adolescent sprint athletes. *International Journal of Sport Nutrition and Exercise Metabolism, 23,* 409–417. https://doi.org/10.1123/ijsnem.23.4.409

Bargh, M. J., King, R. F. G. J., Gray, M. P., & Jones, B. (2016). Why do team-sport athletes drink fluid in excess when exercising in cool conditions? *Applied Physiology, Nutrition, and Metabolism, 42,* 271–277. https://doi.org/10.1139/apnm-2016-0445

Boisseau, N., Le Creff, C., Loyens, M., & Poortmans, J. R. (2002). Protein intake and nitrogen balance in male non-active adolescents and soccer players. *European Journal of Applied Physiology, 88,* 288–293. https://doi.org/10.1007/s00421-002-0726-x

Bradley, W. J., Cavanagh, B. P., Douglas, W., Donovan, T. F., Morton, J. P., & Close, G. L. (2015a). Quantification of training load, energy intake, and physiological adaptations during a rugby preseason: A case study from an Elite European Rugby Union Squad. *Journal of Strength and Conditioning Research, 29,* 534–544. https://doi.org/10.1519/JSC.0000000000000631

Bradley, W. J., Cavanagh, B. P., Douglas, W., Donovan, T. F., Twist, C., Morton, J. P., & Close, G. L. (2015b). Energy intake and expenditure assessed 'in-season' in an Elite European Rugby Union Squad. *European Journal of Sport Science, 15,* 469–479. https://doi.org/10.1080/17461391.2015.1042528

Bradley, W. J., Hannon, M. P., Benford, V., Morehen, J. C., Twist, C., Shepherd, S., Cocks, M., Impey, S. G., Cooper, R. G., Morton, J. P., & Close, G. L. (2017). Metabolic demands and replenishment of muscle glycogen after a Rugby League Match Simulation Protocol. *Journal of Science and Medicine in Sport, 20,* 878–883. https://doi.org/10.1016/j.jsams.2017.02.005

Burke, L. M. (2020). Ketogenic low-CHO, high-fat diet: The future of elite endurance sport? *Journal of Physiology, 599,* 819–843. https://doi.org/10.1016/10.1113/JP278928

Chryssanthopoulos, C., Williams, C., Nowitz, A., & Bogdanis, G. (2004). Skeletal muscle glycogen concentration and metabolic responses following a high glycaemic carbohydrate breakfast. *Journal of Sports Sciences, 22,* 1065–1071. https://doi.org/10.1080/02640410410001730007

Costello, N., Deighton, K., Dalton-Barron, N., Whitehead, S., McLaren, S., & Jones, B. (2019a). Three-day changes in resting metabolism after a Professional Young Rugby League Match. *Sport Performance and Science Reports, 49,* 1–3.

Costello, N., Deighton, K., Preston, T., Matu, J., Rowe, J. & Jones, B. (2019b). Are professional young rugby league players eating enough? Energy intake, expenditure and balance during a pre-season. *European Journal of Sport Science, 19*, 123–132. https://doi.org/10.1080/17461391.2018.1527950

Costello, N., Deighton, K., Preston, T., Matu, J., Rowe, J., Sawczuk, T., Halkier, M., Read, D. B., Weaving, D., & Jones, B. (2018). Collision activity during training increases total energy expenditure measured via doubly labelled water. *European Journal of Applied Physiology, 118*, 1169–1177. https://doi.org/10.1007/s00421-018-3846-7

Costill, D. L., Pascoe, D. D., Fink, W. J., Robergs, R. A., Barr, S. I., & Pearson, D. (1990). Impaired muscle glycogen resynthesis after eccentric exercise. *Journal of Applied Physiology, 69*, 46–50. https://doi.org/10.1152/jappl.1990.69.1.46

Desbrow, B., Tarnopolsky, M., Burd, N. A., Moore, D. R., & Elliott-Sale, K. J. (2019). Nutrition for special populations: Young, female, and masters athletes. *International Journal of Sport Nutrition and Exercise Metabolism, 29*, 220–227. https://doi.org/10.1123/ijsnem.2018-0269

Gavarry, O., Lentin, G., Pezery, P., Delextrat, A., Chaumet, G., Boussuges, A., & Piscione, J. (2018). A cross-sectional study assessing the contributions of body fat mass and fat-free mass to body mass index scores in male youth rugby players. *Sports Medicine - Open, 4*, 17. https://doi.org/10.1186/s40798-018-0130-7

Geeson-Brown, T., Jones, B., Till, K., Chantler, S., & Deighton, K. (2020). Body composition differences by age and playing standard in Male Rugby Union and Rugby League: A systematic review and meta-analysis. *Journal of Sports Sciences, 38*, 2161–2176. https://doi.org/10.1080/02640414.2020.1775990

Hannon, M. P., Parker, L. J. F., Carney, D. J., McKeown, J., Speakman, J. R., Hambly, C., Drust, B., Unnithan, V. B., Close, G. L., & Morton, J. P. (2021). Energy requirements of male academy soccer players from the English Premier League. *Medicine and Science in Sports and Exercise, 53*, 200–210. https://doi.org/10.1249/MSS.0000000000002443

Hengist, A., Watkins, J. D., Smith, H. A., Edinburgh, R. M., Betts, J. A., Roe, G. A. B., & Gonzalez, J. (2021). The effects of glucose-fructose co-ingestion on repeated performance during a Day of Intensified Rugby Union Training in Professional Academy Players. *Journal of Sports Sciences, 39*, 1144–1152. https://doi.org/10.1080/02640414.2020.1860473

Hudson, J. F., Cole, M., Morton, J. P., Stewart, C. E., & Close, G. L. (2020). Daily changes of resting metabolic rate in Elite Rugby Union Players. *Medicine and Science in Sports and Exercise, 52*, 637–644. https://doi.org/10.1249/MSS.0000000000002169

Jeukendrup, A. E., & Killer, S. C. (2011). The myths surrounding pre-exercise carbohydrate feeding. *Annals of Nutrition and Metabolism, 57*, 18–25. https://doi.org/10.1159/000322698

Jones, B., Till, K., King, R., Gray, M., & O'Hara, J. (2016). Are habitual hydration strategies of Female Rugby League Players sufficient to maintain fluid balance and blood sodium concentration during training and match-play? A research note from the field. *Journal of Strength and Conditioning Research, 30*, 875–880. https://doi.org/10.1519/JSC.0000000000001158

Kreitzman, S. N., Coxon, A. Y., & Szaz, K. F. (1992). Glycogen storage: Illusions of easy weight loss, excessive weight regain, and distortions in estimates of body composition. *The American Journal of Clinical Nutrition, 56*, 292S–293S. https://doi.org/10.1093/ajcn/56.1.292S

MacKenzie-Shalders, K. L., Byrne, N. M., King, N. A., & Slater, G. J. (2019). Are increases in skeletal muscle mass accompanied by changes to resting metabolic rate in rugby athletes over a pre-season training period? *European Journal of Sport Science, 19*, 885–892. https://doi.org/10.1080/17461391.2018.1561951

Maughan, R. J., Burke, L. M., Dvorak, J., Larson-Meyer, D. E., Peeling, P., Phillips, S. M., Rawson, E. S., Walsh, N. P., Garthe, I., Geyer, H., Meeusen, R., Loon, L. Van, Shirreffs, S. M., Spriet, L. L., Stuart, M., Vernec, A., Currell, K., Ali, V. M., Budgett, R. G. M., Ljungqvist, A., Mountjoy, M., Pitsiladis, Y., Soligard, T., Erdener, U., & Engebretsen, L. (2018). IOC consensus statement: Dietary supplements and the high-performance athlete. *International Journal of Sport Nutrition and Exercise Metabolism, 28,* 104–125. https://doi.org/10.1136/bjsports-2018-099027

Morehen, J. C., Bradley, W. J., Clarke, J., Twist, C., Hambly, C., Speakman, J. R., Morton, J. P., & Close, G. L. (2016). The assessment of total energy expenditure during a 14-day in-season period of Professional Rugby League Players using the doubly labelled water method. *International Journal of Sport Nutrition and Exercise Metabolism, 26,* 464–472. https://doi.org/10.1123/ijsnem.2015-0335

Nana, A., Slater, G. J., Stewart, A. D., & Burke, L. M. (2015). Methodology review: Using dual-energy X-ray absorptiometry (DXA) for the assessment of body composition in athletes and active people. *International Journal of Sport Nutrition and Exercise Metabolism, 25,* 198–215. https://doi.org/10.1123/ijsnem.2013-0228

Nilsson, L. H., Fürst, P., & Hultman, E. (1973). Carbohydrate metabolism of the liver in normal man under varying dietary conditions. *Scandinavian Journal of Clinical and Laboratory Investigation, 32,* 331–337. https://doi.org/10.3109/00365517309084356

Phillips, S. M. (2012). Dietary protein requirements and adaptive advantages in athletes. *British Journal of Nutrition, 108,* S158–S167. https://doi.org/10.1017/S0007114512002516

Pontzer, H., Yamada, Y., Sagayama, H., Ainslie, P. N., Andersen, L. F., Anderson, L. J., Arab, L., Baddou, I., Bedu-Addo, K., Blaak, E. E., Blanc, S., Bonomi, A. G., Bouten, C. V. C., Bovet, P., Buchowski, M. S., Butte, N. F., Camps, S. G., Close, G. L., Cooper, J. A., Cooper, R., Das, S. K., Dugas, L. R., Ekelund, U., Entringer, S., Forrester, T., Fudge, B. W., Goris, A. H., Gurven, M., Hambly, C., Hamdouchi, A. El, Hoos, M. B., Hu, S., Joonas, N., Joosen, A. M., Katzmarzyk, P., Kempen, K. P., Kimura, M., Kraus, W. E., Kushner, R. F., Lambert, E. V, Leonard, W. R., Lessan, N., Martin, C., Medin, A. C., Meijer, E. P., Morehen, J. C., Morton, J. P., Neuhouser, M. L., Nicklas, T. A., Ojiambo, R. M., Pietiläinen, K. H., Pitsiladis, Y. P., Plange-Rhule, J., Plasqui, G., Prentice, R. L., Rabinovich, R. A., Racette, S. B., Raichlen, D. A., Ravussin, E., Reynolds, R. M., Roberts, S. B., Schuit, A. J., Sjödin, A. M., Stice, E., Urlacher, S. S., Valenti, G., Etten, L. M. Van, Mil, E. A. Van, Wells, J. C. K., Wilson, G., Wood, B. M., Yanovski, J., Yoshida, T., Zhang, X., Murphy-Alford, A. J., Loechl, C., Luke, A. H., Rood, J., Schoeller, D. A., Westerterp, K. R., Wong, W. W., & Speakman, J. R. (2021) Daily energy expenditure through the human life course. *Science, 373,* 808–812. https://doi.org/10.1126/science.abe5017

Potgieter, S., Visser, J., Croukamp, I., Markides, M., Nascimento, J., & Scott, K. (2014). Body composition and habitual and match-day dietary intake of the FNB Maties Varsity Cup Rugby Players. *South African Journal of Sports Medicine, 26,* 35–43.

Schenk, S., Davidson, C. J., Zderic, T. W., Byerley, L. O., & Coyle, E. F. (2003). Different glycemic indexes of breakfast cereals are not due to glucose entry into blood but to glucose removal by tissue. *American Journal of Clinical Nutrition, 78,* 742–748. https://doi.org/10.1093/ajcn/78.4.742

Silva, A. M., Santos, D. A., Matias, C. N., Minderico, C. S., Schoeller, D. A., & Sardinha, L. B. (2013). Total energy expenditure assessment in Elite Junior Basketball Players: A validation study using doubly labeled water. *Journal of Strength and Conditioning Research, 27,* 1920–1927. https://doi.org/10.1519/JSC.0b013e31827361eb

Smith, D. R., Jones, B., Sutton, L., King, R. F. G. J., & Duckworth, L. C. (2016). Dietary intakes of Elite 14- to 19-year-old English Academy Rugby Players during a preseason training period. *International Journal of Sport Nutrition and Exercise Metabolism, 26*, 506–515. https://doi.org/10.1123/ijsnem.2015-0317

Smith, D. R., King, R. F. G. J., Duckworth, L. C., Sutton, L., Preston, T., O'Hara, J. P., & Jones, B. (2018). Energy expenditure of Rugby Players during a 14-day in-season period, measured using doubly labelled water. *European Journal of Applied Physiology, 118*, 647–656. https://doi.org/10.1007/s00421-018-3804-4

Thomas, D. T., Erdman, K. A., & Burke, L. M. (2016). Position of the Academy of Nutrition and Dietetics, Dietitians of Canada, and the American College of Sports Medicine: Nutrition and athletic performance. *Journal of the Academy of Nutrition and Dietetics, 116*, 501–528. https://doi.org/10.1016/j.jand.2015.12.006

Till, K., Morley, D., O'Hara, J., Jones, B. L., Chapman, C., Beggs, C. B., Cooke, C., & Cobley, S. (2017). A retrospective longitudinal analysis of anthropometric and physical qualities that associate with adult career attainment in Junior Rugby League Players. *Journal of Science and Medicine in Sport, 20*, 1029–1033. https://doi.org/10.1016/j.jsams.2017.03.018

Torun, B. (2005). Energy requirements of children and adolescents. *Public Health Nutrition, 8*, 968–993. https://doi.org/10.1079/phn2005791

Trumbo, P., Schlicker, S., Yates, A. A., & Poos, M. (2002). Dietary reference intakes for energy, carbohydrate, fiber, fat, fatty acids, cholesterol, protein and amino acids. *Journal of the American Dietetic Association, 102*, 1621–1630. https://doi.org/10.1016/s0002-8223(02)90346-9

Walsh, M., Cartwright, L., Corish, C., Sugrue, S., & Wood-Martin, R. (2011). The body composition, nutritional knowledge, attitudes, behaviors, and future education needs of senior schoolboy rugby players in Ireland. *International Journal of Sport Nutrition and Exercise Metabolism, 21*, 365–376. https://doi.org/10.1123/ijsnem.21.5.365

Wee, S. L., Williams, C., Tsintzas, K., & Boobis, L. (2005). Ingestion of a high-glycemic index meal increases muscle glycogen storage at rest but augments its utilization during subsequent exercise. *Journal of Applied Physiology, 99*, 707–714. https://doi.org/10.1152/japplphysiol.01261.2004

15
INJURY RISK AND REDUCTION STRATEGIES IN YOUNG RUGBY PLAYERS

Michael Hislop and Keith Stokes

Introduction

Rugby is played throughout much of the world across various codes and in numerous forms (World Rugby, 2018), many of which may help to avert the effects of a sedentary lifestyle through engaging in moderate to vigorous levels of physical activity (Griffin et al., 2021). However, the magnitude and acceptability of injury risk across rugby have been questioned, and notably so in the contact-orientated forms of the game at youth playing levels (Carter, 2015; Freitag et al., 2015a). Perceptions that the risk of injury in youth contact rugby is excessively high when compared with other popular sports of similar playing level have advanced calls for rugby to be modified at youth playing levels by removing contact events that contribute to the elevated injury risk, such as the tackle situation (Pollock & Kirkwood, 2016). The calls to modify the game and the debate stimulated subsequently (e.g., MacDonald & Myer, 2017; Tucker et al., 2016) bring focus on the need to (1) understand the risks to which players are exposed and the context in which risks are being compared; (2) identify factors that may heighten (i.e., risk factors) or lessen risk (i.e., protective factors), (3) design and develop strategies that mitigate risk by inhibiting risk factors or facilitating protective factors; and (4) evaluate said strategies for their efficacy (van Mechelen et al., 1992).

Developing a risk reduction strategy features as a fundamental step in well-known injury risk management frameworks such as the Sequence of Prevention or Translating Research into Injury Prevention Practice models (Finch, 2006; van Mechelen et al., 1992), although there has been little guidance provided on how to develop strategies. Despite the wide array of strategies found to reduce rugby-related injury risk (Barden et al., 2021), the processes by which these strategies have been designed and developed are largely absent from the literature. Such information can provide useful insight into the appearance, structure and

DOI: 10.4324/9781003104797-15

content of interventions while offering a framework for design of interventions in the future (Donaldson et al., 2016; Padua et al., 2014). Therefore, this chapter will first summarise the current research base surrounding injury risk and risk reduction strategies in young rugby players, before sharing a practical example of how a strategy in the form of a movement control (or 'neuromuscular') training programme was designed for use in schoolboy rugby players aged 14–18 years in England.

Research Overview

Impacts of Injury

When considering the risk of injury, it is important to bear in mind the range of mechanisms through which injury can impose a burden and the stakeholders affected by that burden. The immediate consequences of injury often centre on time missed from rugby, but possible exclusion in other sports and forms of physical activity must also be considered. Secondary impacts of injury may include disruptions to time in education or work for players, and occasionally parents/guardians in the case of youth players (Abernethy & MacAuley, 2003). There can also be direct financial consequences of injury, as demonstrated by an economic evaluation of injuries in male youth rugby players reporting mean costs of follow-up treatment as $731 USD per injury (Brown et al., 2015). A recent study investigating women's rugby union in New Zealand between 2013 and 2017 using data collated by the national health provider identified that 51% of total claims and 47% of total costs sustained during rugby union activity originated in females aged younger than 19 years (King et al., 2019). Furthermore, the age bracket associated with the greatest mean cost per moderate-to-serious injury claim per year was found to be players aged 15–19 years at $5,387 NZD (King et al., 2019).

Though many injuries are relatively minor, and players will return to play without complication, some injuries may result in damage that can compromise health and lifestyle during later life. Studies in retired elite and amateur rugby players point to a link between injuries suffered during playing careers and health complications in later-life, such as an increased prevalence of joint pain, osteoporosis and osteoarthritis when compared with non-contact sport playing controls (Davies et al., 2017; Hume et al., 2022). The impacts of injuries to the immature and developing musculoskeletal system in youth rugby players are also relevant (Iwamoto et al., 2005). The contact forms of rugby can entail a risk of permanently disabling (or catastrophic) head and spinal cord injuries that, while rare, can severely compromise post-injury quality of life and incur extensive financial costs through ongoing medical care and post-injury lifestyle adjustment (Badenhorst et al., 2018). Published data from South Africa and France point to catastrophic injury incidence rates of between 0.3 and 0.6/100,000 players in youth rugby and 3.5 and 5.1/100,000 players in adult rugby, depending on catastrophic injury definition (Brown et al. 2013; Reboursiere et al., 2018). Concerns around exposure to repeated head acceleration or impact events have intensified among contact and collision sports worldwide, with evidence pointing to a link between contact or collision sports participation at elite playing levels (with and without a history of concussion) and changes in brain structure (Wright et al., 2021; Zimmerman et al., 2021), decreased cognitive function (Cunningham et al., 2018; Hume et al., 2017) and heightened incidence of neurodegenerative disease (McKee et al., 2009). With these possible consequences of injury in mind, attempts to manage injury risk in rugby may carry benefits that extend beyond lessening the amount of time that players miss from rugby and other physical pursuits to also include reducing financial implications, alleviating complications in later life health and enhancing the public profiles of the sports.

Injury Outcomes in Youth Rugby

Rugby Union

The volume of research illustrating the injury risks posed by rugby at youth playing levels has grown noticeably since early studies appearing in the late 1970s to early 1980s (Davidson et al., 1978; Sparks, 1981), as highlighted in Table 15.1.

Forming a clear picture of youth rugby injury risk from studies published to-date remains challenging due to the lack of consistency in how studies have been conducted. Table 15.1 illustrates the various definitions, data collection processes, and ways in which studies have reported injury data. Reporting definitions have encompassed injuries affecting performance or requiring medical attention (Junge et al., 2004; Leung et al., 2017), presenting at healthcare facilities (O'Rourke et al., 2007), incurring subsequent time-loss for a given number of days (Roux et al., 1987; Sparks, 1981), or leading to absence from subsequent planned training sessions or matches (Lee & Garraway, 1996; Nicol et al., 2011). Data collection practices include players self-reporting injuries (Nathan et al., 1983; Roux et al., 1987), reporting by recognised team liaisons (McIntosh et al., 2010; Nicol et al., 2011), or interrogating internal medical records (Davidson et al., 1978; Sparks, 1981). Injury data have also been reported in various ways, notably in how incidence data have been standardised by calculating person-time at risk. For example, studies have reported injury incidence or prevalence rates per number of player-hours of exposure (Sewry et al., 2018; Solis-Mencia et al., 2019), player-exposures (Willigenburg et al., 2014, 2016) and player-seasons (Lee & Garraway, 1996; Marshall & Spencer, 2001).

Similar degrees of variability have been documented in youth rugby match injury incidence from studies reporting physical complaints or injuries requiring medical treatment (14–130 injuries/1,000 player-match-hours; Davidson et al., 1978; Junge et al., 2004), and injuries resulting in subsequent time-loss from physical activity or sport (>24 hours' time-loss: 15–138 injuries/1,000

TABLE 15.1 Summary of Overall Match and Training Injury Incidence Rates in Youth Rugby Union (separated by Recording Definition)

Author (Year)	Country	Participants	Injury Recorder	Group	Overall	Match	Training
Medical attention/physical complaint							
Bird et al. (1998)	New Zealand	Male and female players, 1993	Research team	Colts male (U21)		11/100 player-matches	1.2/100 player-practices
				School male first XV (U18–19)		6/100 player-matches	0.9/100 player-practices
				School female first XV (U18–19)		5/100 player-matches	
Brown et al. (2012)	South Africa	Male players aged 12–18 years, national youth tournaments, 2011	Research team			48/1,000 player-match-hours	
Brown et al. (2015)	South Africa	Male players aged 12–18 years, national youth tournaments, 2011	Research team			55/1,000 player-match-hours	
Davidson et al. (1978)	Australia	Male school players aged 12–18 years, inter-school matches, 1969–1976	School Nurse			14/1,000 player-hours	

(Continued)

TABLE 15.1 (Continued)

| Author (Year) | Country | Participants | Injury Recorder | Group | Injury Incidence ||||
					Overall	Match	Training
Davidson (1987)	Australia	Male school players aged 11–18 years, inter-school matches, 1969–1986	School Doctor/Nurse			19/1,000 player-hours	
Durie (2000)	New Zealand	Players aged 12–18, 1998	School Clinician			28/1,000 player-hours	
Junge et al. (2004)	New Zealand	School players aged 14–18 years, first and second XV, 2001	Research team physician			130/1,000 player-hours	22/1,000 player-hours
Leung et al. (2017a)	Australia	Male players aged 9–18 years, inter-school matches, 2016	School first aid provider			24/1,000 player-match-hours	
McIntosh et al. (2010)	Australia	Male players aged 12–20 years participating in club and school rugby, 2002–2003	Primary data collectors (University students)			64/1,000 player-match-hours	
McManus and Cross (2004)	Australia	State-level players from U15 and U16 squads, 1997	Research team		13/1,000 exposure-hours		

Peck et al. (2013)	USA	Male and female players at a US service academy, 2006–2011	Athletic trainer	Male	4/1,000 athlete-exposures
				Female	3/1,000 athlete-exposures
Pringle et al. (1998)	New Zealand	Club players aged 6–15 years	Trained observers		16/1000 match-hours
>24 hours' time-loss					
Archbold et al. (2017)	Ireland	Male school players aged 16–18 years in first XV squads, 2014–2015	School data champion		29/1,000 player-match-hours
Archbold et al. (2021)	Ireland	Male school players aged 14–15 years, 2016–2017	School data champion		15/1,000 player-match-hours
Barden and Stokes (2018)	England	Male college players aged 16–19 years, 2012–2015	College medical staff	Elite	77/1,000 player-match-hours
				Sub-elite	34/1,000 player-match-hours
Brown et al. (2012)	South Africa	Male players aged 12–18 years, national youth tournaments, 2011	Research team		23/1,000 player-match-hours

(*Continued*)

TABLE 15.1 (Continued)

Author (Year)	Country	Participants	Injury Recorder	Group	Injury Incidence Overall	Match	Training
Brown et al. (2015)	South Africa	Male players aged 12–18 years, national youth tournaments, 2011–2012	Research team			22/1,000 player-match-hours	
Collins et al. (2008)	USA	Male and female high school players, 2005–2006	Designated reporter	Male		15/1,000 athlete-exposures	1.3/1,000 athlete-exposures
				Female		20/1,000 athlete-exposures	1.0/1,000 athlete-exposures
Fuller et al. (2011)	International	International male under-20 players, junior world championship and trophy events, 2008 and 2010	Team medical personnel			57/1,000 player-hours	
Hartwig et al. (2019)	Australia	Male school and representative-level players aged 14–16 years, 2016–2017	Player self-report			54/1,000 player-match-hours	7/1,000 player-exposure-hours
Haseler et al. (2010)	England	Club youth players aged 8–17 years, 2008–2009	Research team			24/1,000 player-match-hours	

Kerr et al. (2008)	USA	Male and female collegiate players, 2005–2006	Athletic trainers/ emergency medical technicians.	Male	23/1,000 athlete-exposures 17/1,000 match-hours 6/1,000 athlete-exposures
				Female	23/1,000 athlete-exposures 17/1,000 match-hours 6/1,000 athlete-exposures
Leahy et al. (2022)	Ireland	Male school players aged 16–19 years, 2018–2020	School data champion		54/1,000 player-match-hours
Palmer-Green et al. (2013)	England	Male school and academy players aged 16–18 years, 2006–2008	School nurse or physician Physical therapist	School Academy	35/1,000 player-match-hours 47/1,000 player-match-hours
Palmer-Green et al. (2015)	England	Male school and academy players aged 16–18 years, 2006–2008	School nurse or physician Physical therapist	School Academy	2.1/1,000 player-training-hours 1.3/1,000 player-training-hours
Sewry et al. (2018)	South Africa	Male players aged 12–18 years, national youth tournaments, 2011–2016	Research team		20/1,000 player-match-hours

(*Continued*)

278 Michael Hislop and Keith Stokes

TABLE 15.1 (Continued)

Author (Year)	Country	Participants	Injury Recorder	Group	Injury Incidence Overall	Match	Training
Sewry et al. (2019)	South Africa	Male school players aged 15–16 years, 2017	Unknown			29/1,000 player-match-hours	
Solis-Mencia et al. (2019)	Spain	Male national squad players, aged 17–18 years, 2014–2017	Team physician			138/1,000 player-match-hours	1.2/1,000 player-exposure-hours
Willigenburg et al. (2014)	USA	Male University players, 2012–2013	Licensed medical professional			26/1,000 athlete-exposures	8/1,000 athlete-exposures
Willigenburg et al. (2016)	USA	Male University players, 2012–2014	Licensed medical professional			40/1,000 athlete-exposures	8/1,000 athlete-exposures
>7 days' time-loss							
Nathan et al. (1983)	South Africa	Male school players aged 9–19 years, 1982	Player self-report			8/1,000 player-hours	1/1,000 player-hours
Roux et al. (1987)	South Africa	Male high school players, 1983	Player self-report			7/1,000 player-hours	0.5/1,000 player-hours
Sparks (1981)	England	Male school players aged 13–18 years, 1950–1979	Internal records		20/1,000 exposure-hours		
Sparks (1985)	England	Male school players aged 13–18 years, 1980–1983	Internal records		19/1,000 player-hours	40/1,000 player-hours	

Missed match/training

Study	Country	Population	Data collector	Details	Rate
Junge et al. (2004)	New Zealand	School players aged 14–18 years playing first and second XV, 2001	Research team physician		28/1,000 match-hours; 4/1,000 exposure-hours
Lee and Garraway (1996)	Scotland	School and club players, 1993–1994	Team liaison	School (11–19 years); Club (11–19 years)	87/1,000 player-seasons; 218/1,000 player-seasons
Marshall and Spencer (2001)	USA	High school players, 1998–2000	Not provided		2/1,000 athlete-exposures; 46/100 player-seasons
McIntosh et al. (2010)	Australia	Male school and club rugby players aged 12–20 years, 2002–2003	Primary data collectors (University students)		21/1,000 player-match-hours
Nicol et al. (2011)	Scotland	Male and female school players aged 11 years and older	School data champion		11/1,000 player-match-hours
Ogaki et al. (2020)	Japan	Male collegiate players, 2017–2019	Athletic trainer		123/1,000 player-match-hours; 4/1,000 player-exposure-hours
Takemura et al. (2009)	Japan	Male University players, 2005	Team trainer or physiotherapist		48/1,000 player-match-hours; 1/1,000 player-hours

player-match-hours; missed match/training: 11–123 injuries/1,000 player-match hours; Nicol et al., 2011; Solis-Mencia et al., 2019). As well as injury definition, it must be noted that study setting, participant demographic and data collection process may influence the observed variability of injury outcomes. A meta-analysis of injury outcomes in rugby union and league players aged younger than 21 years published in 2015 estimated a match injury incidence of 27 injuries/1,000 player-match-hours (95% CI 13–54) irrespective of whether injuries required medical attention or incurred time-loss (Freitag et al., 2015b). Several studies published since the meta-analysis align with the pooled outcome in documenting match injury incidence rates between 13 and 54 injuries/1,000 player-match-hours (Hartwig et al., 2019; Sewry et al., 2018). Training-related injury incidence has been reported infrequently in youth rugby cohorts, with variability in reported incidence rates typically lower than observed with match injury incidence (>24 hours' time-loss: 1–7 injuries/1,000 player-training-hours; Collins et al., 2008; Hartwig et al., 2019).

In addition to the frequency at which injuries occur, it is also useful to understand the severity of injuries in terms of the amount of time that players can miss. Mean match injury severity has been documented between 19 and 34 days lost per injury (Barden & Stokes, 2018; Haseler et al., 2010). Documented mean training injury severity has been shown to fall within a similar range to mean match injury severity (Palmer-Green et al., 2015). Severity data have also been presented as proportions of overall injury incidence attributed to categories of time-loss. For example: 10–41% of match injuries have been shown to result in less than seven days' time-loss, 24–62% in 8–28 days' time-loss, and 12–49% in more than 28 days' time-loss (Haseler et al., 2010; Solis-Mencia et al., 2019). Injury burden has been reported in youth rugby as a means of presenting a singular figure that accounts for injury frequency and severity. Documented match injury burden has been reported between 379 to 1,545 days' absence/1,000 player-match-hours (Barden and Stokes, 2018; Sewry et al., 2019), while training injury burden has been estimated between 23 and 59 days absence/1,000 player-training-hours (Palmer-Green et al., 2015).

Rugby League

Compared with youth rugby union, descriptive epidemiological studies of injury in youth rugby league cohorts have been reported less frequently (King et al., 2022). Many of the same methodological challenges that beset injury surveillance research in youth rugby union may also apply to youth rugby league, namely, inconsistencies in injury definitions, data collection processes and reporting practices. Table 15.2 presents a summary of descriptive epidemiological studies conducted in rugby league.

Much of the current evidence base for injury epidemiology in youth rugby league originates from Australia and New Zealand (Gabbett, 2008; Pringle et al., 1998) and has typically studied male players involved in elite player development

TABLE 15.2 Summary of Overall Match and Training Injury Incidence Rates in Youth Rugby League (separated by Recording Definition)

Author (Year)	Country	Participants	Injury Recorder	Group	Injury Incidence Overall	Injury Incidence Match	Injury Incidence Training
Medical attention/physical complaint							
Booth et al. (2019)	Australia	Developmental players aged 15–18 years, 2015–2016	Research team			36/1,000 player-match-hours	4/1,000 player-training-hours
Booth and Orr (2017)	Australia	Elite development squad, 2015	Physiotherapist/medical trainer			8/1,000 player-match-hours	
Gabbett (2006)	Australia	Sub-elite junior rugby league players, pre-season period	Head trainer				56/1,000 player-training-hours
Inglis et al. (2019)	Australia	Junior rugby league players aged 13–16 years, 2015	Research team	Under-16 team Under-14 team Under-14 team		83/1,000 player-match-hours 70/1,000 player-match-hours 56/1,000 player-match-hours	
King (2006)	New Zealand	Male players aged 15–18 years, national junior competition, 2005	Team trainer prospectively recorded injuries			217/1,000 player-match-hours	

(Continued)

TABLE 15.2 (Continued)

Author (Year)	Country	Participants	Injury Recorder	Group	Injury Incidence Overall	Injury Incidence Match	Injury Incidence Training
Orr and Cheng (2016)	Australia	Male representative players aged 15–18 years, 2012	Physiotherapist/ rehabilitation trainer/medical practitioner			37/1,000 match-hours	
Orr et al. (2021)	Australia	Male and female junior community club players aged 5–18 years, 2016	Club-affiliated trainer	Male	8/1,000 player-exposure-hours		
				Female	22/1,000 player-exposure-hours		
Pringle et al. (1998)	New Zealand	Club players aged 6–15 years	Trained observers			25/1,000 match-hours	
>24 hours' time-loss							
Tee et al. (2019)	England	Male academy players, 2017	Injury surveillance officer			85/1,000 player-match-hours	
Missed match							
Booth and Orr (2017)	Australia	Male elite development squad, 2015	Physiotherapist/ medical trainer			2/1,000 player-match-hours	
Gabbett (2008)	Australia	Male under-19 junior rugby league players, 2003–2006	Head trainer			57/1,000 player-match-hours	
Tee et al. (2019)	England	Male academy players, 2017	Injury surveillance officer			67/1,000 player-match-hours	

pathways (Booth & Orr, 2017; Tee et al., 2019). Comparatively, little research has been conducted in youth female rugby league players and within recreational settings (Orr et al., 2021). Nonetheless, the incidence of match injuries requiring medical attention has been documented between 8 and 217 injuries/1,000 player-match-hours (Booth & Orr, 2017; King, 2006), with lower and narrower ranges of between 2 and 67 injuries/1,000 player-match-hours in studies adopting time-loss injury definitions (Booth and Orr, 2017; Tee et al., 2019). A recent review of injury epidemiology in rugby league revealed a pooled estimate of match injury incidence in junior rugby league (aged younger than 12 years) of 15 injuries/1,000 player-match-hours (95% CI 13–16; King et al., 2022). In addition, the incidence of training injuries requiring medical attention has been reported as between 4 and 56 injuries/1,000 player-training-hours (Booth et al., 2019; Gabbett, 2006).

Injury severity data for youth rugby league have been reported infrequently and in different forms. Where injury severity has been reported, this indicates approximately two matches are missed (Orr & Cheng, 2016), or 16–22 days are lost per match injury on average (Orr et al., 2021; Tee et al., 2019). Further breakdown of injuries by categories of subsequent time-loss suggests that 45–77% of match injuries may be transient in nature (i.e., no subsequent matches missed), while 23–55% may result in absence from at least one subsequent match (one missed match: 9–23%; two to four missed matches: and 7–23%; five or more missed matches: 8–10%; Booth & Orr, 2017; Orr & Cheng, 2016). Two studies have reported injury burden in youth rugby league as 94 days' absence/1,000 player-hours for overall match and training injuries and 1,898 days' absence/1,000 player-hours for match injury (95% CI 1,813–1,983; Orr et al., 2021; Tee et al., 2019).

Comparisons with Other Youth Sports and Rugby-Playing Settings

Although descriptive epidemiological studies can assist with understanding the magnitude of injury risk that rugby poses to youth players, risks may only be viewed as 'high' or 'low' in comparison with other activities. For these comparisons to be meaningful, it is inherent that comparable data is available that describes the risks between sports or between settings within the same sport (Quarrie et al., 2017). In the case of youth rugby, comparisons of injury risk could feature other sports played at the youth level or other rugby-playing populations. However, studies comparing injury outcomes between youth rugby and other youth sports are sparse. Where comparable data have been sourced from similarly matched playing demographics and collected using consistent study methodologies, there is evidence to suggest that the incidence of injury in rugby may be two to three times greater than in soccer (Junge et al., 2004), and three-times greater than American Football (Willigenburg et al., 2016). One study in youth rugby players aged 6–15 years identified match injury incidence rates in rugby league to be 50% greater than rugby union. Comparisons between youth rugby and other rugby-playing settings are more straightforward. Recent pooled estimates of injury incidence in adult community (47 injuries/1,000 player-match-hours, 95% CI 34–59) and elite rugby (91 injuries/1,000 player-match-hours, 95% CI 77–106) suggest higher rates of injury in these settings than in youth rugby (Williams et al., 2022; Yeomans et al., 2018). A recent review of injury epidemiology in rugby league also indicated that match injury rates increased noticeably from junior cohorts (15 injuries/1,000 player-match-hours) to older and more advanced playing levels (88–432 injuries/1,000 player-match-hours; King et al., 2022). In summary, the present evidence base suggests that injury outcomes in youth rugby may exceed those of less contact and collision-orientated sports but are similar to other contact and collision sports. In addition, injury outcomes in youth rugby appear to be lower than those documented in older and more advanced playing levels of the sport.

Injury Patterns in Youth Rugby

Irrespective of reporting definition, injuries to the lower limb (22–56% of all injuries), head/neck (8–50% of all injuries) and upper limb regions (7–35% of all injuries) have been commonly reported, with few injuries affecting the trunk region (2–16% of all injuries; Nicol et al., 2011; Sewry et al., 2018). Injuries to the ankle (7–22% of all injuries) and knee (5–21% of all injuries) are particularly prominent within the lower limb, while the shoulder/clavicle (2–22% of all injuries) and head/face (9–45% of all injuries) are similarly prominent injury locations (Nicol et al., 2011; Takemura et al., 2009). Injuries to the upper and lower limbs can also impose a substantial burden in terms of time-loss (lower limb – 165–896 days' absence/1,000 player-match-hours; upper limb 209–615 days' absence/1,000 player-match-hours; Barden & Stokes, 2018; Sewry et al., 2019).

Joint and ligament injuries are commonly reported and may contribute to between 15 and 52% of all recorded injuries among youth rugby players (Sewry et al., 2018; Tee et al., 2019). Joint and ligament injuries are also a source of substantial burden with an estimated 173–958 days' absence/1,000 player-match-hours (Barden & Stokes, 2018; Tee et al., 2019). Bone fractures (3–20% of injuries) and muscle strains (6–26% of injuries) have also been reported as common injury types (Brown et al., 2012; Orr et al., 2021), although typically imposing a lower burden than joint injuries (bone fracture: 21–103 days' absence/1,000 player-match-hours; muscle strain: 150–602 days' absence/1,000 player-match-hours; Barden & Stokes, 2018; Tee et al., 2019).

Contact situations have been widely recognised as prominent inciting events for injury in youth rugby, with 76–89% of match injuries documented as occurring during contact activities (Palmer-Green et al., 2013; Tee et al., 2019). Within contact situations, the tackle situation is notable in accounting for 48–84% of all match injuries (Archbold et al., 2017; Orr et al., 2021). Findings from studies in youth rugby to have separated injuries into those occurring to the tackler and ball carrier suggest that injury outcomes are marginally greater for the ball carrier, with tackling and being tackled reported in 37–55% and 45–63%

of tackle-related injuries, respectively (Burger et al., 2014; Sewry et al., 2019). The tackle situation also contributes heavily to time-loss, with tackling shown to incur a burden of 32–325 days' absence/1,000 player-match-hours and being tackled 158–443 days' absence/1,000 player-match-hours (Palmer-Green et al., 2013; Sewry et al., 2019). Cross-referencing of injured body locations by playing event in one study revealed that being tackled was the most common cause of lower limb injuries (35–44% of lower limb match injuries) and tackling the most common cause of upper limb injuries (48–53% of upper limb match injuries; Palmer-Green et al., 2013).

Injury Risk Factors in Youth Rugby

Injury incidence and severity have been shown to increase as a function of the increasing age group in youth rugby (Haseler et al., 2010; Orr et al., 2021). A study conducted at a junior community club indicated that injury incidence increased by five injuries/1,000 player-match-hours per year group (Haseler et al. 2010) from U9 to U17, although evidence from other settings suggests that differences in injury incidence between adjacent age groups become more profound once players reach adolescence (Leung et al., 2017). Many of the studies to have investigated age as a risk factor have studied single-year age bandings, but a recent study in Northern Irish senior school teams that featured a two-year age banding (ages 16–18 years) identified that relatively older players in the cohort (aged >16.9 years) were associated with a 45% greater risk of injury than their younger counterparts (Archbold et al., 2017).

Youth rugby players reporting a previous injury have been associated with 6–85% greater risk of injury than players without a history of injury (Archbold et al., 2017, 2021). Furthermore, the effect of specific injury histories has been investigated, with players reporting a recent history of concussion associated with increased risk of concussion (20–75%; Hollis et al., 2009, 2011) and overall injury (26–45%; Archbold et al., 2017, 2021) when compared to counterparts without such a history

A small number of studies investigating the influence of biological sex on injury in intercollegiate rugby union players have identified similar or moderately greater match injury incidence in female players when compared with male counterparts (Kerr et al., 2008; Peck et al., 2013). Further investigation of injury patterns between the respective cohorts indicated that female players experienced greater incidences of lower limb injuries, particularly knee ligament injuries, and concussion than male players (Kerr et al., 2008; Peck et al., 2013). Conversely, male players appeared to experience greater frequencies of non-concussive head injuries, bone fractures and lacerations than female players (Kerr et al., 2008; Peck et al., 2013).

Studies investigating match injuries have suggested that injuries occur more frequently towards the end of matches in youth rugby (Burger et al., 2014, 2017). These findings have generally been seen as indicative of the effect of fatigue on injury outcomes. Fatigue has been shown to impair tackle technique under controlled settings for amateur players (Davidow et al., 2020), although evidence from elite-level rugby suggests that time-in-game may not affect tackle proficiency (Tierney et al., 2018).

Playing position has not been thought to influence overall injury risk in youth rugby, with the findings of several studies highlighting trivial or equivocal differences in injury incidence between forwards and backs (Kerr et al., 2008; Palmer-Green et al., 2013). However, investigation of injury patterns between positional units has suggested that forwards may experience a greater frequency of injuries to the head and shoulder, as well as haematomas and concussion than backs (Leahy et al., 2022). It has been suggested that differences in injury patterns may reflect the differing positional requirements between forwards and backs, with forwards typically engaging in a greater frequency of physical confrontations (Leahy et al. 2022; McManus & Cross, 2004).

The roles of anthropometric profile and components of physical fitness as injury risk factors in youth rugby remain uncertain despite the interest shown in these factors in other aspects of youth rugby development (Darrall-Jones et al., 2015, 2016; Jones et al., 2018). One of the few studies to investigate the role of anthropometry and physical fitness specifically in a youth rugby cohort identified that heavier players (>77 kg) were 32% more likely to be injured than their lighter peers (Archbold et al., 2017). The same study failed to detect an association between upper or lower body strength measures and injury, although counterintuitively players that reported regularly engaging in weight training were associated with a 65% greater risk (Archbold et al., 2017). A two-season cohort study in elite junior rugby league players discovered that self-reported rugby league training age and resistance training age were not clearly associated with overall injury risk but increasing cardiovascular training age was associated with a 65% increase in the likelihood of injury per additional year of training accrued (Booth et al., 2019). Movement screening was used to assess the relation between movement competency and non-contact injury risk in another study of elite youth rugby league players, although no clear associations between screening scores and non-contact injury incidence were forthcoming (Dyer et al., 2019).

Several dated studies indicate that injury rates across a playing season appear to peak following the commencement of the playing season (termed 'early season bias'), and after mid-term breaks in the case of school programmes (Nathan et al., 1983; Roux et al., 1987). While reasonable to speculate on the influence of environmental factors such as climatic conditions and ground hardness (Alsop et al., 2000), these findings also invite the possibility that inadequate preparation for the demands of the playing season may predispose players to injury until they can acclimate to these physical demands (Upton et al., 1996). However, the advancements made since these early studies in access to physical preparation resources could mitigate the increased risk of early season injuries in youth rugby (Weakley et al., 2019). In the absence of more contemporary evidence, it is challenging to confirm or deny the presence of the early season bias in injury occurrence.

Youth rugby players commonly participate in different settings and across different playing levels as some migrate through representative or talent development pathways (Hartwig et al., 2019). One study to have compared injury outcomes between different playing levels in youth rugby union indicated that match injury incidence recorded in academy settings exceeded that of school rugby programmes by 34% (Palmer-Green et al., 2013). Furthermore, some of the greatest match injury incidence rates across youth rugby were documented in national and international playing settings (Fuller et al., 2011; Solis-Mencia et al., 2019). Possible explanations for the greater injury incidence identified at higher playing levels in youth rugby could include selection policies that prioritise players with more advanced physical profiles (Jones et al., 2018), which may consequently impact on the nature of match activity such that the academy-level matches impose greater requirements on players than school matches (Read et al., 2018). Findings of increased injury incidence in higher playing levels may also raise the question over the preparation of players to play at these higher playing levels. An epidemiological study of training injuries revealed lower training injury incidence in academy settings than school settings (Palmer-Green et al., 2015), while evidence suggests that training exposure in academy rugby settings may better prepare players for the activity profiles representative of match-play than does training exposure in school rugby settings (Phibbs et al., 2018).

Differences in playing levels within the school rugby sector may also manifest in differing injury outcomes. Schools that operate an elite rugby programme are reported to exhibit match injury incidence rates 49–126% greater than schools of lower playing levels (Archbold et al., 2017; Barden and Stokes, 2018). The influence of playing across more than one playing level in youth rugby has also been investigated, with school players reporting involvement in representative rugby associated with a 42% greater risk of injury when compared with players not involved in representative rugby (Archbold et al., 2017). A study of Australian youth rugby players playing across multiple playing levels indicated that each additional hour of match-play in a given week increased the odds of injury by 41% in the following week (Hartwig et al., 2019). These findings suggest that the influence of increasing playing level on injury outcomes in youth rugby may be mediated by the differing physical requirements of match-play between playing levels and the additional loading placed on youth players participating across multiple playing levels.

Injury incidence has been shown to be markedly different between match-play and training in youth rugby. Where comparable data exist, match injuries have been shown to exceed training injuries by 16–35-fold in incidence and 17–66-fold in burden (Palmer-Green et al., 2013, 2015). A prominent theory for the discrepancy in injury outcomes involves the differing activity profiles that players are exposed to during match-play and training. Studies comparing the activity profiles between matches and training suggest that youth players encounter more extensive movement demands during match-play than during training (Hartwig et al., 2011; Phibbs et al., 2018). Furthermore, many of the activities inherent in match-play take place in a less controlled environment where players may be more inclined to take risks and display aggression than during training sessions.

With relatively high risks of injury occurring during contact situations, it is important that players develop an appropriate degree of technical proficiency to execute contact skills safely and effectively (Hendricks & Lambert, 2010). Aspects of technical skill relating to the tackle have been shown in recent studies to influence injury risk, for example 'placing the head to the correct side of the ball carrier', 'using the shoulder to make contact with the ball carrier', and 'leg drive upon contact' when tackling has been associated with a lower risk of concussion (Hendricks et al., 2015). Subsequent work also demonstrated that 'using the shoulder to make contact with the ball carrier' and 'using the arms to wrap the ball carrier' characterised non-injury tackle events for the tackler, while 'Leg drive on contact with the tackler', 'performing an evasive manoeuvre', and 'fending away from contact' were associated with non-injury tackles for the ball carrier (Burger et al., 2016, 2017)

Concussion in Youth Rugby

Concussion is characterised as a traumatic brain injury caused by biomechanical forces imparted to the brain either by direct or indirect impact, with neurological impairment manifesting in a range of clinical signs or symptoms that can evolve and resolve over varying time frames (McCrory et al., 2017). A positive history of concussion has been recognised as a risk factor for concussion in youth rugby union (Hollis et al., 2009, 2011), while concussions sustained during times of brain maturation and functional development may also lead to prolonged recovery periods in youth athletes (Davis et al., 2017; Manzanero et al., 2017). The impact of concussion and general contact sports participation on cognitive and academic outcomes in youth rugby players have been explored, although evidence remains mixed. A study in elite youth rugby league players indicated a history of concussion did not appear to impact on aspects of cognitive performance (Gardner et al., 2020), while a study in similarly aged school rugby union players demonstrated that cognitive performance and academic progress were impaired in rugby-playing cohorts (with and without a history of concussion) when compared non-contact sport controls (Alexander et al., 2015).

Early studies in youth rugby indicated that concussion accounted for 5–6% of injuries and with incidence rates of 1.5-2.2 concussions/1,000 player-match-hours reported (Kerr et al., 2008; Sparks, 1981). More recent estimates point to an increased presence of concussion in terms of incidence (4–6 concussions/1,000 player-hours) and as a proportion of all injuries (18–38%) (Archbold et al., 2021; Sewry et al., 2019). Match-related concussion incidence has been estimated to be a as great as 20/1,000 player-match-hours in an elite college rugby programme, with an associated burden of 119–403 days' absence/1,000 player-match-hours (Barden & Stokes, 2018; Sewry et al., 2019). One study to have investigated mechanisms of concussion in youth rugby indicated all concussions occurred through contact events, notably the tackle (50%) and ruck (40%) situations (Hendricks et al., 2016). Other possible predisposing factors for concussion may include technical proficiency (Hendricks et al., 2015), playing position (Leahy et al., 2022), playing level (Barden & Stokes, 2018) and biological sex (Peck et al., 2013).

Concussion identification and management in community rugby settings remain highly challenging and rely heavily on stakeholders being sufficiently aware of the signs and symptoms and the correct protocols to follow in managing players (Clacy et al., 2019; Salmon et al., 2021b). Factors that further complicate concussion management in community-level youth rugby include differing views between and within various stakeholder groups on responsibility for identifying concussion (Clacy et al., 2017, 2019), depending on medically qualified personnel for diagnosis and management despite the inconsistent presence of this stakeholder group during training sessions and matches (Clacy et al., 2019), and relying on players to disclose symptoms (Beakey et al., 2018; Salmon et al., 2020). Symptom non-disclosure is a prominent issue, with 26–72% of surveyed youth rugby players responding that they would continue to play despite suspecting that they may have experienced a concussion (Delahunty et al., 2015; Kearney & See, 2017), or agreeing that a player should play in an important game despite suspecting that they had suffered a concussion (Sye et al., 2006). Factors underpinning non-disclosure of concussions among players have been explored, with player attitudes and the role of other stakeholders (coaches, parents/guardians, peers) identified as being influential (Beakey et al., 2018; Salmon et al., 2021a).

Concussion management also entails the process that injured players follow in returning to sport. The Graduated Return to Play Protocol (GRTP) for community-level rugby union varies by age, with junior players not permitted to fully return to sport until at least 23 days following the injury under guidance issued by World Rugby. A study of Australian community-level rugby union players conducted between 2005 and 2007 highlighted that 87% of players with concussion returned to team training or match-play within one week of the injury, and a further 8% (95% of total) by three weeks of the injury (Hollis et al., 2012). However, recent studies are more positive in demonstrating that less than 5% of youth players with concussion returned to play before 23 days, which may indicate improved awareness and behaviours over time (Archbold et al., 2017, 2021). Access to medical advice on returning to play for injured players remains problematic, with between 25% and 78% of players reporting that decisions to return to play following concussion were made independently of medical advice (Delahunty et al., 2015; Hollis et al., 2012).

Injury Reduction Strategies in Youth Rugby

Protective equipment represents one of the most commonly investigated means of reducing injury risk in youth rugby (Barden et al., 2021), with examples of protective equipment permitted for use in rugby including mouthguards and protective headgear. Mouthguards have been reported as the most commonly worn piece of protective equipment by youth rugby players (Archbold et al., 2021; Marshall et al., 2001). The high rate of use may be related to policies implemented in some settings that mandate players must wear a mouthguard to participate in rugby-related training and matches (Broad & Welbury, 2015). The use of mouthguards appears beneficial, with orofacial injury incidence shown to be 44% lower in players that wear mouthguards compared with those that do not (Marshall et al., 2005). Furthermore, the introduction of a national policy mandating mouthguard use for matches was reported to coincide with a 43% reduction in dental injury rates in New Zealand (Quarrie et al., 2005). Compared with mouthguards, protective headgear use is reportedly less frequent in youth rugby (Archbold et al., 2021; Marshall et al., 2001). The efficacy of protective headgear has been shown to depend on injury type. For example, there is little evidence to support the efficacy of headgear for overall head and facial injuries, but a reduced risk of superficial scalp and face injuries has been observed among players wearing protective headgear (Jones et al., 2004). Furthermore, results of some observational studies point towards a reduction in concussion incidence in players that report wearing protective headgear during matches (Hollis et al., 2009; Kemp et al., 2008), while other observational studies do not support this association (Archbold et al., 2017; Stokes et al., 2021). An intervention study conducted in youth rugby players also upheld the lack of effect of padded headgear on reducing overall head injury or concussion outcomes, although it must be noted that compliance with using headgear was notably low in this study (McIntosh et al., 2009).

Given the influential roles that stakeholders can have on shaping player behaviour, educational initiatives targeting key stakeholders such as coaches and match officials offer a means of managing injury risk (Brown et al., 2018). The 'Rugby Smart' (New Zealand) and 'BokSmart' (South Africa) programmes are prominent examples of national education programmes that are used in rugby and have been studied extensively. The introduction of the 'Rugby Smart' programme in New Zealand coincided with the reduction of 54% in spinal injuries and 89% in scrum-related spinal injuries (Quarrie et al., 2007). Furthermore, implementation of 'Rugby Smart' has also been reported to correspond with reductions in certain injury types, such as knee (21% reduction), neck/spine (23% reduction) and leg injuries excluding the knee and ankle (by 19%), with improvements in player behaviours in relation to safe tackle, ruck and scrummaging techniques also noted (Gianotti et al., 2009). Building on the 'Rugby Smart' programme, the 'BokSmart' programme was implemented in South Africa to target a similar stakeholder group of coaches and match officials. The 'BokSmart' programme's introduction coincided with a 40% reduction in catastrophic injury incidence among junior rugby players, corresponding to 2.5 fewer catastrophic injuries per year (Brown et al., 2016). The potential mechanisms underpinning the effectiveness of the 'BokSmart' programme may include improvements in knowledge among coaches and match officials and safety behaviours exhibited by players (Brown et al., 2014, 2021).

Neuromuscular training programmes have typically been targeted at sports in which a relatively high proportion of lower limb non-contact injuries are reported (Longo et al., 2012; Soligard et al., 2008). However, recent studies have identified that a pre-activity movement control exercise programme delivered by coaches as part of pre-match and training warm-ups can similarly reduce injury risk in schoolboy and adult male rugby players (Barden et al., 2022; Hislop et al., 2017). Lower match-related injury outcomes were documented in teams using the movement control programme when compared with usual practice protocols, such as head/neck injury incidence (28% lower), upper limb injury burden (34% lower), soft-tissue injuries (40–52% lower) and concussion (29% lower). Analysing the effects of programme dose revealed that more frequent use of the programme magnified the observed reductions in injury outcomes, with match injury incidence shown to be 32–39% lower in teams that used the programme three or more times per week (on average) when compared with teams that did not use the programme as frequently (Barden et al., 2022; Hislop et al., 2017).

Practical Applications

The previous section provided a summary of the current research surrounding injury risk and risk reduction in youth rugby. Studies investigating strategies to reduce injury risk in youth rugby (or in other rugby-playing populations that could apply to youth rugby) have largely focused on reducing the risk of injuries that pose a significant threat to the subsequent health of players and the public profile of rugby. Conversely, few studies have investigated initiatives that might reduce the risk of milder yet more frequent injuries to the musculoskeletal system. Evidence emerging from several other field-based sports has illustrated the potential for pre-activity movement control or 'neuromuscular' training programmes, delivered by coaches as part of pre-training and match warm-up routines, as effective means of reducing non-contact induced soft-tissue injury risk (Emery et al., 2015). However, the effects of these programmes when used in more contact-orientated sports with differing injury profiles remained unknown until recently.

This practical application section details the Activate Injury Prevention Exercise Programme that was designed to reduce injury risk in schoolboy rugby players aged 14–18 years. The programme was developed and evaluated by the University of Bath (Hislop et al., 2016, 2017) and is now being implemented by various national governing bodies and World Rugby (international federation for rugby union).

Designing a Risk Reduction Strategy

Designing an injury risk reduction strategy is typically attempted following initial work to identify the prominent injuries suffered in a population of interest and the factors that may influence these injuries (Finch, 2006; van Mechelen et al., 1992). As the previous section of this chapter alludes to, much of the current scientific evidence base in youth rugby describes the injury patterns and few studies have identified modifiable injury risk factors. Consequently, scientific evidence may be of limited use in informing the design of an injury risk reduction strategy in youth rugby and so other sources of guidance must be sought.

Overemphasising scientific evidence during the development of a strategy over knowledge of the environment into which the strategy will be applied runs the risk that the strategy will be found ineffective because it fits poorly with the implementation context and so uptake is poor (Donaldson et al., 2016). On the other hand, overreliance on current practice or anecdotal evidence at the expense of scientific evidence could also undermine the strategy's effectiveness because the principles and mechanisms through which the strategy reduces injury risk have not been sufficiently applied (Finch, 2006). Consequently, developing an injury risk reduction strategy should reach a compromise that recognises the strengths and limitations of respective sources of information and leverages the strengths of these sources throughout the development process (Donaldson et al., 2016). Incorporating these information sources into a systematic, cohesive development process is likely to lead to a strategy that is both informed by scientific evidence and appropriate for the context into which it will be implemented.

The development process for the Activate programme included four key stages, which are detailed below.

Literature Review of Existing Programmes

The first stage of the development process was to review the scientific literature for exercise programmes used to reduce injury risk in sporting populations (hereafter referred to as 'preventive exercise programmes'). The goal of this first stage was to gain an understanding of the preventive exercise programmes that already existed, specifically:

- The aims of the programmes. If the programmes were intended to reduce injury risk, which injuries (locations and types) were targeted?
- The content of the programme (did programmes feature multiple training methods? Were any specific exercises included?)
- The structure of the programmes (i.e., did programmes contain different parts or levels of progression? If multiple training methods were included, how long was typically devoted to different training methods?)
- How long the programmes typically took to complete
- Which stakeholders were typically responsible for delivering the programme (did stakeholders require specialist knowledge or training to deliver the programme?)
- Other features of note that might influence the success or failure of the programme.

Table 15.3 summarises the preventive exercise programmes identified in the review. All reviewed programmes featured multiple training methods, among which resistance training, perturbation and plyometric activities, and rehearsal of landing/change of direction mechanics featured prominently. A separate review of preventive exercise programmes similarly concluded that multifaceted protocols including resistance and balance training tended to optimise outcomes in terms of injury risk reductions (Lauersen et al., 2014). Preventive exercise programmes may also need to introduce progression by increasing the difficulty of exercises being completed or the volume of repetitions to continually impart enough of a training stimulus to users. An additional benefit of progression is that the novel training stimulus may help to maintain user engagement while optimising the training benefits. The lack of exercise progression and sport-specific activities were cited as possible reasons for why the FIFA '11' programme (pre-cursor to the FIFA '11+') was not shown to reduce injury risks (Steffen et al., 2008). Changes made and presented in the updated FIFA '11+' programme appeared to reinforce these observations, with the updated progressive and sport-specific '11+' associated with greater compliance and notable reductions in injury risk (Soligard et al., 2008).

By combining the information sourced from the literature review with knowledge of whether the programmes had been shown to reduce injury risk, the review highlighted features of efficacious programmes that should be adopted and pitfalls of inefficacious programme that should be avoided in developing efficacious preventive exercise programmes in the future.

A further finding from the review was that all included programmes tended to focus on reducing the risk of lower limb injuries that were induced by non-contact mechanisms (i.e., landing and changing direction). Given the findings presented in the previous section of this chapter regarding injury patterns and mechanisms, adopting one of existing programmes may be appropriate in reducing the risk of lower limb injuries in youth rugby players but would neglect the upper body region that also incurs a notable injury burden. Consequently, the development of a novel training programme focused on reducing lower and upper body injury risk was deemed necessary.

Convene a Multidisciplinary Technical Project Group

Following the literature review, the next step in the development process aimed to comprehend the extent to which the information sourced from the scientific literature was applicable to the youth rugby context. A Technical Project Group (TPG) was convened to engage a range of stakeholders whose knowledge, experiences and perceptions could bring balance to discussions around the programme's content (i.e., scientific evidence and expert opinion) and context (i.e., end-user perceptions). The TPG was comprised of academics experienced in the design and implementation of preventive exercise programmes in other youth sports settings, clinicians working in youth and adult rugby settings, and active

TABLE 15.3 Summary of Existing Preventive Exercise Programmes Reviewed as part of the First Stage in the Development Process

Programme Name	Planned Duration	Training Methods	Progressions	Supporting Research	Research Demographic
Prevent Injury and Enhance Performance (PEP) Programme	20 minutes	• Running-based warm-up • Stretching – Trunk and Lower Limbs • Resistance Exercises • Plyometric exercises • Soccer-specific agility exercises	No	Mandelbaum et al. (2005) Gilchrist et al. (2008)	Female soccer players, aged 14–18 years Female soccer players, mean age 20 years
F-MARC '11+'	20 minutes	• Running-based warm-up • Active stretching • Lower limb resistance exercises • Lower limb balance exercises • Plyometric exercises • Soccer-specific agility exercises	Yes	Soligard et al. (2008) Longo et al. (2012) Grooms et al. (2013)	Female soccer players, aged 13–17 years Male basketball players, aged 11–24 years Male soccer players, aged 18–25 years
'HarmoKnee'	20–25 minutes	• Running-based warm-up • Muscle activation exercises • Lower limb balance exercises • Lower limb resistance exercises • Trunk/hip stability exercises	No	Kiani et al. (2010)	Female soccer players, aged 13–19 years
Knee Injury Prevention Programme (KIPP)	20 minutes	• Resistance exercises • Plyometric exercises • Balance exercises • Agility exercises	Yes	LaBella et al. (2011)	Female soccer/basketball players, mean age 16 years
Anterior Knee Pain Preventive Training Programme (AKP PTP)	15 minutes	• Lower limb closed-chain resistance exercises • Lower limb balance exercises • Lower limb stretching exercises	No	Coppack et al. (2011)	Female and male military recruits, aged 17–25 years

Injury Risk and Reduction Strategies **295**

coaches with backgrounds in strength and conditioning and community-level rugby. The TPG's remit primarily involved deciding upon the structure that the Activate programme would assume, in addition to informing discussions as to the barriers that users may encounter in implementing the programme, the delivery method for the programme, the stakeholders best placed to deliver the programme, and what resources would be needed to assist stakeholders in applying the programme.

Figure 15.1 illustrates the considerations made during the meeting in relation to the structure and content of evidence-based preventive exercise programmes and the logistical/environmental constraints within the implementation context. The following outputs came from this meeting:

- The agreed programme structure would be required to:
  - Contain a variety of training methods
  - Progress exercises at regular intervals either through increasing the repetition volume or the difficulty of exercises
  - Last no longer than 15–20 minutes in duration, once stakeholders had been familiarised with the programme
  - Incorporate an introductory level of exercises that could be implemented during the pre-season period to familiarise users with the programme

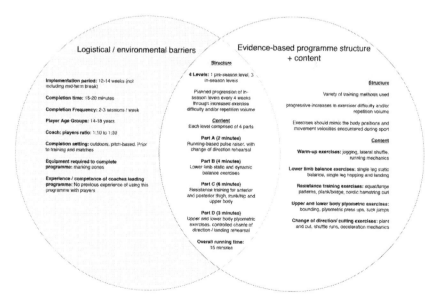

FIGURE 15.1 Venn Diagram Outlining Considerations for Developing the Activate Injury Prevention Exercise Programme to Account for both Logistical and Environmental Barriers to Using the Programme and the Existing Scientific Evidence Base for Preventive Exercise Programme Structure and Content (adapted from Hislop, 2017).

- School rugby coaches were identified as being best placed to deliver the programme to players
- Support for coaches involved in delivering the programme should include a face-to-face workshop delivered during the off or pre-season period to introduce coaches to the programme. Further information should be accessible and in the form of a programme manual detailing the programme structure and implementation procedures, cue cards that could be used as a memory aid by coaches as they delivered the programme, and video clips of individual exercises being completed to provide a visual reference.

Following the TPG meeting, the programme structure was populated with exercises and progressions. Exercises were included with input from other preventive exercise programmes. Certain exercises were backed by a particularly strong evidence base, such as the Nordic Hamstring Extension (Arnason et al., 2008; Mjølsnes et al., 2004). Where the evidence for training methods in reducing the risk of certain injury types, or the physical capabilities of the target beneficiaries of the programme were uncertain, the TPG were consulted for their input. For example, evidence-based training methods adopted in reducing the risk of upper limb injuries were lacking in the literature and so the selection of exercises and progressions targeting the upper limb were largely decided by the TPG.

The structure and content of the introductory workshop were also considered. The rationale and potential benefits of the programme should be explained to coaches, while endorsement of the programme by the national governing body for rugby union would be publicised. In addition, the development process and particularly the input from coaching peers during the process should be outlined to improve acceptability. Discussions between the workshop leader and coaches attending the workshop should also instil knowledge among coaches of when, where and how the programme should be delivered. Finally, the workshop should feature a practical demonstration of a sample session using the programme so that coaches have a visual reference of programme delivery under typical conditions, particularly the process applied in coaching the exercises to players. The workshop leader would begin by explaining the rationale for the programme to players, provide a demonstration of each exercise, before using two to three relevant movement cues to reinforce good execution or correct errors observed among players.

Pilot Testing

Following confirmation of the programme structure and content by the TPG, the next stage featured having the programme tested by coaches under realistic use conditions. This step would be crucial in satisfying whether the programme would be acceptable to deliverers and players, while engaging with end users provided opportunity to receive feedback on suggested changes to the programme ahead of a more comprehensive roll-out. The programme was implemented in six teams from two schools.

All coaches attached to U15, U16 and U18 teams attended an introductory workshop in which instructions were relayed on how to implement the programme with their players, and a practical demonstration of a sample session using the programme was given using a small group of players to reflect the likely scenario under which the programme would be delivered. Coaches also received support materials (manual, cue cards and a DVD containing video clips of individual exercises) at this workshop. Coaches were advised to deliver the programme as often as possible with their players and received prompts to advance to a new level throughout the playing season.

Piloting the programme over an entire season rather than during a small number of sessions was felt to be advantageous because this approach more accurately reflected the realities of using the programme on a regular basis (Donaldson et al., 2016). A further consequence of piloting the programme over the entire season was that coaches were able to comprehensively review and feedback on their experiences with the programme, including the following features:

- Progression through different levels of the programme
- Growing accustomed to coaching individual exercises
- Encountering barriers to using the programme and strategies used in overcoming barriers where possible
- Reporting modifications to the programme or delivery
- Using the programme support materials

Seek Feedback from End Users

Following the playing season, feedback was sought from coaches delivering the programme. One of the two schools piloting the programme dropped out during the playing season due to reasons external of piloting the programme, however feedback was still sought from coaches at both schools.

Although the programme content was generally felt to be appropriate to the players' collective physical development needs, the programme was not perceived to be adequately stimulating for the older age groups while younger age groups felt the content was adequate. To promote uptake of the programme and provide players with a sufficient training stimulus, coaches supported the programme being modified between the age groups while still retaining the same training methods. Consequently, the programme structure was offset between each age group, as Figure 15.2 illustrates. This change led to the creation of two additional levels within the programme to cater to the U16 and U18 age groups.

One prominent change to the programme content was the inclusion of resistance training exercises targeting the neck region. This need was corroborated by consulting the scientific literature, with studies suggesting that neck strength profiles varied notably amongst youth rugby players aged 11–18 years

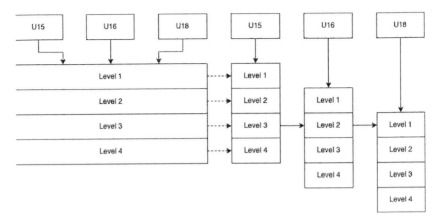

FIGURE 15.2 Changes to Activate Programme Structure Following End User Feedback (adapted from Hislop, 2017).

(Hamilton et al., 2012), and that U18 players were reported to have distinctly lower neck strength profiles than adult counterparts despite having similar peripheral strength profiles (Hamilton et al., 2014). The TPG agreed with this recommendation, following which examples of conditioning activities targeting the neck region were sought. No appropriate protocols were forthcoming from the scientific literature, and so examples of international best practice were incorporated into the Activate programme (Viljoen, 2009). Given the reported variations in neck strength within and between youth rugby age groups (Hamilton et al., 2012), it seemed appropriate that the neck conditioning exercises and progressions should be similar in difficulty across all age groups. The inclusion of the neck conditioning activities forced the volume of other exercises to be reduced to keep to the agreed time limit of 15–20 minutes. Further feedback from the coaches favoured excluding the Nordic Hamstring Extension from pre-match warm-ups due to players reporting feelings of muscle soreness following completion of the exercise.

Figures 15.3–15.6 illustrate an example set of exercises from Level 1 of the U15 version of the Activate Injury Prevention Exercise Programme. All exercises within the four parts are designed to be completed over the course of training sessions and pre-match warm-ups. Part A of the programme includes pulse-raising activities, with some change of direction rehearsal. Part B follows, incorporating lower limb static and dynamic balancing exercises. Most of the exercises and time dedicated to the programme in a session are devoted to resistance training activities that target specific areas of the body and include the front and back of the thigh, trunk, upper limb and neck regions (Part C). The programme concludes with part D, which contains exercises to practice landing and change of direction mechanics, and plyometric exercises targeting the upper and lower limb regions.

The programme can be used outdoors or on an indoor sports hall and requires no equipment other than marking cones. Other equipment such as rugby

Injury Risk and Reduction Strategies **299**

Part A

Running activities to warm-up and develop control and technique when changing direction

Snake Run

Sets: 1   Repetitions: 2   Distance: 15 metres

Coaching Points:
- Using the full width of the channel, alternate swerving from left to right while running
- Drive the outside leg across the body to swerve

Key Cues:
- Chest up

Walking Crunch

Sets: 1   Repetitions: 2   Distance: 15 metres

Coaching Points:
- Shuffle forward two steps and then raise one leg up straight in front of the body
- Bring the opposite elbow to the knee of the raised leg by bending at the waist

Key Cues:
- Brace through the trunk
- Hip, knee, ankle in line

Plant and Cut

Sets: 2   Repetitions: 2   Distance: 15 metres

Coaching Points:
- Begin running diagonally to the left or right
- Plant the outside foot and cut to run diagonally in the other direction
- Alternate between cutting left and right

Key Cues:
- Chest up
- Brace through the trunk
- Hip, knee, ankle in line

FIGURE 15.3 Sample Running and Change of Direction Exercises from Level 1 of U15 Version of Programme (sourced from World Rugby, 2022).

Part B

Balancing exercises to develop movement control and stability in the lower body and trunk

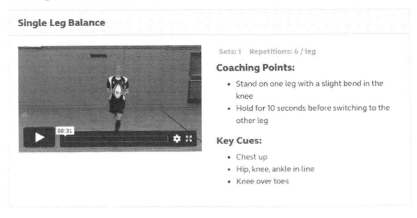

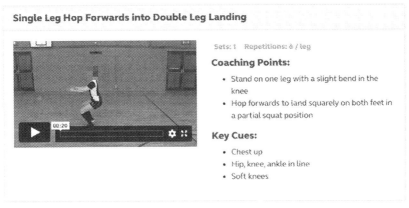

FIGURE 15.4 Sample Lower Limb Balance and Landing Exercises from Level 1 of U15 Version of Programme(sourced from World Rugby, 2022).

balls can be introduced providing that their introduction does not detract from the purpose of completing the exercises. Other modifications to delivering the programme are welcome and coaches are encouraged to modify the delivery to suit their circumstances, providing that the programme remains purposeful, enjoyable, and safe. Figure 15.7 illustrates an example layout for completing the programme.

Coaches should introduce their players to the programme during the pre-season period so that everyone is familiarised with the programme by the time the season begins. It is possible for the programme to be taken on at later stages of the playing season, but coaches should still start at the first level of the programme. Progressing to new levels of exercises should be considered after 4–8 weeks depending on playing season length and how often the programme will

Injury Risk and Reduction Strategies **301**

Part C

Bodyweight or partner resistance activities to develop strength and control through the lower body, upper body, and neck area

Zombie Squat

Sets: 1   Repetitions: 8

Coaching Points:
- Stand with feet a little wider than shoulder-width apart and arms raised in front at shoulder-height
- Squat down until thighs are parallel with the ground before returning to starting position
- Keep heels in contact with the ground throughout the exercise

Key Cues:
- Chest up
- Brace through the trunk
- Hip, knee, ankle in line

Double Leg Glute Bridge

Sets: 1   Repetitions: 8

Coaching Points:
- Lie face-up with hips and knees flexed
- Plant feet close to buttocks
- Raise hips and back from the ground to make a straight line from the shoulders to the knees

Key Cues:
- Brace through the trunk

Front Bridge

Sets: 1   Repetitions: 1   Duration: 30 seconds

Coaching Points:
- Start facing down and resting on the forearms and balls of feet
- Brace through the trunk to keep shoulders and hips aligned and away from the ground

Key Cues:
- Pinch the shoulders together
- Shoulders level with hips
- Brace through the trunk

FIGURE 15.5 Sample Resistance Training Exercises from Level 1 of U15 Version of Activate Programme (sourced from World Rugby, 2022).

Part D

Landing, change of direction, and plyometric training to develop power and control

FIGURE 15.6 Sample Landing and Plyometric Exercises from Level 1 of U15 Version of Activate Programme (sourced from World Rugby, 2022).

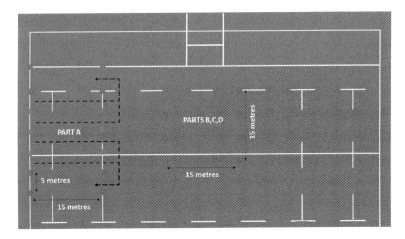

FIGURE 15.7 Sample Pitch Layout for Completing the Activate Programme (sourced from World Rugby, 2022).

be used each week. Certain exercises may also be modified within each level to help individual players within the playing group.

Coaches should be prepared for the programme to take a little longer than planned when introducing new exercises to their players. However, this duration will lessen as players become familiar with completing the exercises. Another important feature is the coaching process, which includes observing players and providing feedback. Coaches should begin by explaining why players are completing the exercises, followed by providing demonstrations of exercises (either using themselves or a player), and reiterating key movement cues to players. To help coaches with observing and correcting movements, a shortlist of movement cues has been provided, of which two to three apply to each exercise:

- Head Neutral/Head Lifted
- Chest Up
- Pinch the shoulders together
- Shoulders level with hips
- Brace through the trunk
- Soft Knees
- Hip, Knee, Ankle in Line
- Knee over Toes

Key Take Home Messages

- Reducing injury risk in a given sport or playing group relies heavily on access to robust and accurate epidemiological data that illustrates priority injuries.
- Priority injuries may be those that occur the most frequently; incur a substantial burden in terms of time-loss, complications in later-life health, or financial costs of treatment; or that carry the greatest damage to the reputation of the sport.
- Once priority injuries have been identified, further work is necessary in identifying factors that may increase or decrease the risk of these priority injuries occurring.
- The process of designing and developing an injury risk reduction strategy features several steps that should access various important sources of information: scientific literature, expert knowledge and end-user experience. It is important that a balance is found between these sources of information, as overreliance on one source could undermine the effectiveness of the strategy.
- The development of a risk reduction strategy must also consider the way the strategy will be delivered, who will be responsible for delivering the strategy, and the support required for delivering the strategy.
- Involving end users of injury reduction strategies throughout the design and development process is recommended. Their involvement can help to ensure that developed strategies balance the need to be evidence-informed with the need to be context-appropriate.

References

Abernethy, L., & MacAuley, D. (2003). Impact of school sports injury. *British Journal of Sports Medicine, 37*, 354–355. https://doi.org/10.1136/bjsm.37.4.354

Alexander, D. G., Shuttleworth-Edwards, A. B., Kidd, M., & Malcolm, C. M. (2015). Mild traumatic brain injuries in early adolescent rugby players: Long-term neurocognitive and academic outcomes. *Brain Injury, 29*, 1113–1125. https://doi.org/10.3109/02699052.2015.1031699

Alsop, J. C., Chalmers, D. J., Williams, S. M., Quarrie, K. L., Marshall, S. W., & Sharples, K. J. (2000). Temporal patterns of injury during a rugby season. *Journal of Science and Medicine in Sport, 3*, 97–109. https://doi.org/10.1016/s1440-2440(00)80072-9

Archbold, H. A., Rankin, A. T., Webb, M., Davies, R., Nicholas, R., Eames, N. W. A., Wilson, R. K., Vincent, J., McKeever, D., & Duddy, K. (2021). Injury patterns in U15 rugby players in Ulster schools: A Rugby Injury Surveillance (RISUS) Study. *Translational Sports Medicine, 4*, 524–533. https://doi.org/10.1002/tsm2.248

Archbold, H. A., Rankin, A. T., Webb, M., Nicholas, R., Eames, N. W., Wilson, R. K., Henderson, L. A., Heyes, G. J., & Bleakley, C. M. (2017). RISUS study: Rugby Injury Surveillance in Ulster Schools. *British Journal of Sports Medicine, 51*, 600–606. https://doi.org/10.1136/bjsports-2015-095491

Arnason, A., Andersen, T. E., Holme, I., Engebretsen, L., & Bahr, R. (2008). Prevention of hamstring strains in elite soccer: An intervention study. *Scandinavian Journal of Medicine and Science in Sports, 18*, 40–48. https://doi.org/10.1111/j.1600-0838.2006.00634.x

Badenhorst, M., Brown, J. C., Lambert, M. I., Van Mechelen, W., & Verhagen, E. (2018). Quality of life among individuals with rugby-related spinal cord injuries in South Africa: A descriptive cross-sectional study. *BMJ Open, 8*, e020890. https://doi.org/10.1136/bmjopen-2017-020890

Barden, C., Bekker, S., Brown, J. C., Stokes, K. A., & McKay, C. D. (2021). Evaluating the implementation of injury prevention strategies in rugby Union and League: A systematic review using the RE-AIM framework. *International Journal of Sports Medicine, 42*, 112–121. https://doi.org/10.1055/a-1212-0649

Barden, C., Hancock, M. V., Stokes, K. A., Roberts, S. P., & McKay, C. D. (2022). Effectiveness of the activate injury prevention exercise programme to prevent injury in schoolboy rugby union. *British Journal of Sports Medicine*, bjsports-2021-105170. https://doi.org/10.1136/bjsports-2021-105170

Barden, C., & Stokes, K. (2018). Epidemiology of injury in Elite English Schoolboy Rugby Union: A 3-year study comparing different competitions. *Journal of Athletic Training, 53*, 514–520. https://doi.org/10.4085/1062-6050-311-16

Beakey, M., Tiernan, S., & Collins, K. (2018). Why do adolescent rugby players under-report concussion? An examination into the variables that influence their behavioural intention to report across three samples. *European Journal of Sports Medicine, 4*, 65–76.

Bird, Y. N., Waller, A. E., Marshall, S. W., Alsop, J. C., Chalmers, D. J., & Gerrard, D. F. (1998). The New Zealand Rugby Injury and Performance Project: V. Epidemiology of a season of rugby injury. *British Journal of Sports Medicine, 32*, 319–325. https://doi.org/10.1136/bjsm.32.4.319

Booth, M., Cobley, S., & Orr, R. (2019). Does a higher training age attenuate injury risk in junior elite rugby league players? *International Journal of Sports Science & Coaching, 14*, 779–785. https://doi.org/10.1177/1747954119883620

Booth, M., & Orr, R. (2017). Time-loss injuries in sub-elite and emerging rugby league players. *Journal of Sports Science & Medicine, 16*, 295.

Broad, M., & Welbury, R. (2015). Club policies for mouth protectors and dental emergency cover in Scottish Rugby Union (SRU) affiliated junior teams. *Primary Dental Journal, 4*, 38–43. https://doi.org/10.1308/205016815816682263

Brown, J. C., Gardner-Lubbe, S., Lambert, M. I., Van Mechelen, W., & Verhagen, E. (2014). The BokSmart intervention programme is associated with improvements in injury prevention behaviours of rugby union players: An ecological cross-sectional study. *Injury Prevention*, injuryprev-2014–041326. https://doi.org/10.1136/injuryprev-2014-041326

Brown, J. C., Gardner-Lubbe, S., Lambert, M. I., van Mechelen, W., & Verhagen, E. (2018). Coach-directed education is associated with injury-prevention behaviour in players: an ecological cross-sectional study. *British Journal of Sports Medicine, 52*, 989–993. https://doi.org/10.1136/bjsports-2016-096757

Brown, J. C., Hendricks, S., Lambert, M. I., Van Mechelen, W., & Verhagen, E. (2021). BokSmart rugby safety education courses are associated with improvements in behavioural determinants in attending coaches and referees: presurvey–postsurvey study. *Injury Prevention, 27*, 363–368. https://doi.org/10.1136/injuryprev-2020-043903

Brown, J. C., Lambert, M. I., Verhagen, E., Readhead, C., van Mechelen, W., & Viljoen, W. (2013). The incidence of rugby-related catastrophic injuries (including cardiac events) in South Africa from 2008 to 2011: A cohort study. *BMJ Open, 3*. https://doi.org/10.1136/bmjopen-2012-002475

Brown, J. C., Verhagen, E., Knol, D., Van Mechelen, W., & Lambert, M. I. (2016). The effectiveness of the nationwide BokSmart rugby injury prevention program on catastrophic injury rates. *Scandinavian Journal of Medicine and Science in Sports, 26*, 221–225. https://doi.org/10.1111/sms.12414

Brown, J. C., Verhagen, E., Viljoen, W., Readhead, C., Van Mechelen, W., Hendricks, S., & Lambert, M. I. (2012). The incidence and severity of injuries at the 2011 South African Rugby Union (SARU) Youth Week tournaments. *South African Journal of Sports Medicine, 24*. https://doi.org/10.17159/2078-516X/2012/v24i2a345

Brown, J. C., Viljoen, W., Lambert, M. I., Readhead, C., Fuller, C., Van Mechelen, W., & Verhagen, E. (2015). The economic burden of time-loss injuries to youth players participating in week-long rugby union tournaments. *Journal of Science and Medicine in Sport, 18*, 394–399. https://doi.org/10.1016/j.jsams.2014.06.015

Burger, N., Lambert, M. I., Viljoen, W., Brown, J. C., Readhead, C., den Hollander, S., & Hendricks, S. (2017). Mechanisms and factors associated with tackle-related injuries in South African Youth Rugby Union Players. *American Journal of Sports Medicine, 45*, 278–285. https://doi.org/10.1177/0363546516677548

Burger, N., Lambert, M. I., Viljoen, W., Brown, J. C., Readhead, C., & Hendricks, S. (2014). Tackle-related injury rates and nature of injuries in South African youth week tournament rugby union players (under-13 to under-18): An observational cohort study. *BMJ Open, 4*, e005556. https://doi.org/10.1136/bmjopen-2014-005556

Burger, N., Lambert, M. I., Viljoen, W., Brown, J. C., Readhead, C., & Hendricks, S. (2016). Tackle technique and tackle-related injuries in high-level South African Rugby Union under-18 players: Real-match video analysis. *British Journal of Sports Medicine, 50*, 932–938. https://doi.org/10.1136/bjsports-2015-095295

Carter, M. (2015). The unknown risks of youth rugby. *BMJ, 350*, h26. https://doi.org/10.1136/bmj.h26

Clacy, A., Goode, N., Sharman, R., Lovell, G. P., & Salmon, P. M. (2017). A knock to the system: A new sociotechnical systems approach to sport-related concussion. *Journal of Sports Sciences, 35*, 2232–2239. https://doi.org/10.1080/02640414.2016.1265140

Clacy, A., Goode, N., Sharman, R., Lovell, G. P., & Salmon, P. M. (2019). A systems approach to understanding the identification and treatment of sport-related concussion in community rugby union. *Applied Ergonomics, 80,* 256–264. https://doi.org/10.1016/j.apergo.2017.06.010

Collins, C. L., Micheli, L. J., Yard, E. E., & Comstock, R. D. (2008). Injuries sustained by high school rugby players in the United States, 2005–2006. *Archives of Pediatrics & Adolescent Medicine, 162,* 49–54. https://doi.org/10.1001/archpediatrics.2007.1

Coppack, R. J., Etherington, J., & Wills, A. K. (2011). The effects of exercise for the prevention of overuse anterior knee pain: A randomized controlled trial. *American Journal of Sports Medicine, 39,* 940–948. https://doi.org/10.1177/0363546510393269

Cunningham, J., Broglio, S., & Wilson, F. (2018). Influence of playing rugby on long-term brain health following retirement: A systematic review and narrative synthesis. *BMJ Open Sport & Exercise Medicine, 4,* e000356. https://doi.org/10.1136/bmjsem-2018-000356

Darrall-Jones, J. D., Jones, B., & Till, K. (2015). Anthropometric and physical profiles of English Academy Rugby Union Players. *Journal of Strength and Conditioning Research, 29,* 2086–2096. https://doi.org/10.1519/JSC.0000000000000872

Darrall-Jones, J. D., Jones, B., & Till, K. (2016). Anthropometric, sprint, and high-intensity running profiles of English Academy Rugby Union Players by position. *Journal of Strength and Conditioning Research, 30,* 1348–1358. https://doi.org/10.1519/JSC.0000000000001234

Davidow, D., Redman, M., Lambert, M., Burger, N., Smith, M., Jones, B., & Hendricks, S. (2020). The effect of physical fatigue on tackling technique in Rugby Union. *Journal of Science and Medicine in Sport, 23,* 1105–1110. https://doi.org/10.1016/j.jsams.2020.04.005

Davidson, R. M., Kennedy, M., Kennedy, J., & Vanderfield, G. (1978). Casualty room presentations and schoolboy rugby union. *Medical Journal of Australia, 1,* 247–249. https://doi.org/10.5694/j.1326-5377.1978.tb112516.x

Davies, M. A. M., Judge, A. D., Delmestri, A., PT Kemp, S., Stokes, K. A., Arden, N. K., & Newton, J. L. (2017). Health amongst former rugby union players: A cross-sectional study of morbidity and health-related quality of life. *Scientific Reports, 7,* 11786. https://doi.org/10.1038/s41598-017-12130-y

Davis, G. A., Anderson, V., Babl, F. E., Gioia, G. A., Giza, C. C., Meehan, W., Moser, R. S., Purcell, L., Schatz, P., Schneider, K. J., Takagi, M., Yeates, K. O., & Zemek, R. (2017). What is the difference in concussion management in children as compared with adults? A systematic review. *British Journal of Sports Medicine, 51,* 949–957. https://doi.org/10.1136/bjsports-2016-097415

Delahunty, S. E., Delahunt, E., Condon, B., Toomey, D., & Blake, C. (2015). Prevalence of and attitudes about concussion in Irish schools' rugby union players. *Journal of School Health, 85,* 17–26. https://doi.org/0.1111/josh.12219

Donaldson, A., Lloyd, D. G., Gabbe, B. J., Cook, J., Young, W., White, P., & Finch, C. F. (2016). Scientific evidence is just the starting point: A generalizable process for developing sports injury prevention interventions. *Journal of Sport and Health Science, 5,* 334–341. https://doi.org/10.1016/j.jshs.2016.08.003

Durie, R. (2000). A prospective survey of injuries in a New Zealand schoolboy rugby population. *New Zealand Journal of Sports Medicine, 28,* 84–90.

Dyer, C. S., Callister, R., Sanctuary, C. E., & Snodgrass, S. J. (2019). Functional Movement Screening and injury risk in elite adolescent rugby league players. *International Journal of Sports Science & Coaching, 14,* 498–506. https://doi.org/10.1177/1747954119853650

Emery, C. A., Roy, T. O., Whittaker, J. L., Nettel-Aguirre, A., & van Mechelen, W. (2015). Neuromuscular training injury prevention strategies in youth sport: A systematic review and meta-analysis. *British Journal of Sports Medicine, 49*, 865–870. https://doi.org/10.1136/bjsports-2015-094639

Finch, C. F. (2006). A new framework for research leading to sports injury prevention. *Journal of Science and Medicine in Sport, 9*, 3–9; discussion 10. https://doi.org/10.1016/j.jsams.2006.02.009

Freitag, A., Kirkwood, G., & Pollock, A. M. (2015a). Rugby injury surveillance and prevention programmes: Are they effective? *BMJ, 350*, h1587. https://doi.org/10.1136/bmj.h1587

Freitag, A., Kirkwood, G., Scharer, S., Ofori-Asenso, R., & Pollock, A. M. (2015b). Systematic review of rugby injuries in children and adolescents under 21 years. *British Journal of Sports Medicine, 49*, 511–519. https://doi.org/10.1136/bjsports-2014-093684

Fuller, C. W., Molloy, M. G., & Marsalli, M. (2011). Epidemiological study of injuries in Men's International Under-20 Rugby Union Tournaments. *Clinical Journal of Sport Medicine, 21*, 356–358. https://doi.org/10.1097/JSM.0b013e31821f5085

Gabbett, T. J. (2006). Performance changes following a field conditioning program in junior and senior rugby league players. *Journal of Strength and Conditioning Research, 20*, 215–221. https://doi.org/10.1519/R-16554.1

Gabbett, T. J. (2008). Incidence of injury in junior rugby league players over four competitive seasons. *Journal of Science and Medicine in Sport, 11*, 323–328. https://doi.org/10.1016/j.jsams.2007.06.003

Gardner, A. J., Howell, D. R., & Iverson, G. L. (2020). The association between multiple prior concussions, cognitive test scores, and symptom reporting in youth rugby league players. *Brain Injury, 34*, 224–228. https://doi.org/10.1080/02699052.2019.1683894

Gianotti, S. M., Quarrie, K. L., & Hume, P. A. (2009). Evaluation of RugbySmart: A rugby union community injury prevention programme. *Journal of Science and Medicine in Sport, 12*, 371–375. https://doi.org/10.1016/j.jsams.2008.01.002

Gilchrist, J., Mandelbaum, B. R., Melancon, H., Ryan, G. W., Silvers, H. J., Griffin, L. Y., Watanabe, D. S., Randall, W. D., & Dvorak, J. (2008). A randomized controlled trial to prevent noncontact anterior cruciate ligament injury in female collegiate soccer players. *American Journal of Sports Medicine, 36*, 1476–1483. https://doi.org/10.1177/0363546508318188

Griffin, S. A., Perera, N. K. P., Murray, A., Hartley, C., Fawkner, S. G., Kemp, S. P., Stokes, K. A., & Kelly, P. (2021). The relationships between rugby union, and health and well-being: A scoping review. *British Journal of Sports Medicine, 55*, 319–326. http://dx.doi.org/10.1136/bjsports-2020-102085

Grooms, D. R., Palmer, T., Onate, J. A., Myer, G. D., & Grindstaff, T. (2013). Soccer-specific warm-up and lower extremity injury rates in collegiate male soccer players. *Journal of Athletic Training, 48*, 782–789. https://doi.org/10.4085/1062-6050-48.4.08

Hamilton, D. F., Gatherer, D., Jenkins, P. J., Maclean, J. G., Hutchison, J. D., Nutton, R. W., & Simpson, A. H. (2012). Age-related differences in the neck strength of adolescent rugby players A cross-sectional cohort study of Scottish schoolchildren. *Bone and Joint Research, 1*, 152–157. https://doi.org/10.1302/2046-3758.17.2000079

Hamilton, D. F., Gatherer, D., Robson, J., Graham, N., Rennie, N., Maclean, J. G., & Simpson, A. H. (2014). Comparative cervical profiles of adult and under-18 front-row rugby players: Implications for playing policy. *BMJ Open, 4*, e004975–e004975. https://doi.org/10.1136/bmjopen-2014-004975

Hartwig, T. B., Gabbett, T. J., Naughton, G., Duncan, C., Harries, S., & Perry, N. (2019). Training and match volume and injury in adolescents playing multiple contact team sports: A prospective cohort study. *Scandinavian Journal of Medicine and Science in Sports, 29*, 469–475. https://doi.org/10.1111/sms.13343

Hartwig, T. B., Naughton, G., & Searl, J. (2011). Motion analyses of adolescent rugby union players: A comparison of training and game demands. *Journal of Strength and Conditioning Research, 25*, 966–972. https://doi.org/10.1519/JSC.0b013e3181d09e24

Haseler, C. M., Carmont, M. R., & England, M. (2010). The epidemiology of injuries in English youth community rugby union. *British Journal of Sports Medicine, 44*, 1093–1099. https://doi.org/10.1136/bjsm.2010.074021

Hendricks, S., & Lambert, M. (2010). Tackling in Rugby: Coaching strategies for effective technique and injury prevention. *International Journal of Sports Science & Coaching, 5*, 117–135. https://doi.org/10.1260/1747-9541.5.1.117

Hendricks, S., O'Connor, S., Lambert, M., Brown, J. C., Burger, N., Mc Fie, S., Readhead, C., & Viljoen, W. (2015). Contact technique and concussions in the South African under-18 Coca-Cola Craven Week Rugby tournament. *European Journal of Sport Science, 15*, 557–564. https://doi.org/10.1080/17461391.2015.1046192

Hendricks, S., O'Connor, S., Lambert, M., Brown, J. C., Burger, N., Mc Fie, S., Readhead, C., & Viljoen, W. (2016). Video analysis of concussion injury mechanism in under-18 rugby. *BMJ Open Sport & Exercise Medicine, 2*, e000053–e000053. https://doi.org/10.1136/bmjsem-2015-000053

Hislop, M. (2017) *Injury risk factors and preventive strategies in schoolboy Rugby Union*. Unpublished thesis, University of Bath.

Hislop, M. D., Stokes, K. A., Williams, S., McKay, C. D., England, M., Kemp, S. P., & Trewartha, G. (2016). The efficacy of a movement control exercise programme to reduce injuries in youth rugby: A cluster randomised controlled trial. *BMJ Open Sport & Exercise Medicine, 2*, e000043. https://doi.org/10.1136/bmjsem-2015-000043

Hislop, M. D., Stokes, K. A., Williams, S., McKay, C. D., England, M. E., Kemp, S. P. T., & Trewartha, G. (2017). Reducing musculoskeletal injury and concussion risk in schoolboy rugby players with a pre-activity movement control exercise programme: A cluster randomised controlled trial. *British Journal of Sports Medicine, 51*, 1140–1146. https://doi.org/10.1136/bjsports-2016-097434

Hollis, S. J., Stevenson, M. R., McIntosh, A. S., Li, L., Heritier, S., Shores, E. A., Collins, M. W., & Finch, C. F. (2011). Mild traumatic brain injury among a cohort of rugby union players: Predictors of time to injury. *British Journal of Sports Medicine, 45*, 997–999. https://doi.org/10.1136/bjsm.2010.079707

Hollis, S. J., Stevenson, M. R., McIntosh, A. S., Shores, E. A., Collins, M. W., & Taylor, C. B. (2009). Incidence, risk, and protective factors of mild traumatic brain injury in a cohort of Australian nonprofessional male rugby players. *American Journal of Sports Medicine, 37*, 2328–2333. https://doi.org/10.1177/0363546509341032

Hollis, S. J., Stevenson, M. R., McIntosh, A. S., Shores, E. A., & Finch, C. F. (2012). Compliance with return-to-play regulations following concussion in Australian schoolboy and community rugby union players. *British Journal of Sports Medicine, 46*, 735–740. https://doi.org/10.1136/bjsm.2011.085332

Hume, P. A., Quarrie, K. L., Lewis, G. N., & Theadom, A. (2022). NZ-RugbyHealth study: Self-reported injury experience and current health of Former Rugby Union and Non-contact Sport Players. *Sports Medicine*. https://doi.org/10.1007/s40279-021-01630-7

Hume, P. A., Theadom, A., Lewis, G. N., Quarrie, K. L., Brown, S. R., Hill, R., & Marshall, S. W. (2017). A comparison of cognitive function in Former

Rugby Union Players compared with Former Non-Contact-Sport Players and the impact of concussion history. *Sports Medicine, 47*, 1209–1220. https://doi.org/10.1007/s40279-016-0608-8

Inglis, P. R., Doma, K., & Deakin, G. B. (2019). The incidence and occurrence of injuries to junior rugby league players in a tropical environment. *Journal of Human Kinetics, 67*, 101. https://doi.org/10.2478/hukin-2018-0075

Iwamoto, J., Abe, H., Tsukimura, Y., & Wakano, K. (2005). Relationship between radiographic abnormalities of lumbar spine and incidence of low back pain in high school rugby players: A prospective study. *Scandinavian Journal of Medicine and Science in Sports, 15*, 163–168. https://doi.org/10.1111/j.1600-0838.2004.00414.x

Jones, B., Weaving, D., Tee, J., Darrall-Jones, J., Weakley, J., Phibbs, P., Read, D., Roe, G., Hendricks, S., & Till, K. (2018). Bigger, stronger, faster, fitter: The differences in physical qualities of school and academy rugby union players. *Journal of Sports Sciences, 36*, 2399–2404. https://doi.org/10.1080/02640414.2018.1458589

Jones, S. J., Lyons, R. A., Evans, R., Newcombe, R. G., Nash, P., McCabe, M., & Palmer, S. R. (2004). Effectiveness of rugby headgear in preventing soft tissue injuries to the head: A case-control and video cohort study. *British Journal of Sports Medicine, 38*, 159–162. https://doi.org/10.1136/bjsm.2002.002584

Junge, A., Cheung, K., Edwards, T., & Dvorak, J. (2004). Injuries in youth amateur soccer and rugby players--comparison of incidence and characteristics. *British Journal of Sports Medicine, 38*, 168–172. https://doi.org/10.1136/bjsm.2002.003020

Kearney, P. E., & See, J. (2017). Misunderstandings of concussion within a youth rugby population. *Journal of Science and Medicine in Sport, 20*, 981–985. https://doi.org/10.1016/j.jsams.2017.04.019

Kemp, S. P. T., Hudson, Z., Brooks, J. H. M., & Fuller, C. W. (2008). The epidemiology of head injuries in English professional rugby union. *Clinical Journal of Sport Medicine, 18*, 227–234. https://doi.org/10.1097/JSM.0b013e31816a1c9a

Kerr, H. A., Curtis, C., Micheli, L. J., Kocher, M. S., Zurakowski, D., Kemp, S. P., & Brooks, J. H. (2008). Collegiate rugby union injury patterns in New England: A prospective cohort study. *British Journal of Sports Medicine, 42*, 595–603. https://doi.org/10.1136/bjsm.2007.035881

Kiani, A., Hellquist, E., Ahlqvist, K., Gedeborg, R., Michaélsson, K., & Byberg, L. (2010). Prevention of soccer-related knee injuries in teenaged girls. *Archives of Internal Medicine, 170*, 43–49. https://doi.org/10.1001/archinternmed.2009.289

King, D., Hume, P. A., Hardaker, N., Cummins, C., Clark, T., Pearce, A. J., & Gissane, C. (2019). Female rugby union injuries in New Zealand: A review of five years (2013–2017) of Accident Compensation Corporation moderate to severe claims and costs. *Journal of Science and Medicine in Sport, 22*, 532–537. https://doi.org/10.1016/j.jsams.2018.10.015

King, D. A. (2006). Incidence of injuries in the 2006 New Zealand national junior rugby league competition. *New Zealand Journal of Sports Medicine, 34*, 21.

King, D. A., Clark, T. N., Hume, P. A., & Hind, K. (2022). Match and training injury incidence in rugby league: A systematic review, pooled analysis, and update on published studies. *Sports Medicine and Health Science*. https://doi.org/10.1016/j.smhs.2022.03.002

LaBella, C. R., Huxford, M. R., Grissom, J., Kim, K. Y., Peng, J., & Christoffel, K. K. (2011). Effect of neuromuscular warm-up on injuries in female soccer and basketball athletes in urban public high schools: Cluster randomized controlled trial. *Archives of Pediatrics and Adolescent Medicine, 165*, 1033–1040. https://doi.org/10.1001/archpediatrics.2011.168

Lauersen, J. B., Bertelsen, D. M., & Andersen, L. B. (2014). The effectiveness of exercise interventions to prevent sports injuries: A systematic review and meta-analysis of randomised controlled trials. *British Journal of Sports Medicine, 48*, 871–877. https://doi.org/10.1136/bjsports-2013-092538

Leahy, T. M., Kenny, I. C., Campbell, M. J., Warrington, G. D., Purtill, H., Cahalan, R., Comyns, T. M., Harrison, A. J., Lyons, M., Glynn, L. G., & O'Sullivan, K. (2022). Injury trends for School Rugby Union in Ireland: The need for position-specific injury-prevention programs. *Sports Health*, 19417381221078531. https://doi.org/10.1177/19417381221078531

Lee, A. J., & Garraway, W. M. (1996). Epidemiological comparison of injuries in school and senior club rugby. *British Journal of Sports Medicine, 30*, 213–217. https://doi.org/10.1136/bjsm.30.3.213

Leung, F. T., Franettovich Smith, M. M., Brown, M., Rahmann, A., Mendis, M. D., & Hides, J. A. (2017). Epidemiology of injuries in Australian school level rugby union. *Journal of Science and Medicine in Sport, 20*, 740–744. https://doi.org/10.1016/j.jsams.2017.03.006

Longo, U. G., Loppini, M., Berton, A., Marinozzi, A., Maffulli, N., & Denaro, V. (2012). The FIFA 11+ Program is effective in preventing injuries in Elite Male Basketball Players a cluster randomized controlled trial. *American Journal of Sports Medicine, 40*, 996–1005. https://doi.org/10.1177/0363546512438761

MacDonald, J., & Myer, G. D. (2017). 'Don't let kids play football': A killer idea. *British Journal of Sports Medicine, 51*, 1448–1449. https://doi.org/10.1136/bjsports-2016-096833

Mandelbaum, B. R., Silvers, H. J., Watanabe, D. S., Knarr, J. F., Thomas, S. D., Griffin, L. Y., Kirkendall, D. T., & Garrett, W. (2005). Effectiveness of a neuromuscular and proprioceptive training program in preventing anterior cruciate ligament injuries in female athletes: 2-Year follow-up. *American Journal of Sports Medicine, 33*, 1003–1010. https://doi.org/10.1177/0363546504272261

Manzanero, S., Elkington, L. J., Praet, S. F., Lovell, G., Waddington, G., & Hughes, D. C. (2017). Post-concussion recovery in children and adolescents: A narrative review. *Journal of Concussion, 1*, 2059700217726874. https://doi.org/10.1177/2059700217726874

Marshall, S. W., Loomis, D. P., Waller, A. E., Chalmers, D. J., Bird, Y. N., Quarrie, K. L., & Feehan, M. (2005). Evaluation of protective equipment for prevention of injuries in rugby union. *International Journal of Epidemiology, 34*, 113–118. https://doi.org/10.1093/ije/dyh346

Marshall, S. W., & Spencer, R. J. (2001). Concussion in Rugby: The hidden epidemic. *Journal of Athletic Training, 36*, 334–338.

Marshall, S. W., Waller, A. E., Loomis, D. P., Feehan, M., Chalmers, D. J., Bird, Y. N., & Quarrie, K. L. (2001). Use of protective equipment in a cohort of rugby players. *Medicine and Science in Sports and Exercise, 33*, 2131–2138. https://doi.org/10.1097/00005768-200112000-00024

McCrory, P., Meeuwisse, W., Dvorak, J., Aubry, M., Bailes, J., Broglio, S., Cantu, R. C., Cassidy, D., Echemendia, R. J., Castellani, R. J., Davis, G. A., Ellenbogen, R., Emery, C., Engebretsen, L., Feddermann-Demont, N., Giza, C. C., Guskiewicz, K. M., Herring, S., Iverson, G. L., Johnston, K. M., Kissick, J., Kutcher, J., Leddy, J. J., Maddocks, D., Makdissi, M., Manley, G. T., McCrea, M., Meehan, W. P., Nagahiro, S., Patricios, J., Putukian, M., Schneider, K. J., Sills, A., Tator, C. H., Turner, M., & Vos, P. E. (2017). Consensus statement on concussion in sport—The 5th international conference on concussion in sport held in Berlin, October 2016. *British Journal of Sports Medicine, 51*, 838–847. https://doi.org/10.1136/bjsports-2017-097699

McIntosh, A. S., McCrory, P., Finch, C. F., Best, J. P., Chalmers, D. J., & Wolfe, R. (2009). Does padded headgear prevent head injury in rugby union football? *Medicine and Science in Sports and Exercise, 41*, 306–313. https://doi.org/10.1249/MSS.0b013e3181864bee

McIntosh, A. S., McCrory, P., Finch, C. F., & Wolfe, R. (2010). Head, face and neck injury in youth rugby: Incidence and risk factors. *British Journal of Sports Medicine, 44*, 188–193. https://doi.org/10.1136/bjsm.2007.041400

McKee, A. C., Cantu, R. C., Nowinski, C. J., Hedley-Whyte, E. T., Gavett, B. E., Budson, A. E., Santini, V. E., Lee, H. S., Kubilus, C. A., & Stern, R. A. (2009). Chronic traumatic encephalopathy in athletes: Progressive tauopathy after repetitive head injury. *Journal of Neuropathology & Experimental Neurology, 68*, 709–735. https://doi.org/10.1097/NEN.0b013e3181a9d503

McManus, A., & Cross, D. S. (2004). Incidence of injury in elite junior rugby union: A prospective descriptive study. *Journal of Science and Medicine in Sport, 7*, 438–445. https://doi.org/10.1016/s1440-2440(04)80261-5

Mjølsnes, R., Arnason, A., Østhagen, T., Raastad, T., & Bahr, R. (2004). A 10-week randomized trial comparing eccentric vs. concentric hamstring strength training in well-trained soccer players. *Scandinavian Journal of Medicine and Science in Sports, 14*, 311–317. https://doi.org/10.1046/j.1600-0838.2003.367.x

Nathan, M., Goedeke, R., & Noakes, T. D. (1983). The incidence and nature of rugby injuries experienced at one school during the 1982 rugby season. *South African Medical Journal, 64*, 132–137.

Nicol, A., Pollock, A., Kirkwood, G., Parekh, N., & Robson, J. (2011). Rugby union injuries in Scottish schools. *Journal of Public Health, 33*, 256–261. https://doi.org/10.1093/pubmed/fdq047

Ogaki, R., Otake, G., Nakane, S., Kosasa, Y., Kanno, Y., Ogura, A., & Takemura, M. (2020). Descriptive epidemiology of injuries in Japanese male collegiate rugby union players. *The Journal of Physical Fitness and Sports Medicine, 9*, 223–233. https://doi.org/10.7600/jpfsm.9.223

O'Rourke, K. P., Quinn, F., Mun, S., Browne, M., Sheehan, J., Cusack, S., & Molloy, M. (2007). A comparison of paediatric soccer, gaelic football and rugby injuries presenting to an emergency department in Ireland. *Injury, 38*, 104–111. https://doi.org/10.1016/j.injury.2006.06.010

Orr, R., & Cheng, H. L. (2016). Incidence and characteristics of injuries in elite Australian junior rugby league players. *Journal of Science and Medicine in Sport, 19*, 212–217. https://doi.org/10.1016/j.jsams.2015.03.007

Orr, R., Hamidi, J., Levy, B., & Halaki, M. (2021). Epidemiology of injuries in Australian junior rugby league players. *Journal of Science and Medicine in Sport, 24*, 241–246. https://doi.org/10.1016/j.jsams.2020.09.002

Padua, D. A., Frank, B., Donaldson, A., de la Motte, S., Cameron, K. L., Beutler, A. I., DiStefano, L. J., & Marshall, S. W. (2014). Seven steps for developing and implementing a preventive training program: Lessons learned from JUMP-ACL and beyond. *Clinics in Sports Medicine, 33*, 615–632. https://doi.org/10.1016/j.csm.2014.06.012

Palmer-Green, D. S., Stokes, K. A., Fuller, C. W., England, M., Kemp, S. P., & Trewartha, G. (2013). Match injuries in English youth academy and schools rugby union: An epidemiological study. *American Journal of Sports Medicine, 41*, 749–755. https://doi.org/10.1177/0363546512473818

Palmer-Green, D. S., Stokes, K. A., Fuller, C. W., England, M., Kemp, S. P., & Trewartha, G. (2015). Training activities and injuries in English youth academy and schools rugby union. *American Journal of Sports Medicine, 43*, 475–481. https://doi.org/10.1177/0363546514560337

Peck, K. Y., Johnston, D. A., Owens, B. D., & Cameron, K. L. (2013). The incidence of injury among male and female intercollegiate rugby players. *Sports Health, 5*, 327–333. https://doi.org/10.1177/1941738113487165

Phibbs, P. J., Jones, B., Read, D. B., Roe, G. A. B., Darrall-Jones, J., Weakley, J. J. S., Rock, A., & Till, K. (2018). The appropriateness of training exposures for match-play preparation in adolescent schoolboy and academy rugby union players. *Journal of Sports Sciences, 36*, 704–709. https://doi.org/10.1080/02640414.2017.1332421

Pollock, A. M., & Kirkwood, G. (2016). Removing contact from school rugby will not turn children into couch potatoes. *British Journal of Sports Medicine*, bjsports-2016-096220. https://doi.org/10.1136/bjsports-2016-096220

Pringle, R. G., McNair, P., & Stanley, S. (1998). Incidence of sporting injury in New Zealand youths aged 6–15 years. *British Journal of Sports Medicine, 32*, 49–52. https://doi.org/10.1136/bjsm.32.1.49

Quarrie, K. L., Brooks, J. H. M., Burger, N., Hume, P. A., & Jackson, S. (2017). Facts and values: On the acceptability of risks in children's sport using the example of rugby — A narrative review. *British Journal of Sports Medicine, 51*, 1134–1139. https://doi.org/10.1136/bjsm.32.1.4910.1136/bjsports-2017-098013

Quarrie, K. L., Gianotti, S. M., Chalmers, D. J., & Hopkins, W. (2005) An evaluation of mouthguard requirements and dental injuries in New Zealand rugby union. *British Journal of Sports Medicine, 39*, 650–654. http://doi.org/10.1136/bjsm.2004.016022

Quarrie, K. L., Gianotti, S. M., Hopkins, W. G., & Hume, P. A. (2007). Effect of nationwide injury prevention programme on serious spinal injuries in New Zealand rugby union: Ecological study. *BMJ, 334*, 1150. https://doi.org/10.1136/bjsm.32.1.4910.1136/bmj.39185.605914.AE

Read, D. B., Jones, B., Phibbs, P. J., Roe, G. A. B., Darrall-Jones, J., Weakley, J. J. S., & Till, K. (2018). The physical characteristics of match-play in English schoolboy and academy rugby union. *Journal of Sports Sciences, 36*, 645–650. https://doi.org/10.1136/bjsm.32.1.4910.1080/02640414.2017.1329546

Reboursiere, E., Bohu, Y., Retière, D., Sesboüé, B., Pineau, V., Colonna, J. P., Hager, J. P., Peyrin, J. C., & Piscione, J. (2018). Impact of the national prevention policy and scrum law changes on the incidence of rugby-related catastrophic cervical spine injuries in French Rugby Union. *British Journal of Sports Medicine, 52*, 674–677. https://doi.org/10.1136/bjsm.32.1.4910.1136/bjsports-2016-096122

Roux, C. E., Goedeke, R., Visser, G. R., van Zyl, W. A., & Noakes, T. D. (1987). The epidemiology of schoolboy rugby injuries. *South African Medical Journal, 71*, 307–313.

Salmon, D., Badenhorst, M., Walters, S., Clacy, A., Chua, J., Register-Mihalik, J., Romanchuk, J., Kerr, Z. Y., Keung, S., & Sullivan, S. J. (2021a). The rugby tug-of-war: Exploring concussion-related behavioural intentions and behaviours in youth community rugby union in New Zealand. *International Journal of Sports Science & Coaching*, 17479541211047661. https://doi.org/10.1177/17479541211047661

Salmon, D., Mcgowan, J., Sullivan, S. J., Murphy, I., Walters, S., Whatman, C., Keung, S., Clacy, A., & Romanchuk, J. (2020). What they know and who they are telling: Concussion knowledge and disclosure behaviour in New Zealand adolescent rugby union players. *Journal of Sports Sciences, 38*, 1585–1594. https://doi.org/10.1080/02640414.2020.1749409

Salmon, D., Romanchuk, J., Sullivan, S. J., Walters, S., Clacy, A., Register-Mihalik, J., Kerr, Z. Y., Whatman, C., & Keung, S. (2021b). Concussion knowledge, attitude and reporting intention in rugby coaches and high school rugby players. *International Journal of Sports Science & Coaching, 16*, 54–69. https://doi.org/10.1177/1747954120961200

Sewry, N., Verhagen, E., Lambert, M., van Mechelen, W., Marsh, J., Readhead, C., Viljoen, W., & Brown, J. (2018). Trends in time-loss injuries during the 2011-2016 South African Rugby Youth Weeks. *Scandinavian Journal of Medicine and Science in Sports, 28*, 2066–2073. https://doi.org/10.1111/sms.13087

Sewry, N., Verhagen, E., Lambert, M., van Mechelen, W., Readhead, C., Viljoen, W., & Brown, J. (2019). Seasonal time-loss match injury rates and burden in South African under-16 rugby teams. *Journal of Science and Medicine in Sport, 22*, 54–58. https://doi.org/10.1016/j.jsams.2018.06.007

Soligard, T., Myklebust, G., Steffen, K., Holme, I., Silvers, H., Bizzini, M., Junge, A., Dvorak, J., Bahr, R., & Andersen, T. E. (2008). Comprehensive warm-up programme to prevent injuries in young female footballers: Cluster randomised controlled trial. *BMJ, 338*, 95–99. https://doi.org/10.1136/bmj.a2469

Solis-Mencia, C., Ramos-Alvarez, J. J., Murias-Lozano, R., Aramberri, M., & Salo, J. C. (2019). Epidemiology of injuries sustained by Elite Under-18 Rugby Players. *Journal of Athletic Training, 54*, 1187–1191. https://doi.org/10.4085/1062-6050-510-18

Sparks, J. P. (1981). Half a million hours of rugby football. The injuries. *British Journal of Sports Medicine, 15*, 30–32. https://doi.org/10.1136/bjsm.15.1.30

Steffen, K., Myklebust, G., Olsen, O. E., Holme, I., & Bahr, R. (2008). Preventing injuries in female youth football – A cluster-randomized controlled trial. *Scandinavian Journal of Medicine and Science in Sports, 18*, 605–614. https://doi.org/10.1111/j.1600-0838.2007.00703.x

Stokes, K. A., Cross, M., Williams, S., McKay, C., Hagel, B. E., West, S. W., Roberts, S. P., Sant'Anna, R. T., Morrison, E., & Kemp, S. (2021). Padded Headgear does not reduce the incidence of match concussions in Professional Men's Rugby Union: A case-control study of 417 cases. *International Journal of Sports Medicine, 42*, 930–935. https://doi.org/10.1055/a-1345-9163

Sye, G., Sullivan, S. J., & McCrory, P. (2006). High school rugby players' understanding of concussion and return to play guidelines. *British Journal of Sports Medicine, 40*, 1003–1004. https://doi.org/10.1136/bjsm.2005.020511

Takemura, M., Nagai, S., Iwai, K., Nakagawa, A., Furukawa, T., Miyakawa, S., & Kono, I. (2009). Injury characteristics in Japanese collegiate rugby union through one season. *Football Science, 6*, 39–46. https://doi.org/10.7600/jpfsm.6.343

Tee, J. C., Till, K., & Jones, B. (2019). Incidence and characteristics of injury in under-19 academy level rugby league match play: A single season prospective cohort study. *Journal of Sports Sciences, 37*, 1181–1188. https://doi.org/10.1080/02640414.2018.1547100

Tierney, G. J., Denvir, K., Farrell, G., & Simms, C. K. (2018). Does player time-in-game affect tackle technique in elite level rugby union? *Journal of Science and Medicine in Sport, 21*, 221–225. https://doi.org/10.1016/j.jsams.2017.06.023

Tucker, R., Raftery, M., & Verhagen, E. (2016). Injury risk and a tackle ban in youth Rugby Union: Reviewing the evidence and searching for targeted, effective interventions. A critical review. *British Journal of Sports Medicine, 50*, 921–925. https://doi.org/10.1136/bjsports-2016-096322

Upton, P. A., Roux, C. E., & Noakes, T. D. (1996). Inadequate pre-season preparation of Schoolboy Rugby Players—A survey of players at 25 Cape Province High Schools. *South African Medical Journal, 86*, 531–533.

van Mechelen, W., Hlobil, H., & Kemper, H. C. (1992). Incidence, severity, aetiology and prevention of sports injuries. A review of concepts. *Sports Medicine, 14*, 82–99. https://doi.org/10.2165/00007256-199214020-00002

Viljoen, W. (2009) *Neck injury prevention*. Cape Town: BokSmart, unpublished.

Weakley, J. J. S., Till, K., Darrall-Jones, J., Roe, G. A. B., Phibbs, P. J., Read, D. B., & Jones, B. L. (2019). Strength and conditioning practices in adolescent rugby players: Relationship with changes in physical qualities. *Journal of Strength and Conditioning Research, 33*, 2361–2369. https://doi.org/10.1519/JSC.0000000000001828

Williams, S., Robertson, C., Starling, L., McKay, C., West, S., Brown, J., & Stokes, K. (2022). Injuries in Elite Men's Rugby Union: An updated (2012–2020) meta-analysis of 11,620 match and training injuries. *Sports Medicine, 52*, 1127–1140. https://doi.org/10.1007/s40279-021-01603-w

Willigenburg, N. W., Borchers, J. R., Quincy, R., Kaeding, C. C., & Hewett, T. E. (2016). Comparison of injuries in American Collegiate Football and Club Rugby: A prospective cohort study. *American Journal of Sports Medicine, 44*, 753–760. https://doi.org/10.1177/0363546515622389

Willigenburg, N. W., Geissler, K. E., Roewer, B. D., Caldwell, T., Salazar, L. D., Borchers, J. R., Higgins, T., & Hewett, T. E. (2014). Injuries in American collegiate club rugby: A prospective study. *Annals of Sports Medicine and Research, 1*, 1005.

World Rugby (2018). *Global participation in rugby*. World Rugby.

World Rugby (2022). Activate Injury Prevention Exercise Programme, [online], available: https://passport.world.rugby/injury-prevention-and-risk-management/activate-injury-prevention-exercise-programme/under-15-age-13-15-years/level-1/ [Accessed 27/05/2022].

Wright, D. K., Gardner, A. J., Wojtowicz, M., Iverson, G. L., O'Brien, T. J., Shultz, S. R., & Stanwell, P. (2021). White matter abnormalities in retired Professional Rugby League Players with a history of concussion. *Journal of Neurotrauma, 38*, 983–988. https://doi.org/10.1089/neu.2019.6886

Yeomans, C., Kenny, I. C., Cahalan, R., Warrington, G. D., Harrison, A. J., Hayes, K., Lyons, M., Campbell, M. J., & Comyns, T. M. (2018). The incidence of injury in Amateur Male Rugby Union: A systematic review and meta-analysis. *Sports Medicine, 48*, 837–848. https://doi.org/10.1007/s40279-017-0838-4

Zimmerman, K. A., Laverse, E., Samra, R., Yanez Lopez, M., Jolly, A. E., Bourke, N. J., Graham, N. S. N., Patel, M. C., Hardy, J., Kemp, S., Morris, H. R., & Sharp, D. J. (2021). White matter abnormalities in active elite adult rugby players. *Brain Communications, 3*, fcab133. https://doi.org/10.1093/braincomms/fcab133

16
THE YOUNG FEMALE RUGBY PLAYER

Sean Scantlebury and Omar Heyward

Introduction

The Growth of Female Rugby

Female rugby has grown substantially in global popularity. In the 2016 Rio Olympics, female rugby sevens was introduced, which helped to increase the spotlight on females in the rugby codes. Internationally, the number of Australian females playing rugby league in 2018 increased by 29% (Cummins et al., 2020), whilst female rugby union saw a 28% increase in participation to 2.7 million registered players from 2017 to 2019 worldwide (British Broadcasting Corporation, 2019). Additionally, there has been major investment into female rugby. For example, in England there has been the introduction of top-tier competitions (Rugby Football Union [RFU]: Premier 15's; Rugby Football League [RFL]: Women's Super League [WSL]), supporting the growth and profile of the female game. Furthermore, in 2019 the England senior female rugby union squad became the first professional female rugby union team in the world when the RFU awarded 28 fulltime playing contracts ahead of the Six Nations Championship (The Rugby Football Union, 2019). This contrasts with the men's rugby union team, which became professional in 1995 (The Rugby Football Union, 2010).

The advent of professionalism in male rugby resulted in longitudinal position-specific improvements in physical characteristics, such as greater height, body mass and lower fat mass (Fuller et al., 2013). Similar increases in body mass, strength, power and sprint momentum, alongside decreased body fat are evident in female rugby union players transitioning between amateur and professional generations (Hill et al., 2018; Tucker et al., 2021; Woodhouse et al., 2022). However, the rate of increase in these qualities across a five-year period (~6.5%)

DOI: 10.4324/9781003104797-16

amongst elite female rugby union is greater than the first 10 years following professionalism in male rugby (~3.8%; Hill et al., 2018), emphasising the rapid development of the female game (Woodhouse et al., 2022).

Alongside improvements in anthropometric and physical qualities, the intensity of female international rugby union has increased since the transition from amateur to professional status (Woodhouse et al., 2021). Woodhouse et al. (2021) found the average running demands, sprints and high intensity (>4 m/s^2) accelerations and decelerations (m/min) to increase across multiple playing positions in a top two ranked international team between 2015 and 2019. Therefore, as female rugby continues to grow in popularity, anthropometric and physical qualities improve and the game intensifies, it is important to expand the evidence base which can be used to inform practice across different rugby codes (i.e., union, league, sevens) and age groups (i.e., youth, senior).

Considerations for the Youth Female Player

Both female sport professionalism and participation have seen faster growth rates than the underpinning female-specific sport science evidence base (Jones et al., 2019). In comparison to research in male sport, a lack of female-specific literature remains (Cummins et al., 2020; Emmonds et al., 2019). The evidence gap is likely multi-factorial and may be due to sporting context (e.g., limited duration of female sport professionalisation, infrastructure and sport science support; Emmonds et al., 2019), sociological factors (Sharrow, 2017) and biological differences (e.g., endocrinology) between the sexes. The application of sport science research findings that use male participants may not be appropriate for female athletes. There are several sex-specific considerations (e.g., menstrual cycle, pelvic health) for female athletes that must be accounted for. Additionally, previous research has investigated unique aspects of consideration in female rugby, where the top two identified themes were psycho-social aspects and menstrual cycle (Heyward et al., 2020).

Although psycho-social aspects have been identified as a key consideration in female rugby, there is currently no available literature regarding sex-specific coaching effectiveness (Heyward et al., 2020). Empathy and connection have been suggested to be of higher value to females than males (Cunningham & Roberts, 2012). Thus, an emphasis on developing strong professional relationships with female rugby players has been previously identified as an important factor for coaches (Heyward et al., 2020). With respect to the menstrual cycle (see Box 16.1) in female rugby union, unpublished data from a survey investigating menstrual cycle characteristics (n=213) identified 12.7 $\pm$ 1.3 years as the average age at menarche, menstrual cycle length as 29.2 $\pm$ 4.2 days and menses length as 5.0 $\pm$ 1.5 days (Heyward et al., unpublished). During menses, 51% of elite female athletes reported their training and performance to be negatively affected (Bruinvels et al., 2016). Whilst no data are available in youth female rugby, in elite women's rugby 93% of players reported menstrual cycle symptoms (e.g., stomach cramps, reduced energy). Furthermore, in Australian senior football codes (rugby league, rugby union/sevens, Australian football), one-third of athletes were reported to use hormonal contraceptives (Clarke et al., 2021). Reasons for hormonal contraceptive use were described as avoiding pregnancy (71%), regulating cycle (38%) and reducing menstrual pain (36%). Menstrual cycle monitoring in rugby has been reported as low as 22% (Heyward et al., 2020). It may therefore be an important consideration for youth female athletes to be educated on menstrual health and monitoring, contraceptive use, and symptom management. Menstrual cycle management strategies for rugby players have been previously identified and include increasing education, establishing a point of contact, incorporating regular monitoring and establishing menstrual cycle profiles (see Box 16.2; Findlay et al., 2020).

Box 16.1 The Menstrual Cycle

- **The menstrual cycle** is the regular, biological process for reproduction that occurs within the uterus and ovaries (Reed & Carr, 2015).
- **Menarche** is the first occurrence of menstruation and typically occurs at 12.5 years of age (Chumlea et al., 2003).
- **Cycle length** is the number of days between the onset of menses in one cycle to its onset in the following cycle.
- **Eumenorrhea** is associated with reproductive function and has positive implications for both short and long-term health in female athletes (Logue et al., 2020).

On average, a eumenorrheic women will typically experience menses (which usually last three to seven days) every 21–35 days (Reed & Carr, 2015).

Further areas of consideration for the youth female rugby player may be breast injuries and urinary incontinence. In elite female athletes, contact breast injuries and frictional breast injuries are common (36%; Brisbine et al., 2019). Athletes in contact and combat sports (e.g., rugby, boxing) report a higher frequency of breast injuries compared to athletes of other sports (47.3% vs. 33.7%). In football code athletes (rugby codes and Australian football), 58% of players have experienced a contact breast injury in either training or match-play (Brisbine et al., 2020). Of the football code athletes who suffered a breast injury, 48% perceive the injury to negatively affect performance. The most common three negative performance effects of breast injuries were *'distracted by the pain'* (19%), *'less likely to dive or tackle'* (16%) and *'unable to run conformably'* (14%). Although data for breast injuries are not currently available for youth athletes, this may be an important consideration for the health, wellbeing and performance of young rugby players. Additionally, urinary incontinence in female rugby players may also be a consideration.

> **Box 16.2 Managing the Menstrual Cycle**
>
> A high percentage (51%) of elite female athletes report their training and performance to be negatively impacted by the menstrual cycle (Bruinvels et al., 2016). Therefore, practical recommendations for optimising health, well-being and athletic performance in rugby players during the menstrual cycle have been suggested (Findlay et al., 2020).
>
> - **Increasing education:** Develop awareness, openness, knowledge and understanding of the menstrual cycle within the sporting environment and beyond.
> - **Establish a point of contact:** Identify an individual within the athlete support team whom athletes are comfortable approaching with menstrual cycle concerns.
> - **Incorporate regular monitoring:** Daily monitoring of cycle phase and symptomology to help inform medical treatment and modify training when necessary.
> - **Establish menstrual cycle profiles:** Athletes should undergo a comprehensive menstrual cycle history profiling with the inclusion of related medical details, (e.g., iron status, contraceptive use), symptoms and perceived impact on performance.

In a varsity female rugby cohort ($n=95$), 54% of athletes experienced urinary incontinence. Of the players who leaked urine, 90% reported leaking during match-play, and 88% reported leaking when being tackled (Sandwith & Robert, 2021). Despite the high prevalence of incontinence, up to 89% of players were not bothered by their incontinence. Early education of pelvic health and pelvic floor training exercises may be important for the youth female rugby player.

The Female Rugby Player and Injury

The number of research studies in female rugby has increased considerably in the last 10 years (see Table 16.1) with most research focussing on injury and physical performance (see Figure 16.1; Heyward et al., 2022). Continuing to increase the evidence base available for female rugby is important to support the growth of the game (Cummins et al., 2020). Heyward et al. (2022) conducted a scoping review of the available literature in female rugby before using expert opinion (via a Delphi study) to establish future research priorities. Thirty-one experts (categorised as elite player ($n = 4$), sport science ($n = 11$), sports medicine ($n = 9$), or governance ($n = 7$) domains) participated in the study. The theme of injury achieved the highest priority rating (4.5 out of 5) between experts. Within the

TABLE 16.1 The Number of Research Studies in Female Rugby by Decade

Evidence-Based Themes	Year Period Published							
	<1990		1990–2000		2001–2010		2011–Jan 2021	
	Number of Studies	%	Number of Studies	%	Number of Studies	%	Number of Studies	%
Fatigue and recovery	0	0	0	0	0	0	6	100
Injury	1	2	5	10	10	21	32	67
Match characteristics	0	0	0	0	0	0	26	100
Nutrition	0	0	0	0	0	0	6	100
Physical performance	1	3	2	6	2	6	27	84
Psychology	0	0	0	0	0	0	5	100
Total	**2**	**2**	**7**	**6**	**12**	**10**	**102**	**82**

% represents the percent of studies in each evidence-based theme, for each year period. Information from (Heyward et al., 2022).

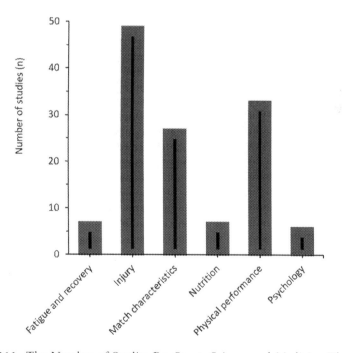

FIGURE 16.1 The Number of Studies Per Sports Science and Medicine Theme in Female Rugby (information from Heyward et al., 2022).

theme of injury, concussion occurrence, risk factors, mechanisms, return-to-play management and female response to concussion were the two highest priorities.

Concussion has emerged as a major health and safety issue in sport. Therefore, robust monitoring of head and concussive injuries is recommended (Orr et al., 2021). Evidence suggests that following sports-related concussion, female athletes experience greater symptom severity and take longer to recover compared with male athletes (Bauman et al., 2017; Thibeault et al., 2019). A recent systematic review investigating concussion in senior female rugby found the mean injury burden for concussions to be 33 days lost (King et al., 2022). The pooled analysis match injury incidence of female concussion was higher for rugby league (10.3 per 1,000 match hours) than rugby union (2.8 per 1,000 match hours) or rugby 7s (8.9 per 1,000 match hours). The primary mechanisms for concussion occurring in female rugby union were being tackled (ball carrier) or tackling another player (51.7%; King et al., 2022). Such findings are consistent with youth female rugby literature as the tackle was found to be the main cause of injury in youth female rugby union ([percentage of injuries caused] tackler: 32.5%, ball carrier: 28.6%; Collins et al., 2008) and rugby league (tackling unspecified: 62.9%, ball carrier: 8.1%, tackler: 11.3%; Orr et al., 2021). The tackle being the predominant cause of injury is consistent with findings in male youth rugby union which found tackle-related injuries to account for 60% of all injuries (Burger et al., 2017). Proficient contact skills in matches have been associated with a reduced risk of injury for both the ball-carrier and tackler (Hendricks et al., 2018). Therefore, developing correct tackle technique through coaching and building technical capacity through training is conceivably the most appropriate strategy for reducing the risk of injury in youth female rugby.

FIGURE 16.2 Key Injury Surveillance Figures from the 2021 Women's Rugby League Super League.

Unpublished data from the RFL found concussion to be the most frequent time loss injury from match-play across the 2021 women's rugby league Super League season ($n = 20$; Figure 16.2). Such findings are consistent with published research in youth female rugby. Both Collins et al. (2008) and Lopez et al. (2020) found high rates of concussion in high school rugby union (14.3% of all injuries) and U19 rugby sevens players (22.2% of all time-loss injuries), respectively. Orr et al. (2021) found lower rates of suspected concussion in youth rugby league players (3.2% of all injuries) despite the head being the second most impacted area behind the lower extremities. The authors suggested the prevalence of concussion may have been underestimated as concussion requires a clinical diagnosis by a doctor. Community sports such as youth female rugby rarely have doctors present at practice or matches which may lead to an under reporting of concussion incidence (Orr et al., 2021). The prevalence of concussion across senior and youth female rugby, alongside other potentially severe injuries (e.g., knee ligament injuries; Figure 16.2) highlights the importance of identifying risk factors which predispose female athletes to injury. Identifying injury risk factors that impact females playing rugby will help guide intervention plans aimed at reducing the incidence of injury.

Injury Risk Factors and Barriers to Their Management

As well as biological differences between male and female rugby players, there are contextual differences (e.g., amateur vs professional sport; Donaldson et al. 2015). For example, factors such as insufficient training time, a lack of resources or equipment and staff provision may limit the ability of practitioners to implement the same injury management strategies applicable to men in female rugby (Emmonds et al., 2019). Therefore, developing a consensus on injury risk factors that are specific to females who play rugby provides a foundation on which injury prevention strategies may be built. Scantlebury et al. (2022) conducted a Delphi study to achieve consensus on injury risk factors that impact females playing rugby league. The Delphi panel consisted of 12 experts (one medical doctor, five strength and conditioning coaches, three physiotherapists and three research scientists). The first round of the Delphi process asked experts to list injury risk factors specific to females who play rugby league under five pre-determined categories: '*individual player characteristics*', '*lifestyle and environment*', '*training and match factors*', '*a lack of provision*' and '*other*'. A total of 82 injury risk factors were identified following round one. Rounds two and three asked experts to rate their level of agreement whether they perceived the injury risk factor increased the risk of injury on a five-point Likert scale ranging from 1 to 5 (1 = *strongly disagree*, 5 = *strongly agree*). Overall, 53 injury risk factors achieved consensus (≥70% agreement between experts; Figure 16.3).

The incorporation of stakeholders (e.g., rugby coaches) into the research process has been advocated to increase the application of injury prevention data into practice (Fullagar et al., 2019; Jones et al., 2019). Stakeholders can bridge the gap

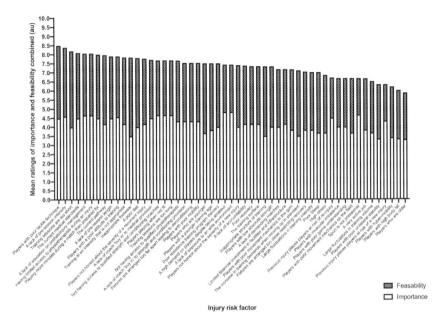

FIGURE 16.3 The Combined Mean Ratings of Importance and Feasibility for each of the Injury Risk Factors (Scantlebury et al., 2022).

between research and practice by defining the importance of injury risk factors within a specific context, their feasibility to manage these factors and the barriers which may restrict their management (Donaldson et al., 2019). Therefore, Scantlebury et al. (2022) asked the coaches of six WSL teams and one international team to rate the importance (i.e., the importance that the injury risk factor increased the risk of a female rugby league player getting injured) and feasibility (i.e., the feasibility that the injury risk factor can be managed and reduced) of the 53 injury risk factors which achieved consensus following the Delphi-process. Furthermore, coaches were asked to list any barriers which may prevent the mitigation of each of the 53 injury risk factors. Ultimately, each injury risk factor had a coach-perceived rating of importance to manage, feasibility to manage and a list of barriers that may restrict management. Coaches were asked to rate the importance and feasibility of each injury risk factor out of five (i.e., 1 = *Not important/feasible*, 5 = *very important/feasible*). The average rating of importance and feasibility for each injury risk factor was calculated, combined and ranked (Figure 16.3). Ranking the injury risk factors by combined importance and feasibility highlights injury risk factors that should be targeted as a priority to increase player safety and performance.

Before injury prevention strategies can be implemented, the context-specific barriers which restrict injury risk factor management must be considered and removed. Coaches identified 43 barriers that restrict injury risk factor management. The 43 barriers were categorised into eight broader themes: '*Multiple commitments limits time to train*', '*A lack of education*', '*A small player pool*', '*A limited training and playing age*', '*A lack of development pathway*', '*A lack of facilities*', '*Player attitudes towards training*', '*A lack of qualified staff provision*'. A comprehensive list of injury risk factors and barriers which restrict their management can be found in Scantlebury et al. (2022). Providing solutions that reduce the impact of the barriers perceived by WSL and international rugby league coaches to restrict the management of injury risk factors will help the formation of injury prevention strategies. Therefore, the practical recommendations section of this chapter will focus on providing solutions to reduce the coach perceived barriers to injury risk factor management.

Practical Applications

This section provides practical solutions to reduce the impact of the barrier themes perceived by rugby league coaches to restrict injury risk factor management. Three constraint-driven solutions are included (1) increasing player and coach education, (2) improving the physical development of youth female rugby players before transitioning to open age rugby and (3) increasing the minimum standards of provision (i.e., staff, facilities).

A lack of education was perceived to be a barrier theme preventing the management of 28 of the 53 injury risk factors. An important initial step towards improving education is to understand the most effective methods of providing information to players and coaches (Fullagar et al., 2019; Jones et al., 2019). Establishing the most effective methods of knowledge transfer may vary depending on the individual's preferred method of delivery, their learning style and their access to information (Fullagar et al., 2019; González-Haro et al., 2010; Trakman et al., 2019). Previous literature has found coaches prefer attaining knowledge through face-to-face interaction (Fullagar et al., 2019; Mesquita et al., 2010) or attending workshops (Williams & Kendall, 2007). Alternatively, athletes prefer to obtain knowledge through qualified staff members or internet articles (Trakman et al., 2019). Therefore, to facilitate the transfer and application of knowledge from research into practice, it is crucial to make information available in a multitude of ways. Hosting education workshops on specific topics (e.g., managing the menstrual cycle) will provide coaches the opportunity to obtain knowledge and interact with fellow coaches, whilst providing access to qualified staff and releasing information via media platforms may improve player education. Methods to increase the efficiency of training should be a key focus for coach and player education. Female rugby is a predominantly amateur sport which means players are often forced to train around their work schedule. Subsequently, having multiple commitments that limit time to train was identified as a barrier theme. Whilst providing sufficient funding to enable full-time training may not be a viable option at present, educating players and staff on appropriate training and recovery practices may maximise the training time that is available. Previous literature has identified strategies to optimise training (e.g., short, intense bouts of interval training are an effective method of improving cardiorespiratory and metabolic function; Buchheit & Laursen, 2013) and recovery (e.g., nutritional strategies, Heaton et al., 2017; stretching and massage, Halson, 2013). Therefore, delivering this information to coaches and players in a non-time-restricted manner (e.g., pre-recorded online workshops) will help alleviate the impact of limited training time.

The popularity of women and girls rugby league is at an all-time high with the playing community increasing by 53% from 2017 to 2021 (Rugby Football League, 2021). The increase in participation can be seen across all age groups with a 23% increase at U12's in mixed-gender competitions, an 85% increase in 12–16-year-olds playing in girls-only competitions and a 36% increase in over 16's playing in women-only competitions. Despite the benefits of increased participation, the increase in physicality as players progress from youth rugby (<16 years old) to open-age rugby (>16 years old) may predispose players to injury. Previous research (Orr et al., 2020) quantifying injury incidence in youth rugby league players found the injury incidence (medical attention and time loss) of U13-U18 female players (22.2 injuries/1,000 player hours) to be higher than the overall injury incidence when all age groups (U6-U18) and both sexes were combined (5.9 injuries/1,000 player hours). This was attributed to the U16 to U18 age group where 16- and 17-year-olds were playing against older females in an U18 competition (Orr et al., 2021). Therefore, it is important players prepare for the increased physicality associated with the transition from youth to senior rugby. Increased lower-body power and muscular strength are associated with superior skills such as tackling and ball carrying ability in male rugby league (Waldron et al., 2014) as well as decreased risk of injury (Gabbett et al., 2012) and enhanced recovery following match-play (Johnston et al., 2015; McCormack et al., 2020). Furthermore, participation in neuromuscular training prior to 18 years of age can reduce anterior cruciate ligament injury incidence by 72% in female athletes (Myer et al., 2013). Consequently, it is recommended that youth female rugby players develop their physical fitness in a structured manner prior to participation in senior rugby.

Lloyd and Oliver (2012) developed the youth physical development model for females which provides guidance regarding training progressions from early childhood to adulthood. For example, during early and middle childhood, female athletes should place a greater focus on developing fundamental movement skills (e.g., squat, hinge, push, pull, brace) before placing greater emphasis on agility, strength, power, speed and endurance as they mature. Whilst the model provides guidelines based on chronological age, growth rate, and maturational status, consideration should be given to the initial training status of the athlete. For example, an adolescent female with a limited training history should place more focus on developing fundamental movement skills before commencing with the training content which aligns with their chronological age.

Despite research finding 65% of strength and conditioning coaches working in female rugby to be masters educated (Heyward et al., 2020), a lack of qualified staff provision was perceived by rugby league coaches to be a barrier to the management of 22 injury risk factors. Employing qualified full-time staff members (e.g., physiotherapists, strength and conditioning coaches) may not be possible due to the financial restrictions associated with female rugby (Emmonds et al., 2019). However, integrating a minimum qualification standard and providing education and career professional development opportunities to allow staff to obtain the required qualifications would increase the standard of provision in female rugby. For example, it is recommended rugby clubs fund courses such as the Immediate Medical Management on the Field of Play (IMMOFP) course or the Pre-Hospital Immediate Care in Sport (PHICIS) course for physiotherapists or the United Kingdom Strength and Conditioning (UKSCA) accreditation for strength and conditioning coaches. Investing in these courses for staff will improve the standard of provision, reducing the coach perceived barrier to injury risk factor management of a lack of qualified staff.

Factors associated with reducing injury risk include well-developed physical qualities (McCormack et al., 2020), and consistent training (Gabbett, 2016). Subsequently, strength and conditioning coaches have highlighted injury risk reduction as one of the predominant reasons they prescribe sprint and plyometric training for female rugby players (Heyward et al., 2020). For example, as anterior cruciate ligament injuries are a substantial burden in female rugby (Fuller et al., 2017; Toohey et al., 2019), the incorporation of landing mechanics into the training program may help reduce injury risk (Petushek et al., 2019). However, despite 81% of strength and conditioning coaches indicating 45–60 minutes of resistance training sessions were prescribed two to three days a week across all training phases in female rugby codes, rugby league coaches perceived limited access to gym and field-based training facilities to be barriers to the management of ten injury risk factors. This appears logical as the inability to provide players with access to gym facilities or a suitable training pitch restricts their ability to improve physical (e.g., absolute strength) and technical (e.g., tackle technique) qualities. This in turn predisposes players to increased injury risk. Therefore, improving minimum standards to require female rugby league clubs to provide consistent gym (e.g., 45–60 minutes, two to three days a week) and field access (e.g., 60–120 minutes, two to three days a week) to players is imperative.

Overall, increasing player and coach education via multiple platforms (e.g., face-to-face workshops, online media), preferentially in a non-time restricted manner may help increase player and coach knowledge on a variety of important subjects such as the development of physical fitness. Improving physical qualities should be a paramount consideration for youth female rugby players. Therefore, depending on the training age of the individual, fundamental movement skills should be developed in early childhood, prior to the development of sports-specific skills, agility, speed, power, strength, hypertrophy and endurance from middle childhood to adulthood. The ever-increasing physical demands of female rugby highlights the need to improve each of these bio-motor abilities to prepare players for competition as they progress through age grades. Increasing the minimum standards required of rugby clubs (e.g., suitable gym and pitch facilities, qualified staff) will help provide the necessary training environment required for players to develop their physical qualities, in turn, improving performance and reducing the likelihood of injury.

Key Take Home Messages

- Participation in female rugby has risen with a concurrent improvement in physical characteristics and an intensification of match demands.
- There are unique sex-specific points of consideration for youth rugby players, including psycho-social aspects, menstrual cycle, breast health and urinary incontinence that must be considered when working with young female athletes.
- There is a need to increase the evidence base used to inform practice in female rugby. Injury, particularly concussion occurrence, risk factors, mechanisms, return to play management and female response to concussion have been identified as high priority areas for future research.
- The head and lower extremities are the predominant areas of injury in senior and youth female rugby, with a high prevalence of concussion. The tackle (both tackler and ball carrier) is the main mechanism causing injury. Therefore, an emphasis should be placed on developing appropriate tackle technique in youth female rugby players to not only improve performance but also to reduce the incidence of injury.
- Consensus has been established for 53 injury risk factors specific to females who play rugby league. Furthermore, eight barrier themes perceived by rugby league coaches to restrict injury risk factor management have been identified: '*Multiple commitments limit time to train*', '*A lack of facilities*', '*A lack of qualified staff provision*', '*A lack of education*', '*The players attitude to training*', '*A small player pool*', '*A limited training and playing age*' and '*A lack of developmental pathway*'.
- Three constraint-driven suggestions are provided to reduce the impact of coach perceived barriers to injury risk factor management: increasing player and coach education through multiple platforms (e.g., online media, coaching workshops), improving the physical development of youth female rugby players through structured training before transitioning to open age rugby and increasing the minimum standards of provision (e.g., minimum qualification requirements for staff, consistent availability of suitable training facilities).

References

Bauman, S., Ray, M., & Joseph, P. P. (2017). Gender differences in clincial presentation and recovery of sports related concussion. *British Journal of Sports Medicine, 51*, A35. http://dx.doi.org/10.1136/bjsports-2016-097270.89

Brisbine, B. R., Steele, J. R., Phillips, E. J., & McGhee, D. E. (2019). The occurrence, causes and perceived performance effects of breast injuries in elite female athletes. *Journal of Sports Science & Medicine, 18*, 569–576. https://www.ncbi.nlm.nih.gov/pmc/articles/PMC6683617

Brisbine, B. R., Steele, J. R., Phillips, E. J., & McGhee, D. E. (2020). Breast injuries reported by female contact football players based on football code, player position and competition level. *Science and Medicine in Football, 4*, 148–155. https://doi.org/10.1080/24733938.2019.1682184

British Broadcasting Corporation. (2019). World Rugby launches campaign to increase participation in women's game [Internet]. [cited 2022 Jun 28]. Available from: https://www.bbc.co.uk/sport/rugby-union/48348245

Bruinvels, G., Burden, R., Brown, N., Richards, T., & Pedlar, C. (2016). The prevalence and impact of heavy menstrual bleeding (menorrhagia) in elite and non-elite athletes. *PLoS One, 11*, e0149881. https://doi.org/10.1371/journal.pone.0149881

Buchheit, M., & Laursen, P. B. (2013). High-intensity interval training, solutions to the programming puzzle. *Sports Medicine, 43*, 313–338. https://doi.org/10.1007/s40279-013-0029-x

Burger, N., Lambert, M. I., Viljoen, W., Brown, J. C., Readhead, C., Den Hollander, S., & Hendricks, S. (2017). Mechanisms and factors associated with tackle-related injuries in South African youth rugby union players. *The American Journal of Sports Medicine, 45*, 278–285. https://doi.org/10.1177/0363546516677548

Chumlea, W. C., Schubert, C. M., Roche, A. F., Kulin, H. E., Lee, P. A., Himes, J. H., & Sun, S. S. (2003). Age at menarche and racial comparisons in US girls. *Pediatrics, 111*, 110–113. https://doi.org/10.1542/peds.111.1.110

Clarke, A. C., Bruinvels, G., Julian, R., Inge, P., Pedlar, C. R., & Govus, A. D. (2021). Hormonal contraceptive use in football codes in Australia. *Frontiers in Sports and Active Living, 3*, 634866. https://doi.org/10.3389/fspor.2021.634866

Collins, C. L., Micheli, L. J., Yard, E. E., & Comstock, R. D. (2008). Injuries sustained by high school rugby players in the United States, 2005–2006. *Archives of Pediatrics & Adolescent Medicine, 162*, 49–54. https://doi.org/10.1001/archpediatrics.2007.1

Cummins, C., Melinz, J., King, D., Sanctuary, C., & Murphy, A. (2020). Call to action: A collaborative framework to better support female rugby league players. *British Journal of Sports Medicine, 54*, 501–502. http://dx.doi.org/10.1136/bjsports-2019-101403

Cunningham, J., & Roberts, P. (2012). The Feminine Brand – A new brand model built around female motivation. In J. Cunningham, & P. Worsfold (Eds.), *Inside her pretty little head: A new theory of female motivation and what it means for marketing* (pp. 163–176). Marshall Cavendish International Asia Pte Ltd.

Donaldson, A., Callaghan, A., Bizzini, M., Jowett, A., Keyzer, P., & Nicholson, M. (2019). A concept mapping approach to identifying the barriers to implementing an evidence-based sports injury prevention programme. *Injury Prevention, 25*, 244–251. http://dx.doi.org/10.1136/injuryprev-2017-042639

Donaldson, A., Cook, J., Gabbe, B., Lloyd, D. G., Young, W., & Finch, C. F. (2015). Bridging the gap between content and context: Establishing expert consensus on the content of an exercise training program to prevent lower-limb injuries. *Clinical Journal of Sport Medicine, 25*, 221–229. 10.1097/JSM.0000000000000124

Emmonds, S., Heyward, O., & Jones, B. (2019). The challenge of applying and undertaking research in female sport. *Sports Medicine-Open, 5*, 1–4. https://link.springer.com/article/10.1186/s40798-019-0224-x

Findlay, R. J., Macrae, E. H., Whyte, I. Y., Easton, C., & Forrest, L. J. (2020). How the menstrual cycle and menstruation affect sporting performance: Experiences and perceptions of elite female rugby players. *British Journal of Sports Medicine, 54*, 1108–1113. http://dx.doi.org/10.1136/bjsports-2019-101486

Fullagar, H. H., McCall, A., Impellizzeri, F. M., Favero, T., & Coutts, A. J. (2019). The translation of sport science research to the field: A current opinion and overview on the perceptions of practitioners, researchers and coaches. *Sports Medicine, 49*, 1817–1824. https://link.springer.com/article/10.1007/s40279-019-01139-0

Fuller, C. W., Taylor, A. E., Brooks, J. H., & Kemp, S. P. (2013). Changes in the stature, body mass and age of English professional rugby players: A 10-year review. *Journal of Sports Sciences, 31*, 795–802. https://doi.org/10.1080/02640414.2012.753156

Fuller, C. W., Taylor, A. E., & Raftery, M. (2017). 2016 Rio Olympics: An epidemiological study of the men's and women's Rugby-7s tournaments. *British Journal of Sports Medicine, 51*, 1272–1278. http://dx.doi.org/10.1136/bjsports-2016-097301

Gabbett, T. J. (2016). The training—injury prevention paradox: Should athletes be training smarter and harder? *British Journal of Sports Medicine, 50*, 273–280. http://dx.doi.org/10.1136/bjsports-2015-095788

Gabbett, T. J., Ullah, S., & Finch, C. F. (2012). Identifying risk factors for contact injury in professional rugby league players–application of a frailty model for recurrent injury. *Journal of Science and Medicine in Sport, 15*, 496–504. https://doi.org/10.1016/j.jsams.2012.03.017

González-Haro, C., Calleja-González, J., & Escanero, J. F. (2010). Learning styles favoured by professional, amateur, and recreational athletes in different sports. *Journal of Sports Sciences, 28*, 859–866. https://doi.org/10.1080/02640411003734077

Halson, S. L. (2013). Recovery techniques for athletes. *Sports Science Exchange, 26*, 1–6. http://doi.org/10.1136/jmg.2003.014902

Heaton, L. E., Davis, J. K., Rawson, E. S., Nuccio, R. P., Witard, O. C., Stein, K. W., Baar, K., Carter, J., & Baker, L. B. (2017). Selected in-season nutritional strategies to enhance recovery for team sport athletes: A practical overview. *Sports Medicine, 47*, 2201–2218. http://doi.org/0.1007/s40279-017-0759-2

Hendricks, S., Till, K., Oliver, J. L., Johnston, R. D., Attwood, M., Brown, J., Drake, D., MacLeod, S., Mellalieu, S., Treu, P., & Jones, B. (2018). Technical skill training framework and skill load measurements for the rugby union tackle. *Strength & Conditioning Journal, 40*, 44–59. http://doi.org/10.1519/SSC.0000000000000400

Heyward, O., Elliot-Sale, K.J., Roe, G., Emmonds, S., Hornby, K., Stokes, K.A., & Jones, B. (unpublished). Oral contraceptive use and non-use in Championship and Premiership women's rugby union: Perceived symptomology, management strategies and performance and wellness effects.

Heyward, O., Emmonds, S., Roe, G., Scantlebury, S., Stokes, K., & Jones, B. (2022). Applied sports science and sports medicine of women's rugby: Systematic-scoping review and Delphi study to establish future research priorities, *BMJ Open Sport & Exercise Medicine, 7*, e001108. https://doi.org10.1136/bmjsem-2021-001108

Heyward, O., Nicholson, B., Emmonds, S., Roe, G., & Jones, B. (2020). Physical preparation in female rugby codes: An investigation of current practices. *Frontiers in Sports and Active Living, 2*, 584194. https://doi.org/10.3389/fspor.2020.584194

Hill, N. E., Rilstone, S., Stacey, M. J., Amiras, D., Chew, S., Flatman, D., & Oliver, N. S. (2018). Changes in northern hemisphere male international rugby union players' body mass and height between 1955 and 2015. *BMJ Open Sport & Exercise Medicine, 4*, e000459. http://dx.doi.org/10.1136/bmjsem-2018-000459

Johnston, R. D., Gabbett, T. J., Jenkins, D. G., & Hulin, B. T. (2015). Influence of physical qualities on post-match fatigue in rugby league players. *Journal of Science and Medicine in Sport, 18*, 209–213. https://doi.org/10.1016/j.jsams.2014.01.009

Jones, B., Till, K., Emmonds, S., Hendricks, S., Mackreth, P., Darrall-Jones, J., Roe, G., McGeechan, I., Mayhew, R., Hunwicks, R., Potts, N., Clarkson, M., & Rock, A. (2019). Accessing off-field brains in sport; an applied research model to develop practice. *British Journal of Sports Medicine, 53*, 791–793. http://dx.doi.org/10.1136/bjsports-2016-097082

King, D. A., Hume, P. A., Hind, K., Clark, T. N., & Hardaker, N. (2022). The incidence, cost, and burden of concussion in women's rugby league and rugby union: A systematic review and pooled analysis. *Sports Medicine*, 1–14. http://doi.org/10.1007/s40279-022-01645-8

Lloyd, R. S., & Oliver, J. L. (2012). The youth physical development model: A new approach to long-term athletic development. *Strength & Conditioning Journal, 34*, 61–72. http://doi.org/10.1519/SSC.0b013e31825760ea

Logue, D. M., Madigan, S. M., Melin, A., Delahunt, E., Heinen, M., Donnell, S. J. M., & Corish, C. A. (2020). Low energy availability in athletes 2020: An updated narrative review of prevalence, risk, within-day energy balance, knowledge, and impact on sports performance. *Nutrients, 12*, 835–853. https://doi.org/10.3390/nu12030835

Lopez, V., Jr, Ma, R., Weinstein, M. G., Hume, P. A., Cantu, R. C., Victoria, C., Queler, S. C., Webb, K., & Allen, A. A. (2020). United States under-19 rugby-7s: Incidence and nature of match injuries during a 5-year epidemiological study. *Sports Medicine – Open, 6*(1), 41. https://doi.org/10.1186/s40798-020-00261-y

McCormack, S., Jones, B., & Till, K. (2020). Training practices of academy rugby league and their alignment to physical qualities deemed important for current and future performance. *International Journal of Sports Science & Coaching, 15*, 512–525. https://doi.org/10.1177/1747954120924905

Mesquita, I., Isidro, S., & Rosado, A. (2010). Portuguese coaches' perceptions of and preferences for knowledge sources related to their professional background. *Journal of Sports Science & Medicine, 9*, 480–489. https://www.ncbi.nlm.nih.gov/pmc/articles/PMC3761720/

Myer, G. D., Sugimoto, D., Thomas, S., & Hewett, T. E. (2013). The influence of age on the effectiveness of neuromuscular training to reduce anterior cruciate ligament injury in female athletes: A meta-analysis. *The American Journal of Sports Medicine, 41*, 203–215. https://doi.org/10.1177/0363546512460637

Orr, R., Hamidi, J., Levy, B., & Halaki, M. (2021). Epidemiology of injuries in Australian junior rugby league players. *Journal of Science and Medicine in Sport, 24*, 241–246. https://doi.org/10.1016/j.jsams.2020.09.002

Petushek, E. J., Sugimoto, D., Stoolmiller, M., Smith, G., & Myer, G. D. (2019). Evidence-based best-practice guidelines for preventing anterior cruciate ligament injuries in young female athletes: A systematic review and meta-analysis. *The American Journal of Sports Medicine, 47*, 1744–1753. https://doi.org/10.1177/0363546518782460

Reed, B.G., & Carr, B. R. (2015). The normal menstrual cycle and the control of ovulation. In *Endotext*. South Dartmouth, MA: MDText.com, Inc. PMID: 25905282

Rugby Football League. (2021). *These girls can* [Internet]. [cited 2022 Jun 28]. Available from: http://secure.rugby-league.com/ign_docs/TheseGirlsCan.pdf

Rugby Football Union. (2010). History of the RFU [Internet]. [cited 2022 Jun 28]. Available from: https://web.archive.org/web/20100422210444/http://www.rfu.com/AboutTheRFU/History.aspx

Rugby Football Union. (2019). England Women announce contracts and squad [Internet]. [cited 2022 June 28]. Available from: https://www.englandrugby.com/news/england-women-contracts-red-roses-and-squad/

Sandwith, E., & Robert, M. (2021). Rug-pee study: The prevalence of urinary incontinence among female university rugby players. *International Urogynecology Journal, 32*, 281–285. http://doi.org/10.1007/s00192-020-04510-2

Scantlebury, S., Ramirez, C., Cummins, C., Stokes, K., Tee, J., Minahan, C., Emmonds, S., McCormack, S., Phillips, G, & Jones, B. (2022). Injury risk factors and barriers to their mitigation for women playing rugby league: A Delphi study. *Journal of Sports Sciences*, 1–14. https://doi.org/10.1080/02640414.2022.2085433

Sharrow, E. A. (2017). "Female athlete" politic: Title IX and the naturalization of sex difference in public policy. *Politics, Groups, and Identities, 5*, 46–66. https://doi.org/10.1080/21565503.2016.1268178

Thibeault, C. M., Thorpe, S., Canac, N., Wilk, S. J., & Hamilton, R. B. (2019). Sex-based differences in transcranial Doppler ultrasound and self-reported symptoms after mild traumatic brain injury. *Frontiers in Neurology, 10*, 590. http://doi.org/10.3389/fneur.2019.00590

Toohey, L. A., Drew, M. K., Finch, C. F., Cook, J. L., & Fortington, L. V. (2019). A 2-year prospective study of injury epidemiology in elite Australian rugby sevens: exploration of incidence rates, severity, injury type, and subsequent injury in men and women. *The American Journal of Sports Medicine, 47*, 1302–1311. https://doi.org/10.1177/0363546518825380

Trakman, G. L., Forsyth, A., Hoye, R., & Belski, R. (2019). Australian team sports athletes prefer dietitians, the internet and nutritionists for sports nutrition information. *Nutrition & Dietetics, 76*, 428–437. https://doi.org/10.1111/1747-0080.12569

Tucker, R., Lancaster, S., Davies, P., Street, G., Starling, L., De Coning, C., & Brown, J. (2021). Trends in player body mass at men's and women's Rugby World Cups: A plateau in body mass and differences in emerging rugby nations. *BMJ Open Sport & Exercise Medicine, 7*, e000885. http://dx.doi.org/10.1136/bmjsem-2020-000885

Waldron, M., Worsfold, P. R., Twist, C., & Lamb, K. (2014). The relationship between physical abilities, ball-carrying and tackling among elite youth rugby league players. *Journal of Sports Sciences, 32*, 542–549. https://doi.org/10.1080/02640414.2013.841975

Williams, S. J., & Kendall, L. (2007). Perceptions of elite coaches and sports scientists of the research needs for elite coaching practice. *Journal of Sports Sciences, 25*, 1577–1586. https://doi.org/10.1080/02640410701245550

Woodhouse, L. N., Tallent, J., Patterson, S. D., & Waldron, M. (2021). Elite international female rugby union physical match demands: A five-year longitudinal analysis by position and opposition quality. *Journal of Science and Medicine in Sport, 24*, 1173–1179. https://doi.org/10.1016/j.jsams.2021.03.018

Woodhouse, L. N., Tallent, J., Patterson, S. D., & Waldron, M. (2022). International female rugby union players' anthropometric and physical performance characteristics: A five-year longitudinal analysis by individual positional groups. *Journal of Sports Sciences, 40*, 370–378. https://doi.org/10.1080/02640414.2021.1993656

17
PLANNING YOUR COACHING FOR YOUNG RUGBY PLAYERS

Michael Ashford and Jamie Taylor

Introduction

It is first important to note that this book has considered a wide breadth of academic evidence across multiple roles and responsibilities of those working with young rugby players. The chapters have included evidence-informed and applied implications for strength and conditioning coaches, those tasked with organising and shaping the laws of competition within youth rugby, sports psychologists, sports scientists and coaches. Additionally, as authors, we are both active practitioners in the field of rugby union, presently working as coach developers and coaches within a Talent Development programme. Thus, to best address the planning process and offer our conceptualisation of key theoretical and applied concepts, we have decided to frame planning through the lens of coaching specifically (but hope the concepts can be applied by other practitioners and those working as part of a multidisciplinary team).

First, it is essential to start this chapter by establishing why planning is important for those involved in shaping the experiences of young rugby players. Therefore, we will introduce four key factors which capture why planning is integral to the coaching process. First, is the notion that all coaching is a goal-directed process, where coaches observe, intervene and make decisions towards intended goals (Collins et al., 2016; Harvey et al., 2015). Planning has consistently been accepted as a central component of the coaching process (cf. Jones et al., 1995; Thorpe, 1984). For instance, Lyle (2002, p. 125) captured planning as the '*link between aspirations, intentions and activity*'. The key tenet of Lyle's (2002) frame of planning is the idea that there is a consistent link between intentions and coaching activity which suggests that coach effectiveness rests on the existence of a consistent point of reference. Within the domain of sports psychology, Martindale and Collins (2005) conceptualised this point of reference as the creation of desired intentions for impact, which refers to intentions which best address the needs and/or wants of those they're working with over an accepted duration of time. Put simply, planning for young rugby players should *begin with the end in mind* and work backwards from there.

Second, Abraham and Collins (2011a) conceptualised the idea of nested planning and thinking, which separates a person's decision-making into those that are (1) fast and intuitive, and (2) slow and deliberate (Kahneman, 2011; Kahneman & Klein, 2009). They defined the fast and intuitive decision-making process as *naturalistic* (Harvey et al., 2015; Klein, 2007) and slow and deliberate decision-making as *classical* (Abraham & Collins, 2011a). The notion of nested planning engages a coach and/or practitioner in a classical decision-making process of working backwards from a desired intention for impact at the macro level, considering political and strategic needs of the wider context over the long-term (e.g., a quadrennial cycle). Importantly, this macro scale goes beyond traditional periodisation (Bompa & Haff, 2009) and, in addition to goals being temporal (e.g., a season long cycle), they also take account of the strategic and political context of a social environment. Macro goals allow for deliberately meso sub-phases to be planned, with a more tactical than strategic orientation (e.g., six-week blocks of time). Then planning for the micro level, capturing activities taking place in the near future in a moment in time that engage coaches in naturalistic decision making (e.g., a training session). Additionally, although this might initially be a linear process for the coach, subsequent phases of replanning and tweaking should occur to take account of changing contextual demands. Nested planning as an approach is underpinned by the philosophy of Professional Judgment and Decision Making (PJDM). Which, in essence, is a practical approach to coach decision-making, that asks the coach to work backwards from their intentions for impact, using multiple levels of nested planning to formulate their coaching approach.

Schon (1991) suggested that practitioners (across any domain) can explore the gap between their expectations and reality after delivery has taken place, which he referred to as reflection on-action. Additionally, he also highlighted that reflection considering the relationship between expectations and reality can take place during delivery, which he termed reflection in-action (Schon, 1991). Argyris and Schön (1974) suggested that effective coaches are better able to shape informed expectations that closely align to the realities of their coaching practice as they deliver. Therefore, by engaging in nested planning and the formulation of clear intentions for impact, coaches can formulate markers of coaching effectiveness (Lyle, 2021; Martindale & Collins, 2005). These points of reference allow coaches to reflect on the relationship between the process (was the approach taken coherent with the intention for impact?) and outcome (was the intended impact met?). By exploring this relationship, critical reflection on-action or in-action (Collins & Collins, 2020; Schon, 1991) can take place to explore the gaps between intentions and reality providing an opportunity to replan within and for future sessions. It can also serve as a platform for sensemaking (i.e., exploring why an individual player is unable to grasp a particular attacking shape of running options outside of the scrum-half), especially with a disjuncture between expectations and reality (Klein, 2007; Klein et al., 2006).

Third, it is clear from many domains that plans very rarely manifest themselves as originally intended. Coaching is no different (Klein, 2007). Establishing clear intentions for impact, better prepares a coach or practitioner to be responsive to the needs of the player in the short-term, without losing sight of the bigger picture (Collins et al., 2016; Harvey et al., 2015). This pattern of planning, reflection and re-planning must happen continuously as situational and contextual demands change over time (Hoffman et al., 2014). For instance, replanning can be as simple as adapting the methods used in a session due to an unexpected number of players attending, or as complex as understanding appropriate post-match feedback for a player experiencing high challenge, or poor performance (Stead et al., 2022; Taylor & Collins, 2021). Subsequently, beginning with a clear end in mind, shaping intentions for impact allows for flexibility and adaptation of coaching methods in the face of complex and ever-changing situations (Abraham et al., 2014).

Fourth, orchestrating the complexity of the youth sport social environment means planning over macro, meso and micro scales is critical to efficacious coaching. Heightened levels of complexity are largely influenced by the social context in which the coach/practitioner operates (Collins, 2019) and the needs and wants of the players involved (Collins et al., 2012b; Taylor & Collins, 2019). These complexities are likely to be amplified by the nature of youth sport, where participants have different needs and 'just letting them play' is unlikely to be appropriate (MacNamara et al., 2015; Nash & Taylor, 2021). This puts increased decision-making demand on the coach seeking to offer an appropriate experience for all their participants. Nested planning allows coaches to shape their practice based on multiple levels of need (Abraham & Collins, 2011a; Abraham et al., 2014). These needs can be segmented into five underpinning components, which Collins (2022) referred to as the five rings of: technical, tactical, physical/movement, mental and lifestyle/wellbeing.

Now we have considered why planning is important, we will capture how these concepts can be used practically within a coach or practitioners' day-to-day practice. However, before we begin, this chapter is not an attempt to *reinvent the wheel* where the planning process is concerned. Multiple conceptions of planning are already accessible which offer appropriate mechanisms for its successful execution, many of which will be cited and considered throughout the course of this chapter. For instance, we will draw heavily on the work of Abraham, Collins and colleagues (2011a, 2011b, 2014, 2022) which have offered a thorough examination of the planning and coach decision-making process. In addition to reading this book chapter, we advise you to access these sources to deepen your understanding of your planning for young rugby players. Therefore, for clarity, the purpose of this final chapter is to contextualise the nested planning process and offer key considerations for those working with young rugby players and offer evidence-informed recommendations for practice (Neelen & Kirschner, 2020).

Establishing Intentions for Impact

In their planning book chapter, Abraham et al. (2014, 2022) make use of the coach decision making framework (Abraham & Collins, 2011b) which presents a coach with three integral sources of knowledge, understanding **who** they are coaching, understanding **what** they are coaching and understanding **how** they are coaching. Whilst beginning with the end in mind is an integral starting place for successful planning, there are several key factors to address before finalising desired intentions for impact. First, coaches should engage in deep thinking to understand **who** they are coaching, which captures the participants age/stage of development, and biopsychosocial needs and wants. In reference to understanding who a coach/practitioner is supporting, the development of young rugby players is a dynamic and non-linear process and players can embark on different pathways as they progress (Abbott et al., 2005). Collins et al. (2012b, p. 228) present the idea that due to the non-linear nature of development, there is a need for *'flexibility, individual optimisation and return routes'* as features of the environment. Additionally, coaches should acknowledge and address the motivational factors that underpin a player's reason for participation, as not all players wish to eventually progress to the elite level of the game. Therefore, we reference the Three Worlds Continuum (Box 17.1) which captures a player's motivations across and between different situations (Collins et al., 2012b). The implications being that technical and tactical coaches, strength and conditioning coaches, sport psychologists, sports scientists and practitioners alike, should understand the motivations of their players as individuals before any planning takes place.

Box 17.1 The Three Worlds Continuum (Adapted from Collins et al., 2012b, pp. 228–229)

Elite Referenced Excellent (ERE)	'Excellence in the form of high-level sporting performance where achievement is measured against others with the ultimate goal of winning at the highest level possible, or'
Personal Referenced Excellence (PRE)	'Excellence in the form of participation and personal performance, where achievement is more personally referenced by, say, completing a marathon or improving one's personal best'
Participation for Personal Well-being (PPW)	'Taking part in physical activity to satisfy needs other than personal progression'.

Additionally, player development needs to be seen as a biopsychosocial phenomenon, where biological, psychological and social factors interact, forming the unique needs of the individual you're coaching (Collins et al., 2012b; Collins & Cruickshank, 2022).

Here we begin to address the highly individual nature of youth rugby, where young rugby players possess different motivations, at different ages/stages of development biopsychosocially within different contexts (Abraham et al., 2022; Collins et al., 2012a, 2012b). Let us consider a hypothetical example, where coaches and practitioners are supporting a group of U14 male rugby league players in a club environment. The wider group of players consider friendships and social factors as their motivation for participation, whilst the social context of the club pressurises a focus on results and performance. In contrast, two individual players wish to take rugby league seriously and perceive it as a plausible career in the future. In this example, the coach is required to weigh up numerous factors (e.g., player performance, friendships, social experiences and results) before forming their intentions for impact. We suggest that a useful starting point would be case conferencing or needs analysis. This could be done through extended open conversation with players, parents, coaches and club committee members. This allows the coach to weigh up the biopsychosocial needs of their players and of the wider environment.

In addition to understanding **who** is being coached, understanding **what** is going to be coached also feeds into the development of appropriate intentions for impact (Abraham & Collins, 2011a; Abraham et al., 2014). Importantly however, at all levels of planning, there needs to be a clear underpinning **why** for a coach's action. The five rings model (Collins, 2022), although presenting five distinct components, actively encourages the coach to integrate each of these factors. Indeed, as an additional challenge, the coach will need to integrate these factors both for each individual player and across their training group. As an example, the coach may be working with a mix of players who engage partly for personal wellbeing purposes and others with ambitions of playing at higher levels of the sport (Collins et al., 2012). Catering towards this mix, the coach recognises the need for the building of perceived and actual competence across the five rings to support long-term participation and development. Yet, to cater to their needs, the coach may choose to make these objectives more overt to the aspiring player and more covert to the less ambitious player. Nested planning helps to inform that coach's emphasis and *why*. Some implications of each 'ring' have been suggested by the authors of each chapter within this book. As a signposting tool, each chapter has been aligned to each of the five rings below. We suggest revisiting relevant chapters to support/enhance understanding and facilitate the planning process (see Table 17.1).

For example, Chapter 10 offers an example of a mental model of rugby union, which captures the complexities of the technical and tactical requirements for each moment of the game. By first considering the age/stage of the players

TABLE 17.1 Alignment of Book Chapters to the Five Rings of Athlete Development

The Five Rings (Collins, 2022)	Tactical	Technical	Physical and Movement Skills	Mental	Lifestyle and Welfare
Relevant Chapters	1, 3, 5, 6, 10	1, 3, 4, 5, 6, 10, 11	1, 2, 3, 4, 5, 6, 7, 8, 12, 13, 15	1, 2, 3, 4, 5, 9	1, 2, 5, 12, 13, 14, 15, 16

a coach works with, they can assess the demands of the game (i.e., the big 5) in accordance with the laws at that stage of development. For example, within the laws of English Age Group Rugby, U15 rugby union players are introduced to lifting in the lineout, which means they are presented an increased technical and tactical demand in this moment of the game. Additionally, the introduction of this part of the game results in increased physical demands, such as jumping power, strength alongside increased mental factors, such as developing confidence and self-efficacy in the execution of movements. This also happens at a time when players will be moving through a range of physical and cognitive developmental changes (e.g., maturation), along with the social consequences of these changes (e.g., peer relationships).

Auditing Your Planning: The Big 5

Given the complexity of the aims of the coaching process, despite an organisational drive towards the use of tools like SMART goal setting, this type of approach has recently been questioned (Swann et al., 2022). Pertinent to the coach, setting highly specific, measurable goals may be undesirable given that 'not everything that can be counted counts but not everything that counts can be counted' (attributed to multiple sources, maybe Einstein!). So, therefore, this presents us with a challenge. One suggested approach would be the use of the 'Big 5' reflective questions (Collins & Collins, 2020) which are a series of questions that can flexibly be deployed proactively (in planning) and reactively (post event). An example is shown in Table 17.2.

Importantly, this allows for the coach to proactively engage in pre-mortem type thinking, anticipating future problems (Kahneman & Klein, 2009) and considering alternative courses of action. Similarly, post-event, auditing the process that they took, rigorously avoiding post-hoc justification of action, by referencing initial intentions for impact. In turn, allowing for adaptive action framed against intentions. Given the concepts that have been presented, Box 17.2 summarises the process where coaches (and practitioners) would shape desired intentions for impact, begin the nested planning process and employ the Big 5 to audit planning proactively and reactively.

TABLE 17.2 Options for Using the Big 5 as a Planning Audit (Adapted from Collins & Collins, 2020)

Proactive	Reactive
What do you plan on doing?	What happened?
What other ways can you do that?	Describe what other ways you could have done that?
Why have you chosen this option?	What made you choose that option?
What contextual factors would make you choose a different option?	What would have made you choose a different option?
How will you know you made a good decision?	What would you have done if…?

Box 17.2

Establishing your intentions for impact – some questions to consider

- Why do your players participate? (*ERE, PRE, PPW*)
- What is the age/stage of the participants?
- What does this mean for the demands of the game in the format which is going to be played?
- What are the key challenges that require introduction? (e.g., lifting in the lineout, scrummaging technique, new positions)
- What do they/you/stakeholders hope to achieve by the end of the season?
- What are the goals of the context in which you work? (*club, community, school, county, talent development, region, international*)
- What is the purpose of this environment? (*Enjoyment, development, winning, dependent on the individuals, all*)

Example intentions for impact – creating coherence between stakeholders

Context - U15 male club rugby union environment

    Motivations – mix of ERE, PRE & PPW depending on individual

    Club goals – provide a successful and enjoyable training and playing experience for young rugby players to develop.

1. Support players to develop an appropriate base skill set (catch, pass, carry, move, offload, tackle, contact skills) which can be executed with confidence in competitive situations in appropriate situations.
2. Introduce and refine players technical ability, tactical understanding, physical and movement skills, mental skills and considerations of welfare in unit specific techniques and skills (scrum, lineout, kick-off).
3. Provide an enjoyable whilst challenging playing experience where player development is a central factor and desire for success is fostered.

Level	Strategic & Political Goals	Intentions for Impact	Timeline & Activity		
Macro: 1 Year U15's Season	- Progress all players into U16 age group. - Make the final of county cup, plate or bowl - Ensure 3 players are successful in entry to local Regional Academies DPP programme.	1) Support players to develop an appropriate base skill set (catch, pass, carry, move, offload, tackle, contact skills) which can be executed with confidence in competitive situations in appropriate situations. 2) Introduce and refine players technical ability, tactical understanding, physical and movement skills, mental skills and considerations of welfare in unit specific techniques and skills (scrum, lineout, kick-off). 3) Provide an enjoyable whilst challenging playing environment where player development is a central factor and the desire for success is built.	Pre-Season Intentions for Impact Priority – 2 Secondary – 1 & 3	Block 1 Intentions for Impact Priority – 1 Secondary – 2 & 3	Block 2 Intentions for Impact Priority – 3 Secondary 1 & 2
Meso: Socio, tactical, motivational	- Support development of mental skills in line with technical and tactical challenges - Provide appropriate levels of physical and movement challenge through sessions.	Pre-Season (Weeks 1-8) 1) Introduce technical and tactical demands of set piece requirements (Key challenges – pushing as 6 in scrum, lift, jump, catch, backs launch from set phase – what when why?). 2) Support players to understand specific roles and responsibilities within a wider way of playing. 3) Target "big rocks" of players skill sets (catch, pass, carry, move offload, tackle, contact skills.	Block 1 (Weeks 8-20)	Block 2 (Weeks 21 – 38)	
Micro Sessions	Develop session and meeting plans with intentions for impact, behavioural approach, learning design and athlete experience detail	1	2	3	4	5	6	7	8

FIGURE 17.1 A Sample Nested Plan for a U15 Rugby Union Team (adapted from Abraham & Collins, 2011a; Abraham et al., 2014, 2022).

Nested Planning to Meet the Desired Intentions for Impact

Up until this point, we have considered four key factors which explain why planning is so important within the coaching process. Additionally, we have introduced the concept of nested planning, the importance of understanding **who** you are coaching, understanding **what** you are coaching and the importance of beginning with the end in mind by developing desired intentions for impact (Abraham et al., 2014; Martindale & Collins, 2005). Given the complex nature of the ideas already discussed, a coach is then tasked with piecing each of these concepts together into a coherent nested plan (Abraham & Collins, 2011a). Once clarity regarding desired intentions for impact is established (and this is shared/coherent across and between all coaches/staff working with the players) a coach can begin to populate the meso-associated time frames they are working towards (i.e., across the duration of a season). In Box 17.2, we offered a hypothetical example of some desired intentions for impact for a group of U15 male rugby union players in a club environment. To best portray the nested planning process, we have used this example within Figure 17.1, which demonstrates the integration and coherence between the macro, meso, and micro components of a nested plan, inclusive of player needs and key challenges.

Nested planning over longer periods of time involves classical decision-making regarding what a coach prioritises. As an example, coaches may choose to prioritise the way they want to defend (i.e., defend the man vs. defend the ball), their kicking strategy (i.e., for territory vs. to compete for possession) or the way they want to attack (i.e., build pressure through possession vs. offload and score quickly). Importantly, no evidence exists to suggest that specific tactical priorities exceed others. Instead, coaches should consider the time it will take for the players to learn specific tactical solutions and the technical, mental, physical and movement skills and lifestyle demands they create (Ashford et al., 2021; Tee et al., 2018). Furthermore, just because a coach prioritises a specific area of the game (and the aligned needs/challenges that come with it) does not imply that other moments of the game should be neglected. Additionally, younger rugby players (*age* <16) will have a reduced memory capacity and cognitive load, which refers to the amount of new (*tactical*) knowledge structures that can be introduced to them which could be transferred to the long-term memory (Cope & Cushion, 2020). Therefore, to avoid cognitive overload and maximise a young players potential to learn, we suggest that coaches and practitioners follow the *rule of three*, where a maximum of three **new** tactical structures are introduced within a block of learning. Given these concepts, Box 17.3 offers some reflective questions and wider statements to consider in the development of an age-appropriate nested plan.

Box 17.3 Identifying What You Want to Prioritise and Why?

- How do you want to attack? (progress the ball up the field, penetrate the defensive line, score)
- How do you want to defend? (*prevent opponent from progressing, control territory, stop opponent from scoring*)
- How do you want to contest possession? (*lineout, scrum, kick off, ruck, maul, tackle – recycle & continue in possession – contest & win out of possession*)
- Considering the way you want to play – what learning will you prioritise first?
- Why? (*because it will take the longest amount of time? Or the shortest? Or because you can build upon previous learning?*)

Planning for Long-Term Learning

- Don't confuse performance in training with learning.
- Learning often involves behaviour change and takes time.
- Therefore, plan for an appropriate amount of time for the development of; technical skills, tactical understanding and solutions, mental skills, physical and movement skills and lifestyle/well-being factors to take place.
- Remember, young rugby players will only have mental space for a limited amount of new material in their working memory. Therefore, stick to the rule of three!

From a Big Picture to a Moment in Time

Now we have discussed how nested planning can be applied into a youth rugby setting, we will now bring planning closer to the moment by moment decisions that a coach makes. A nested plan captures desired intentions for impact and the decisions of what to prioritise and why (Abraham & Collins, 2011a, 2022). As a starter, Muir et al. (2011) offered the coaching planning and practice reflective framework which considered how a coach's behaviours, practice design and learner engagement aligned to the intended session objectives (see Abraham et al., 2022). However, so far limited attention has been paid to why coaches might adopt a specific approach.

There are of course a broad range of methods that a coach can use, captured by the idea of 'coaching approach' and 'learning design', both of which are used to shape the athlete experience (Ashford et al., 2021). First, the coaching approach, which is the orientation of the coach towards their practice, made up of the interactions and behaviours a coach uses. Second, the learning design of the coach, or in essence, the types of different activities that are set up for players to engage with (Muir et al., 2011). In their planning chapter, Abraham and colleagues (2022) discussed the importance of constructive alignment, which is a concept developed in education by Biggs (2003). Constructive alignment refers to the development of approaches and activities that align to the associated learning outcomes.

Often, the consideration of coaching methods that facilitate and shape player learning is explored from the coaches perspective. Conversely, we suggest that coaches and practitioners engage in a pre-mortem to critically explore the athlete experience from proposed methods of delivery, that is, what thoughts, feelings and experiences the player is given in line with the desired intentions (Argyris & Schön, 1974; Schon, 1991). Importantly, these outcomes are best achieved through the shaping of the player experience (Taylor & Collins, 2020, 2022), a factor that seems to have broadly been overlooked in the coaching literature so far, in pedagogical terms at least. This contrasts with education more broadly that has put a significant weighting on the experience of learners (Soderstrom & Bjork, 2015). Either way, we would suggest that as a feature of nested planning, the coach considers the type of experience they want their players to have, the extent to which the content they are offered is meaningful to them individually, the depth of their understanding and how challenging the experience is (Abraham & Collins, 2011a). Thus, at all levels of the nested plan, there is a need to consider the approach(es) and learning design that is most likely to induce the desired athlete experience. Importantly, this distinguishes nested planning and PJDM from other approaches in the literature that may advocate for a specific pairing of both coaching approach and learning design. This is clearly at odds with the suggestion that coaching needs to be done in a specific way, regardless of participant needs. It is for this reason that the approach is strongly aligned to the concept of research-informed practice, rather than presenting a single way to coach based on a philosophical positioning. For instance, a significant breadth of applied recommendations and implications are presented throughout this book, all of which may be suitable given specific demands and player needs. In essence, we are advocating for the idea that 'everything works somewhere, nothing works everywhere' (Wiliam, 2016, p. 63).

Conclusion

Supporting the development of young rugby players is inherently complex, not just because of the physical demands imposed by the game, but additionally, the wide breadth and depth of knowledge and understanding required to meet players wants and needs alongside the socio-political challenges of shaping an appropriate player experience. Consequently, nested planning is an essential mechanism for coaching efficacy, as it supports us to navigate this inherent level of complexity. This level of complexity is not subjective to coaching but universal across all disciplines where young rugby players are being supported. The process of beginning with the end in mind through evidence-informed intentions for impact should be universal to all disciplines from the strength and conditioning coach, through to the sports psychologist. We encourage all coaches and practitioners to deepen their understanding of **what** knowledge underpins the process of developing a nested plan which results in players meeting desired intentions for impact. Additionally, this understanding should be extended to the methods which capture **how** this player experience will be shaped. Finally, and most importantly, we encourage all coaches and practitioners who support young rugby players to employ PJDM to consider **why** their decision-making, both classical and naturalistic, and the methods used in practice, coaching approach and learning design were (or weren't) appropriate. To summarise this process Thinking Box 17.4 offers a summary of the nested planning process, we hope this facilitates your practice.

> **Box 17.4 Summarising the Nested Planning Process**
>
> 1. Formulate a clear **Why** for your practice by:
> 2. *Understanding **Who** you are working with* – case conferencing & needs analysis to explore, identify and analyse your players biopsychosocial needs.
> 3. *Understanding **What** is to be worked on* – consider the demands of the game within your context (e.g., establishing a 'way of playing' and the technical, mental, physical and movement and lifestyle demands associated).
> 4. *Beginning with the end in mind* – create desired intentions for impact.
> 5. *Prioritise technical/tactical solutions* and nest these experiences over a macro timescale (i.e., a season, or four-year cycle).
> 6. *Understanding **How** desired intentions for impact will be achieved* – the methods of coaching that best support your desired intentions and the underpinning evidence of where they should be applied.

7 *Audit your planning process* – using the Big 5. Replan, engage in critical reflect-in action and reflect-on action.
8 *Monitor* the alignment between intentions and reality through objective and subjective analysis methods (see Chapter 10 for examples).

Planning and Replanning for and in a Moment in Time

1 *Coaching approach* – how do I/we shape the players experience through the way I/we behave and interact?
2 *Learning design* – how do I/we shape the players experience through the design of the activities I/we create?
3 *Monitor* (reflect in-action) – how do I ensure I focus my/our attention to observe and intervene when the situation is optimal?

Key Take Home Messages

- Planning affords a practitioner the opportunity to (1) begin with the end in mind through desired intentions for impact, (2) use nested planning and thinking to make informed coaching decisions, (3) be flexible and adaptable; and (4) navigate complex individual player needs.
- Planning should begin by taking time to understand **who** you're working with, their needs, wants and characteristics that will influence the way they learn. Use case conceptualisations and needs analyses with players and stakeholders (i.e., parents, teachers, peers).
- Next, take time to understand **what** you're working towards and the wider technical, tactical, physical and movement, mental and lifestyle and wellbeing considerations.
- Utilising this knowledge and understanding, begin with the end in mind by developing evidence-informed desired intentions for impact over a macro timescale (e.g., quadrennial cycle or single season) and working backwards from there to a meso (e.g., six weeks) and micro (e.g., single training session).
- Prioritise what should come first, second and third, etc. by considering the length of time learning may take.
- Employ the Big 5 Reflective questions to reflect proactively (*what might happen and why*) and reactively (*what happened and why*) to plan, deliver, reflect and replan to effectively meet the desired intentions for impact.
- Given your desired intentions for impact, replan on a session-by-session basis which coaching methods would best shape the athlete experience. Coaching methods include the **coaching approach** (i.e., planning for the behaviours and interactions that shape the player experience) and the **learning design** (i.e., the way in which activities set for players facilitate their learning).

- Finally, expert coaches have been found to be lifelong learners who consistently explore the alignment between their expectations in their coaching practice and the realities of the player experience they create. Continuously seek to engage in a cycle of nested planning, replanning, delivery, reflection and again, replanning to test and tweak the effectiveness of your practice.

References

Abbott, A., Button, C., Pepping, G. J., & Collins, D. (2005). Unnatural selection: talent identification and development in sport. *Nonlinear Dynamics, Psychology, and Life Sciences*, 9(1), 61–88.

Abraham, A., & Collins, D. (2011a). Taking the next step: Ways forward for coaching science. *Quest*, 63, 366–384. https://doi.org/10.1080/00336297.2011.10483687

Abraham, A., & Collins, D. (2011b). Effective skill development+-t - How should athletes' skills be developed. In D. Collins, A. Button, & H. Richards (Eds.), *Performance psychology: A practitioner's guide* (pp. 207–230). London: Churchill Livingstone, Elsevier.

Abraham, A., Collins, D., & Martindale, R. (2006). The coaching schematic: Validation through expert coach consensus. *Journal of Sports Sciences*, 24, 549–564. https://doi.org/10.1080/02640410500189173

Abraham, A., Collins, D., Morgan, G., & Muir, B. (2009). Developing expert coaches requires expert coach development: Replacing serendipity with orchestration. In A. Lorenzo, S. J. Ibanez, & E. Ortega (Eds.), *Aportaciones Teoricas Y Practicas Para El Baloncesto Del Futuro*. Seville: Wanceulen Editorial Deportiva. 10.13140/RG.2.1.4062.5046

Abraham, A., Sáiz, S. L. J., Mckeown, S., Morgan, G., Muir, B., North, J., & Till, K. (2014). Planning your coaching: A focus on youth participant development. In C. Nash (Ed.), *Practical sports coaching*, pp. 16–53. Abingdon, Oxfordshire: Routledge.

Abraham, A., Sáiz, S. L. J., Mckeown, S., Morgan, G., Muir, B., North, J., & Till, K. (2022). Planning your coaching: A focus on youth participant development. In C. Nash (Ed.), *Practical sports coaching* (2nd ed.), pp. 18–44. Abingdon, Oxfordshire: Routledge.

Argyris, C., & Schön, D. A. (1974). *Theory in Practice: Increasing professional effectiveness*. San Francisco, CA: Jossey-Bass.

Ashford, M., Abraham, A., & Poolton, J. (2021). What cognitive mechanism, when, where, and why? Exploring the decision making of University and Professional Rugby Union Players during competitive matches. *Frontiers in Psychology*, 12, 609127. https://doi.org/10.3389/fpsyg.2021.609127

Biggs, J. B. (2003) *Teaching for quality learning at university* (2nd ed.). Buckingham: Open University Press/Society for Research into Higher Education.

Bompa, T. O., & Haff, G. G. (2009). *Periodization theory and methodology of training* (5th ed.). Champagne, IL: Human Kinetics.

Collins, D. (2019). The principles of elite coaching: Blending knowledge, experience, and novelty. In *Routledge Handbook of elite sport performance* (pp. 5–14). Abingdon, Oxfordshire: Routledge.

Collins, D. (2022). Macrostructures and microsystems In. D. Collins, & A. Cruickshank. *Sports psychology essentials* (pp. 215–231). Abingdon, Oxfordshire: Routledge.

Collins, D., Abraham, A., & Collins, R. (2012a). On vampires and wolves—Exposing and exploring reasons for the differential impact of coach education. *International Journal of Sport Psychology*, 43, 255. https://doi.org/10.7352/IJSP.2012.43.255

Collins, D., Bailey, R., Ford, P. A., MacNamara, Á., Toms, M., & Pearce, G. (2012b). Three worlds: New directions in participant development in sport and physical activity. *Sport, Education and Society, 17*, 225–243. https://doi.org/10.1080/13573322.2011.607951

Collins, D., & Collins, L. (2020). Developing coaches' professional judgement and decision making: Using the 'Big 5'. *Journal of Sports Sciences, 39*, 115–119. https://doi.org/10.1080/02640414.2020.1809053

Collins, D., Collins, L., & Carson, H. J. (2016). "If it feels right, do it": Intuitive decision making in a sample of high-level sport coaches. *Frontiers in Psychology, 7*, 504. https://doi.org/10.3389/fpsyg.2016.00504

Collins, D., & Cruickshank, A. (2022). *Sports psychology essentials.* Routledge.

Cope, E., & Cushion, C. (2020). A move towards reconceptualising direct instruction in sport coaching pedagogy. *Profession, 18*, 19.

Cushion, C. (2007). Modelling the complexity of the coaching process. *International Journal of Sports Science & Coaching, 2*, 395–401. https://doi.org/10.1260/174795407783359650

Harvey, S., Lyle, J. W. B., & Muir, B. (2015). Naturalistic decision making in high performance team sport coaching. *International Sport Coaching Journal, 2*, 152–168. http://dx.doi.org/10.1123/iscj.2014-0118

Hoffman, R. R., Ward, P., Feltovich, P. J., DiBello, L., Fiore, S. M., & Andrews, D. H. (2014). *Accelerated expertise: Training for high proficiency in a complex world.* Oxfordshire: Psychology Press, Routledge.

Jones, D. E., Housner, L. D., & Kornspan, A. S. (1995). A comparative analysis of expert and novice basketball coaches' practice planning. *Applied Research in Coaching and Athletics Annual, 1*(2), 201–227.

Kahneman, D. (2011). *Thinking fast and slow.* Macmillan.

Kahneman, D., & Klein, G. (2009). Conditions for intuitive expertise: A failure to disagree. *American Psychologist, 64*, 515–526. https://doi.org/10.1037/a0016755

Klein, G. (2007). Flexecution as a paradigm for replanning, part 1. *IEEE Intelligent Systems, 22*, 79–83. https://doi.org/10.1109/MIS.2007.4338498

Klein, G., Moon, B., & Hoffman, R. R. (2006). Making sense of sensemaking 2: A macrocognitive model. *IEEE Intelligent Systems, 21*, 88–92. https://doi.org/10.1109/MIS.2006.100

Lyle, J. (2002). *Sport coaching concepts: A framework for coaching practice.* Oxfordshire: Routledge, Abingdon.

Lyle, J. (2021). Coaching effectiveness: A personal discourse on bringing clarity to an overused concept. *International Sport Coaching Journal, 8*, 270–274. https://doi.org/10.1123/iscj.2020-0025

MacNamara, Á., Collins, D., & Giblin, S. (2015). Just let them play? Deliberate preparation as the most appropriate foundation for lifelong physical activity [Opinion]. *Frontiers in Psychology, 6.* https://doi.org/10.3389/fpsyg.2015.01548

Martindale, A., & Collins, D. (2005). Professional judgment and decision making: The role of intention for impact. *The Sport Psychologist, 19*, 303–317. https://doi.org/10.1123/tsp.19.3.303

Mosston, M. (1966). *Teaching physical education.* Indianapolis, IN: Merrill.

Muir, B., Morgan, G., Abraham, A., & Morley, D. (2011). Developmentally appropriate approaches to coaching children. In I. Stafford (Ed.), *Coaching children in sport* (pp. 39–59). London & New York: Routledge.

Nash, C., & Taylor, J. (2021). 'Just let them play': Complex dynamics in youth sport, why it isn't so simple. *Frontiers in Psychology.* https://doi.org/10.3389/fpsyg.2021.700750

Neelen, M., & Kirschner, P. (2020). *Evidence-informed learning design: Use evidence to create training which improves performance.* London: KoganPage.

Schon, D. A. (1991). *The reflective practitioner: How professionals think in action.* Aldershot: Ashgate Publishing Ltd.

Soderstrom, N. C., & Bjork, R. A. (2015). Learning versus performance: An integrative review. *Perspectives on Psychological Science, 10,* 176–199. https://doi.org/10.1177/1745691615569000

Stead, J., Poolton, J., & Alder, D. (2022). Performance slumps in sport: A systematic review. *Psychology of Sport and Exercise, 61*(102136), 1–9. https://doi.org/10.1016/j.psychsport.2022.102136

Swann, C., Jackman, P. C., Lawrence, A., Hawkins, R. M., Goddard, S. G., Williamson, O., Schweickle, M. J., Vella, S. A., Rosenbaum, S., & Ekkekakis, P. (2022). The (over)use of SMART goals for physical activity promotion: A narrative review and critique. *Health Psychology Review,* advance online publication, 1–16. https://doi.org/10.1080/17437199.2021.2023608

Taylor, J., & Collins, D. (2019). Shoulda, Coulda, Didnae—Why don't high-potential players make it? *The Sport Psychologist, 33,* 85–96. https://doi.org/10.1123/tsp.2017-0153

Taylor, J., & Collins, D. (2020). The highs and the lows – Exploring the nature of optimally impactful development experiences on the talent pathway. *The Sport Psychologist, 34,* 319–328. https://doi.org/10.1123/tsp.2020-0034

Taylor, J., & Collins, D. (2021). Getting in the way: Investigating barriers to optimising talent development experience. *Journal of Expertise, 4,* 315–332.

Taylor, J., & Collins, D. (2022). The talent development curriculum. In C. Nash (Ed.), *Practical sport coaching* (2nd ed.). Abingdon, Oxfordshire: Routledge.

Tee, J. C., & Ashford, M., & Piggott, D (2018). A tactical periodization approach for rugby union. *Strength and Conditioning Journal, 40,* 1–13. https://doi.org/10.1519/SSC.0000000000000390

Thorpe, R. (1984). *Planning and practice* (vol. 6). Leeds: Coachwise 1st4sport.

Wiliam, D. (2016). *Leadership for teacher learning creating a culture where all teachers improve so that all students succeed.* Blairsville, PA: Learning Sciences International.

INDEX

Note: **Bold** page numbers refer to tables and *italic* page numbers refer to figures.

absolute fat mass 52, 263
Activate Injury Prevention Exercise Programme 291, *295*
activate programme structure following end user feedback *298*
adjustables 3, 93
ad libitum drinking 258
aerobic endurance 115
age at peak height velocity (APHV) 19, 53
Age Grade Rugby (AGR) 5; development programme 9–10; principles 6; RFU 5–6; structure 6; talent identification 9–10; U7 to U18, 6–7; youth development 7–8
age grouping 51, 56; annual 61, 62; chronological 19, 51, 80
anaerobic endurance 115
annual-age grouping 61
ASRM *see* athlete self-reported measures (ASRM)
athlete development, five rings of 333, **336**
athlete monitoring cycle 229
athlete self-reported measures (ASRM) 240
athleticism 17, 20
attitude 195, 199
Australian Polynesian players 53

backs 2, 3, 7, 53, **71**, 93–95, 99, 174, 226, 286
ball-carrier technical skills **204**
bandwidth feedback 181

bio-banding 56
biochemical markers 241
bioelectrical impedance analysis (BIA) 113
biopsychosocial modelling 36, **37–38,** 39
Birth Quartile (BQ) Distribution Percentages *76*
body mass *52,* 113
body shape 52
BokSmart programme 290
Booth, M. 70
brief assessment of mood (BAM) 240

carbohydrate (CHO) 252, **254–255,** 255–256
CAYPABLE framework *35,* 35–36
centres of excellence (CoE) 10
CK *see* creatine kinase (CK)
coaching children: biopsychosocial modelling *35,* **37–38,** 39; child's development 35–36; coaching and learning 47–48; decision-making processes *35;* 'how' are we coaching 39–41; movement-focused coach development 42, **46**; movement skills 42; perspectives *35,* 35–36; skills 47; stages of development **45**; structure a session 44; throwing **43**; understanding movement 44; 'what' are we coaching 41; 'who' are we coaching *35,* **37–38,** 39
coaching process: auditing 336, *337*; classical 332; coherence between stakeholders

337; decision-making process 332; establishing intentions 334–336; in-action 332; key factors 331–332; long-term learning 339; macro goals 332; moment decisions 340–341; naturalistic 332; pattern of 333; reflection on-action 332; sample nested plan *338,* 338–339; social environment 333
coefficient of variation (CV) 245
community sports 321
countermovement jump (CMJ) test 114, 237
creatine kinase (CK) 241
cycle length 317

declarative knowledge 195
developmental features: becoming CAYPABLE framework *35,* 35–36; coaching children *35,* 35–36
Development Model of Sport Participation (DMSP) 68
direct instruction 181
documented mean training injury severity 280
dual-energy X-ray absorptiometry (DXA) 113, 263
DXA *see* dual-energy X-ray absorptiometry (DXA)

early diversification 68
early-maturing players 19
early specialisation 68
Ecological Dynamics Framework (EDF) 67
effect size (ES) 245
elite participants 173
energy requirements 250–252
England Rugby Developing Player Programme (ERDPP) 10
England Rugby Player Pathway *9*
eumenorrhea 317
external load 21, 113, 138, 139, 142–144, 224, 226–228
external training load quantification tools 228

fat-free mass (FFM) 52, 250, 263
fatigue response 236–237; ASRM 240; biochemical markers 241; congested fixtures 242–243; hormonal markers 241; match-play 242; measuring and monitoring 237; neuromuscular performance 237, **238–239,** 240; practical considerations 243–246, *244*; training 241–242

fat mass 113, 263, 315; absolute 52, 263
female rugby: cardiorespiratory/metabolic function 324; considerations 316–318; constraint-driven solutions 323; growth 315–316; injury 318, 320–321; injury surveillance *320*; menstrual cycle management 317; research by decade *319*; risk factors and barriers 321–323, *322*; studies *319*
field-based fitness testing protocols 109
fixed prescription *vs.* autoregulatory prescription 142–143
flexible chronological approach 76
forwards 2, 3, 7, 53, **71**, 93–95, 99, 174, 226, 286
4C's framework 41

global navigation satellite systems (GNSS) 91
global positioning system (GPS) 223
Graduated Return to Play Protocol (GRTP) 289
growth, defined as 18

Half Game rule 8
hormonal markers 241
hydration requirements 258–259

Immediate Medical Management on the Field of Play (IMMOFP) 325
inertial head loading 200
injury risk 20–21, 270; concussion 288–289; designing 291–292; exercise programmes 292–293, **294**; factors 285–288; feedback 297, 298, 300, 303; impacts of 271–272; *vs.* other sports 283–284; patterns 284–285; pilot testing 296–297; reduction strategies 289–291; rugby league 280, **281–282,** 283; rugby union 272, **273–279,** 280; TPG 293, 295–296; U15 version of programme *299–302*
inside backs 2, 95
interclass correlation coefficient (ICC) 113
Intermittent Fitness Test 115
Intermittent Recovery Test Level 115
internal load 21, 223, 224, 227, 228
International Olympic Committee 3, 5, 22
isolated technique 173
isometric assessments 113–114
isometric mid-thigh pull (IMTP) 114

kinanthropometry 51–53, *56*; biological maturation 53; collaboration 62; communication 62; 4C's of

implementation 59; grouping strategies 56, 61; growth and maturation 57; guidelines and protocols 57–59; injury risk 55–56; maturity status 54–55; measurement error 58; measurement tools 58; measuring *vs.* estimating maturity 58–59; physical performance 55–56; player assessment 59–60; pragmatic methods 58; talent identification 55–56; talent pathway 61–62; training sessions 60–61
Knockout Cup 8

late-maturing players 19
league, definition of 8
lineouts 2, 7
load monitoring 222
Locking Wheel Nut Model *84*
longitudinal assessment approach 10
long-term athletic development: athleticism 20; balancing training 21; definition 17; factors *18*; growth and maturation 17–20; injury risk 20–21; psychosocial development 21–22; RAMPAGE 25, **26**, 27–28; ten pillars 23, **24**
lower match-related injury 291

macronutrient: anthropometric assessment 260; body composition assessment 263–264; CHO 252, 255–256; dietary assessment 259; fat 257–258; fluid intake 258–259, **261–262**; protein 256–258; use of supplements 259–260
markers 3, 79, 81, 83, 167, 244, 332; biochemical and hormonal 241
match demands: age groups 100; drill design *98*; evaluating training drills 100–102; GNSS *101*; position and phases-of-play 99–100; quantifying 92; research 92; Rugby League 92–94; Rugby Union 94–96; technical-tactical components 92–93; training drills 97–99
maturation 18, 53
maximum sprint speed (MSS) 226
menarche 317
menstrual cycle 317, 318
mental model *185*, 335
micro-electrical-mechanical systems (MEMS) 91
middle forwards 3
miniature adults 16
Mirwald maturity offset method 53–54
multistage fitness-test (MSFT) 115

National Rugby League (NRL) 172
national standardised fitness testing 116, 117
National Strength and Conditioning Association (NSCA) 17
nested planning 158, 333
neuromuscular training programmes 291
non-functional overreaching 21
non-invasive anthropometric measurements 59
nutritional requirements 250

O'Connor, D. 71
Oliver, J. L. 242, 324
on-time maturing players 19, 55, 62
organised chaos 5, 231
outside backs 2, 3, 93, 95, 96, 174
overtraining 21, 102, 142

penalty kicks 2
performance indicators (PI) 93
periodisation 128–129
Personal Disclosure Mutual Sharing (PDMS) 157
physical activity level (PAL) 252
physical qualities: aerobic/ anaerobic capacities 115; agility test 115; anthropometrics 109, 113; body composition 109, 113; change of direction tests 115; chronological age 118, *120*; conducting the assessments 117; data analysis 118; evaluation 118; linear speed 114–115; measuring 108–109; movement skills 115–116; PCA 118; power 114; process for *108*; ProPQ Tool 118; reporting 118; strength testing 113–114; testing assessment 116–117; testing methods **110–112**
PI *see* performance indicators (PI)
Player Development Group (PDG) 10
positive/negative modelling 181
post-facto performance analysis methods 177
predicted adult height (PAH) 53
Pre-Hospital Immediate Care in Sport (PHICIS) 325
principal component analysis (PCA) 118, *119*
procedural knowledge 195
Professional Judgment and Decision Making (PJDM) 332
Profile of Mood States (POMS) 240
PROGRESS framework 159–160
ProPQ Tool 118

psychosocial development: adolescence 154–155; behaviour and language 158; characteristics **152**; coaching frameworks 155–156; definition 151; individual differences 161; promoting learning over winning 156–157; PSC 158–159, *159*; within rugby 151, 154; skills **153**; social environments 161; supportive environment 157–158; TDE 155, *159*
psychosocial skills and characteristics (PSCs) 150, 158–159, *159*; opportunities to practice 159–160; promote transfer 160

questioning 28, 160, 181

Raise, Activate, Mobilise, Prepare, Activity, Games, and Evaluate (RAMPAGE) 25, **26,** 27–28
random practice 181
rating of perceived challenge (RPC) 209
Reactive Agility Test 115
relative age effect (RAE) 19
resting metabolic rate (RMR) 251
risk reduction strategy 270
Rugby Football League (RFL) 42, 116, 315
Rugby Football Union (RFU) 2, *5,* 5–6, *9,* 315; AGR 2, 5–6; talent development framework 166; U16 Academy Festival 180
rugby league 3; injury risk 280, **281–282,** 283
Rugby Smart 290
rugby union 2, 57; physical demands 95–96; talent identification and development in 68; technical-tactical demands 94–95

School Clinical Rugby Measure (SCRuM) test battery 172
scrums 2, 94
seasonal load 223
self-reported training 227–228
Sequence of Prevention 270
session load 225
session rating of perceived exertion (sRPE) 222
sexual maturation 53
skeletal maturation 53
Small Blacks programme 23
smallest worthwhile change (SWC) 245
small-sided games 145–146
somatic maturation 53
squad load *230, 231*
strength and conditioning training: aerobic/anaerobic capacity 135–137; body mass 128; conditioning conclusions 137; conditioning sessions 144–146; developing 138; influence sprint 135; power 129, 135; resistance training 128, 135; resistance training exercises 138, *139,* **140–141,** 142–144; training programmes **130–134**

tackle 194; attitudes 195, 199; ball-carrier technical skills **204**; behaviours 195, 199; contact skill training variables **207–208**; contact training program **211–215**; height 199, 200; injuries 194–195; injury prevention and performance **200**; knowledge 195, 199; monitor 202–203; physical conditioning 201–202; physical movement skills 205; progression 210, 216; skill training framework 206, 209, *209,* 210; skill training models 205–206; skill training programme 210; training 203–205; Youth Rugby Union **196–198**
tackler(s) 194
tackling 44, 172, 194, 199, 201–202, 205
Talent 67
talent development 68
talent identification 68; development processes *83*; environmental constraints 74, 81–82; frozen Screen Clips *73*; multidisciplinary approach 82–84; participation history 70–71, **71**, 78; performer constraints 71, 78–80; physical characteristics 74–75, 80; practical applications 77–78; psychological skills and characteristics 71–72, 78–79; relative age effects 75–76, 81; sociocultural influences 77, 81–82; task constraints 68, 70, 78; technical and tactical skills 72–74, 79–80
talent identification programmes 19
technical and tactical problems 166, 185–187; carrying 180; competition 187; decision-making 181–182; definitions for measures **175–176**; EXPERTS **186**; measurement 184–185; measuring **168–171**; mental model *185*; passing 177, 180; pattern recall 182; performance analysis 174, 177; practical recommendations 167; research studies **178–179**; talent identification 72–74, 79–80; testing batteries 167, 172–173; use of competition 182, **183**; Wellington rules **188**
Technical Project Group (TPG) 293, 295–296
testing batteries 167, 172–173

three worlds continuum 334
Time motion analysis 91
total energy expenditure (TEE) 251
training load 222; see also training practices
training practices: analysis and communication 228–229; challenges 229, 231; competition-to-training ratios 231–232; longitudinal analysis *230*; match-play preparation 226; monitoring player loads 227–228; seasonal load 223; session load 225; squad load *230, 231*; weekly load 223–225
Translating Research into Injury Prevention Practice models 270
triangular competition 7, 8

variable practice 181
video analysis 181
video feedback 181

Waterfall competition 7, 8
weekly load 223–225
Wellington rules **188**
wide- running forwards 3
Women's Super League (WSL) 315

youth development 3–4; strategies to support 7–8
youth rugby 4–5; talent identification and development programme 9–10
Youth Rugby Union **196–198**

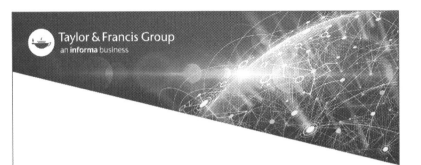

ted in the United States
ker & Taylor Publisher Services